Canadian Business Finance

CANADIAN
BUSINESS
FINANCE

GLEN A. MUMEY
Faculty of Business Administration
and Commerce
University of Alberta

1977

IRWIN-DORSEY LIMITED
Georgetown, Ontario   L7G 4B3

First Printing, February 1977

ISBN 0-256-01787-5

Printed in the United States of America

To Lois

PREFACE

This text is written for the introductory class in business finance. It is intended to provide students with a sense of financial decision-making, while at the same time presenting necessary factual and theoretical material.

It differs from many of its predecessors in its format. The major differences and their rationales are:

1. Asset evaluation decisions and capital budgeting are presented early. There are two reasons. First it seems more natural and consistent with business behavior to first inquire into the question "Which assets do we want?" and then into the question of "How should we get the money?" Second, the introduction of capital budgeting analysis early allows the student to apply this in a variety of situations. I am particularly concerned that capital budgeting methods provide a backdrop for the evaluation of short-lived assets, since, after all, these compete for funds with their long-lived counterparts.

2. Working capital management is approached gradually. Current assets are analyzed as substitutes (albeit imperfect) for fixed assets; the same applies for current and fixed liabilities. The administration of inventories and credit is discussed along with the acquisition decisions on those assets. And maintenance of company liquidity, while dis-

cussed in a cash management section, permeates nearly all other topics, since company liquidity arises from the relative liquidity of all its assets and the relative urgency of the claims against them. No major decision is without liquidity considerations.

3. Similarly, while a chapter addresses risk, I have hoped to make the concept of risk something approaching a universal consideration in financial decisions. The topic reemerges time after time.

4. Ratio analysis is not confined to one section. Ratios and their limitations are discussed in their decision contexts. This as-needed approach seems more consistent with an intracompany approach to finance, in contrast to the "analysis of financial statements" done by an outsider.

The overall intent of these departures from convention are two-fold: to involve the reader in more realistic, multifaceted decision settings, and to encourage him to think broadly enough to avoid localized optimization.

The only essential prerequisite for reading this text is a class in accounting, or some supplemental reading about basic accounting methods. Introductory economics is not necessary but very desirable. No prior work in statistics is needed—though some exposure would enrich the reader's understanding of the risk dimension of finance. Calculus is not required.

I thank the University of Alberta for providing circumstances conducive to research and writing. I also convey my appreciation for the insights and care of the reviewers—Professors Myron Gordon, P. B. Healey, Harold Musson and Calvin Potter.

I alone am responsible for errors.

January 1977   GLEN A. MUMEY

CONTENTS

Captial. Current Ratio. "Acid Test" or "Quick" Ratio. Liquidity Ratios in Perspective. Risk and Financial Condition: *Insolvency and Financing. Measuring Insolvency Potential.* Planning the Company's Financing: *Financing Alternative 1—Bank Borrowing. Financing with Long-Term Debt. Financing with Equity. A Financing Solution.*

Market. Bond Brokerage. Bond Transactions: *Yield. Yield versus Expected Rate of Return.* Bond Yield Variation: *The Yield Curve. Riding the Yield Curve. Risk Premiums. Risk Premiums: A Philosophical Note.* The "Burden" of Debt.

1

THE TOPIC OF FINANCE

In everyday personal usage the term finance is closely related to money. A family in financial trouble is short of money, money borrowed to purchase a house provides the financing for the purchase, and so on.

This everyday concept coincides quite closely with the usage of the word finance in business and government. There finance may be defined as the managing of money; the managerial responsibility may include the procurement of money, control over its disbursement, and the care of money which has been procured and not yet disbursed.

An Alternative View

From another viewpoint, that of the economist, finance takes on a slightly different coloration. In its simplest form, this view regards finance as arrangements for borrowing and lending. A lender gives up the opportunity for immediate consumption, to

1

allow a borrower the opportunity to consume, or to assemble resources for production (i.e., build a steel mill or a highway). In return for the release of resources by the lender, the borrower gives the lender a claim on resources available in the future.

It is easy to expand this simple construct to greater conformity to reality. The transaction between borrower or lender can be characterized as the issuance of a *financial claim* by the borrower, which is bought by the lender. A financial claim is defined as a property interest in purchasing power available in the future. There are many types of financial claims beyond loans; one with which the reader is undoubtedly already familiar is shares of stock in limited companies.

Finance then is thought of by the economist as activities related to transactions in financial claims. Company officers who borrow money for assets, or employ company money for the purchase of interest-bearing financial claims, are practicing finance. So, too, are bank managers, insurance agents, stock exchange clerks, and homeowners who borrow to buy refrigerators.

Use of the Broader Definition

The main difference between the economist's version and the more common variants of what finance means arise from the economist's distinction between real and financial assets. Real assets are goods and services which have been produced but not used up—they include machines, houses, inventories of unsold goods, and even knowledge. Financial assets are the intangible financial claims previously discussed. Typically, financial claims are issued to facilitate the purchase of real assets. In everyday usage, the practice of finance usually includes *decisions* relating to the purchase of real assets, as well as activities relating to financial claims.

For example, in business the decision to buy a new factory would probably be called a financial decision, and financial officers of the company would be involved in this choice. This usage in business has probably arisen from practical considerations; if financial officers had to arrange borrowing or other claims necessary to purchase assets they needed to know about the assets being purchased and they had expertise to contribute to the asset choice process. This book will use the rather untidy managerial definition, since it is concerned with the practice of finance.

Related Concepts

A fuller impression of the concept of finance is conveyed by some related terms such as the following:

Financier. Someone who can provide money for other peoples' ventures.

Financial instrument. A legal document creating a claim for its owner against assets, including money; a "security."

Financial institution. An organization which specializes in providing money to others, buying and selling securities, providing an outlet for the money of others, or creating money.

Financial market. A set of transactions between users and suppliers of money, or buyers and sellers of financial instruments; the term includes related financial institutions.

Financing. Money obtained for the acquisition of assets.

Financing sources. Parties from which financing is obtained: creditors, shareholders, and so on, or sometimes methods used for financing: borrowing, retention of earnings, and so forth.

A Related Definition: Investment

Confusion may sometimes be avoided by recognizing its potentiality. The economists' and popular versions of finance are accompanied by variant definitions of another related word: *investment.* In traditional economics, this refers to production of capital goods, those goods used in the production of other goods. In another, the popular sense, it may refer to any employment of savings, either through purchase of capital goods or of financial claims. Sometimes modifiers are attached to denote these two versions—*capital investment* and *financial investment.* Mostly though the reader must look to the word's context to clarify its meaning.

An additional nuance is provided by the terms *direct investment* and *portfolio investment*. Portfolio investment implies remoteness of the investor from his investment. The portfolio investor holds financial claims, and does not involve himself actively in selecting or managing the capital goods which are ultimately bought by the issuer of the claims. In contrast, a direct investor "gets involved" with capital goods, either as a purchaser himself or as a security owner who can influence or control the management of the capital goods.

The study of finance subdivides into a number of specialized areas of study, which themselves have a set of names. *Public finance* refers to the finance functions as related to the government sector; procurement of money through taxation, borrowing and other ways, and evaluating alternative methods of investing and disbursing the public money. *Portfolio management* describes the task of handling portfolio investments. (Sometimes this area is described as "investments"; the modifier "portfolio" is implied.) *Financial institutions* describes management and other activities within financial institutions, and public policy relating to those institutions. *Personal or consumer finance* treats financial practices at the household level. *Financial markets* addresses the transactions that take place between various business, governments, individuals, and financial institutions. Finally, *business finance* (sometimes financial management) describes the financial practices of business firms.

CANADIAN BUSINESS FINANCE

This book will be devoted to basic descriptions and concepts related to business finance. The setting for most of the analysis will be incorporated businesses in Canada that are owned by private investors. (Alternative terms are corporation, limited company, or more commonly, company.) Some attention will be given to unincorporated small businesses and to the process of forming a limited company. However, the central focus will be on the company that is already in existence, that entity frequently called the "going concern."

The limited company may be defined as an organization which takes on legal existence separate from its owners. It may buy and sell property and enter contracts in its own name. The owners of the company, called shareholders or stockholders, may sell or otherwise transfer their property interest (shares) in the company without affecting its existence. The company may incur debts for which shareholders cannot be held responsible (limited liability). With all these rights goes an important obligation—the company may be subject to corporation income taxes.

While the language of the limited company will be employed, there is no abrupt contrast between financial management in large companies and in small, perhaps unincorporated, businesses. Most of the corporate analysis will be adaptable to smaller firms. Important differences will be noted as they arise in the discussion.

Tasks within Business Finance

Business finance subdivides into two functions, and three types of decisions. The functions are: treasury, and asset management. The treasury function essentially coincides with the traditional economists' view of finance as applied to the company; it is the procurement of money for the purchase of assets. Under the treasury function are included arrangements for borrowing, issuance of company shares and other financial instruments, and the handling of payments to the company's creditors and shareholders.

The second function, asset management, consists of a number of tasks. Cash and bank deposits require attention and control. The company may undertake portfolio investments, which require supervision. Credit and collections from credit customers fall under the purview of finance. Finally, finance is usually defined to include control over the selection, purchase, and replacement of all assets.

Sometimes the word comptrollership is employed to describe the asset management function. Again, though, there is some terminological confusion on this point because comptrollership usually is defined broadly enough to include accounting, and accounting is usually regarded as an area distinct from finance.

Three Classes of Financial Decisions

Finance is more than decision making. There are bills to be collected, cash to be temporarily invested in interest-bearing securities, bankers to be placated, and a host of other work-aday finance jobs. Nevertheless, decisions are at the heart of management, and financial decisions are vital to the company. Three classes of financial decisions are identifiable, the first two relating closely to the asset management and treasury functions. *Asset selection decisions* are the choices that must be made among asset possibilities. *Financing decisions* are those that must be made among methods for financing the assets. Via the equality of left and right sides on the company balance sheet, every asset chosen requires financing. A third class of decisions, which emerges implicitly from the other two, is the *growth rate* or *scale* decision. What total dollar amount of assets should be selected and financed, and how rapidly should this amount increase or decrease?

The three choices may be illustrated by examining a company balance sheet, that of Laura Secord Candy Shops, Limited (Illustration 1–1). Note that Laura Secord had to make decisions about the mixture of assets which are represented on its balance sheet. For example, out of its nearly $19 million

ILLUSTRATION 1–1

LAURA SECORD CANDY SHOPS, LIMITED
Balance Sheet
April 30, 1972

Assets	Amount in Dollars	Proportion (percent of total assets)
Cash	$ 98,000	0.5%
Accounts receivable	2,223,000	11.9
Inventories	3,954,000	21.1
Prepaid expenses	618,000	3.3
Fixed assets	10,012,000	53.5
Other assets	1,808,000	9.7
Total	$18,713,000	100.0%
Liabilities and Equity		
Bank debt (short-term)	$ 4,580,000	24.5%
Accounts payable and		
accruals	1,700,000	9.1
Longer term borrowing	6,433,000	34.4
Other liabilities	677,000	3.6
Common stock and paid-in		
surplus	919,000	4.9
Retained earnings	4,404,000	23.5
Total	$18,713,000	100.0%

in total assets, why did it not spend more than 21.1 percent on inventory, and less than 53.5 percent on fixed assets? No doubt, its top management felt pressure from the marketing division to extend more credit; why were not more funds committed to the accounts receivable position?

Second, Laura Secord's management had to decide how to finance those nearly $19 million in total assets. Why did they chose to borrow over $13 million, or almost 72 percent of the amount required to finance their total assets? Why did they borrow from the sources listed, and why didn't they rely more on nondebt sources, by selling more shares, or inducing share-holders to retain more earnings within the company?

Finally, there is scale and growth. Why did the company have about $19 million in assets on this balance sheet date, rather than $5 million more or less? If size was to be changed by $5 million should this have been attempted over a one-year period or over a decade?

Finance as a Lively Process

The three areas posed in the previous section—investment proportion, financing proportion, and scale—provide a general picture of the subject area embraced by finance. However, like the balance sheet, to which these areas are related, the descriptions of the subjects are rather static in character and do not reveal the full flavour of finance. There is a great deal more to the topic than independently analyzing the three problem areas. The firm to which the balance sheet and problems relate does not stand still and wait for its affairs to be tidily arranged. Instead, the firm is engaged in a process of buying, selling, manufacturing, mining, or whatever, and finance represents but one facet of its affairs. To some extent, the financial manager can control the processes which go on within the firm; in other instances, he must accommodate to these processes. Some examples may help to show the depth of problems confronted by the financial manager.

Suppose than an unforeseen business opportunity emerges and requires quick action. The company president (who does not happen to be a finance man) becomes aware of an opportunity to buy out a competing manufacturer at a seemingly favourable price. The proposed deal must be consummated quickly and requires all cash. The financial manager, called in to advise, is asked to provide his best impressions, perhaps with limited information for study, on whether the investment is a wise one, and whether the necessary monies can be procured. Quickly he must set to work on a problem that combines all three of the topic areas noted in the previous section. Should the asset be bought? Should the necessary money be obtained by disposing of other assets? If not, should it be obtained from previously used financing sources, or should new sources be tapped?

To complicate matters, the financial manager may have to cope with some problems even though his advice on other problems is not taken. He may, for example, recommend against the planned purchase, but other members of the management team may overrule him. Then he must still proceed toward finding the necessary money, either by recommending the disposal of other assets (which will tend to hold the size of the firm constant) or by finding additional financial resources. Furthermore, the requisite asset disposals or financing acquisitions may have to be done within a short period of time and this may limit the opportunities available to the financial manager. Even though he would like to raise additional money by the sale of shares to the general public, the months required for this process may not be available. Some of the company's assets, if sold on short notice, might only bring "distress sale" prices. Monies owed to the company may not be due until far into the future.

Now consider a second example, which could conceivably occur in a firm that has just experienced the scenario in the first example. A strike disrupts the company's transportation outlet so that it cannot make deliveries to customers. Many of the employees in the plants affected by the strike are highly skilled and would be difficult to replace if laid off. The firm's financial manager is asked to survey the financial implications of keeping the plants in production and maintaining the work force. If production continues and sales are interrupted, finished goods inventory will pile up. Do the benefits from maintaining the work force provide an adequate return to justify the potentially massive accumulation of one asset, inventory? If the accumulation of inventory is deemed to be adequately beneficial, how can it be financed?

Each week the employees will have to be paid and the firm's accountants will record the accumulation of more inventory. Does the firm have cash reserves which can be drawn down for this accumulation? How long will collections from previously extended credit, and resulting decline in the accounts receivable position, help to fill this financing gap? Can suppliers of raw materials be prevailed upon to extend additional credit? Can the firm convince its banker that he should assist by providing additional loans even though no end of the strike is in sight?

All of the subproblems in these two examples can be classified within the three-area framework of the previous section. Yet the examples demonstrate that each classification of problem cannot be neatly separated from the others. They appear together and interrelated in the financial experiences of the typical firm.

The examples may rightly suggest that financial management sometimes involves devising tactics to handle crisis situations. More significantly, they should indicate that the financial manager must live in a state of readiness. He must attempt to develop strategies which both contribute to the company's present operations and yet leave it ready to cope with sudden opportunities or calamities.

ADMINISTRATIVE ORGANIZATION FOR FINANCIAL DECISIONS

A typical administrative arrangement for financial matters is represented by the organization chart of X Company Ltd. (Illustration 1–2). Characteristically, a senior financial officer is placed close to the top of the entire management structure, usually at the vice presidential level. On some occasions, the role of senior financial officer will be filled by the president himself.

Typically, the areas of finance and accounting are administratively related. The vice president for finance may be in charge of both functions; a comptroller may also be charged with responsibility for both functions, or portions of both func-

ILLUSTRATION 1–2

An Example of Administrative Relationships

X Company Ltd.

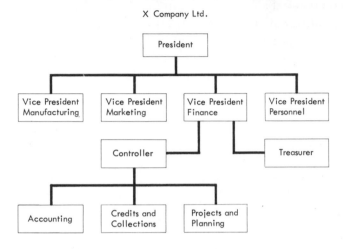

tions. Although these functions are often merged administratively, especially at senior levels, the functions themselves are distinctive.

The accounting function consists of the development of data. Financial management, in turn, relies heavily on accounting information. At various administrative levels, persons designated as accountants or as financial officers may in fact be doing both jobs. Training in finance is an important part of academic and professional accounting education in Canada, so it is not particularly surprising that many accountants are performing financial functions and many financial officers have accounting backgrounds and some accounting responsibilities.

Centralization in Finance

Traditionally financial management has been quite centralized. Not only has the gathering of funds been done at a central corporate level, but also financial decisions of all three types have frequently been made at central points in the administrative organization. While finance has lagged behind other areas in current trends toward managerial decentralization, it too is slowly heading in this direction. In fact, there is a strong reason for expecting decentralization of some financial decision making.

One of the concepts related to the decentralized organization is the decentralized "profit centre." Under this concept, each division of the corporation is responsible for its own profit performance. This is done in an attempt to more precisely fix responsibility and identify divisional managerial teams with superior performance. However, the system becomes rather pointless unless corresponding authority is vested at the divisional level, so that these divisions are free to make decisions that affect their profitability. If even one major area of authority, such as power to make decisions about acquiring assets, is deleted from the division's autonomy, the profit-centre concept is weakened. Responsibility is more easily evaded because divisional officers can blame top management for failures in their operations.

Consider an example, where a company requires that all purchases of assets over $5,000 must be approved centrally. A division, involved in supplying remote mining operations, wishes to buy a $200,000 airplane to be used in making deliveries of urgently needed supplies. Top management turns down this request and during an ensuing period the division's sales fail to grow at an adequate rate. This lack of growth may be attributable to many causes, and in fact may be a direct result of faulty divisional management. However, the divisional manager is now left with an "out"; he can allege that failure to provide the plane and its facility for prompt delivery weakened his competitive sales position.

As in other issues relating to decentralization, there is no clear-cut answer. Elimination of all central management of finance functions appears nonsensical. Surely it would be wasteful for each division to arrange all its own financing sources; for example, to issue its own shares. Certainly too, one would not wish to give a division authority for purchasing single assets of sufficient size to place the entire company under financial strain. Thus, while there is a trend toward divisional autonomy in financial decisions, the trend is not likely to lead to complete decentralization.

OBJECTIVES OF FINANCIAL DECISIONS

Profit Maximization

While corporate decisions may be made under a variety of administrative structures, there is a large element of similarity in the goals toward which these decisions are directed. Companies may be generally described as being directed toward the objective of profit maximization. They are trying to produce services of as much value to their customers as possible (revenue maximization) and at the same time accomplish this end using components of as little value as possible (cost minimization). Indeed, this quest for economic efficiency is a condition for the survival of a particular corporation; without concern about costs and revenues, the privately owned company is almost certain to be overwhelmed by more aggressive competitors.

This is not to suggest that all firms unrelentingly seek profit at all times. Of course there are companies which give to charity without thought of a resulting benefit to the company, which build office buildings more expensive than needed to feed the ego of the president, or which lose profits by rapid expansion because the board of directors wants the company to be a sales leader. However, incidents of this type appear to be aberrations around a central theme. Therefore, this book will employ profit maximization as the best general statement available on what shareholders, creditors, and the public expect companies to do. By extension, asset selection, financing choice, and company size will be regarded as correct if they are consistent with profit maximization and wrong (in a managerial, not an ethical sense) if they depart from that precept.

Refinement of Profit Maximization

For the practice of financial management, the broad objective of profit maximization leaves some unanswered questions. Does timing of profits matter? Are some profit prospects better than others because of considerations relating to risk? The answer to both of these questions is yes. The next sections will enquire into the issues of how the *value* of profits are affected by timing and risk.

TIMING OF PROFITS

Time-Shape of Profits

Profits, or more precisely, the profit prospects of a company, are the result of revenues and costs expected in the future. But in choices among assets or among sources of financing, the futurity of profits prospects may vary between alternatives.

Suppose a manager must choose between two assets. One of these, A, will yield profits of $500 per year for ten years and then will become worthless. The second, B, will generate profits of $1,000 per year for four years, after which it too becomes worthless. Suppose both assets can be purchased for equal prices, and that financial resources permit purchasing only one. A will slowly return total profits of $5,000; B will more quickly return $4,000. Thus there is a choice between "more, eventually" and "less, promptly"; the assets offer profit potential which differ both in quantity and time-shape. Time-shape is defined as the distribution of some phenomenon, in this case flows of profit, over time. The time-shape of the profits on the above assets are shown in Illustration 1–3.

ILLUSTRATION 1–3

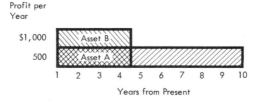

Years from Present

Time Preference

If there were no preferences between present and future profits, time-shape would be irrelevant. But there is a good reason for companies and their shareholders to prefer profits that are near in time to those that are far off. That reason is the existence of positive interest rates.

For the company or person borrowing money, a dollar received this year instead of next year will result in the saving of a year's interest charges. Or if the dollar is not used for loan repayment, it can be invested in an interest-bearing security.

We, therefore, conclude that there is a preference regarding time-shape, and that profit prospects will be valued in an inverse relation to their futurity.

Adjustment Processes

Since shareholders can be characterized as having a dislike for waiting, but also a desire for high profits, what quantity of total profits should the company be willing to sacrifice in return for avoiding long delays in the receipt of those profits? To approach this problem systematically, one needs a method of adjusting or compensating for differences in the timing of prospective profits.

Adjustment processes are common in many everyday circumstances. For example, if an individual is contemplating spending long hours outdoors on a winter day and wants an indication of the severity of the weather, he might check the outside temperature. However, temperature alone does not tell the whole story about the potential discomfort or danger that may be caused by weather conditions; wind velocity is also important. Suppose an individual confronts a choice of exposing himself to the weather today, when the temperature is $-3°$ and there is no wind, or tomorrow, when a temperature of $-20°$ coupled with a 30 kilometer per hour wind is predicted.

To cope with the problem, the individual may well decide to consult a table of wind chill equivalents, such as the one shown in Illustration 1–4.

A glance at this table indicates that in terms of discomfort and danger, a temperature of $-20°$, coupled with a 30 kph wind is equivalent to a temperature of $-42°$ under calm conditions.

ILLUSTRATION 1–4

Wind Chill Equivalents

Actual Temperature ($°C$)	Wind Speed (kph)				
	0	15	30	45	60
$-35°$	$-35°$	$-49°$	$-62°$	$-70°$	$-74°$
$-30°$	$-30°$	$-43°$	$-55°$	$-61°$	$-66°$
$-25°$	$-25°$	$-36°$	$-48°$	$-54°$	$-57°$
$-20°$	$-20°$	$-31°$	$-42°$	$-47°$	$-50°$
$-15°$	$-15°$	$-26°$	$-35°$	$-39°$	$-42°$

Obviously, the chart can be extended to compare not only a windy day and a calm day, but to compare two windy days. For the decision maker, it is temperature adjusted for wind that matters. Similarly, for the financial manager, it is profit adjusted for time that matters. We will leave the matter of the specific adjustment process until the next chapter.

RISK IN PROFITS

The Concept of Risk

To understand risk, one must distinguish between profit possibilities that are planned for or anticipated, and profits that actually result. The first may be called profits ex ante, and the second profits ex post. Financial decisions always involve the maximization of profits ex ante. If a company buys a machine in the hope of increasing the company's output and profits, the expected profits are ex ante in character. One must wait until the machine is bought and put into operation to see whether ex post profits result.

When one forms a profit expectation ex ante, he will surely consider the possibility that his information about the future events that may affect this profit is imperfect, and that therefore ex post profit, what he actually gets, may diverge from his ex ante projection. *Risk may be defined as the extent to which potential for divergence exists between profit ex post and profit ex ante.*

For example, a Canada Savings Bond is usually regarded as riskless. The government promises to make a fixed payment or payments to the bondholder. No significant possibility of the government breaking its promise is foreseen. No divergence is envisioned between the results expected before purchase of the bond (receipt of interest and principal) and the actual results that may ultimately ensue.

On the other hand, a land developer may purchase a piece of property adjoining Thunder Bay in anticipation that within five years he will be able to divide it into lots and resell it at a handsome profit. However, he must rely on an approximation that Thunder Bay's population five years hence will be large enough to sustain an adequate demand for his residential lots. He can only make an educated guess about how transportation routes will change over the next five years in ways which may enhance or retard the salability of his lots. He can only estimate what the costs of servicing the lots—providing lighting, sewer, water, and streets—will be five years hence. The list could go on; when the developer talks about anticipating a profit from the acquisition of his land, he does not know what the profit is actually going to be and can really only talk about his best guess out of a spectrum of ex post profit possibilities.

Risk and Measurement

If profits are to be adjusted for risk, in a manner similar to the adjustment for time (or wind chill), there is need for identifying the magnitude of the risk involved. There are two approaches to this identification of magnitude. First, it can be done judgmentally, by classifying projects within verbally described categories such as high-risk, low-risk, or safe (the equivalent approach to wind chill conversion would be to specify the wind velocity as intense, moderate, or calm). While this seems like a crude method, it is widely used, because of the absence of a universally accepted measurement scale for risk.

A second approach is to attempt to use some measurement scale, even though no measure of risk is as widely accepted as "kilometers per hour" in the realm of wind measurement. One measurement method is to express the range of possible profits.

Consider an asset, Project A, where the best available estimate of profit is $1,500, but where profits could potentially be as high as $5,000 or as low as a $2,000 loss. The best estimate is often simply described as *expected profit*.[1] In this case, the range of possible profit might be described as $7,000, from +$5,000 to −$2,000.

Another and more sophisticated method involves specifying the anticipated profits in the form of a probability distribution. To develop this distribution, a more careful statement about Project A's profit possibilities would have to be made; for example:

---

[1] Expected profit is often used with a more technical meaning—the mean of a profit probability distribution.

Profits on Project A

Probability of Occurrence	Profit
.3	$5,000
.4	$1,500
.3	−$2,000

Once this distribution is identified, standard statistical measures can be applied to measure its expected profit and its risk dimension. For those readers who are familiar with elementary statistical procedures, the most frequent measures employed are the mean, for expected profit, and the standard deviation, for risk. These measures enable a more precise statement about the extent to which results may diverge from expectations.

Measuring risk in a probability distribution, rather than just expressing it as a range of possible profits, also conveys much more meaning. To illustrate, one need only note that the previously shown probability distribution for Project A has the same range of profits as that for a second project, B, shown below. However, this second situation has only a slight chance of producing results different than the expected profit of $1,500.

Profits on Project B

Probability of Occurrence	Profit
.005	$5,000
.005	−$2,000
.99	$1,500

Risk Preference

The availability of interest rates provides a straightforward reason for preferring present profits to future ones. Since the concept of risk is more nebulous than that of time, it is not surprising that the basis for preference with respect to risk is less obvious. Suffice to say that risk aversion is generally accepted as a "fact of life" in finance. Most people do not like to expose themselves to the possibility of financial misfortune which accompanies high-risk projects. As a result, it will be appropriate (later in the text) to explore methods of risk adjustment. Even though there is not full agreement on whether and how it can be measured, formal or informal adjustment for risk is widely used in modern business.

WEALTH MAXIMIZATION

Without looking at detailed method, we have discussed the possibility of adjusting profits for time and risk. These adjustments are in the nature of necessary improvements in the method of profit seeking, rather than a contradiction of the profit goal. This modification of the profit theme to consider value of profits is often called wealth maximization. Throughout the rest of this book we will presume that financial decisions will be directed toward this goal of wealth.

This goal arises from the concern that companies have for the well-being of their shareholders. These shareholders are the owners of the company and their preferences have a great deal of influence in the way the company conducts its affairs. Sometimes these shareholders appear to have little actual power in the operation of the company which they own. Many shareholders do not even bother to exercise their rights to influence the affairs of the company by voting at annual meetings.

Yet companies often seem to be acting on behalf of their shareholders. Perhaps the reason that shareholders do not directly intervene more frequently in the management of their companies is because their wishes are anticipated by the company's officers. Perhaps, too, those officers know that shareholders have the power to "vote" in another way besides the formal balloting at annual meetings; they can express their dissatisfaction with company affairs by selling their shares. The more disenchanted shareholders a company has, who are considering the sale of their shares, the more vulnerable the corporation is to having a majority of its shares purchased by outside groups. In turn, these takeovers by outside groups have not infrequently resulted in the installation of a new set of company managers.

When time and risk adjustment are introduced into corporate financial decision processes, these adjustments do not arise from the whims of the company's management. Instead, they rest on the preferences of shareholders, who are known to have biases against long waiting for profits, and against exposure to risk in the search for profit. This does not mean that corporations or stockholders will refuse to undertake projects of a long duration or high risk. It only means that adjustments should be introduced into the decision process to attempt to ensure that high futurity or risk are accompanied by profits sufficiently high to compensate for these disadvantages.

THE REMAINDER OF THE TEXT

The plan of presentation for the rest of the book has evolved from a logical sequence connecting the various types of financial decisions. This sequence of decisions is:

1. The company decides whether to buy a particular asset, or to change a policy affecting the amount of a type of asset (the asset selection decision).

2. The company will identify the consequences of its asset selection decisions, in terms of money need.

3. Methods for meeting the money needs will be identified and evaluated (the financing decision).

4. The costs of financing will be related to the profit possibilities from the assets, and from this comparison insights will be obtained on whether the overall size of the asset collection and related financing should be enlarged or contracted (the scale decisions).

More specifically, the following three chapters will discuss analytical tools and information needed for financial decisions. Chapters 5 through 8 will describe how assets are managed in Canadian companies, and methods for making financial decisions relating to these assets. Chapters 9–15 will relate to the sources from which Canadian companies obtain their funds, and methods for evaluating and choosing between these sources. Chapters 16 and 17 will discuss decisions relating both to assets and financing sources, including the topics of the appropriate size and the appropriate growth rate. The remaining chapters will be devoted to such special subjects as the beginning and terminating of companies and the financial problems that relate to international business.

SUMMARY

The financial aspects of operating a company include obtaining money for use by the company (the treasury function), and exercising aspects of control over company assets. Asset control involves direct management of the company's cash and credit positions, and participation in decisions about the spending of company money upon these and other assets.

Three classes of financial decisions are identifiable: asset selection, financing, and growth rate or scale.

Financial officers occupy key roles in the management of most companies. The general managerial issue of centralization versus decentralization is applicable in finance.

Financial decisions in companies are presumed to be based on profit maximization. However, the concept of profit needs refinement if it is to be operationally useful. The timing of potential profits, and the risk inherent in profit opportunities, affect the value of profits. Profits may be subject to adjustment for time and risk, the maximization of profits so adjusted is often called wealth maximization.

QUESTIONS AND PROBLEMS

1. Distinguish between the everyday and the economists' concept of finance. Which is broader? Which coincides more closely with company usage?

2. Distinguish between the way in which you use the word investment in everyday conversation and the economists' meaning for the term. Give an example of action that might be taken by a company which would be described as capital investment? Financial investment? Direct investment? Portfolio investment?

3. Define the term profit, and indicate the limitations of this definition as an objective for financial decisions. (Discuss the operational objections, not the ethical ones.)

4. A company contemplates spending $1 million on the development of a new product. The company's first estimate of the results that will ensue from this venture is that it will result in a $3 million total profit during the ensuing five years. What additional information would you like to have about this profit picture if you were going to be involved in making a decision to proceed or not to proceed?

5. The manager of Alpha Company tells you that he foresees considerable risk in the next year's profit outlook. As he puts it, "We might make $5 million, we might make $1 million or we might lose $3 million." What is the range of profit expectation? In assessing the riskiness of this situation, what is the usefulness and what is the limitation of range as a measure of risk?

RELATED READINGS

Donaldson, G.   "Financial Goals: Management vs. Stockholders." *Harvard Business Review,* May–June 1963.

Fama, E., and Miller, M.   *The Theory of Finance.* New York: Holt, Rinehart & Winston, 1972, chaps. 1 and 2.

Findlay, M. C., and Whitemore, G A.   "Beyond Shareholder Wealth Maximization." *Financial Management,* Winter 1974.

Haley, C. W., and Schall, L. D.   *The Theory of Financial Decisions.* New York: McGraw-Hill, 1973, chap 1.

MacDonald, R.   "The Financial Executive and Senior Management." *Finance Executive,* March 1969.

Solomon, E.   *The Theory of Financial Management.* New York: Columbia University Press, 1963, chaps 1 and 2.

Weston, J. F.   *The Scope and Methodology of Finance.* Englewood Cliffs, N.J.: Pentice-Hall, 1966.

2

ASSET CASH FLOWS

The preceding chapter explored the nature and objectives of finance. As we have already noted, finance is intimately related to the coming and going of money. For the financial manager, money flow is an object of both prediction and control. An ensuing chapter (Chapter 4) will discuss means of controlling the use of money so that it is made to serve the wealth-maximizing objectives of the company. Before that control can be exercised, information is needed. What are the consequences, in terms of cash accumulation and/or decumulation, if a particular managerial action is taken? It is the purpose of this chapter to look discerningly at the cash effects of company decisions, particularly those relating to assets.

CASH FLOW PROJECTIONS

The wealth-enhancing aspect of an asset is a thing apart from the asset's material composition. To the financial decision maker a silent, growing tree or a rattling, deteriorating truck may both be engines of cash flow generation. Information about the expected quantity of this flow (positive or negative) is essential for analysis. The information must be in the form of forward-looking projections, which consider not only the amount of cash involved, but also their timing.

The basic form of cash flow projection is a series of point estimates of cash flows in future periods. *Point estimate* is defined in this context as a single number selected ex ante to characterize cash flow possibilities for a period. It contrasts with such other descriptive methods as listing a variety of possibilities, specifying a range of possibilities, or indicating a probability distribution. The point estimate is used because "best estimates" are the main ingredients in most business decisions, and because, even where more sophisticated analysis is used their form is often a point estimate coupled with analysis of the risk dimension that surrounds the estimate.

Cash Flows from Assets

Cash flow projections are utilized in a number of ways. Forecasts of the cash required and the cash generated are prepared for proposed asset acquisitions. Similar forecasts may also be prepared in connection with financing proposals. Finally, and vitally, overall forecasts of all cash entering and leaving the company must be prepared, in an attempt to anticipate and control cash deficiencies (or excesses).

This chapter will concentrate on the first type of projection, although much of the discussion will be applicable to all types. An example of a simple cash flow projection on an asset is given in Illustration 2–1. This example relates to a machine which requires some "start-up" cost, and a maintenance shutdown after five years. The machine generates benefits in the form of labour savings. Disposal is projected after ten years.

Feasibility Studies

Information about asset cash flows is usually obtained with considerable effort. A person or group within the company (not necessarily directly involved with finance) is charged

ILLUSTRATION 2–1

Cash Flow Projections—Purchase of Automatic Lathe

Period	Description	Cash Flow	Net Cash Flow for Period
1977 . . .	Purchase of machine	−$120,000	
	Installation	− 10,000	−$130,000
1978 . . .	Employee training expense	− 5,000	
	Labour saving	20,000	15,000
1979 . . .	Labour saving	30,000	30,000
1980 . . .	Labour saving	30,000	30,000
1981 . . .	Labour saving	30,000	30,000
1982 . . .	Labour saving	25,000	
	Maintenance on machine	− 8,000	17,000
1983–87	Labour saving	30,000 per year	30,000 per year
1988 . . .	Labour saving	30,000	
	Proceeds from disposal (salvage)	25,000	55,000

with assembling information about a proposed asset or collection of assets. This undertaking is often called a *feasibility study*. The central result of the study usually will be a forecast of the cash flows for the asset(s) involved.

These projections, in turn, must be developed from more basic information. Technical qualities of the asset must be considered. (How much labour will the new lathe save?). Market effects may be important. (If a new product is introduced, or if quantity of output is changed, as a result of an asset acquisition, will the product be readily salable, and at what price?) The asset may create significant effects on personnel. (Will the union expect extra benefits in return for tolerating a laboursaving machine?) Government regulatory action may colour the asset decision. (Does the new equipment require modification to conform to provincial safety legislation?) Unless all major effects, and their cash flow implications, can be contemplated the feasibility study may provide inadequate information.

On the other hand, feasibility studies are costly. The benefits of additional information must be balanced against the cost of its procurement. Therefore, one expects to find (and does) that the intensity of feasibility studies varies widely. Small assets may be purchased on the basis of information given by a salesman; the effort on feasibility studies (both private and governmental) on the Mackenzie Valley pipeline will number in thousands of man-years.

CASH FLOWS DISTINGUISHED FROM ACCOUNTING EARNINGS

The concept of profit implicitly used in the previous example, Illustration 2–1, has been simply a comparison of amounts of money coming in with amounts of money going out. While this is within the spirit of the usual definition of profit, it differs from the rules for profit measurement which are employed by companies in the preparation of published accounting statements. This difference does not imply that one or the other method is right or wrong; the manner of profit calculation is dependent upon the purpose for which it is calculated. In published accounting statements, companies are attempting to describe how effectively they performed *in a particular period*. This concern with the profit from activities in a particular period requires a departure from the method of measuring profits simply by money flows.

Consider a simple example. In 1977, LePage Ltd. examines the possibility of spending $5,000 on a machine that is expected to last ten years, and returns $1,000 per year. Perhaps the machine will not be used at all during 1977. If one were to attempt to describe the profit associated with the machine during 1977, it would be nonsensical to report that the machine was a resounding failure because it had resulted in a net cash outflow of −$5,000. Instead, the accountant would not consider the $5,000 original cost as part of profit determination at the time it was spent, but instead would attempt to match that cost with the revenues that would be derived from it. He could do this by employing a method of depreciation such as the simple technique of dividing the cost by the number of years the machine was going to be used ($5,000 ÷ 10 = $500). Then, during each year in which the machine returned a $1,000 cash flow, $500 in capital costs could be charged against those revenues. The accounting earnings on the machine would accordingly be reported as $500 during each year the machine was used.

In contrast with the accounting statement's purpose of accounting for profits *per period*, financial analysis is concerned basically with profits *per decision*. In decisions to buy assets, all money inflows to be received from the asset are relevant, as are all payments to be made in connection with the asset. These inflows and outflows—subject to adjustment for time and risk—are the ingredients for calculating the asset's potential profit.

To return to the Le Page example, the issue for financial analysis is: What is the amount of difference between $1,000 per year for ten years and $5,000 to be surrendered in 1977 after appropriate time and risk adjustments have been made. There is no conceptual need for calculating depreciation, because the decision maker has no interest in obtaining a profit figure for 1977 or any other individual year.

To repeat, the two methods are not in conflict. In the financial version, profit is projected ex ante over the asset's life. In the accounting version, profit is identified ex post for a particular period. Both ultimately match monies in against monies out.

Relevant Cash Flows

When cash flow information is assembled, care must be taken to have the right information at hand for the decision that is to be made. Three important conditions for relevance in asset cash flow projections are:

1. Separating investment information from financing information.

2. Developing information which is *marginal* with respect to the decision at hand.

3. Reducing information to an *after-tax* basis.

These conditions will be discussed in detail in the following sections.

SEPARATION OF ASSET INFORMATION

The Logic of Separation

It is appropriate to undertake separate analyses for assets and their related financial sources. The logic of this generalization arises from the practical separability of decisions relating to (a) whether an asset should be acquired and (b) how the asset should be financed. Buying an asset requires corresponding financing. Often the financing is sought out for the purchase of the particular asset. Nevertheless, there are two separate steps, which should in analysis be taken one at a time. The analytical sequence, and usually the company procedure will run:

1.   Should we buy the asset—is it worth financing?

2.   Is the financing source desirable—should we look elsewhere?

If the decisions are separated, the information relating to them should also be sundered.

This will mean that such items as payment of interest to creditors, or dividends to shareholders, will not be included among the cash flows relating to an asset. Even though an asset may be bought on a "time payment plan," it will be analyzed as if it were to be bought for cash. Later, a choice can be made as to whether the time payment plan offered by the vendor is superior to other methods of raising money for the asset's purchase price.

An Example of Erring by Not Separating

An example can illustrate the logic of this separation. Suppose that a timber company is contemplating borrowing $100,000 for the construction of a forest access road. One approach to assembling the information on this situation would be to simultaneously consider the money that is going to flow in as a result of the project (reduced timber haulage costs, possibility of extracting more timber, timber savings through improved fire prevention, and so on) and the monies that are going to flow out in servicing the associated loan (interest and repayment of principal).

This contrasts with the recommended method of considering the asset's cash flows separately.

The facts of the situation are projected as follows:

Cash in the amount of $100,000 is going to be laid out at the time the road is built. This $100,000 must be committed, irrespective of how it is financed. One can then describe the road-building asset in terms of a current outlay of —$100,000 and a series of expected receipts resulting from the reduced haulage costs and other items. The annual value of the receipts is expected to be $26,000, each year for five years. After five years the road will be deemed worthless, since by then all the timber in the area served by the road will have been removed.

The road is to be financed with a loan from the uncle of the timber company owner, made available at 4 percent interest with principal repayable in equal annual installments over five years.

Using the method of mixing the investment and financing projections, construction costs (which are financed) are excluded, and payments on the financial obligation resulting from construction are included. With this method financial dimensions of the road are:

| Time—
Year of
Operation | Net Operating
Receipts | Financing Payments | | Net Cash
Flow |
		Principal	Interest*	
1 ...	$26,000	−$20,000	−$4,000	$2,000
2 ...	26,000	− 20,000	− 3,200	2,800
3 ...	26,000	− 20,000	− 2,400	3,600
4 ...	26,000	− 20,000	− 1,600	4,400
5 ...	26,000	− 20,000	− 800	5,200

*Interest payments reduce annually, reflecting repayments of principal.

Looked at in the light, the road appears profitable; it pays its financing costs and generates cash in every year of its projected life.

In contrast, cash flow analysis on the asset above shows:

Time	Net Operating Receipts	Construction Cost	Net Cash Flow
Year of Construction		$100,000	−$100,000
1st year of operation	$26,000		26,000
2nd year of operation	26,000		26,000
3rd year of operation	26,000		26,000
4th year of operation	26,000		26,000
5th year of operation	26,000		26,000

From this viewpoint, the road does not project as an unequivo-cal success. In one year an outflow is projected; this is followed by five years of projected inflow. However, the money amounts are not directly comparable. They occur at different times, and the net operating receipts probably are subject to risk. Only after risk and time adjustment will the company know for sure whether the *value* of the cash inflows exceeds the *value* of the outflows.

The loan can then be viewed separately. For example, if the opportunity to deposit money in a chartered bank savings ac-count at 6 percent was the only investment available, the loan would still be acceptable.

MARGINAL CASH FLOWS

We have seen that issues can be obscured by including in-formation about an asset and its related financing in a single analysis. It is also possible to err through another form of over-aggregation. This possibility of error arises because the choice of an asset may not necessarily be a single decision, but a series of separable incremental decisions. If an asset can be pur-chased in various sizes or quantities, or if an existing asset can be added to or exchanged for a different model, various steps of investment in the asset are possible. If separate steps are possible, so are separate decisions.

Marginal cash flows from an asset are those *changes in cash inflows and outflows* associated with a *change in the amount of investment* in that asset. They represent the projected financial effects of a decision to acquire an additional amount of an asset. (The concept may also be applied if there is a proposed reduction in asset size; that is, if the "additional amount" is negative.)

An example of the importance of marginal cash flows fol-lows. This example involves a tire retailer who believes he is losing sales and profits because he does not have a sufficient stock of tires available for sale. The intent of the example is to show how an analysis based on total cash flows can be mislead-ing, and how this analysis may be improved through the use of marginal cash flow data.

The tire retailing company concludes that it is losing $10,000 per month of potential profits because of inabilities to supply goods promptly to its customers. Typically, a customer comes in and wants a tire of a particular size for immediate installation. If the company is unable to supply it, the customer goes to a competitor for his purchase. Furthermore, once given an incentive to go to a competitor, he may direct subsequent business to that competitor.

The company decides that it can cut this loss by $8,000 per month ($96,000 per year) if it increases the stock of tires it keeps on its premises by committing another $200,000 to inventory. During the time that this policy is in effect, the $200,000 investment will have to remain committed. As individual tires are sold out of the inventory, they will have to be promptly replaced if continuing customer satisfaction is to prevail.

These facts indicate a ratio of annual loss avoidance to the amount of the investment of $96,000/$200,000, or 48 percent; a rate of profit that may look very tantalizing to the company.

However, a more selective look at the problem may leave the company with reservations about buying $200,000 worth of additional tires. Suppose the company discovers that by buying only $100,000 of new inventory (concentrating on the most popular tire sizes), could eliminate about $7,000 per month of its losses attributable to being out of stock. Now the decision can be restructured into two separate stages. Should the company buy $100,000 of additional inventory, and then should it buy still another $100,000 of additional inventory?

The data, structured marginally, tell this story:

	Marginal, First Step	Marginal, Second Step	Overall
Investment	$100,000	$100,000	$200,000
Annual loss avoidance	84,000	12,000	96,000
Loss avoidance ÷ investment	84%	12%	48%

Observe that the overall annual loss avoidance per dollar invested, 48 percent, is largely attributable to the first $100,000 of inventory, with its 84 percent benefits per dollar invested. The second step is much less attractive, and might potentially be regarded as unnecessary.

Many financial undertakings can be carried on at different levels of scale. While applying marginal analysis to different levels of scale is time-consuming, and probably is not worthwhile in every case, there are many situations where it can be rewarding.

TAX CONSIDERATIONS

After-Tax Cash Flows

Limited companies are responsible for the regular filing of tax returns with Revenue Canada. On these tax returns, a particular form of accounting earnings must be calculated in accordance with specific tax accounting rules. Earnings identified in this way may be called taxable earnings.

Normally, the measurement of taxable earnings coincides fairly closely with a company's regular accounting procedures. On some points a conflict between authorities may occur; then guidelines established by the Canadian Institute of Chartered Accountants govern on published statements and tax returns are filed in accordance with tax legislation and Revenue Canada rules.

When paid, taxes constitute cash outflows. Therefore, expected taxes must be considered when cash flow projections are being made. The goal of companies' decisions is presumed to be the maximization of the wealth of company owners, not the joint wealth of the owners and the Revenue Canada. Therefore, it is after-tax cash flows that are important in financial analysis.

Confusion may arise in the identification of taxes and after-tax cash flows, because two concepts of profit are mixed together in the necessary calculations. The pertinent profit measure for asset decisions is projected net cash flow. Income tax payments are an element of the cash flow involved in this calculation. In turn, income taxes must be projected with reference to anticipated taxable income, a different measure of profit. Net cash flow is still the measure used for the decision; taxable income is a computational step in obtaining net cash flow.

Tax Projection Simplified

A simplifying assumption is often used to reduce the formidability of tax projection. This assumption is: cash flows are subject to tax unless an exception is considered. Using t to designate the tax rate and $(1 - t)$ to denote the fraction of income left to the company

$$\text{After-tax flow} = (\text{Before tax cash flow}) \, (1 - t).$$

Two important and related exceptions must immediately be noted:

1.   Under normal circumstances, money paid to acquire an asset will not be tax deductible. Therefore, initial costs of assets are not subject to reduction by $(1 - t)$.

2.   Two important allocations of initial cost are deductible for tax purposes. Depreciable assets afford offsets to taxable income in the form of capital cost allowances. Natural resources afford depletion allowance. These deductions are often referred to as types of *tax shelter*. Since a dollar of deduction shelters a dollar of company income from taxation at rate t, saving from a tax shelter is:

$$(\text{Tax shelter}) \, (t).$$

Using this simplified method, after-tax cash flow for any year is described more completely as

$$
\begin{aligned}
\text{After-tax cash flow} = \ & (\text{Payment of initial cost})^{*} \\
& + (\text{net cash from operations}) \, (1 - t) \\
& + (\text{tax shelter}) (t).
\end{aligned}
$$

*   * This will be a negative cash flow.*

For example, a machine is bought for $400,000 in 1977. During 1978, it will yield cash flows from operations of $100,000. It

Net Cash Flow 1977:	Payment of initial cost	−$400,000
	(Tax shelter) (t) = 80,000 (0.45)	36,000
	(Net from operations) (1 − t)	0
		−$364,000
Net Cash Flow 1978:	Payment of initial cost	0
	(Tax shelter) (t) = $64,000 (0.45)	$ 28,800
	(Net from operations) (1 − t) =	
	$100,000 (0.55)	$ 55,000
		$ 83,800

is subject to capital cost allowance deductions of $80,000 in 1977 and $64,000 in 1978. Following the above formula, cash flows are calculated after tax for these two years out of the machine's life, using $t = 0.45$.

More Detailed Modification

Often the method above is sufficient. A more complete method is presented here. It again begins by assuming that all operating cash flows are subject to tax, and thereby are reduced by the factor $(1 - t)$. From that point the following modifications can be made.

1. Possible additions to after-tax cash flow:
    a. Tax deductible noncash expenses. The appropriate correction is to add the expense, multiplied by t, to recognize the previously ignored tax saving.

2. Possible subtractions from after-tax cash flows:
    a. Taxable noncash revenues. For these, subtract $[t(\text{noncash revenues})]$.
    b. Nontax deductible cash payment from operations. Again, subtract $[t(\text{nondeductible payments})]$.

3. Nonoperating items:
    a. Purchase price of assets. This is usually an after-tax outflow.
    b. Disposal price of assets. This is usually an after-tax inflow, subject to modification. (See Chapter 5.)
    c. Special tax credits, that are allowed from time to time as a result of government policy. These are usually after-tax cash inflows.

Tax Rates

Limited companies are subject to income taxation at both federal and provincial levels. As in the case of the personal income tax, company tax is payable to Revenue Canada, which then makes appropriate remission to the provinces. In tax calculation, a 10 percent credit is allowed on federal tax for the payment of provincial tax. Since most provinces presently tax at or near 10 percent, the result may be regarded as a cancellation, with federal rates regarded as combined rates.

Various corporate tax rates exist: a general one and several special rates. At the time this book was written the general rate was

$$t = 0.46.$$

The most important special rate was that for manufacturing and processing companies; they are allowed to use $t = 0.40$.

Energy companies are another important class of companies offered a special rate, in this case $t = 0.25$.

Small companies which meet certain conditions are also given a preferential rate on their first $100,000 of annual taxable earnings. They use $t = 0.25$ or, if they are manufacturers, $t = 0.20$. This special treatment ends when the small company has accumulated a historical total of $500,000 in earnings.

Tax Shelter (Capital Cost Allowance)

The most important tax shelter is the capital cost allowance, or CCA. The amount of shelter is computed on the basis of two principles:

a. *Class depreciation.* Similar assets are grouped into classes. Depreciation is then resolved on all of the assets in each class as a single calculation. When assets are bought, their purchase price is added to the balance maintained for an appropriate class. When assets are sold, a subtraction takes place.

b. *Declining balance calculation.* CCA for any class is calculated by the formula:

CCA = (Unexpired captial cost of class) (class depreciation rate)

Unexpired capital cost (UCC) is in turn defined as:

UCC = (Original cost of all assets in class)
      − (CAA taken on class in all previous periods).

Class depreciation rates are specified by tax law; some examples are: Masonry buildings, 4 percent; wood buildings, 5 percent; most industrial machinery, 20 percent; automobiles and trucks, 30 percent; and airplanes, 40 percent. These rates are maximum rates allowable; normally it is to the advantage of the taxpayer to employ the maximum rate possible.

The calculation of capital cost allowance takes the following form:

Let subscripts denote years, with 1 denoting the first year the class was used, 2 the second year, and so on. Then the CCA calculation for the class for any year can be determined in two stages. First find UCC and then apply the class rate:

$$UCC_1 = (\text{Asset purchases} - \text{disposals})_1$$
$$CCA_1 = UCC_1 \, (\text{class rate})$$
$$UCC_2 = UCC_1 - CCA_1 + (\text{asset purchases} - \text{disposals})_2$$
$$CCA_2 = UCC_2 \, (\text{class rate})$$
$$UCC_3 = UCC_2 - CCA_2 + (\text{asset purchases} - \text{disposals})_3$$
$$CCA_3 = UCC_3 \, (\text{class rate}).$$

In each subsequent year, a new UCC is identified and multiplied by the CCA rate to obtain that year's capital cost allowance.

A Detailed Example

Anderson Company Ltd. has been shipping all of its merchandise to customers via common carrier. It now is evaluating the purchase of some large trucks. It contemplates a fleet of ten trucks, to be bought for $50,000 per truck. It expects that these trucks will reduce the company's transportation charges by $700,000 per year. Maintenance and operation of the trucks will cost $500,000 per year. Thus, net cash flows from operations of $200,000 per year are expected. Additionally, sale of the trucks after five years, at an expected total price of $80,000, is contemplated. The cash flow stream is depicted in Illustration 2–2. A tax rate of 40 percent is employed.

Suppose the only important tax shelter arises from capital cost allowance, at a 30 percent rate. CCA calculation and adjustment is shown in Illustration 2–3.

A Note of Caution

A word of caution is in order at this point. Tax rules normally do not change drastically from year to year, with respect to general principles; but specific aspects of the rules are fre-

ILLUSTRATION 2–2

Net Cash Flows
(in thousands of dollars)

Year of Truck Use	From Operations	Operating Cash Flows (1 − t)	Purchase and Sale	Total Cash Flows before CCA
Time of purchase (year 0)			−$500	−$500
1	+$200	+$120		+ 120
2	+ 200	+ 120		+ 120
3	+ 200	+ 120		+ 120
4	+ 200	+ 120		+ 120
5	+ 200	+ 120	+ 80	+ 200

quently changed. Thus, in practice, it is necessary to consult up-to-date tax information, or someone with tax expertise, before estimates of after-tax cash flow are formulated for any major financial decision.

GENERAL ASPECTS OF CASH FLOWS

Principles for Projections

It is apparent that the development of financial projections on assets can be a time-consuming, and therefore costly, proc-

ILLUSTRATION 2–3

Adjustment of After-Tax Cash Flows
(in thousands of dollars)

(1) Year of Truck Use	(2) Cash Flow before CCA (from Illus. 2-2)	(3) CCA at 30%	(4) Unexpired Capital	(5) Tax Shelter CCA (t)	(6) After-Tax Cash Flows (Col. 2 − Col. 5)
0	−$500	$150	$350	+$60	−$440
1	+ 120	105	245	+ 42	+ 162
2	+ 120	74	171	+ 30	+ 150
3	+ 120	51	120	+ 20	+ 140
4	+ 120	36	84	+ 14	+ 134
5	+ 200	*	0	*	+ 220

* The approximate equality of the remaining UCC ($84,000) and the salvage value ($80,000) result in approximately no CCA in year 5. For limited discussion of salvage value, see Chapter 5. For more detailed discussion, it will be necessary to consult a tax text.

ess. One may think of the process of making projections as itself constituting an investment process. In return for costs of making projections, benefits are expected to ensue in the form of reduced errors in asset purchase decisions. When we think along profit-maximizing lines, this suggests that projection effort should be directed most intensely toward projects where the potential for error control is greatest.

This rationale suggests that several situations merit special attention:

a. Large-scale asset acquisitions.

b. Acquisitions which are made recurrently, and where, while individual assets may be small, the type of asset is held on a large scale.

c. Situations where information appears to be either easily obtainable and/or particularly essential in a decision.

The reason for the first situation is obvious; errors on large projects cost big money. It may be quite reasonable to spend an extra $10,000 for preliminary research on a $1 million project, but absurd on a $10,000 one.

Similarly, in the second situation, a company may devote much effort to developing information for credit decisions, not because any individual account receivable is large but because the whole receivable position is. In this situation, the effort is likely to be toward predicting events that affect large numbers of credit accounts, such as changes in broad business conditions; or in deciding, developing, and analyzing types of information that are applicable to a wide number of cases, such as determining whether "credit ratings" are helpful in forecasting the repayment prospects on credit extensions.

The third situation signals a need for judgment in individual cases. If even ultraconservative estimates of future cash flows are sufficient to justify purchase of an asset, there is little point in trying to develop more realistic (optimistic) projections. Similarly, if obviously optimistic estimates will result in rejection of a project, there is again little to be gained by increased realism. Again, if projections of the future are regarded as very imprecise, because of the need for costly or unobtainable information (e.g., a costly market survey), it may be better to tolerate the possibility of error in the projection, than to try to improve the projection.

As projections for specific purposes are considered, in subsequent chapters, some examples of projection procedures that attempt to reduce projection cost will be introduced. Beyond these techniques, common sense and ingenuity are required by the financial manager in this difficult task of deciding whether marginal amounts of effort should be devoted to the further fine-lining of projections.

Evaluating Information: Post Audits

Projections about the future are almost inevitably imperfect. Even excellently prepared estimates will almost surely not exactly coincide with actual events. While estimates will always be estimates, care can still be taken to ensure that they are not made under conditions of bias or error. For example, some individuals within a company who form predictions may be consistently optimistic or consistently pessimistic. Furthermore, particular estimating procedures employed may be erroneous.

To improve projections, and therefore decisions, the information once developed should be regularly appraised. To illustrate the advantage of appraisal, suppose that a factory has considered the purchase of a machine which was expected to reduce its need for labour. The cost of the device was estimated, as well as the cash flows that would result from reduced labour use. The estimated reduction in labour force was eight men, and this was seen as sufficient justification for buying the machine.

After the machine was installed, it could not practically be removed from the factory and resold. Therefore, there was no direct reason to reconsider the machine after it was emplaced. However, as operating results became known after the machine had been used for some time, it developed that maintenance on the machine itself required one workman (not anticipated) and that the machine only replaced six labourers instead of the intended eight. The result was a net saving of the employment of five men, not eight as projected.

A study of the machine, after it had been installed, would

reveal this projection error. Nothing could be done about this machine, but the information that this projection was erroneous could be used to improve subsequent projections. Without this after-the-fact evaluation, similar errors in projection might be repeated many times without detection. With the use of after-the-fact evaluation, or postaudit, needs for corrections in the process of making projections can be identified.

SUMMARY

Information about future prospects is required in the making of decisions about whether to purchase assets. For the financial officer, the most important attribute of the asset is the amount of cash inflows and outflows that will be associated with the asset, and the timing of these inflows and outflows. Therefore, it is customary to develop cash flow projections, series of point estimates of cash inflow and outflow over time, for assets under consideration. Feasibility studies of varying degrees of intensity are often undertaken to predict these flows.

It is important to distinguish between projected cash flows and projected accounting earnings; the former is most important in the asset acquisition decision.

It is usually desirable to separate the decision of whether to buy an asset from the decision about how the asset should be financed if it is bought.

Assets can usually be purchased in varying quantities. Marginal information, incremental series of cash flows associated with incremental amounts of asset purchased, are desirable data for decisions about such assets.

To the wealth-seeking company, it is after-tax cash that matters. Accordingly, inflows and outflows resulting from the imposition of federal and provincial income taxes must be incorporated in the refined cash flow projection.

Projection itself involves a cost; information is normally not free. Therefore, judgment must be exercised about the degree of effort that should be committed to attempting to predict cash flows.

Predictions can be improved in the future by attempting to discover patterns of error in past projections through the use of postaudits.

QUESTIONS AND PROBLEMS

1. What is a point estimate?

2. A company contemplates purchase of a machine. Original cost is $100,000 for purchase of the machine. Installation costs of $20,000 will be required. The purpose of the machine is to produce cost savings, but during the first two years of its life these savings are not expected to ensue, because of initial operating problems, training costs, and so on. After that, for the following five years the machine is expected to throw off cost savings of 3,000 hours of labour per year, with labour valued at $12 per hour. At this point, the end of the machine's seventh year, $40,000 cost for reconditioning and repairs is expected. This overhaul of the machine will enable it to continue to generate its labour savings for another three years. At the end of the tenth year of its life, it will be removed and sold for scrap at an estimated disposal price of $5,000.

   From this data develop a cash flow projection for the asset.

3. The asset described in the preceding question may also be bought in a larger size, for $200,000. This asset will save 5,000 hours of labour per year, will require a $100,000 overhaul in the seventh year, and will have an estimated salvage value of $15,000. Its installation costs are the same as the previous asset. Identify the marginal cash flows obtainable by purchasing the larger asset.

4. Turtle Trust Company has been asked by a client to aid in the evaluation of a real estate investment. The client has estimated that the proposed asset, a business building, will produce net earnings of $50,000 per year for 10 years, and $80,000 per year for the following 15 years. These earnings projections have taken depreciation into account; that depreciation was calculated using a straight-line method, a ten-year life, and an initial cost of $850,000.

   Putting yourself in the shoes of the Turtle Trust financial officer, and using only the information given, reassemble the data into cash flow projection (do not consider income taxes).

   Compare the usefulness of your reassembled projection to that of the income projection developed by your client.

5. With reference to the above question, the income projection was developed from additional assumption: that $500,000 of borrowed money would be used for part payment in acquiring the building, and that the interest on this money would be $50,000

per year for ten years, after which the borrowed $500,000 would be repaid in a lump sum.

Would you use this additional information as well in re-assembling the income projection into a cash flow projection? If so, why and how? If not, why not?

6. What is a tax shelter?

7. Mr. Wallace, a junior financial officer, is asked by his company's comptroller to prepare cash flow projections for a number of prospective assets. Before completing his projections Mr. Wallace checks with the comptroller about an income tax rate to be used in the projections. The comptroller tells him to ignore tax considerations because he is interested only in the *relative* attractiveness of the assets. "If an asset is best or worse before tax, it is going to be best or worst after tax, so why spend the effort on converting data to after-tax form." Mr. Wallace disagrees with this position. Do you? Why or why not?

RELATED READINGS

Bodenhorn, D. "A Cash Flow Concept of Profit." *Journal of Finance*, March 1964.

Canadian Master Tax Guide. Published annually by Commerce Clearing House Canadian Limited.

Hirshleifer, J. "On the Theory of Optimal Investment Decisions." *Journal of Political Economy*, August 1958.

Jaedicke, R. K., and Sprouse, R. T. *Accounting Flows: Income, Funds, and Cash.* Englewood Cliffs, N.J.: Prentice-Hall, 1965, pp. 1–28.

Porterfield, J. T. S. *Investment Decisions and Capital Costs.* Englewood Cliffs, N.J.: 1965, pp. 5–20.

Riddell, B. *The New Taxes.* Toronto: MacLean-Hunter, 1973.

3

ADJUSTMENT FOR TIME

In Chapter 2 information about amounts and timing of asset cash flows has been examined. As we have already noted, both characteristics—quantity and timing—are ingredients in the wealth-maximizing endeavour. In this chapter, an adjustment process for comparing these two aspects of cash flows will be explored. The central result of the adjustment will be to collapse the two dimensions into a single, composite measure as the wind chill equivalent temperatures summarize the combined effect of wind and cold.

PRESENT VALUE

Adjusting for Time: Present Value

The present value method is virtually identical in form to the wind chill table (Illustration 1–4) described in Chapter 1. In this method, a present value table is assembled. The table takes amounts of money available at varying times in the future, and expresses their equivalents in money amounts available at the present.

Here is an example of such a table:

Present Value of $1

Number of Years in the Future	Present Value
0	$1.00
1	0.94
2	0.89
3	0.84
4	0.79
5	0.75

The above table is used in the following manner. Suppose a company is choosing between two parcels of land, which are identical in price. Both of the assets will yield just one future cash inflow. Parcel A is expected to sell for $3,000 after one year. Parcel B will sell for $3,500 after four years. Both of these amounts of money, with varying amounts of futurity, can, by the above table, be converted to their equivalents in money available at present. The conversion for parcel A is

$$\$3,000 \times 0.94 = \$2,820.$$

The adjustment for parcel B is

$$\$3,500 \times 0.79 = \$2,765.$$

The two cash flow streams have now been converted to amounts which are directly comparable. By converting both to their present value equivalents, they are reduced to a common time dimension. Now a direct present value comparison can be made: Parcel A is modestly superior to parcel B.

The Table's Development: Compound Interest

The foundation of a present value table is a straightforward development from the mathematical properties of compound interest. *Compound interest* is defined as interest calculated over more than one period, with each period's interest determined on the basis of both principal and previously accumulated interest. It differs from *simple interest*, where "interest on interest" is not reckoned.

To exemplify, consider a loan agreement where $1,000 is borrowed at 6 percent interest for two years, with both interest and principal repayable at the end of the two-year period. If simple interest is employed, the repayable amount is simply $1,000 plus two years' interest on that $1,000, for a total amount of $1,120.

If interest is compounded annually, the calculation becomes:

Amount originally borrowed	$1,000.00
6% interest on $1,000	60.00
Total amount owing at end of year 1 . . .	$1,060.00
6% interest on $1,060	63.60
Total amount owing at end of year 2 . . .	$1,123.60

The compounding process can be described with a simple algebraic expression by noting that every year the compounding takes place, the amount of debt with interest already accumulated is increased by a factor (1 + interest rate). In the above example, the factor is 1.06, and one observes:

$$\$1,000 \times 1.06 = \$1,060.00$$
$$\$1,060 \times 1.06 = \$1,123.60.$$

The algebraic expression of compound interest will be based on the following terms:

P = A present amount of money.
r = Rate of interest.
F = A future amount of money.
n = Number of time periods involved.

Now the compounding process can be described as:

$$F = P(1 + r)^n$$

Once this expression has been identified, it can be employed to solve another type of problem. Consider the following question, "How much money would one have to invest now, at a compound interest of 6 percent, if he were to be able to have $1,000 available in five years?" Here a future amount of money, F, is given and it is necessary to solve for a present amount of money, P. The solution to this follows from the previous formula; that formula can be rearranged to

$$P = \frac{F}{(1 + r)^n}$$

or

$$P = F[1/(1 + r)^n].$$

When the interest rate is 6 percent and the time involved is five years,

$$1/(1 + r)^n = 1/(1.06)^5 + \text{about } 0.75.$$

Completing the solution,

$$P = \$1{,}000 \times 0.75 = \$750.$$

To obtain $1,000 five years hence, one would need to have $750 now.

This relationship casts considerable light on the question: How does one compare amounts of money of varying degrees of futurity? A future money amount is regarded as reproducible by the investment of a present amount of money now. For example, if X Company is offered $1,000 five years hence, it could say that such an amount is worth $750 right now, because that is the amount X Company would have to invest immediately at 6 percent in order to have $1,000 available in the future.

This line of reasoning was the foundation for the present value table in the previous section. That table was constructed on the basis of $1/(1.06)^n$, where various values of n are designated in the left-hand column. Those values in the right-hand column are often called *discount factors;* they are employed to "discount" a future amount to present value equivalence.

So far we have worked with a 6 percent interest rate; to provide more general usefulness, present value tables are constructed on the basis of a number of interest rates. These rates, when used in present value calculations, are often called *discount rates.* An example of such a table is given below and a more detailed version is included in Table A–1 in the Appendix at the end of the book.

It is apparent that the choice of discount rate, and with it

Present Value of $1 ($F = \$1$)

Number of			Interest Rates (r)		
Years (n)	6%	8%	10%	15%	20%
1	0.94	0.93	0.91	0.87	0.83
2	0.89	0.86	0.83	0.76	0.69
3	0.84	0.79	0.75	0.66	0.58
4	0.79	0.74	0.68	0.57	0.48
5	0.75	0.68	0.62	0.50	0.40
10	0.56	0.46	0.38	0.25	0.16
20	0.31	0.22	0.15	0.12	0.03

the related set of discount factors, is essential if the present value method of time adjustment is actually to be employed. However, that hard question may be set aside until later; first, it is desirable to explore the properties of present value tables more fully. These tables, and their underlying mathematics, are the most potent tools employed in contemporary financial analysis.

Present Value of Annuities

A second type of present value table is just a lazy man's adaptation of the first model—in some (but only some) applications of time adjustment, it removes some of the work. Where there are money payments of the same amount over a number of consecutive years, starting one year from the present, the present value of all of the payments can be obtained as:

Present value of series = (Annual amount) (discount factor$_1$ + discount factor$_2$ . . . + discount factor$_n$),

where subscripts denote years and where n is the last year of the series. A series of equal annual payments is called an annuity, and the sum of the discount factors for each year in the series may be called an *annuity discount factor*. Annuity discount factors for various values of n and r are presented in an *annuity table*, often identified as the present value of $1 per period.

As an example of the use of an annuity table, one might wish to know the present value of the rents on a building which are anticipated to be $2,000 per year for the next 20 years. Rather than laboriously identifying a discount factor for each year, multiplying that factor by $2,000, and then summing these products for each of the 20 years, an annuity table can be employed. Here is a simple example of such a table, calculated with 6 percent discount rate.

Number of Years Received	Present Value of $1 Received Annually
1	0.94
2	1.83
3	2.67
4	3.47
5	4.21
10	7.36
20	11.47

To employ the table in solving the rent problem, one simply refers to the appropriate value on the annuity table, 11.47, and multiplies that by $2,000 to obtain the present value of the stream of future rents, $22,940.

The method of construction of the annuity table, to repeat, is just a summing of discount factors from the "Present Value of $1" table. To illustrate, the annuity table gives the present value of $1 per year for three years as $2.67, where a 6 percent discount rate is used. Turning to the "Present Value of $1" table, one may obtain and sum the discount factors for each of the first three years:

$$0.94 + 0.89 + 0.84 = \$2.67$$

A detailed table (see Table A–2) giving the present value of annuities under different interest rates is included in the Appendix at the end of the book.

Mathematically, the annuity table may be described as the summing of a geometric progression. The formula underlying the table is:

$$P = \frac{A}{r} [1 - \frac{1}{(1 + r)^n}].$$

Sometimes it is useful to work with an annuity presumed to be of infinite time duration. Such an annuity is described as a *perpetuity*. Where n approaches infinity, $1/(1 + r)^n$ approaches a value of zero. Substituting into the above formula, a perpetuity is given a present value of

$$P = \frac{A(\text{perpetual})}{r} \cdot$$

A Computational Note

The annuity table presumes a series of annual payments starting one year from the present (end of the current year or year 1). The present value of a series of payments starting further in the future may be obtained by subtraction. For example, suppose someone wishes to know the present value of a $5,000 annuity commencing at the end of year 5, and continuing until the end of year 20. He may reason that this is equivalent to an annuity running from year 1 through year 20, except that payments were not received in year 1 through 4. Accordingly, he finds the annuity discount factor for $n = 20$, and subtracts the annuity discount factor for $n = 4$. If a rate of 6 percent were employed, the calculation would be $11.470 - 3.465 = 8.005$ as the appropriate annuity discount factor. The present value of the $5,000 annuity $= \$5,000 \times 8.005 = \$40,025$.

Mixed Present Value Problems

Frequently, in financial calculations, both of the two present value tables may be conveniently employed. Consider a simplified version of the facts in a typical machine purchase decision. The machine will result in labour savings of $10,000 per year over a five-year period. At the end of five years, the prospective purchaser plans to alter his production arrangements, and, therefore, expects to sell the machine at an estimated disposal value (or *salvage value*) of $40,000. Using a 10 percent discount rate, what is the present value of these benefits?

It is usually regarded as permissible to alter the facts a little for convenience in calculation. One convention often used is to assume end-of-year money amounts. In this problem, the labour saving will ensue throughout each year, perhaps evenly at a rate of $833 per month ($10,000/12), or $27.40 per day

($10,000/365). However, for ease of calculation, it will be assumed to occur in lump sums at the end of each year.

The problem now may be restated as finding the present value of two items:

1. $10,000 at each year-end for five years (labour saving).

2. $40,000 at end of fifth year (salvage).

On item (1) the annuity table is appropriate since a series of equal payments is involved. Present value of (1) is $10,000 × 3.791 = $37,910, where 3.791 is read from the annuity table (Table A–2) in the Appendix.

For item (2), with a single payment, the "Present Value of $1" table (Table A–1, Appendix) is appropriate. This is found to be $40,000 × 0.621 = $24,840. The total present value of the benefits received from the machine is found by adding the present values of the two benefit components = $37,910 + $24,840 = $62,750.

Net Present Value

The most common use of the concept of present value in business is that of asset evaluation. Should a particular asset be purchased or not? Typically purchase of the asset will require an immediate cash outlay from the purchasing company. Then, as time passes, the asset is expected to generate money receipts. The financial evaluation of the asset purchase requires a comparison of these cash outlays and inflows.

One naïve test of asset acceptability may first come to mind: an asset would unquestionably be unsatisfactory if the only information available about it was that its projected cash inflows were less than outflows. For example, it would be nonsensical to pay $1,000 for an asset which over its lifetime is expected to yield benefits totaling $800 (including salvage value). This test of acceptability, which requires

$$\text{Money inflows} > \text{money outflows},$$

will reject glaringly bad projects, but it is not stringent enough to reject all undesirable projects.

The deficiency in the test should be apparent from previous discussion. The test does not consider timing of cash flows. For example, a machine which will cost an immediate $1,000 and which will return $110 per year for ten years will pass the money inflows > money outflows test; $1,100 >$1,000. However, the money receipts occur much later than outflows, and timeliness of money payments is important. Timeliness can be recognized by modifying the test to the following decision rule:

Present value of inflows > present value of outflows

In the above example, if a 10 percent discount rate is employed,

Present value of $1,000 purchase price = $1,000.
Present value of $110 per year for 10 years = $676

Applying the modified test,

[Present value of inflows, $676] < [present value of outflows, $1,000],

the asset is rejected.

This decision rule may be expressed in alternative form:

Present value of inflows − present value of outflows > 0.

In turn the right-hand side of this expression may be described by the term *net present value*, NPV:

NPV = Present value of inflows − present value of outflows.

The rule described above may then be restated as

NPV > 0.

In the example, again,

NPV = $676 − $1,000 = −324.

When the timing of receipts is considered, the value of money disbursed for the machine will exceed the value of receipts.

DISCOUNT RATES

Choice of Discount Rate: Current Practice

In present value or NPV calculations, a discount rate is required. Up to this point we have skirted the question of how this rate is determined. The method that appears to prevail in current business is to start with a basic interest rate and then add a premium to compensate for risk:

Discount rate = Riskless rate + risk premium.

In turn, these terms may be defined as:

Riskless rate is the rate of interest currently prevailing on securities with no risk of nonpayment. Usually, this rate would be determined by observing the interest rate on newly issued Government of Canada Bonds.

Risk premium is an addition to the riskless rate to reflect risk conditions. In practice, just as risk is usually assessed judgmentally rather than precisely measured, the risk premium is assigned judgmentally. Observation of corporate practice suggests that these premiums may range from 4 percent to 25 percent or more in current usage. For example, a petroleum company may consider an investment in exploration of a new oil field to be quite risky, and an investment in a pipeline to be quite safe. Accordingly, it might, if the riskless rate was 8 percent, establish a discount rate of 30 percent for the exploration (risk premium of 22 percent) and 12 percent for the pipeline (risk premium of 4 percent).

In a later chapter devoted to risk, the topic of risk premium determination will be considered again. Various approaches have been attempted to establish systematic rules for risk-premium determination. However, it is worth repeating that a systematic approach to risk-premium determination is not evident in current business practice.

And this is not surprising; one could hardly expect otherwise until businesses are able to adopt practicable methods for measuring the risk dimension itself.

The reader will note that, though this chapter started by dealing with adjustment for time (present value and NPV), risk adjustment has also slipped in. By making the choice of discount rate on the basis of risk considerations, present values and NPVs are made lower for risky projects than for safe ones. One can easily observe the effect of this risk-associated difference in discount rates. Consider two machines, both of which are expected to return $10,000 per year in cost savings for five years. On one, there is little chance for deviation from the expected return of $10,000 per year; its returns are discounted at 8 percent to produce a present value of $68,000. On the second machine, there is a large chance for variation around the expected amount. If a 20 percent discount rate was deemed appropriate for this risky situation, that would value the second machine at $40,000.

In practical terms, this calculation would tell the financial manager that the first machine is an acceptable purchase if it can be bought for less than $68,000, while the second machine is only desirable if it can be acquired for less than $40,000. Notice that the method of using high discount rates for high-risk projects is, in this application to machine purchase policy, used to ensure that risky machines are purchased only if they are expected to produce extraordinarily high receipts.

Reasons for Associated High Discount Rates with Risk

There are several good reasons for setting high discount rates, or alternatively, expecting high receipts on risky assets. First, risky situations are not sought after so eagerly by competitors, so it is reasonable to expect that higher receipts are potentially obtainable on high-risk ventures.

Second, the acquisition of a high-risk asset normally means that the acquiring company moves closer to being characterized as a higher risk company; this in turn, as we shall discuss in later chapters, may mean that financing charges made to the company by its creditors and other financing sources will be higher. Therefore, it is reasonable to expect more receipts from high-risk projects because they contribute to higher financing costs.

Third, the company's share prices may be adversely affected by the company's exposure to risk, unless the money received from the risky project is handsome enough to offset the impact of the risk. This third point is an important one, because it can be used to answer the question, "What if the particular group of people who constitute the company's shareholders are individuals who personally don't mind taking risks?" Even if these shareholders are not directly concerned about risk, they are still likely to be concerned about the prices of the shares they own. Thus, the company will even be serving the interests of exceptional shareholders, who aren't directly concerned with risk, by insisting on high performance from high-risk projects.

RATE OF RETURN

Choice of a discount rate is a vexacious issue. One approach to financial calculations appears (but only appears) to avoid the necessity of choosing a rate, by instead solving for one. This rate, found by calculation from other facts, is called variously rate of return, internal rate, or return on investment (ROI).

Suppose Carlisle Ltd.'s real estate department bought attractive land outside of Calgary five years ago for $150,000, as an intended plant site. Later, plans were changed so the plant site was not needed, and it was recently sold for $250,000. A shareholder of the company who became aware of this transaction said that he "was disappointed that the company had money tied up in land yielding such a modest appreciation during a period when a trust company savings account would have paid 7 percent compound interest." He said he would like to know what "rate of interest" the real estate had actually yielded.

To solve such a problem, one needs to reexamine the character of the discount factors which have previously been used. They give the present value of a future dollar where a discount rate and time span is specified. Alternatively, a discount factor may be regarded as a ratio, $P:F$. In previous usage, we have worked with known value of F, r, and n; now we may observe that with known values of P, F, and n, the present value table may be used to obtain r.

Consider the Carlisle example again:

$P = \$150,000$, the initial price of the land.
$F = \$250,000$, the amount for which the land was later sold.
$n = 5$, the number of years the land was held.
P/F, discount factor implied by above facts $= 150,000/250,000 = 0.6$

Now one may go to the "Present Value of $1" table (Table A–1, Appendix), and find the r that is associated with $P/F = 0.6$, $n = 5$. Reading rightward from $n = 5$, the discount factor closest to 0.6 is 0.621. Reading upward, $r =$ about 10 percent.

(Interpolation could be used for more precise results.)[1] Thus, the apprehensive Carlisle shareholder can be reassured.

Rate of Return as an Acceptance Test

The rate of return is sometimes used in practice as a measure of prospective performance on assets. In fact, the method competes with NPV in current practice as an asset evaluator. The relative attractiveness of rate of return is largely superficial, though. While a rate can be identified on an asset, and used to describe the prospects of the asset, the usual acceptance decision rule specified is

Rate of return > Appropriate minimum rate (or *target rate*).

In turn, the best statement about setting the target rate is

Target rate = Riskless rate + risk premium,

the same formula as that for the choice of an appropriate discount rate. Thus, the information requirement is just as great for either the NPV or rate of return methods. Used in the manner described here, it is not surprising to note that they yield identical results; out of a group of assets being considered, all of the assets rejected by NPV will be rejected by rate of return, and all accepted by one method will also be accepted by the other.

Rate of Return in More Detail

If rate of return leads to the same results as NPV, why should one be familiar with this method, too? There are three reasons: First, both methods are used in practice, and the student of finance should be familiar with current practice—embarrassment may be avoided, if for no other reason. Second, not all asset choices are accept/reject decisions of the type just discussed, and the two methods do not yield the same results in other situations—to be considered later. Third, the rate of return mode of calculation is almost universally employed to de-

---

[1] Mathematically, in the case of a single future receipt and a single present payment, $r = \sqrt[n]{F/P} - 1$. This follows directly from the compound interest formula, $F = P/(1 + r)^n$.

termine the cost of financing the company's assets—more on this will come later.

Because of its importance, consideration of a more detailed rate of return problem is justifiable. Suppose JKL Telephones, Ltd. contemplates the installation of electronic switching equipment. It estimates end-of-year amounts as:

1976	Cost of equipment	−$3,000,000
1977	Additional cost of training	
	personnel and other start-up costs	− 1,000,000
1978–1987	Labour savings each year, no salvage	
(10 years)	value	700,000

To act on this information, a comprehensive definition of rate of return is needed. *Rate of return is a discount rate that, when used to calculate present values, will result in NPV = 0.* Note that this definition is consistent with the previous calculation; the rate found then was that rate associated with the discount factor P/F; if F was discounted by that factor it would equal P and hence NPV would be zero. In more complex problems, the discount rate which sets NPV = 0 must be found experimentally.

To return to the JKL data one may "try on" a discount rate, say, $r = 12$ percent. Accordingly, one obtains at the end of 1976,

Description	12% Discount Factors	Present Value
Present value of JKL switching equipment outflows:		
−$3,000,000 initially	1.000	−$3,000,000
−$1,000,000, 1 year hence	.893	− 893,000
Total present value of outflows		−$3,893,000
Present value of JKL switching equipment inflows:		
$700,000 per year for 10 years, starting 1 year hence		
(11-year annuity discount factor of 5.988) −		
(1-year annuity discount factor of 0.893)	5.095	
Total present value of inflows		3,566,500
Net present value, sum of all payments		− 326,500

If NPV is negative in the trial calculation, the experimental value of r is too high. (The converse also holds.) Another trial may be run at $r = 0.10$

Present value of outflows	-$3,909,000
Present value of inflows	+ 3,910,200
Net present value	$ 1,200

On a project this size, NPV = $1,200 may be regarded as approximating NPV = 0, so rate of return = 10%.

OTHER USES OF PRESENT VALUE TABLES

Considered as a P/F ratio, the discount factor may be used to solve another broad class of financial problem of the type, "How much will accumulate at the end of a period?" For example, a company may have $100,000 in surplus cash at the present time, and an opportunity to invest that cash in a savings account which offers 6 percent compound interest. It wishes to know how much money will have accumulated at the end of five years, when it plans to use these funds for a plant expansion. This question can be converted to a ratio form: What future amount will accumulate from every dollar invested at present, or alternatively, where the rate of interest is 6 percent and the number of years involved is five, what is the value of F/P?

Recalling the ratio character of discount factors, the answer to this question is now easy. F/P is the reciprocal of P/F, so

$$F/P = 1/\text{discount factor}.$$

The discount factor for five years at 6 percent is 0.747.

$$1/.747 = 1.339.$$

Therefore, $100,000 invested now for five years will increase to almost $134,000.

Similarly, the ratio character of the discount factor can be used to solve another class of problems. For example, suppose you were interested in the question, "How long would it take to accumulate $50,000 if one is able to invest $25,000 at present at the rate of interest of 15 percent?" Here a present amount of money (P) of $25,000 is being compared with a target future amount (F) of $50,000. Thus, the discount factor that will describe this situation is known:

$$P/F = \$25,000/\$50,000 = 0.50.$$

The situation can be described by a discount factor of 0.50, and an interest rate (r) of 15 percent. We need to know the number of years (n). One can now go to the Present Value of $1 table (Table A–1, Appendix) and look down the column of discount factors under 15 percent until he comes to 0.497 (approximately 0.5), the discount factor derived from the facts above. Then, looking leftward to the "years" column he can observe that the discount factor 0.497 is associated with five years. Thus, the individual will have to wait five years to realize his objective of getting $50,000.

SUMMARY

Information about prospective assets is customarily developed in at least two dimensions—the amount and timing of cash flows. Time adjustment is a method for expressing an equivalence between these dimensions.

The principle time adjustment technique is represented by a present value table which is in turn developed from the concept of compound interest. The present value table may express the present value of $1 to be received in the future, or the present value of a series of $1 payments flowing through the future.

A stream of cash flows over time, may contain both positive and negative quantities during the various time periods. Net present value is the algebraic sum of the present values of a series of cash flows; NPV may be a positive or negative. A common test of asset acceptability rests on the decision rule NPV > 0.

Discount rates are required for present value calculations; these are usually set judgmentally, based on a riskless rate and a risk premium. Higher discount rates, and reciprocally, lower present values, are associated with higher risk in conventional usage.

The internal rate of return is an experimentally identified discount rate which will cause the NPV of a series of cash flows to be 0. This rate of return may be used as an asset evaluator; the rule is rate of return > target rate.

Present value relationships may be used to solve a variety of financial problems, such as the time needed to obtain an investment objective.

QUESTIONS AND PROBLEMS

1. Find the present value of $10,000 to be received five years hence, using a discount rate of 10 percent. Use the present value table (Table A–1, appendix).

2. Solve the problem, using algebra.

3. A business venture is expected to return $20,000 after five years. As a business man you regard 15 percent as the minimum acceptable return on ventures of this type. What is the most you would be willing to pay in order to participate in this business opportunity?

4. An apartment building is expected to produce rentals of $12,000 per year over the next 20 years. At the end of 20 years it is assumed that the building will be worthless. Find the present value of the rents, using a discount rate of 12 percent.

5. What would be the value of the above building if it was expected to last 25 years instead of 20? What is the extra value associated with extending the life of a building from 20 years to 25 years?

6. Company X borrows $100,000 from Company Y on a promissory note with the following terms:

    $100,000 principal must be paid at the end of three years; payment of principal in advance is not permitted. Interest payments of 12 percent per annum are due at the end of each year.

    a. Identify the cash flow stream for the note, a type of asset.
    b. Company B decides to sell A's notes to a third party, immediately after acquiring it. The third party, Company C, is willing to buy the note if it can make 15 percent on its investment. What amount will Company C offer for the note?

7. A tract of timber can be purchased now for $1 million. Timber will be allowed to grow for 15 years. At that time it is estimated that the value of the tract will have increased to five times its purchase price. Determine NPV for the tract, using a discount rate of 10 percent.

    Try the same calculation with a discount rate of 20 percent.

8. A business has been hiring a trucking firm to make deliveries to some of its customers and contemplates buying a truck to save on these delivery charges. Discuss how the NPV method

could be used in making this decision. How would you determine a discount rate?

9. How does the use of high-risk premiums in discount rate determination cause a company to avoid risky projects?

10. Future value = $200,000, present value = $100,000, five year's time is involved. Find internal rate of return.

11. An employee decides to return to school for a year to acquire a new technical skill. Tuition for the year's course of study is $2,000. The employee is currently earning $15,000 per year. One year's income will be lost if he takes the class. His enrollment in the class will increase his earnings by $1,500 per year over the next 15 years. Find internal rate of return (ignore income tax considerations).

12. What considerations would be involved in determining a target rate for the decision about whether to undertake the year of education in the above problem? What nonmoney considerations would be involved in a decision about whether to undertake the year's education?

13. If an individual saves $1,000 in 1980 and is able to earn 10 percent compound interest on this money for ten years, how much will be accumulated by 1990?

14. Using compound interest, how long does it take for money to double if 12 percent interest is available?

RELATED READINGS

Cissell, R., and Cissell, H. *Mathematics of Finance*. 4th ed. Boston: Houghton Mifflin, 1972.

Jean, W. "Terminal Value or Present Value in Capital Budgeting Programs." *Journal of Financial and Quantitative Analysis*, January 1971.

Mao, J. C. T. *Corporate Financial Decisions*. Palo Alto, Calif.: Pavan, 1976, chap. 5.

4

CAPITAL BUDGETING

Capital budgeting is the name frequently given to the process of deciding which assets to purchase. Historically the term capital budgeting, has frequently referred to the preparation of a plan, or budget, for the expenditures on long-lived assets. However, the methods involved have applicability in analysis of short-lived as well as long-lived assets.

And there is good reason for applying capital budgeting methods consistently to all company assets. Without full spectrum interasset comparison, a company may be tolerating relatively inferior assets unwittingly. Worse yet, those inferior assets may be using up investment dollars that could have been more productively deployed elsewhere.

Asset Choice: Basic Economics

The capital budgeting problem is part of a wider class of budgeting problems; in general these problems have a solution which may be described as:

$$\boxed{\begin{array}{l}\text{Marginal benefit per}\\ \text{unit of cost of A}\end{array}} = \boxed{\begin{array}{l}\text{Marginal benefit per}\\ \text{unit of cost of B}\end{array}} = \cdots \boxed{\begin{array}{l}\text{Marginal benefit per}\\ \text{unit of cost of N}\end{array}}$$

where A, B, . . . N refer to items being purchased. Verbally, this optimal budget principle may be reexpressed as: "A dollar should never be spent on one item when it can generate greater benefit by being spent on another item." When a budget is optimally allocated it is used in such a way that no more improvement is possible. This condition of "no more improvement possible" is satisfied when the *equimarginal* relationship is established; namely, that marginal benefits per dollar spent are equalized with respect to each of the items among which a budgetary choice is being made.

The Objective in the Budgeting Process

The equimarginal rule, if it can be rigorously applied, will proportion a company's funds in a manner that will best serve the company's objectives—at least on the basis of the information known at the time that decisions have to be made. Note that the rule presumes that benefits, or corporate objectives, are defined. This question was addressed in Chapter 1, when the objective of the company was presumed to be wealth maximization. Thus in the case of the company, marginal benefit is presumed to mean marginal net receipts of money, adjusted for time and for risk.

VARIOUS EVALUATION METHODS

One might conclude, especially if he agreed that all companies shared the wealth-maximizing objective, that virtually all companies would then agree on a process for evaluation of prospective assets. That, however, is not the case. There are a number of criteria by which assets are selected that are in common usage. Some of these methods, particularly those involving the calculation of present values, are thought to be theoretically stronger than others. However, these "purer" methods have not gained full ascendancy in practical usage. We shall examine a number of methods in current use and attempt to assess their strengths and weaknesses.

The first methods to be examined may be characterized as *capital budgeting without rationing*. With these methods, each potential asset is accepted or rejected on its own merits. A test is applied, and if the asset satisfies the test's decision rule (such as NPV > 0), its purchase is approved. Underlying this method is the presumption that financing is available for all acceptable assets. In economic analysis, capital budgeting without rationing is consistent with a perfectly elastic capital supply—financing available without limit at a given capital cost per dollar used.

Cost of capital is broadly defined as:

Capital cost = (Dollars per year required to compensate all suppliers of funds to the company) ÷ (total assets).

It is similar to the interest rate paid on borrowed money but relates to the cost of all funds used by the company, whether provided by owners or creditors. Measurement and more refined definition of capital cost are discussed in Chapter 11.

Nonrationing capital budgeting methods may be subdivided into those which use present value calculations and those that do not. The present value or discounting methods include net present value and internal rate of return. Two nondiscounting methods will be introduced later.

CAPITAL BUDGETING WITHOUT RATIONING (DISCOUNTING METHODS)

The logical process involved in capital budgeting without rationing is shown in Illustration 4–1. This format relates to discounting methods. The various steps in the illustration are described as follows:

1. A discount rate for the NPV method or target rate for the IRR method is established. This rate would usually reflect both the company's cost of obtaining funds and risk in the asset under consideration. Because risk will usually vary among assets under consideration, a family of rates, for projects falling into different risk categories, is commonly used.

2. The appropriate rate is either applied in an NPV calculation or compared with the project's IRR.

ILLUSTRATION 4-1

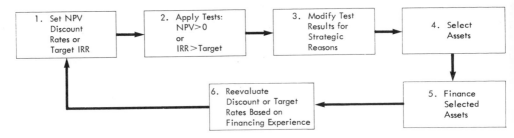

3.   The test results may be modified because of broader strategic considerations that have not been quantified into the asset's cash flow projections. For example, a new plant with NPV < 0, might be regarded as acceptable because of the learning experience it would provide for the company in the production and marketing of a new product line.

4.   On the basis of both the quantitative test and nonquantitative considerations, potential asset purchases are accepted or rejected.

5.   Consistent with the assumption of available capital, it is assumed that assets purchases accepted can be financed.

6.   Information from the experience in financing assets is regularly fed back into the setting of discount or target rates, since capital cost is an important ingredient in determining these rates.

The most basic type of capital budgeting choice process involves the establishment of an acceptance criterion such as NPV > 0. Any asset proposal may be subjected to the test. If the proposal meets the acceptance conditions the asset is purchased, and if it doesn't it is rejected.

Such a test is consistent with the equimarginal principle. If assets are considered in marginal quantities, increments of an asset will be added up to the point where the last increment of the asset considered is probably close to the minimum acceptable standard. Since all assets are subject to the same procedure, there should be a tendency for the marginal benefit per dollar invested on each asset to be close to the minimum standard for acceptability. That is, using an NPV test, increments of assets would tend to be added until marginal NPVs on all assets were close to zero. Note that with such a test, a high marginal benefit per dollar invested is regarded as a signal that, on that asset, there may be further benefits to be exploited.

We may now turn to various tests that are in common use. While they may all have the general intent of wealth maximization, they differ in the way by which they test any project's contribution to this goal.

Marginal Net Present Value

We have already looked at the mechanics of the NPV test for acceptability: Marginal NPV > 0. We have also looked at the rationale for applying this test on a marginal basis, both when the desirability of developing marginal information was considered in Chapter 2, and also when the rationale of the equimarginal principle was examined.

The principal strength of the NPV method is its close relationship to the definition of wealth, defined as prospective net cash flows adjusted for time and risk. By specifying a discount rate which not only reflects an adjustment for time, but also the prevalent mode of compensating for risk, projected marginal cash outflows and inflows associated with a project are both reduced to present values, or amounts of wealth. Thus, the Marginal NPV > 0 test becomes, when verbally reexpressed, "Are there net additions to wealth associated with adding to this particular asset?" Since the ultimate extent of wealth maximization is the acceptance of all wealth-enhancing projects, the NPV test is directly consistent with the wealth-maximizing precept.

Another advantage of NPV lies in the possibility of relating cost of capital to the asset choice process. The risk-reflecting discount rates employed in the NPV calculation can be directly related to the company's cost of acquiring funds via the feedback process shown in Illustration 4–1.

The fact that the NPV method does not have full acceptance in the business world suggests that it may have disadvantages as well as these advantages just noted. These disadvantages will emerge as other acceptance criteria are compared with the NPV method.

Rate of Return

As discussed previously, the rate of return method for accept/reject decisions consists of first identifying the project's marginal internal rate of return, that rate which brings the present value of all marginal cash inflows and outflows to zero, and then testing that rate against a target rate: marginal rate of return > target rate.

Suppose that a project requires a $100,000 outlay this year, and a $10,000 outlay next year. Following that it will return $50,000 per year for the next five years, after which it will be salable for a salvage value of $15,000. All values are assumed to be after tax. The experimental obtaining of rate of return is shown in the following table:

		Discounted Values Using Various Discount Rates		
Year	Cash Flow	15%	25%	26%
0	−$100,000	−$100,000	−$100,000	−$100,000
1	− 10,000	− 8,700	− 8,000	− 7,940
2	50,000	37,800	32,000	31,500
3	50,000	32,900	25,600	25,000
4	50,000	28,600	20,500	19,850
5	50,000	24,850	16,400	15,750
6	65,000	28,080	17,030	16,250
Sum (NPV)		$ 43,530	$ 3,530	$ 410

We observe that the rate of return is approximately 26 percent. This rate can then be tested against the target rate of return that is deemed commensurate to the riskiness of the asset.

The similarity between the NPV and rate of return methods is quite apparent. Both are based on present value calculations. In fact, where they are employed on accept/reject decisions, both methods will normally yield the same results. This equality of results rests on the plausible assumption that the discount rate used in the NPV method, and deemed reflective of the capital cost and risk conditions, will be identical to the target rate of return established in the rate of return method.

The equivalence is easily substantiated by recalling the nature of the rate of return calculation. Successive rates of return were tried until one yielded NPV = approximately 0. Any lower discount rate would have yielded an NPV > 0.

Thus, as long as the target rate or discount rate is less than the rate of return, the same project evaluated by the NPV method will yield NPV > 0, the NPV acceptance condition.

This point is illustrated in the arithmatic example above by first considering a target rate of 25 percent. Then the project is not only acceptable on a rate of return basis at, but also at a 25 percent discount rate that yields a positive NPV of $3,530. Alternatively, had a 28 percent target rate been selected, the project would have been rejected since the project's rate of return of approximately 26 percent is less than 28 percent; similarly discounting the projected cash flow at 28 percent yields, as the reader can verify, a negative NPV of −$5,505.

If NPV and rate of return yield the same results, are there any differences? The answer is yes. First, as we shall shortly observe, capital budgeting decisions may be made in a rationing context, and there the results are not necessarily the same with these two methods.

Second, there are some minor bases of preference in the case of the nonrationing decision. To the extent that decisions on capital budgeting may involve presentations to persons who are unfamiliar with the term "net present value," rate of return is a more commonly used and perhaps more widely understood expression. On the other hand, computationally the rate of return method is more difficult, since it involves a trial and error process. It is also more indirect. Who cares what the rate of return really is, so long as it is greater than the target rate; i.e., so long as discounting at the target rate yields NPV > 0.

A third problem with rate of return will be noted in passing. In unusual instances, the mathematical properties of internal rate of return identification make possible an ambiguous solution, where a particular asset may have more than one rate of return. If this multiple rate of return problem is suspected, an NPV test, discounting at the target rate, will resolve any question about the project's acceptability.

At this point in our analysis NPV and rate of return are approximately tied. Both methods also have wide acceptance in practice. Since marginal NPV is consistent with the concept of equimarginal wealth maximization, marginal rate of return must, at this point, also be regarded as consistent with a wealth-maximizing objective.

LIQUIDITY AND OTHER STRATEGIC CONSIDERATIONS

In warfare a distinction is made between strategy and tactics. Tactics refers to plans and procedures employed in specific situations. Strategy is more general, governing the relationships between special situations. Tactics are used to win battles. Strategy is concerned with winning the war (and the ensuing peace settlement). Strategists may override tacticians; it may be better to deprive a field commander of resources needed to win a battle and hold these in reserve for more critical battles which may follow.

One may liken the NPV or IRR tests to tactical decisions. All the facts that can be quantified about a particular asset are analyzed. While this analysis is vital, it may be incomplete. Information that is not quantified, and viewpoints broader than that of the analysts, may also require consideration and may result in a reversal of an original accept/reject choice.

It is impossible to catalogue all of the strategic considerations that may be interposed into the asset decision process. However, some illustrative strategic questions may be posed:

1. Does the asset impose legal consequences; for example, will the new plant addition enlarge output to the point where anti-combines prosecution may result?

2. Does the asset bring one division of our company into competition with another?

3. Does the asset provide valuable learning experience?

4. Does the asset have an impact on public relations, or labour relations?

It is important to note that the possible conflict between these strategic considerations and the initial asset analysis is not, or at least need not be, a conflict over the objective of wealth maximization. A project may be deemed acceptable or unacceptable from the viewpoint of wealth maximization at a tactical level. Subsequent reversal of the tactical decision need only imply that the overall wealth maximization of the company was better served by foregoing advantage at the tactical level.

Liquidity

One extra-quantitive consideration often introduced to modify initial accept/reject decisions relates to liquidity. Liquidity may be understood by first considering this attribute at its extreme. An asset is regarded as ultimately liquid if it is immediately available for the purchase of other assets or the discharge of liabilities. Cash on hand and bank demand deposits usually qualify for description as ultimately liquid assets.

Liquidity refers to the ease with which an asset can be made available for spending. One definition of a liquid asset is "an item that can be readily converted into cash without significant loss." There is no accepted measure of *degree* of liquidity, so the extent of the attribute in any asset must be assessed judgmentally.

The importance of liquidity lies mainly in the ability it affords to cope with the unexpected. Should unforeseen expenses arise, or should unanticipated investment opportunities occur, liquid assets provide one means for handling these situations. By expeditiously handling these expenses or opportunities, the wealth of the company may be preserved or enhanced.

An Illustration of Liquidity

A company is considering asset purchases which will increase the output of one of its plants. One of these involves plant enlargement, the second the stockpiling of raw materials to eliminate seasonal plant shutdowns. Suppose both assets are regarded to be of equal riskiness and an appropriate time adjustment process indicates that a marginal investment in the plant will yield a higher NPV than a similar investment in inventory. It is possible that a firm might rationally act in a manner contrary to that suggested by the NPV comparison, and buy the inventory anyway.

The reason: should difficulties or unusual opportunities develop unexpectedly in some other component of the corporate entity, the inventory commitment would be more reversible, or liquid. Once the plant is built it lasts for many years, but a seasonal inventory accumulation will usually involve a de-cumulation of the inventory later in the season; in the follow-ing season the inventory is again built up. Thus, every season there is an opportunity to decide to revert to the old low level of production by avoiding the recommitment of funds to the raw materials stockpile.

Possible Confusion between Illiquidity and Risk

In considering the liquidity of assets, it is important to dis-tinguish between considerations of liquidity and risk. To the extent that an asset is readily salable, this tends to limit the riskiness of the asset; if the asset fails to fulfill its intended purpose, it can be sold. If liquidity and low risk are associated, it is appropriate to account for both of these attributes. For example, a calculation of NPV might be made with a lower discount rate for an asset that lacked risk because it was read-ily salable at a relatively certain price, and then the asset might be given some additional preference because of its liquidity.

Note that the two do not necessarily go hand in hand. For example, a machine which results in labour saving on an as-sembly line may be a safe investment, in the sense that its benefits can be confidently predicted. But at the same time it may be very illiquid—once the machine has been installed, it may be completely uneconomical to remove it and resell it.

An asset may also be liquid and risky. A mining operation, for example, may be of such nature that it will exploit its ore body fully within a year. However, the ore may be valuable, or virtually worthless, depending on the vagaries of the metal market. Such an asset is reasonably liquid, in the sense that if it yields any benefits it will yield them quickly, but at the same time it is risky.

CAPITAL BUDGETING WITHOUT DISCOUNTING

Payback

Unlike the NPV and rate of return, payback does not involve present value calculations. Instead, payback may be thought of as an answer to the question, "How long will it take to get our money back?" More formally, a *payback period* is identified by starting at the present, and summing undiscounted cash flows one year at a time until the sum of the cash flows equals zero. (An interpolation may be necessary.)

An example will again illustrate. A project has the following cash flows:

Year 0	Asset is purchased	−$100,000
Year 1	Asset is in operation	+ 20,000
Year 2	Asset is in operation	+ 30,000
Year 3	Asset is in operation but requires major remodeling	− 10,000
Year 4	Asset is in operation	+ 40,000
Year 5	Asset is in operation	+ 40,000
Year 6	Asset is in operation	+ 40,000
Year 7	Asset is salvaged	+ 25,000

With this information, a schedule of accumulated cash flows can also be identified.

Year	Cash Flows	Cumulative Cash Flows
0	−$100,000	−$100,000
1	+ 20,000	− 80,000
2	+ 30,000	− 50,000
3	− 10,000	− 60,000
4	+ 40,000	− 20,000
5	+ 40,000	+ 20,000
6	+ 40,000	+ 60,000
7	+ 25,000	+ 85,000

It is now apparent that the accumulation of cash flows on the project reaches 0, hence paying off the investment in the project, between years 4 and 5. Interpolation would identify the payback period as 4.5 years.

The accept/reject rule, using the payback method, is

Payback on prospective asset < target payback.

In turn, the target or minimal acceptable payback is identified by the company on a judgmental basis, and may be varied in response to risk conditions. That is, projects that are perceived to have higher risk may be subject to testing with a relatively short target payback period.

Disadvantages of Payback

The payback method has some well-known conceptual disadvantages. First, it fails to consider information beyond the payback period. We may note, in the example above, that the prospective performance of the asset under consideration during years 6 and 7, was entirely ignored in the calculation; payback would have been indentified as 4.5 years, irrespective of whether the project had been expected to yield nothing or $1 million during years 6 and 7.

A second disadvantage of the payback lies in its ignoring of time-shape within the payback period. Another example will illustrate the nature of this problem in an exaggerated form; data includes only the first three years of each asset's life:

	Asset 1		Asset 2	
Year	Annual Cash Flow	Cumulative Cash Flow	Annual Cash Flow	Cumulative Cash Flow
0 . . .	−$100,000	−$100,000	−$100,000	−$100,000
1 . . .	70,000	− 30,000	0	− 100,000
2 . . .	15,000	− 15,000	0	− 100,000
3 . . .	15,000	0	100,000	0

Note that both projects have equal payback periods. Yet, if timing of money flows is important, asset 1 is clearly superior. It yields most of its "payback" very soon while the "payback" on asset 2 comes later.

If these two conceptual difficulties are not enough, there are some more problems in implementation. First, there is no obvious connection between the target payback period and the company's cost of capital. Capital costs can provide some overall guideline for the establishment of NPV discount rates or rate of return target rates but they provide no ready feedback into the establishment of the target payback period.

Additionally, payback rates enjoy little usage and make little sense in evaluating assets that are bought with the intent of subsequent disposal. For example, judging a temporary raw material stockpile as superior to a building, on the basis of a one-year target payback test, would seem absurd. (While this problem is sufficiently major to warrant special mention it should be noticed that it is essentially a special case of the first objection raised; a comparison of a building and an inventory would fail to reckon the considerable benefits that might obtain from the building after the payback period.)

Advantages of Payback

The disadvantages of the payback method are widely known and rather obvious, and yet the payback method remains at least as popular as either of the previously discussed methods. What are its advantages? First, and perhaps least important, it is computationally easy, and does not require knowledge of present value techniques. (Since payback is used by companies employing complex production technologies, explaining its use here on the basis of the company's inability to understand present value seems rather implausible.) Second, it has limited information requirements; the information must be projected only far enough into the future to establish that undiscounted cash inflows equal outflows, and at most no longer than the target payback period. Third, the method also gives recognition to liquidity, since payback is directly related to the asset's reconversion to cash.

It is also worth noting that the conceptual problems of the payback methods may be offsetting ones. This may be observed by classifying the cash flow time-shapes from assets as being after the initial investment, either ascending or descending. An asset with ascending cash flows is a slow starter but picks up momentum with time—examples might include assets which require learning or gradual market penetration. A descending asset is one that yields its results quickly, but not sustainably— an example would be an asset associated with a product that can be priced high until competitors are attracted.

Now to return to the two basic conceptual objections to payback. First it ignores cash flows after the payback period; this characteristic results in inadequate recognition for ascending assets. The second disadvantage is failure to consider the timing of cash flows within the payback period; this characteristic results in inadequate recognition of descending assets. Thus, the two conceptual weaknesses of the payback method may be partially self-cancelling.

While payback is not devoid of advantages, its lack of direct connection to the wealth-maximizing process makes it, at least conceptually, a method inferior to NPV or rate of return. While the method should be known, and even respected, by students of finance, it appears to lack the potential for scientifically based decisions that the other methods contain.

Accounting Return

This fourth method appears to be less widely used in practice than the other three, but it still has its followers.

Accounting rate of return is defined as:

$$\text{Accounting rate of return} = \frac{\text{Expected annual accounting earnings from asset}}{\text{Initial cost of asset}}$$

It differs from the other three methods in that it draws on different information. While we have presumed with the other three methods that projections of cash flows would be employed as the information base for decisions, this method instead works with estimates of profit, as measured by conventional accounting. The decision rule then becomes

Projected account rate of return > Target accounting rate of return

At first glance, the method may appear attractive in that it works with more familiar information. If the performance of assets is going to eventually be reported on the basis of conventional accounting, why shouldn't similar data be employed in the asset choice process? The answer lies in the fact that conventional accounting reports result by period while a decision to acquire an asset involves the assessment of the prospects over the entire life of the asset.

For example, suppose that an asset can be acquired for $100,000 and yields expected accounting profits of $10,000 in the first year of its life, $20,000 in the second year of its life, and other varying returns in the future. Should this project be described as yielding 10 percent accounting rate of return, on the basis of comparing the first year's returns with the initial outlay, should it be described instead on the basis of a comparison between the initial outlay and profit projected for some other year, or should some sort of averaging be effected? (And if an averaging method is elected, should it give equal weight to profits earned in every year?)

This limitation by itself seems serious enough to make further discussion of the accounting rate of return method unwarranted. It may be that, in the companies where the method is used, assets are sufficiently similar so that the choice of accounting return for any year serves as an adequate index of that asset's performance relative to others. However, the propriety of the method is then based on the existence of isolated circumstances; and it is at best a proxy for a more logically supportable method.

Capital Budgeting without Rationing, Summarized

We have now looked at a number of different ways of making accept/reject decisions with respect to assets. For consistency with the equimarginal principle, all of these methods should be practised with the use of marginal information about prospective assets. Two methods in current practice, NPV and rate of return, are usually regarded as standing on the most solid, logical ground; for accept/reject decisions there is little basis for preference between these.

A third method, payback, enjoys widespread use but suffers from serious conceptual problems; nevertheless, it has elements of practical attractiveness. A fourth method, accounting rate of return, appears to enjoy relatively little usage and to have little conceptual attraction.

CAPITAL RATIONING

Capital rationing is defined as capital budgeting undertaken subject to a fixed amount of available funds. The capital rationing method requires a ranking scheme; even though all assets may seem favourable, only the most favourable must be selected, up to a purchase amount determined by the supply of funds available. (In economist's parlance, this method presumes a perfectly inelastic capital supply.)

The logical sequence of capital returning is shown in Illustration 4–2. Explanations of the sequence are:

ILLUSTRATION 4–2

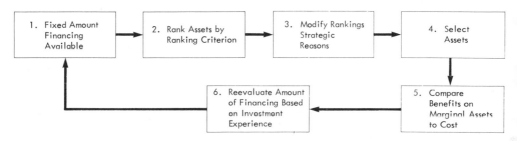

1. Starting point: ration of money is available.

2. Assets are ranked by ranking methods (to be discussed promptly).

3. Modifications, as in capital budgeting without rationing.

4. Assets are chosen in rank order until ration is exhausted.

5. Ideally, the lowest ranking assets accepted (marginal assets) should now be evaluated by a conventional test. Are these marginal assets characterized by NPV > 0 or IRR > target rate?

6. If the above answer is yes, enlarging the ration can be considered for the next period. If no, reducing.

Capital Rationing by Rate of Return

The capital rationing method consists of selecting a ranking criterion, and then ranking various prospective assets, or increments of assets, on the basis of this criterion. Once all assets are ranked, the selection process consists of starting with the highest ranked asset and continuing to accept projects of decreasing rank until all available funds are exhausted. For example, the rate of return may be used as a ranking criterion.

Consider an example where marginal rates of return have been calculated on a set of asset alternatives.

Asset	Marginal Funds Required	Marginal Rate of Return (percent)
Machine A	$100,000	30%
Machine A—larger version	50,000	20
Machine B	200,000	25
Machine B—larger version	100,000	18
Machine B—still larger	100,000	14
Additional receivables	50,000	16
More additional receivables	50,000	16
Tract of land	150,000	22

These alternative assets may now be ranked on the basis of rates of return. Along with this ranking a cumulative commitment of funds is identified—the cumulative figure indicates the amount of funds required to accept a particular project and all those ranking above it.

Rank	Asset	Marginal Funds	Cumulative Funds	Marginal Rate of Return (percent)
1	Machine A	$100,000	$100,000	30%
2	Machine B	200,000	300,000	25
3	Tract of land	150,000	450,000	22
4	Machine A—larger version	50,000	500,000	20
5	Machine B—larger version	100,000	600,000	18
6	Additional receivables	50,000	650,000	16
7	More additional receivables	50,000	700,000	16
8	Machine B—still larger	100,000	100,000	14

This ranking of projects, and its associated cumulative funds, now provides a basis for capital rationing. If a fixed amount of $500,000 is available, projects ranked 1 through 4 can be accepted: at that point the supply of funds will be exhausted.

This approach, like the accept/reject approach, is roughly consistent with the equimarginal principle for correct budgeting. We can observe in the above figures that there is a tendency for the marginal rates of return on projects to equalize. For example, the minimum size of machine A yielded a marginal rate of return of 30 percent, but a second increment of machine A was then acquired, bringing the marginal rate of return on the total purchase of machine A to 20 percent. This was close to equality with the other projects accepted (25 percent on an initial amount of machine B, and 22 percent on the tract of land).

NPV as a Ranking Criterion

As we have seen in the example, rate of return can be used directly as a method of ranking assets in a capital rationing situation. NPV needs to be modified slightly, and then it too can be used. Because funds are presumed limited, ranking under the capital rationing situation must be done on a per dollar invested basis. This condition poses no problem with rate of return, since the rate of return is, in fact, a ratio which can be described as a rate of appreciation per dollar invested.

However, NPV is measured as a total amount of dollars. Two projects may both produce prospective NPVs of $100,000 but one project may require the commitment of $1 million to attain this while the other attains it with a commitment of $100,000. In the accept/reject context, these projects could both be accepted, because of their positive NPVs, but where a choice among projects is required, one requiring the lesser investment is superior.

This difficulty has been overcome by adapting NPV to ratio form. This ratio, which may be called a *net profitability index*, is set forth as

$$\text{Net profitability index} = \frac{\text{NPV}}{\text{Initial cash outlay}^1}.$$

---

[1] The net profitability index is a special form of the profitability index, described as

$$\text{Profitability index} = \frac{\text{Present value of cash outflows}}{\text{Present value of cash outflows}}.$$

The superiority of the net index lies in the fact that it uses as a denominator only the cash that will be required initially. Thus it identified NPV per dollar required immediately, a format consistent with the rationing of immediately available funds.

Both methods can be used in lieu of an NPV test. When NPV > 0, net profitability index > 0, and profitability index > 1.

This ratio is also described, particularly in the public sector, as a *net benefit:cost ratio.*

Net Profitability Index or Rate of Return

There has been a great deal of controversy over which is more appropriate in the capital rationing situation—attempting to obtain the highest rate of return or attempting to obtain the highest NPV (using the net profitability index). An example may illustrate the nature of the controversy.

	Cash Flows	
Year	Asset 1	Asset 2
0	−$ 100,000	−$100,000
1	41,000	71,000
2	41,000	71,000
3	41,000	71,000
4–9	0	0
10	1,000,000	0

The following information can be calculated from the above data. The NPV calculations and related net profitability indexes are based on a discount rate of 15 percent.

	Asset 1	Asset 2
Rate of return	40%	50%
NPV (15%)	$241,000	$62,000
Net profitability index	2.41	0.62

These calculations indicate that the two methods may lead to different conclusions. Using the rate of return method, asset 2, is substantially superior. However, using an NPV method, asset 1 is four times better than asset 2. These contrasts turn entirely on the discount rates that are used in the calculations. In the rate of return method, the discount rates which set NPV = 0 turn out to be high, with accompanying low discount factors. For example, the terminal $1 million on asset 1 has a present value when discounted at 40 percent of only $35,000

($1,000,000 $\times$ 0.035). On the other hand, when the 15 percent rate employed on the NPV calculation is used, that $1 million is valued with a discount factor of 0.247, and is assigned a present value of $247,000.

The choice of method depends on which discount rate is more appropriate. While there are many ifs and ands to the controversy, a straightforward answer is that, if the owners of the company are attempting to hold assets of the maximum possible value (wealth maximization) the appropriate discount rate is that used by the marketplace in valuing the company, or the rate that is appropriate for an asset of this particular risk category. Since that valuation rate, probably quite closely related to capital cost, is the appropriate discount rate for the NPV method, NPV rankings appear to be superior to rate of return rankings.

To return to the above example, if in general a 15 percent discount rate is deemed appropriate for the valuation of assets such as these, this rate should be directly applied. If the company must choose between these two projects, it should give recognition to the fact that the final $1 million is of considerable value in an environment where the usual rate of return on projects of this type is 15 percent.

In the previous discussion of accept/reject criteria, we left the choice between rate of return and NPV at a virtual standoff. However, if one thinks of these two methods as general-purpose criteria, which can be used not only in accept/reject tests but also as ranking criteria, NPV (with its rationing variant, the net profitability index) must now be regarded as the superior contender.

Payback and Capital Rationing

Payback can be, and in practice is, applied in a capital rationing context. In this context it probably fares no better in a comparison with NPV than it did in the nonrationing decision setting. On the other hand, because of the deficiencies of the rate of return method as a ranking criterion, with its possible inclusion of irrationally high discount rates, payback, with its compensating conceptual errors, does not appear so inferior to IRR in the capital rationing context.

Nonrationing versus Capital Rationing

After examining capital budgeting techniques both with and without rationing, it is appropriate to ask whether one method is better than another. Insight into the comparison can be obtained by considering the consequences of erroneous application.

a. If rationing is applied, and if more funds *could have* been obtained, projects with NPV > 0, or IRR > target rate, might be erroneously rejected.

b. If rationing is not applied, and a fund shortage develops, projects may have to be rejected even though they would have compared favourably to those already accepted. An explicit ranking process would have forced this comparison.

If the accept/reject method is based on financial plentitude, the capital rationing method is based on financial scarcity. In the second method only a fixed amount of funds are presumed available for commitment among prospective assets.

In a sense, the choice between the methods is a choice between extremes. It is unrealistic to assume that most companies can have immediate access to all the funds they want at some given capital cost consistent with the company's accept/reject criteria. However, it may seem even more unrealistic to presume that a company can secure no more funds, if its alternative is to otherwise reject extremely attractive investment opportunities.

Because most companies, especially larger ones, have relatively prompt access to additional financing sources, the assumption of readily available capital seems closer to the actuality of the real world than the presumption of a rigidly restricted capital supply. Thus the nonrationing mode of financial decisions seems to be a more generally suitable method than the capital rationing format.

Uses of Capital Rationing

We have already noted the assumption of a rigid limitation of funds underlying capital rationing. While this rigidity may not be a general condition, there are certainly specific instances where scarce funds have to be allocated among competing uses. For example, asset choice decisions taking place in a division of a company may fit the capital rationing mode. The central capital budgeting process of the company may be undesirably rigid so that the financial management within a division of a company must take a given amount of funds as a fact of life, and attempt to do the best it can with them. In a case of this type, capital rationing appears appropriate.

A final qualification is needed here, of course. If the management of the division finds that in its capital rationing process it is rejecting extremely desirable projects because of shortage of funds, the financial managers within that division ought to communicate that fact quite forcefully to the central management of the company.

ADDITIONAL VIEWPOINTS ON CAPITAL BUDGETING

The Need for Capital Budgeting

If the assets actually selected by various business firms all followed a standard pattern, one might be inclined to think that it would be possible for an individual company to simply follow practices of other firms, rather than worry about developing its own individualized asset choice process. A brief look at company practice will indicate that companies do, in fact, make individualized asset selection, and that there is no fixed pattern of ratios among assets on which one can fall back. A look at the holdings of major asset categories by various Canadian industries will confirm this (see Illustration 4–3).

ILLUSTRATION 4–3

Asset Proportions, by Canadian Industry

Asset Category	Proportion (percent of all categories) by Industry				
	Manufac- turing	Mining	Public Utilities	Wholesale Trade	Retail Trade
Cash and short-term investments	6%	8%	2%	9%	10%
Accounts receivable	21	10	5	37	19
Inventories	25	5	2	35	45
Buildings and equipment	43	37	99	14	23
Land and depletable assets	4	41	4	5	4

Note: Columns may not total 100 percent because of rounding.
Source: Statistics Canada, *Corporate Financial Statistics.*

Not only is there wide variance of asset proportions between industries, but major differences also exist between industry subclassifications. For example, within manufacturing, comparisons may be made between different types of manufacturing firms (Illustration 4–4).

ILLUSTRATION 4–4

Asset Proportions, by Types of Canadian Manufacturing Firms

Asset Category	Proportion (percent of all categories) by Type		
	Food and Beverage	Textiles	Paper and Allied Products
Cash and short-term investment	9%	5%	5%
Accounts receivable	18	26	15
Inventories	31	34	17
Buildings and equipment	39	35	59
Land and depletable assets	2	—	5

Note: Columns may not total 100 percent because of rounding.
Source: Statistics Canada, *Corporate Financial Statistics.*

As one would expect, when the classification of companies is narrowed further, some increase in commonality of usage is observed. Yet important divergences still persist, even among closely related companies. For examples, consider data from past balance sheets of three sets of companies. The first pair are both meat-packers, Canada Packers Limited and J. M. Schneider, Limited. The second pair are both manufacturers of houshold products, Sklar Manufacturing Limited, and John Inglis Co. Limited. The third pair are mining and metals companies, Noranda Mines Limited and Rio Algom Mines Limited. Comparisons between the three pairs of companies are shown in Illustration 4–5.

These illustrations lead to one important conclusion. Asset selection is an individualized undertaking. A company can gain only limited guidance in observation of the practice of other firms. It must form its own independent decisions about asset proportions. A company's assets must fit the opportunities and conditions that are unique to it.

ILLUSTRATION 4–5

Asset Proportion in Related Pairs of Companies, Approximately December 31, 1971

	Proportion (percent of all categories)		
Asset Category	Canada Packers/ Schneider	Sklar/Inglis	Noranda/ Rio Algom
Cash and short-term investment . . .	−/−	−/−	7%/ 2%
Accounts receivable	30%/16%	38%/27%	16 /35
Inventories	38 /28	35 /50	19 /16
Fixed assets	32 /56	27 /22	59 /47

Note: Columns may not total 100 percent because of rounding.
Source: The Financial Post Corporation Service.

A Positive Viewpoint for Asset Selection

In the next several chapters, we will be examining the setting and process for making financial decisions relating to different types of assets. The role of the company's financial officers customarily varies somewhat with respect to the handling of various assets. For example, financial officers will directly manage some assets, such as cash, securities, and many aspects of the company's receivables position. In the case of receivables, financial officers may have the opportunity to approve or deny credit for particular customers, to establish the terms under which credit is granted, and to determine the rigour with which collection policies are pursued.

In other instances, the role of financial officers will be a more distant one. For example, the financial officers may participate in the setting of limits on the amount of raw material to be accumulated, but beyond that, they may have little role in the handling of this component of the company's inventory.

This distance from many transactions, where financial management functions in an evaluative capability, may suggest to the reader that the financial manager is something of a corporate policeman who spends a great deal of his time saying "no" to other people's projects. If this image exists, it is unfortunate. Evaluation of assets ought not to be viewed primarily as a process of screening out unsatisfactory projects, even though that is essential in an evaluative process. Instead, the asset selection process should be viewed as a search for opportunities.

Asset ownership forms an indispensable part of a company's activities. While some corporations fail because they spend excessive amounts on assets, others also fail because they maintain inadequate amounts. Firms which control their plant acquisition process too tightly, may operate with outmoded equipment. Those who curb their inventory acquisitions too intensively may be plagued with shortages. Those who restrict their receivables too stringently, and are unwilling to grant sufficient credit, may lose customers. Any of these examples of overthriftiness may make a firm vulnerable to displacement by more aggressive competitors.

One may also recall the equimarginal condition. Satisfaction of this equation requires not only that projects with low marginal returns be eliminated, but also that high-yielding projects be pressed forward. Suppose that the marginal return on one of a company's assets is much greater than that on others. This may serve as a signal that insufficient investment is being undertaken in the asset with the high marginal returns. There may be unexhausted opportunities; perhaps an additional step of investment could be made, at a lower marginal return than previous investment on that asset, but still greater than the marginal performance of other assets. The firm's financial decisions are just as remiss if they fail to exploit an opportunity as if they allow the commitment of funds to an unsatisfactory project.

SUMMARY

Capital budgeting describes the process of choosing among long-lived assets, or more broadly, the process of choosing among all assets. Rational capital budgeting should be consistent with the equimarginal principle of economics.

In principle under capital budgeting without rationing, all assets which satisfy acceptance criteria are purchased. With rationing assets are ranked and a prespecified quantity of money is allocated among the highest ranking alternatives. Actual choices are often compromises between the two methods.

Net present value and internal rate of return may be used with either method. Without rationing NPV and IRR produce identical results. With rationing, results may differ and NPV is preferred.

Another method, payback, also enjoys considerable use. This method evaluates projects by considering the time necessary to recoup the original investment.

Quantitative evaluative criteria such as NPV, IRR, or payback are often tempered with strategic considerations. One important strategic aspect of choice is the effect of the asset upon the company's overall liquidity.

The role of the financial manager in capital budgeting should not be limited to rejecting unsatisfactory projects; wealth enhancing asset choice requires encouragement of search for attractive projects as well.

QUESTIONS AND PROBLEMS

1. Distinguish between the narrower and broader meanings of capital budgeting. Describe the problem associated with implementing the narrower concept.

2. Explain why the use of marginal or incremental data is essential to optimal capital budgeting.

3. Suppose that a company practicing capital budgeting without rationing decides that it is accepting too many assets. What logical basis could it use for such a judgment? How could it correct the problem?

4. Define cost of capital.

5. A farm manager considers two alternatives as a choice of power on his farm. (a) Buy two 100 horsepower tractors priced at $25,000 each, along with two items of tillage equipment for use with the tractors—these items are a disk harrow, priced at $7,000, and a cultivator, priced at $6,000. (b) Buy a 200 horsepower tractor which sells for $55,000. Along with this buy two larger tillage implements (which cannot be used simultaneously, with only one tractor) for $11,000 each.

    The farm manager is satisfied that these tasks can be performed as effectively with one unit as with the other. The larger unit will save the hire of one tractor operator, with an estimated labour saving of $5,000 per year on seasonal labour.

All equipment is expected to have a ten-year life with end-of-period salvage value at 25 percent of original cost. Ignoring income tax considerations, identify marginal rate of return on the 200 horsepower tractor and related equipment.

6. Distinguish between strategy and tactics both in war and finance.

7. Compose an original example of an asset that is liquid and safe? Illiquid and safe? Illiquid and risky?

8. Using marginal data from the tractor example in Question 5, find the payback period for the incremental money needed to purchase the larger tractor and associated equipment.

9. Specify the two major criticisms of the payback method, and indicate how the errors associated with these criticisms may tend to partially offset one another.

10. Under what circumstances would one expect the use of capital rationing?

11. Why would a "lazy" company treasurer prefer the use of capital rationing to capital budgeting without rationing?

12. In Chapter 1 reference was made to three major types of financial decisions. Which type is affected by the choice between rationing and not rationing? What potential error may be introduced in this decision?

13. Describe a net profitability index, and indicate why this modification of NPV is necessary under capital rationing.

14. The text describes the discount rate used in the net profitability index approach to capital rationing as "appropriate." How does the rate of return method result in the introduction of inappropriate discount rates?

RELATED READINGS

Baumol, W., and Quandt, R. "Investment and Discount Rates under Capital Rationing—A Programming Approach." *The Economic Journal,* June 1965, pp. 317–29.

Bierman, H., and Smidt, S. *The Capital Budgeting Decision.* 3d ed. New York: Macmillan, 1971.

The Conference Board. *Managing the Resource Allocation Process.* New York: National Industrial Conference Board, 1963.

Edge, C. *The Appraisal of Capital Expenditures.* Hamilton, Ont.: The Society of Industrial and Cost Accountants of Canada, 1959.

Henrici, S. "Eyeing the ROI." *Harvard Business Review,* May–June 1968.

Johnson, R. W. *Capital Budgeting.* Belmont, Calif.: Wadsworth, 1970.

Kilpatrick, I. *Capital Expenditures, Key to Profits.* Toronto: Sir Isaac Pitman (Canada) Ltd., 1971.

Klammer, T. "Empirical Evidence of the Adoption of Sophisticated Capital Budgeting Techniques." *Journal of Business,* 1972.

Mao, J. "Internal Rate of Return as a Ranking Criterion." *Engineering Economist,* Winter 1966.

———. "Survey of Capital Budgeting: Theory and Practice." *Journal of Finance,* May 1970.

Myers, S. "A Note on Linear Programming and Capital Budgeting." *Journal of Finance,* March 1972.

Quirin, D. *The Capital Expenditure Decision.* Homewood, Ill.: Richard D. Irwin, Inc., 1967.

Weingartner, M. "Some New Views on the Payback Period and Capital Budgeting Decisions." *Management Science,* August 1969.

5

FIXED ASSETS

Fixed assets are normally defined as those assets which are bought for relatively permanent use in a company's regular business activities. For purposes of financial analysis there are several reasons for treating these assets as a special category. First, because of their relative permanence, time adjustment becomes very critical in decisions relating to the assets. Second, though there are many exceptions, the assets tend to be illiquid; long-lived assets that are bought for the purposes of a particular company may not be readily reconverted into cash. Third, analysis affecting fixed assets is often separated in company practice.

GENERAL CONCEPTS RELATING TO FIXED ASSETS

Of course, the boundary between fixed assets and other asset varieties is quite blurred. For example, a company may acquire land with mixed intentions; the land may eventually be used for plant expansion, but at the same time, it could be promptly resold if the funds were needed for other purposes. Thus it may be permanent or it may be temporary, depending upon yet unknown future conditions. Conversely, some assets customarily not regarded as fixed may share fixed asset attributes. For example, a company may establish a credit policy which allows customers to pay for goods within 60 days, with the knowledge that once established, it will be difficult to retreat from the policy. Are the receivables acquired in connection with this policy (though individual accounts come and go) relatively permanent or impermanent?

Categories of Fixed Assets

Within fixed assets, several major categories can be identified. Not only is there physical dissimilarity between these categories, but there are also important differences in tax usage. The three categories are land, including the ownership of natural resources, buildings and equipment, and intangible items such as patents.

In the typical Canadian company, buildings and equipment constitute the largest dollar commitment to a single asset category. Exceptional situations occur; in the important resource-based industries the land category may dominate the left-hand side of the balance sheet.

The third category actually appears to be a rather minor one. However, this category can be broadened considerably if it is used to cover certain occurrences that are not explicitly called asset acquisitions. For example, an advertising program developed to reinforce the general image of a company may require major expenditures at present, which are expected to show results over a long period of time. In effect, an asset is being "purchased"; the asset is relatively permanent and intimately connected with the company's business activities. So it is properly considered to be a fixed asset in fact, if not in form. Another closely related example of such a "fixed asset that isn't called an asset" is a personnel development program. A company may spend large amounts of money training employees in the hope of recovering this money through higher quantity and quality of output from its labour force in the future. Again, in fact an asset is being created, and logic suggests, even though current accounting practice does not, that such an "asset" acquisition should be analyzed in comparison with other assets.

Projecting Cash Flows from Fixed Assets

A preceding chapter has already considered the identification of cash flows from assets. Projections for fixed assets can be made along the same lines, although there are certain exceptions, particularly in connection with tax matters.

There are two general motives for acquiring fixed assets. They can either generate additional revenue by enhancing the quantity or quality of a company's output, or they may result in cost savings. Beyond these operating sources of cash inflows (both of which may be present in a single asset) disposal of the asset itself may constitute another source of cash inflow. This last source is likely to be less important in fixed assets than in other assets, because of the fairly long lives of the fixed assets.

There are three tax aspects affecting cash flows from fixed assets which require further elaboration. These are capital cost allowances, capital gains tax treatment and immediate tax write-offs. The impact of each of these items will be discussed in the following sections.

TAX ASPECTS

Capital Cost Allowances

The effect of capital cost allowances on cash flows has already been discussed in Chapter 2. This effect is associated with buildings and equipment; it results from the recognition in tax law that the fixed asset is normally used up in the normal course of a company's operations. The year-at-a-time method for considering capital cost allowance which was shown in Chapter 2 was very useful in illustrating the manner by which capital cost allowance affects cash flows. However, there is a simpler method available for employment in practical analysis.

In developing the simple method, one begins by recognizing that, apart from purchase and salvage, in any year a company's after-tax cash flow from a depreciable asset is:

$$\text{After-tax cash flow} = \text{Operating cash flow } (1-t)$$
$$+ \text{ (tax shelter from CCA) } t$$

The two components, operating cash flow and tax shelter, are likely to have different lives. At some point the asset will cease to be economically useful and its cash flows will terminate. However, the tax shelter is likely to live beyond the asset, and in fact has the mathematical attributes of perpetual life.

The perpetual life of the tax shelter rests on two assumptions:

a. The asset is part of a class of assets in the company; there are always other assets in this CCA class.

b. The asset does not generate salvage value.

Of these assumptions (a) is quite realistic especially for the large company. Assumption (b) is only set forth initially; greater generality will follow.

When the asset is purchased, the unexpired capital cost of the asset class is enlarged by the asset's initial cost. This initial change in unexpired capital cost (UCC) sets into effect a series of changes in the company's annual capital cost allowances (CCA). Using subscripts to denote time $(\text{CCA})_0 = d(\text{UCC})_0$ where d is the class depreciation rate. During the next year $(\text{UCC})_1 = (\text{UCC})_0 (1-d)$, and $(\text{CCA})_1 = (\text{CCA})_0 (1-d)$. In each ensuing year, the effect of this asset on the company's capital cost allowance decreases by the factor $(1-d)$; thus the effect is eroded each year but it never fully expires.

This property gives the tax shelter from an asset a life that continues even though the asset itself has been abandoned. The present value of this endless stream of tax shelter from an asset purchase may be obtained with a simply derived[1] formula.

---

[1] The formula is the sum of an infinite geometric progression. Present value of CCA in year n is $Cd(1-d)^n / (1+r)^{n+1}$, where $Cd(1-d)^n$ is the CCA calculated at the end of year n and $(1+r)^{n+1}$ is the discount factor which brings this CCA to a present value. The sum of the geometric progression

$$P = \frac{Cd}{1+r} + \frac{Cd(1-d)}{(1+r)^2} + \frac{Cd(1-d)^2}{(1+r)^3} \cdots$$

is

$$P = C\left(\frac{d}{d+r}\right).$$

Where C is the original cost of the asset and r the discount rate,

$$\text{Present value of CCA tax shelter} = C\left(\frac{d}{d+r}\right).$$

The present value of tax savings from this shelter is

$$C\left(\frac{d}{d+r}\right)t.$$

For example, suppose a company plans to acquire a new machine, which falls in a capital cost allowance class where a 20 percent rate is stipulated. The company expects that the machine will be scrapped after ten years; however, the disposal of the machine at zero value will have no effect on the UCC account for machines in this class. Suppose the company's tax rate is 40 percent, the machine's initial cost is $100,000, and the company employs a 10 percent discount rate.

Substituting into the formula:

$$\text{Present value of tax saving} = C(d/d + r)t = \$1,000,000$$
$$[0.20/(0.20 + 0.10)](0.40) = \$266,667.$$

A complete identification of NPV can follow. Assume that operating cash flows from the machine are projected at $500,000 per year for four years. Using the annuity discount factor of 3.170 ($n = 4$, $r = 0.10$), and again $t = 40$ percent, the operating cash flows have a present value after tax of

$$P = \$500,000 \ (3.170) \ (1 - .40) = \$951,000.$$

All cash flows from the asset are then on a present value after-tax basis:

Initial cost	−$1,000,000
CCA tax saving	266,667
Operating cash flows	951,000
NPV	$ 217,667

This procedure is also adaptable to the IRR method of capital budgeting; then the trial-and-error search for the r that sets NPV $= 0$ must include experimental substitutions of the r in $d/d + r$.

Capital Cost Allowance Formula with Salvage Value

The method is also adaptable when an asset is expected to have a salvage value. When salvage takes place, cash will be received from the asset disposal. Additionally, UCC for the asset class is decreased by the amount of the salvage. If S is the salvage value, the joint effect in the *year of salvage* can be described as

$$S - S\left(\frac{d}{d+r}\right)t.$$

Since salvage is expected to take place in the future, these cash flows must be discounted. Letting n_s denote year when salvage is expected,

$$\text{Present value, after tax, of salvage} = \frac{S - S\left(\dfrac{d}{d+r}\right)t}{(1+r)^{n_s}}.$$

In the previous example, had a $300,000 salvage value been expected after four years, its present value after tax would have been:

$$\frac{\$300,000 - \$300,000\left(\dfrac{0.2}{0.2+.01}\right)(40\%)}{(1.10)^4} = \$150,263.$$

Following further in the example, NPV identification with salvage would then become

Initial costs	−$1,000,000
CCA tax saving	266,667
Operating cash flows	951,000
Salvage	150,263
NPV	$ 367,930

One can observe that asset disposals of the type described above receive favourable tax treatment relative to other cash flows; the net receipt

$$S - S(d/d+r)t,$$

also may be described as

$$S[1 - \left(\frac{d}{d + r}\right) t].$$

Had it been an operating cash flow, tax would have reduced the flow by the factor $(1 - t)$.

Capital Gains Tax

Tax relief is afforded on other types of asset disposals, besides the one-depreciable-asset-out-of-a-class type described in the previous section. Disposal on nondepreciable assets or one-of-a-kind depreciable assets may be subject to tax at a *capital gains* rate. As a general rule to qualify for capital gains treatment, the disposal must involve an asset which was not bought with the principal purpose of being resold. For example, sale of land or buildings which had been intended for relatively permanent use probably would be allowed as capital gains; disposal of an inventory usually would not.

If an asset disposal qualifies for capital gain tax treatment, tax will be calculated as

$$\text{Taxable capital gain} = \frac{\text{Selling price} - \text{purchase price}}{2}.$$

Accordingly, cash flows from this type of disposal attract tax as follows:

$$\text{Tax} = \frac{(\text{Selling price} - \text{purchase price})}{2} t.$$

After-tax receipts are described as

Purchase price + (selling price − purchase price) $(1 - 0.5t)$.

Thus part of the cash inflow is not subject to tax and part is subject to reduction by the tax factor of $(1 - 0.5t)$ rather than the ordinary $(1 - t)$.[2]

_____

[2] On a one-of-a-kind asset which has previously been depreciated the treatment is more complex; in general

$$\text{Tax} = t(\text{purchase price} - \text{UCC}) + \frac{t(\text{selling price} - \text{purchase price})}{2},$$

with the first term representing a "recapture" of previously used tax shelter.

For example, a company may consider holding a tract of land for possible development as a parking lot. When considering whether or not to acquire the land, the company may want to consider the possibility of disposing of the land. Suppose the land is originally purchased for $100,000 and disposal at a price of $300,000 is contemplated after nine years. If the company is subject to a 40 percent tax rate, the cash receipt upon disposal of the property is calculated as follows:

Selling price	$300,000	$300,000
Cost	100,000	
Capital gain	$200,000	
Amount subject to tax	$100,000	
Tax rate	40%	
Tax		40,000
Selling price − tax = cash flow after tax in year 9		$260,000

Ignoring benefits and costs of operations, and applying a discount rate of 10 percent, NPV is calculated as

9th year receipt, after tax	$260,000	
9 year, 10% PV factor	0.424	
Present value of receipt		$110,240
Purchase price		− 100,000
NPV		$ 10,240

The potential importance of capital gains treatment is evident; if all profit in this example had been taxed, tax would have been $80,000, cash flow in year 9 would have been $220,000, and NPV would have been negative:

$$NPV = \$220,000 \, (0.424) - \$100,000 = -\$6,720.$$

Immediate Write-Offs

Earlier we noted that some actual fixed assets may not be designated as fixed assets under usual accounting practice. Two examples were cited: long-term advertising programs and personnel development programs. If assets of this type are subject to analysis along with other fixed assets, their tax dimension needs to be recognized. In general, assets of this type can have their original cost subject to immediate claim as a tax deductible expense.

For example, suppose that a company spends $1 million on employee training programs this year and expects these programs to result in additional output of 10,000 units per year, valued at $50 per unit. It is believed that the effect of the training program will extend at least five years into the future; the company is subject to a 40 percent tax. In this case an initial investment of $1 million is yielding $500,000 per year for five years, without tax considerations. When tax is considered, benefits from the project are reduced to $300,000 per year, but the after-tax cost of the project is also reduced to $600,000. These after-tax cash flows can then be used for an NPV analysis, or other type of evaluation.

One may note that in effect, assets of this type are subject to a 100 percent capital cost allowance rate.[3]

COSTS RELATED TO ASSET ACQUISITIONS

Related Costs Which Should Be Included in an Asset Acquisition

One of the distinctive aspects of fixed asset evaluation relates to the impact of various tax considerations on future tax flows, as just discussed. A second aspect lies in the potential complexity of the identification of a fixed asset's initial cost. Often, when a fixed asset is acquired, additional related purchases are also necessary.

Some of these collateral items are rather obvious. For example, when a machine is purchased, installation costs associated with the machine should be considered. Or when land is bought and held for some future purpose, real estate taxes payable on the land and other maintenance costs must be taken into account.

When the acquisition of a fixed asset constitutes a major expansion in the company's business operations, the identification of related costs may be more complex. Suppose, for example, a company considers building a new factory, in addition

---

[3] Substitution of 100 percent capital cost allowance rate into the capital cost allowance formula yields $P_e = Ct(d/d + r) = Ct(1/1 + r)$. This is equivalent to a saving of Ct, available one year in the future and discounted accordingly. The assumed delay may be realistic, so use of the formula would represent a refinement over the presumption in the preceding example that "immediate write-off" was equivalent to "immediate tax savings."

to its existing facilities. Some minimum stockpiles of raw material may be essential to operation of the factory; when the factory is in operation, a work-in-process inventory will be inevitable. These minimum inventory requirements should be regarded as part of the initial cost of the factory; they are an integral part of its technology. (Beyond this minimum, the discretionary aspects of inventory accumulation can be treated as a separate decision, and will be discussed in Chapter 6.)

Other unavoidable commitments of funds may also be associated with the factory. For example, some finished goods may inevitably be accumulated, awaiting shipment at the plant, or in the process of transportation. Or an increase in the company's cash balance requirements may result because of the increased volume of payrolls and purchases associated with the new plant.

Costs Which Should Be Subject to Separate Analysis

At the same time, one must take care to avoid overaggregation. For example, one might at first conclude that, if the company customarily sells on credit, an additional accumulation of receivables may be necessary if a new plant is to be placed online. However, the cost of additional receivables should only be co-mingled in the plant acquisition decision if the company decides that its credit policy is unalterable. Otherwise, the company might presume that goods from the new plant could be sold for cash, and *then* decide if it should in fact grant credit. In that case, it will be proper to estimate the future cash flows from the plant on the basis of the cash price, estimate the cost of the plant without any associated receivables, and then separately consider the credit decision.

Some decision makers get around these complexities by adding a standard amount to the direct cost of some of their fixed assets, to allow for related nonfixed assets. While such a method may be too crude for large and complex asset acquisitions, one can see the logic in using a method whereby one adds on one quarter or one third of the fixed asset acquisition cost to provide for "working capital." Obviously, such a policy, if adopted, must be developed on the basis of the individual experience of a company.

TECHNIQUES FOR PREDICTIONS ON FIXED ASSETS

Break-Even Analysis

Break-even analysis is a technique that can be used to potentially remove some of the complexity from asset purchase decisions, and also to roughly explore the asset's risk dimension. This technique is really a straightforward application of elementary algebra, as an example will illustrate.

A group of individuals organized as Snow Ventures Ltd., contemplate acquiring land and facilities for the development of a ski slope and related resort. Initial costs, net of the present value of capital cost allowances, are estimated at $1 million. Studies of similar developments indicate that for every customer attracted to the resort during the ski season, cash flows of about $45 after operating costs can be expected, or $25 on an after-tax basis.

The company decides to form its estimations only for the next ten years and to presume that its facility will be salable at the end of ten years for $800,000, net of any related taxes. The only other cash flows projected are the $25 per year for each person using the facility. CCA considerations are ignored because of the project's high land component. The company uses the NPV method, with a 15 percent discount rate.

It is apparent that the NPV calculation is contingent upon an estimate of the number of customers per year, yet that estimate may be difficult to make. Snow Ventures may formulate its problem along the following lines:

Let Q = number of customers per year.

	Years		
	0 *Initial Cost*	*1–10* *Operations*	*10* *Salvage*
Cash flows	−$1,000,000	$ 25Q	$800,000
Discount of annuity factors	1.0	5.019	.247
Present value	−$1,000,000	125.48Q$	$197,600

NPV = −$1,000,000 + 125.48Q$ + $197,600 = $125,48$Q$ − $802,400.

It may now explore the problem by identifying the minimum number of customers who must be attracted each year if the project is to be acceptable. If the test of acceptability is NPV > 0, one can solve algebraically for the number of customers that will cause NPV to equal 0.

$$125.48Q - \$802,400 = 0$$
$$Q = 6,395.$$

This value of Q, where NPV $= 0$, may be called the break-even point; unless the company can expect an annual volume of customers in excess of this amount, the project will be unacceptable.

Calculation of the break-even point may simplify the decision about whether to undertake the ski resort investment. If the developers of Snow Venture are confident that they can attract more than the break-even number of customers, they can accept the project without even making the projection of the actual number of customers that they expect to obtain. Similarly, if they are reasonably sure that they cannot attract 6,395 customers, they can reject the project out of hand.

Additionally, the algebraic relationship developed can be used to explore the consequences of varying levels of customers. For example, Snow Ventures may be reasonably confident that it would be able to attract at least 5,000 and no more than 10,000 customers per year. With the algebraic formulation given above it could easily calculate that its minimum NPV would be:

$$NPV = \$125.48 \ (5,000) - \$802,400 = -\$175,000.$$

It could also identify a maximum estimate of NPV as:

$$NPV = \$125.48 \ (10,000) - \$802,400 = \$452,400.$$

Thus, it would have estimates that a possible deterioration in the wealth position of the company of $175,000 would be possible, but that an enhancement of that wealth position by $452,400 would also be possible.

Further Algebraic Exploration: Sensitivity Analysis

Break-even analysis is often a useful tool; it can lead to the quick acceptance or rejection of some assets, and it can provide insights into the possible consequences of investing in other assets. Algebraic exploration can also be carried on in a more detailed way.

To follow the previous example, suppose that the developers are agreed that an annual customer volume of 5,000–10,000 is a reasonable range of expectations. Suppose, also, that the developers are really not very sure about their estimate of a salvage value of $800,000 for the project, but instead think that, in fact, the terminal value could be anywhere between $500,000 and $1 million. Furthermore, suppose they are not sublimely confident in the $25 per customer cash flow and feel that this figure might vary between $15 and $40.

The problem can be explored in more detail with the following algebraic formulation:

$$\text{Let } Q = \text{Number of customers per year.}$$
$$S = \text{Salvage value.}$$
$$P = \text{Profit per customer.}$$

		Years	
	0	1-10	10
Cash flows	-$1,000,000	PQ	S
Discount or annuity factors	1.0	5.019	0.247
Present value	-$1,000,000	5.019PQ	0.247S

$$NPV = 5.019PQ + 0.247S - \$1,000,000.$$

Algebraic experimentation is now possible by considering various values of P, Q, and S. In this example, we will just consider the upper and lower values for P, Q, and S plus the "best guesses" that the Snow Ventures had made for P and S: $25 for P and $800,000 for S. The information is summarized below:

Alternative Values

P	Q	S
$15	5,000	$ 500,000
25	10,000	800,000
40		1,000,000

NPV calculations, based on these values and the equation,
$$NPV = 5.019PQ + 0.247S - \$1,000,000$$
are summarized in Illustration 5–1.

ILLUSTRATION 5–1

SNOW VENTURES—NPV, where:

	P = $15		P = $25		P = $40	
	Q = 5,000	Q = 10,000	Q = 5,000	Q = 10,000	Q = 50,000	Q = 10,000
S = $ 500,000 . .	−$500,000	−$124,000	−$249,000	$378,000	$127,000	$1,131,000
S = $ 800,000 . .	− 426,000	− 50,000	− 175,000	452,000	201,000	1,205,000
S = $1,000,000 . .	− 376,000	0	− 126,000	502,000	251,000	1,255,000

We can now examine the data and draw a number of conclusions:

1. As it stands now, the project may be regarded as quite risky, with possible NPV values from −$500,000 up through $1,255,000.

2. It will be very important to attempt to get better information about revenues per customer. If those revenues should be as low as $15, the project would be unsatisfactory, even at the most optimistic values of Q and S. Similarly, if profits per customer should turn out to be $40, the project would be unequivocally acceptable.

3. Estimates of salvage value do not appear to be important. In no case does a change in the value of S from its lower limit to its upper limit affect the acceptability of a project. Therefore, there is no point in attempting to refine the estimates of the salvage value.

4. If a better estimate of Q can be obtained, that may be important. However, better information about Q will only be important if P takes on some intermediate value. We observe that if P = $15, or P = $40, the asset is either unacceptable or acceptable, irrespective of whether Q = 5,000 or Q = 10,000. Thus, getting better information about Q is secondary to the obtaining of better information about P.

Analysis of this exploratory type is often called sensitivity analysis. We observe how sensitive the prospective outcomes of a project are to changes in various factors affecting the project. In the Snow Ventures case the project is especially sensitive to the factor, "profit per customer" and is very insensitive to the factor, "salvage value."

This exploration is often carried on in a computerized way. It goes further than simple break-even analysis both in probing the possible value of additional refinements in cash flow estimates and also in exploring the risk dimensions of a project. Sensitivity analysis is gaining widespread acceptance among Canadian companies.

A Limitation of Sensitivity Analysis

A note of caution is in order when sensitivity analysis is employed to explore the risk dimensions of a project. For example, this analysis suggested, in the above example, that the project might have a present value as low as −$500,000. It is true that the range of possible outcomes on the project goes this low; one would, however, want to consider the practical likelihood of the simultaneous occurrence of minimum values of P, Q, and S, all of which are necessary to produce the project's minimum outcome.

While sensitivity analysis is used in practice, and probability analysis has substantially less acceptance, one can observe that a statement about the probability of actually getting such a low value might be useful in the analysis. An evaluation of the asset may be unduly pessimistic if the person evaluating the asset worries too much about prospects which, for example, have a likelihood of 1 in 10,000 of occurring. To generalize, one must consider whether the full range of outcomes identified in a sensitivity analysis are realistic possibilities. Apart from this *caveat*, break-even and sensitivity analyses are useful and widely employed devices.

REPLACEMENTS AND DISPOSALS

Replacement Decisions

Fixed asset purchases are frequently considered as replacements for existing fixed assets. An example will demonstrate that decisions of this type are amenable to marginal analysis. One important aspect to consider for a replacement decision is that usually the important issue is not whether the old asset should eventually be replaced. Instead, the issue relates to whether it should be replaced now or later.

Consider a situation where Adams Ltd. owns ten, three-year-old trucks. It is questioning whether to replace these trucks now or to defer replacement for at least another year. The facts of the situation are as follows:

1. New trucks cost $60,000 each.

2. The old trucks can be sold for $20,000 each.

3. Trucks, whether new or old, are expected to decline in sales value at a rate of 20 percent per year.

4. Eight new trucks will do the work of the ten old ones.

5. Eight new trucks will require the same expenditure on tires, routine maintenance, fuel and oil as the ten old ones.

6. Average extraordinary repairs of $2,500 per truck are estimated for the old trucks during the forthcoming year; if new trucks are purchased the figure will be $200 per truck.

7. Each truck requires one driver, at a cost of $18,000 per year.

8. The company uses a 10 percent discount rate; the relevant Capital Cost Allowance rate is 30 percent. The company always has other assets in the same class. The company's tax rate is 50 percent.

Analysis of Adams Ltd. replacement problem is presented in Illustration 5–2.

By analyzing the differences between the new trucks and the old ones, it becomes apparent that it is better to wait another year. At that time, the calculation can be repeated; perhaps then the maintenance costs on the old trucks will have increased still further, and lower potential output from the old trucks (perhaps because of maintenance downtime) may mean that seven new trucks will replace the ten old ones. Thus, next year's analysis may result in an affirmative decision.

Decisions to Sell Fixed Assets

So far we have looked at acquisitions of assets, either in the form of buying entirely new assets or buying assets to replace existing ones. Asset positions can be allowed to decline too;

ILLUSTRATION 5–2

ADAMS LTD.
Marginal Analysis of Replacement
(changes in cash flows associated with purchase of eight new trucks
as replacements for ten old trucks)

		Real and Potential Cash Flow Differences at Times:	
Description of Difference		Present	During or at End of Year 1
1. Cash outlay when new trucks are purchased and old trucks sold:			
Buy 8 new trucks at −$60,000 . . .	−$480,000		
Sell 10 old trucks at +$20,000 . . .	200,000		
Net cash flow	−$280,000	−$280,000	
2. Value of tax savings from increased capital cost allowances:			
Increase in UCC account	$280,000		
Present value of tax savings: $Ct\ (d/d + r) = \$280{,}000(.50)$ $(0.3/0.3 + 0.1)$	$105,000	+ 105,000	
3. Difference in cash value at end of year, if new trucks are bought:			
New truck value at end of year: $480,000 less 20% decline in value	$384,000		
Value old trucks would have had if kept $200,000 less 20% decline in value	160,000		
Increase in value of trucks at end of year	$224,000		+$224,000
4. Loss of tax shelter if trucks were sold at end of year. This calculation is necessary as an offset to 3., since UCC would be lost if trucks were sold at end of year.			
Decrease in UCC account	$224,000		
$224,000 (0.50) 0.3/0.3 + 0.1) . .	84,000		− 84,000
5. Saving of drivers, after tax, $36,000 (1 − t)$			+ 18,000
Saving of repair bills, after tax:			
Old trucks, 10 at $2,500	$ 25,000		
New trucks, 8 at $250	2,000		
Saving	$ 23,000		
Saving (1 − tax rate)	$ 11,500		+$ 11,500
Total of marginal cash flows, including value of potential cash flows from salvage		−$175,000	+$169,500
10% discount factor		1,000	.909
Net present value for each year		−$175,000	$154,000
Net present value (sum of above)		−$21,000	

conformity to the equimarginal principle may render asset disposals desirable, without replacement. Depending on the character of the asset, disposal decisions can be considered for a whole asset classification or marginal parts of it. In general an asset should be discarded when present value of the cash flows obtainable from the disposal exceed the present value of the cash flows obtainable from using the asset.

Good management requires that existing assets should not be taken for granted but should be subject to this type of NPV examination. This is not to suggest that all assets must be under study at all times. However, in practice, financial managers must keep an open mind and consider occasional prunings from the company's asset position. (This task may require some heroism, particularly if the financial manager had previously recommended purchase of the asset.)

An ongoing example of fixed asset retrenchment has occurred in Canadian railway systems, where railroad companies subject individual branch lines to marginal analysis. Cash flows gained from abandoning a rail line are saving of maintenance and personnel costs, and possible salvage of materials. Cash flows lost include the operating profits from the branch line operation, and the consequences of the possible loss of other business that was once channeled into the railroad company's trunk lines from the branch lines, and is now lost to other carriers.

Problems from Asset Disposals

These rail branch line abandonments, and there have been many, also illustrate another problem associated with asset retrenchment. Communities along the railway branch lines have been very concerned about their abandonment, and as a result this has become a major political issue. While other companies are not subject to as much public regulation as railways, few companies feel that they can totally ignore public opinion. Additionally, labour unions may enter the picture, if jobs are being eliminated. Thus, where major asset retrenchments are being made, consideration may have to be given to special factors which affect the company at a strategic level.

LIQUIDITY

Liquidity and Fixed Assets

At the outset of this chapter, fixed assets were defined as those that were expected to be long lived. In the usual sense of the word, fixed asset is almost synonymous with illiquid asset. However, assets are frequently called fixed on the basis of convention, and many so-called fixed assets have surprising elements of liquidity. Furthermore, liquidity may often be "designed into" fixed assets.

In general, flows of funds into fixed assets can be easily reversed if the assets are useful to other potential buyers. For example, bulldozers owned by construction companies are a standard product which is readily salable to other construction companies, or to other users. Thus, it is possible for a construction company to make a major commitment into the fixed asset, machinery, and yet regard its commitment to that asset as quite liquid. While the company may intend to keep its heavy equipment for a long period of time, it may at the same time feel some confidence that if other opportunities or pressures require funds its machinery position can be liquidated. In fact, this liquidation may not even disrupt the company's use of the type of equipment which is sold, for such equipment may be available on a rental basis.

Liquidity in the Choice Process

In some cases, an asset may be designed for liquidity. Suppose, for example, a company has a chance of using two different factory construction plans. In one design, the building, stripped of its machinery, may be easily adaptable to the uses of other manufacturing companies. The second alternative may be a much more specialized type of building. Here the company might want to augment its NPV comparisons of the two alternative buildings with judgmental consideration of liquidity aspects. This comparison could lead the company to build a higher priced, but more easily liquidated building in preference to a strict "least cost" choice.

SUMMARY

Land, buildings and equipment, and intangibles constitute three major fixed asset categories.

Buildings and equipment are affected by the tax shelter afforded from capital cost allowances. Tax relief on asset disposals may be afforded through capital gains treatment.

Break-even analysis allows a simplified exploration of asset acceptability under a range of *ex ante* circumstances. More involved analysis is provided by simulation and sensitivity analysis.

Marginal analysis becomes particularly essential in replacement and disposal decisions. Disposal decisions are often coloured by extra-economic considerations.

Fixed assets possess varying degrees of liquidity. This strategic element affects choices of asset acceptability and design.

QUESTIONS AND PROBLEMS

1. What is the customary accounting distinction between current and fixed assets?

2. How can the acquisition of assets classified as current result in a relatively permanent commitment of company funds? Provide two examples.

3. Indicate in detail how the annual capital cost allowance for an asset is determined.

4. Company has a marginal tax rate of 40 percent, and uses a discount rate of 15 percent. It purchases an asset for $100,000, the CCA rate of which is 10 percent.
    a. Identify the amount of CCA for the first, second, and third years of the asset's life.
    b. Find the present value of the capital cost allowances that will result over all the years of the asset's life. (Use the formula.)
    c. Find the present value of the tax savings that will result from the asset's CCA.
    d. How is the value of the tax shelter on the above asset affected by the assumption that the asset will last only ten years and have no salvage value? By what amount will it

be affected if the asset lasts ten years and has an estimated salvage value of $50,000?

5. What is the tax effect if profit from the sale of an asset is classified as a capital gain rather than ordinary income? What determines the classification?

6. A company buys a building in Year 0 for $100,000 and sells it in Year 3 for $150,000. The company's tax rate is 40 percent; the gain on the building is classified as a capital gain. Find the after-tax cash inflow from the disposal of the asset. Using a discount rate of 15 percent, what is the asset's NPV?

7. Company X follows a policy that the initial cost of any fixed asset should, in capital budgeting analysis, be expanded by 25 percent as an estimate for related current asset requirements? Explain the possible rationale for such a rule? What are its pitfalls?

8. A company plans to build a new plant and begin production of product X. Product X is a well-established product on which little price variation is expected. Product price is currently $40 per unit. While the company is quite confident about the unit price of X, it is rather uncertain about how much X can be sold.

   The plant for producing X, and associated other investment for entering the X market, will cost $3 million. Raw materials, direct labour, and other noncapital costs are estimated at $20 per unit of X. A ten-year life is projected for the plant which will produce X, and the company expects a 15 percent return on its investment.

   a. Ignoring tax considerations, what is the minimum volume of production in sales the company must sustain if the assets used for product X are to be an acceptable investment?

   b. Repeat the calculation, assuming a 40 percent marginal tax rate and an average capital cost allowance rate of 15 percent?

9. Purchase of a new machine is contemplated. The motive for a purchase is labour saving. The machine may last five years or ten years. It may save 10,000 hours of labour annually or it may save 20,000. Wage rates may be $10 per hour or they may be $15 per hour.

   Ignoring tax considerations, explore the possible present values of benefits from the machine, using a discount rate of 20 percent. Interpret your findings.

10. Indicate the limitations of the analysis in the above problem. What additional type of information would be desirable?

11. Return to the Adams Ltd. example and the related data presented in Illustration 52. In the example, the calculations presented indicated that the trucks under consideration should not be replaced.

   Now some time has elapsed, and the facts of the case have changed. The old trucks have deteriorated and now have a salvage value of only $10,000 each. Six new trucks will do the work of ten old ones. Average extraordinary repairs of $3,000 are now estimated on each of the old trucks during the forthcoming year. Other facts are unchanged.

   In light of the changed circumstances, reexamine the replacement decision for Adams Ltd.

12. How can liquidity be "designed into" fixed assets?

RELATED READINGS

Hollingworth, F. D. "Divestment—It's Tough to Bite the Bullet." *The Business Quarterly,* Summer 1975.

Johnson, R. W., Forsythe, J. D. *Canadian Financial Management.* Boston: Allyn and Bacon, 1974, chap. 8.

Magee, J. F. "Decision Trees for Decision-Making." *Harvard Business Review,* July–August 1964.

———. "How to Use Decision Trees in Capital Investment." *Harvard Business Review,* September–October 1964.

Richardson, L. K. "Do High Risks Lead to High Returns?" *Financial Analysts Journal,* March–April 1970.

Salayar, R. C., and Subrata, K. S. "A Simulation Model of Capital Budgeting under Uncertainty." *Management Science,* October 1966.

Schwabb, B., and Lusztig, P. *Managerial Finance in a Canadian Setting.* Toronto: Holt, Rinehart & Winston, 1973, pp. 69–71.

6

INVENTORY
MANAGEMENT

An inventory is a stock of goods; these goods have the characteristic that they will normally be disposed of during the course of the company's regular business operations. The basic thrust of the chapter will be toward the question of whether or not marginal amounts of various types of inventory should be held. While some different evaluation and decision techniques will be introduced, basically the rationale of capital budgeting will be employed in considering marginal inventory decisions. Revenues and noncapital costs will be projected, and subjected to testing for acceptability.

The transition from fixed asset to inventory analysis introduces a difference in the nature of the investment maintained. In a fixed asset, an investment is made initially; no further investment is required unless "remodeling" or other major maintenance cost is required. (Recurrent, "normal" maintenance expenditures is customarily included in the identification of net operating cash flows.)

In contrast, investment in short-lived assets can be characterized as a process of recovery and renewal. Items are sold out of inventory; others are purchased to replace them. Accounts receivable are regularly collected; new credit is regularly extended. Thus, these investments are of a recycling character. The original investment is constantly being retrieved and reinvested; however, a balance equal to the amount of original investment tends to be maintained. Items from an original inventory may be sold in a few days, but the investment commitment in the inventory may be maintained for decades.

In evaluation of inventory investments, it will be important to identify benefits derived from inventory holding. Therefore, the following section will explore many of the potential benefits that motivate companies to acquire inventories.

PURPOSES FOR HOLDING INVENTORY

Nondiscretionary Inventory

In considering fixed asset decisions we had previously noted that fixed assets, if they are to be used, may result in the "tying up" of minimum levels of inventory. If a manufacturing plant is to operate, it may, for example, require minimum stocks of work-in-process. These minimal inventory levels that are essentially a part of fixed assets, may be called nondiscretionary inventory as part of the fixed asset decision. Such stocks which are integral parts of other projects need not be analyzed as inventory, even though they are included under that caption in company accounts.

Inventory for Production Leveling

One important reason for holding inventory is to allow production to take place at a constant pace. The need for such inventory arises because the demand for a product may be seasonal or sporadic in nature. An attempt to produce goods for a current demand could lead to a disorderly production process, with assembly lines running in frenzy during periods of high demand and lying idle during periods of low demand. One solution to such disorder lies in producing at an even pace and, during periods of low demand, allowing finished goods to accumulate. This finished goods inventory can be subsequently used as a source of supply during periods where demand is greater than the rate of production.

An example can illustrate this type of inventory accumulation:

Assumptions

1. Sales for Archer Ltd. a manufacturer of "snowmobiles" are projected as follows:

Projected Sales (in physical units)

February–July	no sale
August	10,000
September	40,000
October	50,000
November	40,000
December	20,000
January	20,000
Total annual sales	180,000

2. Cost with seasonal production, $900 per unit.

3. Cost with level production of 15,000 units per month, $800 per unit.

4. Inventory with seasonal production: virtually none.

5. Inventory projection with level production of 15,000 per month is shown in Illustration 6–1.

It is easy to observe in Illustration 6–1 that a stockpile of finished goods is built up, and then subsequently drawn down to meet the seasonal sales requirement. The required financial commitment is also apparent. The firm must be prepared to commit a maximum of $76 million to an inventory position. This peak financing requirement will only exist for a month, yet it will have to be provided for. From another viewpoint, the average commitment to inventory over the year will be the sum of the projected total inventory column, divided by 12 months, or $35.3 million.

Benefits are also in evidence on the firm's planned annual production of 180,000 units. Leveling of the production process

ILLUSTRATION 6-1

ARCHER LTD.
Projected Inventory Needs
(in millions of dollars)

Month	(1) Projected Cost of Goods Produced at $800 per Unit (level production)	(2) Projected Cost of Goods Sold at $800 per Unit (based on sales forecast)	(3) Projected Change in Inventory	(4) Projected Total Inventory (accumulation of Col. 3)
February	$12		$12	$12
March	12		12	24
April	12		12	36
May	12		12	48
June	12		12	72
July	12		12	72
August	12	$ 8	4	76
September	12	32	− 20	56
October	12	40	− 28	28
November	12	32	− 20	8
December	12	16	− 5	4
January	12	16	− 5	0

through inventory accumulation will save $100 per unit in costs (through the use of smaller equipment which can be used a longer time, avoidance of overtime pay, and so on) so the benefit attributable to the holding of the inventory will be $18 million per year; with a 40 percent tax rate that reduced to $10.8 million after tax. Note that this annual $10.8 million is obtained in addition to the maintenance of all invested funds, which will recurrently liquidate and then be recommitted to the next season's inventory buildup.

This example has been intentionally simplified. The thoughtful reader will no doubt be left with questions, such as: What are the consequences of wrong projections? What about provision for storing the inventory? What are the consequences of a competitor, using seasonal production, introducing a last minute design change? Answers to questions of this type should emerge as we progress through additional topics in the chapter. Also, the Archer example will be reintroduced and subjected to capital budgeting analysis.

The above examples showed production being leveled through an accumulation of finished goods inventory. In a similar way, inventory can serve to eliminate the consequences between an imbalance of raw materials supply and production. For example, a sawmill may accumulate a stockpile of logs during the logging season and draw down this stockpile throughout the year if it wishes to maintain level production. The investment here would result because the firm elected to accumulate logs and hold these logs for some time rather than attempting to process them immediately upon their arrival. Benefits would again be the cost's savings from a more orderly production process.

Inventory as a Device for Reducing Handling Problems

Inventories can be a versatile servant. We have seen in the preceding section how they can be used to level out production, converting an intermittent production into a continuous production process. They can also be used to convert a continuous process into a noncontinuous one. A firm, for example, may manufacture several products and decide that it is better (rather than to try to manufacture all of the products simultaneously) to manufacture in batches—first a batch of one product and then of another. Just as inventory accumulation could match up regular production with irregular demand, stockpiling of finished goods from irregular production can allow that production to be matched up with demand that continues after the production has been suspended.

Similarly, inventory accumulation can be used to economize ordering, dispatching, and transportation costs. A firm can buy raw materials in large quantity, taking advantage of possible volume discounts in buying, volume discounts in handling, and saving in paper work through the processing of a single rather than a series of transactions. These goods can then be held for eventual use. The obtaining of these savings requires an inventory investment; the savings are only worthwhile if they comprise an adequate benefit from the magnitude of investment required, when subjected to capital budgeting tests.

An interesting example of this type of inventory accumulation is found at the port of Churchill on Hudson Bay. The shipping season from this port is very short—about two months during the summer. The attraction of the port is that it provides a low-cost water transportation route for grain produced in the Prairies. Grain gradually flows from the Prairies to Churchill during the period between harvest time in late summer and the beginning of next year's shipping season. Large inventories of wheat accumulate and then pour quickly from the port to world markets when the ice goes out of the navigation route.

Safety Stocks

So far inventory accumulation has been discussed as if the future were perfectly foreseeable. In the detailed example of production leveling, the projection of inventory accumulation was made without addressing the question of whether or not the underlying sales projections were precise.

For example, the market for snowmobiles is dependent upon some unpredictable variables. One could not confidently foretell that the winter of 1972–73 would be one with little snow, or that farmers (who are good snowmobile customers) would enter the winter of 1973–74 with bank balances reinforced through recent doublings and triplings of producer prices for many food commodities.

There are two sides to this problem of difficulty in prediction: inventories based on best available estimates may be either excessive or inadequate. Since at this point we are concerned with reasons for accumulating inventory rather than for limiting that accumulation, let us consider the danger of running short of inventory. Shortages in inventory can occur because of a number of reasons. Demand for output of a product may be greater than expected with resulting shortages of finished goods or raw materials. Delays in shipping time, often unforeseeable, may result in inadequacies of raw materials and supplies inventories. Strikes by suppliers may cause shortages; the list could go on almost indefinitely.

Running out of inventory may have serious consequences. If the finished goods inventory is exhausted, customers, relying on immediate availability of a product, may be disappointed and may be driven away to better stocked competitors. Running out of raw materials and supplies inventories may cause costly production shutdowns. All of these possible costs associated with running out of inventory are gathered together under the heading of *stockout costs*.

To protect against shortages, extra inventories may be accumulated. To return to the Archer Ltd. example, this company might decide to schedule production for a year at a rate of 18,000 units per month rather than 15,000 with sales projected at 180,000 units during the year. The result of this 18,000 per month production pattern would be to accumulate inventory in excess of planned requirements. Production at 18,000 units per month would result in a total annual production of 216,000 units and a projected ending inventory of 36,000 units (216,000 production minus 180,000 projected sales). This extra inventory accumulated as a buffer against the possibility of shortages, is called a *safety stock*.

In general the determination of a safety stock consists of a balancing of two effects. As the size of the safety stock is increased, the probability of inventory deficiencies and attendant stockout costs is decreased. At the same time, an increasingly larger level of inventory must be financed, and other carrying costs associated with the inventory must be incurred. The striking of a wealth-maximizing balance between these two effects is one of the more difficult aspects of financial management.

Inventory as a Marketing Tool

Not all finished goods inventory is held available for immediate sale. A firm may maintain inventories which are solely for display. In this case the costs of holding these assets are analogous to an expenditure for advertising. The firm finds it easier to sell goods if its customers actually can examine the goods, rather than order them on the basis of a description or picture.

Closely related to keeping a display stock, another situation arises when a firm attempts to maintain an extremely wide variety of inventory for sales advantage. A department store may stock 40 or 50 different models and sizes of television sets, where a warehouse-type discounter may offer only two or three. Again the company is attempting to use marginal inventory as a competitive marketing tool.

Speculative Inventory Accumulation

A firm may buy inventory because of anticipated need based on various projections. Inventory of this type is sometimes called an *anticipation stock*. Inventory may also be accumulated because of difficulty associated with making projections, and the related apprehension about running out of needed items; i.e., safety stocks. In addition an inventory may be bought in expectation of an increase in the market price of the inventory item; this may be called a *speculative* accumulation.

The benefits from a correct expectation of price increase is obvious. The inventory could be resold advantageously, or if the inventory were used in the company's production process the company would have the benefit of a cost advantage over its competitors. There is little that a textbook can say about speculative inventory accumulation, except that it is done. Commodity markets are notoriously difficult to forecast, and certainly there are no easy rules available for evaluating speculative inventory investments.

INVESTMENT AND COST IN INVENTORY HOLDING

Related Investments

Inventory usually requires accompanying storage space. Sometimes this space is relatively insignificant in cost, as when lumber inventories are piled outside on low-cost land. More often extra building space is required, and sometimes specialized equipment, such as refrigeration capability, is also needed. If these storage facilities are to be purchased, rather than rented, it is appropriate to consider the purchase cost as part of the inventory investment. For example, if a firm decides to hold a peak inventory of $500,000 worth of material, to provide for production leveling, and if a $100,000 building is required to store this inventory, the total investment required is $600,000. Only if the benefits from production leveling are great enough to provide an adequate reward for a commitment of a $600,000 investment is the inventory accumulation desirable.

Costs of Holding Inventory

Aside from capital cost, which will be implicitly considered in capital budgeting tests for investment acceptability, there are *carrying costs* (operating costs related to the holding of inventory) to be considered. Rental of storage space, heating and/or cooling costs, handling costs, the maintenance of guards or security arrangements are all carrying costs.

In addition to carrying costs, inventory may be subject to physical change during the time it is left in storage. Usually, the economic character of this change is negative, and the change is referred to as *spoilage*. Examines include the rusting of metal equipment, the possible decay of perishable foods, or insect infestations in grain inventories.

Sometimes physical change for the better constitutes the motive for holding an inventory, or at least can enhance the value of carrying inventory. The "aging" of wine or cheese, or the "curing" of lumber are examples of physical changes which have positive economic aspects.

Risk in Inventory Holding

There are two principal sources of risk in carrying inventory. Physical deterioration in inventory may not be readily predictable; for example, the occurrence of unforeseen warm, humid weather may hasten some decay processes.

In most inventories though, the most important risk will be that associated with price change. This price change is important even when inventories have not been accumulated for speculative purposes. For example, again consider Archer Ltd. which uses level production with a resulting accumulation of finished goods inventory. An unforeseen style change by a competitor could render the snowmobile inventory much less marketable than had been previously anticipated, with a result that the snowmobiles in inventory would have to be sold at a discount. If the inventory had not been accumulated, Archer Ltd. might have been able to learn of the competitor's style change, and perhaps modify the design of its product.

As another example, a manufacturer of fertilizers arranges to buy phosphate rock, one of the major ingredients in many types of fertilizers, by chartering an ocean freighter, where previously he had been obtaining it by rail. He now has an unusually large amount of inventory in transit, or accumulated in advance of use when the ship is unloaded. An expected transportation saving may make this holding of inventory appear to be an attractive investment. However, a sharp decline in the phosphate market would make the fertilizer manufacturer regret his inventory purchase. Had he not bought the large quantity, it is quite possible that he could have, by buying at the lower prices which prevailed later, been able to more than offset extra transportation costs.

This risk dimension is a two-sided one; often firms make windfall gains from inventory holding because of unexpected price appreciations. Nevertheless, a risk dimension exists, and many inventory investments may be grouped among relatively risky assets. Some may be flamboyantly risky (women's fashion merchandise is a notorious case). Near the end of the chapter, techniques for reducing investory risk will be considered.

EVALUATIVE CRITERIA AND TECHNIQUES

NPV Identification

The preceding sections have attempted to set forth the benefits, costs, and risks, that may be associated with inventory holding. These aspects of inventory analysis can be analyzed in a manner similar to that employed on fixed assets, and then subjected to acceptance tests.

It is usual in inventory evaluation to distinguish between peaks and average investment needs. To return to the Archer Ltd. example of production-leveling inventory, peak inventory accumulation of $76 million was required and an average level of about $35.3 million had to be maintained throughout the year. For most analysis, the average is regarded the more useful figure. While it is true that the company will temporarily need above-average amounts of financing, we shall see later that flexible financing arrangements can enable a company to use, and pay for, funds on a temporary, "as needed" basis. Therefore, since the company will not be required to incur capital costs on the peak amount all through the year, the average amount is more consistent with the amount of financing actually required.

(While the average figure is the more correct for inclusion in a capital budgeting test, this should not suggest that a company can ignore the peak figure; in its financial planning Archer Ltd. will have to include arrangements for having $76 million available at some point during the year.)

In addition to maintaining its inventory, Archer Ltd. will have to store it. When the inventory reaches its peak of $76 million, nearly 100,000 snowmobiles will be in storage. Suppose this, in turn, requires a $5 million warehouse facility. This investment will be maintained throughout the year, to bring the average level of investment required to $40.3 million.

This investment is large, but so are the benefits. On annual sales of 180,000 units, production savings of $100 per unit, amounts to $18 million per year. Suppose that additional handling, maintenance, and security costs associated with the inventory holding are $4 million per year to produce a net saving of $14 million before tax. The problem can now be developed into a net present value analysis. The analysis is presented below, based on a 40 percent corporation tax rate. Archer uses a 15 percent discount rate to recognize the degree of risk involved. Data is summarized in Illustration 6–2.

Most of the ingredients for NPV identification are available in Illustration 6–2. The remaining requirement is the time over which benefits are expected. The inventory itself (distinguished from the building to house it) has the characteristics of a perpetual investment. Each year investment can be committed and recovered; this recycling can continue indefinitely. If, as a starting point, one regards the annual rate of deterioration in the building to be negligible, it, too, can be viewed as a perpetual-lined investment. Given the assumption, the stream

ILLUSTRATION 6–2

ARCHER LTD.
Data for Inventory Decision
(in thousands)

Investment required:	
Average inventory	−$35,333
Warehouse	− 5,000
Total	−$40,333
Value of capital cost allowance tax shelter:	
$C(d/d + r)t$, where $t = 40\%$	
$r = 15\%$, and $d = 5\%$	
$5,000 (0.05/0.20) 0.4$	$ 500
Annual net receipts:	
Production cost savings before tax	$18,000
Less carrying costs	− 4,000
Net receipts	$14,000
$(1 − t)$	0.6
Annual receipts after tax	$ 8,400

of benefits, $8,400,000 per year, may be regarded as perpetual lined (with present value of A/r).

```
NPV identification can now proceed:
  Cost  . . . . . . . . . . . . . . . . . . . . . . . . .   −$40,333,000
  Tax saving from CCA  . . . . . . . . . . . . . .        500,000
  Present value of operating cash
    flows (8,400,000/0.15)  . . . . . . . . . . . .     56,000,000
  NPV  . . . . . . . . . . . . . . . . . . . . . . . . .   $16,167,000
```

If the building was assumed to deteriorate more rapidly, more conventional procedure could be employed. For example, if the building was expected to last ten years and have a salvage value of $2 million, the calculation might be made on the basis of $n = 10$, with receipt of salvage, accompanying loss of CCA, and liquidation of the inventory investment occurring at the end of the tenth year.

Archer could also use experimental analysis to consider other possible levels of inventory. One possible solution might be to use a modified production leveling. The company might decide to produce only some models in advance of its seasonal needs. For example, Archer Ltd. might single out one or more of the snowmobile models that it regards as most basic, and least vulnerable to going "out of style." It might find that it could affect significant cost savings with only this partial production leveling, and at the same time it might reduce the risk dimension in its inventory accumulation by not producing in advance those models most vulnerable to competition from design changes.

Rate of Return

Data amenable to NPV identification also can be used for IRR identification. In the Archer example, assuming perpetual return:

NPV = Initial cost + tax saving from CCA
      + present value of operating cash flows.

or substituting from Illustration 5–2, but leaving r as unknown,

NPV = −$40,333,000 + $5,000,000 (0.05/0.05 + r).
      + $8,400,000/$r$.

Setting NPV $= 0$ and searching for r, IRR of about 21 percent is obtained.

Inventory Turnover

One compact method that is widely used in evaluating inventory positions is the inventory turnover ratio. This ratio is calculated as:

$$\text{Turnover ratio} = \frac{\text{Cost of goods sold}}{\text{Average inventory}}.$$

The cost of goods sold figure used in calculating the ratio is normally an average for a year. Often the calculation of average inventory is done by simply adding the year's beginning and ending inventory and dividing by two. Of course, a more sophisticated average, such as the average of monthly inventory positions used in the previous example, could also be employed—this refinement is essential if inventory has significant seasonal peaks.

The intent of the ratio is to literally describe the number of times that inventory "turns over." For example, if annual cost of goods sold was $300,000, and average inventory was $30,000 one could assert that on the average it would be necessary to replenish the whole inventory ten times during the year.

In general, a high inventory turnover ratio has been regarded as desirable; it is supposed to indicate that relatively small inventory investment is sustaining a large amount of business activity. Turnover ratio is sometimes explained in the context of a formula:

$$\text{Rate of return on assets} = \text{Profit margin} \times \text{asset turnover.}$$

Profit margin refers to the fractional relationship between profit and cost of goods sold. The turnover ratio is a ratio between cost of goods sold and quantity of assets. The product of the ratios therefore becomes profit per unit of assets.

The turnover ratio is useful as a quick comparative measure on inventory positions, particularly in retail and wholesale businesses. A low turnover ratio relative to other firms in a similar business can signal that a company is overcommitted on its inventory investment.

While the turnover ratio is useful, and is in fact widely used, it is imperative to recognize that the goal of a business is profit maximization (or wealth maximization) and not maximization of the turnover ratio. In the context of the above formula for profitability on assets, it is quite possible that profit margins and inventory turnover can be reciprocally interrelated. Inventory itself can increase profit margins; for example, a firm with large inventories may avoid stockout costs, and reduce other costs, such as those associated with small transportation shipments or with irregular production schedules.

Even in merchandising businesses where the turnover measure is widely used, a low inventory turnover ratio may be unsatisfactory from a profit-making view. Consider the following example:

1. A women's clothing store, Palace of Fashion Ltd., sustains sales activity resulting in cost of goods sold of $1 million per year. It does this on the basis of a $200,000 average inventory, which consists of an inexpensive line of women's clothing, stocked only in standard sizes. Its current sales rate is $1,500,000 per year.

2. Selling, general, and administrative costs are estimated $200,000 per year plus 10 percent of costs of goods sold.

3. The company's tax rate is 46 percent.

4. The income statement is presented as follows:

Sales	$1,500,000
Cost of goods sold	1,000,000
Margin on sales	500,000
Selling, general and	
administrative costs	400,000
Net earnings before tax	$ 100,000
$(1 - t)$	0.54
Net earnings after tax	$ 54,000

Palace's inventory turnover ratio is currently 5.0 ($1,000,000/$200,000). The company now considers the possibility of doubling its inventory, to enlarge its size range and to eliminate some previously existing stockouts. It has sufficient storage and display space for the inventory. It estimates that the new inventory will increase its sales by $600,000 per year up to a total of

$2,100,000. The cost of goods sold on these marginal sales will be $400,000 (at the same ratio as before).

Selling, general, and administrative expenses are expected to follow the same pattern and increase by 10 percent of the additional cost of goods sold. Thus, the company expects the following effects from its $200,000 addition to inventory:

Increase in sales	$600,000
Increase in cost of goods sold	400,000
Increase in gross margin	$200,000
Increase in selling, general, and administrative expenses . . .	40,000
Increase in net earnings before income tax	$160,000
$(1 - t)$	0.54
Increase in net earnings after tax	$ 86,400

The company is therefore considering an annual return of $86,400 on a $200,000 investment. In rate of return terms, this is a 43 percent IRR. Alternatively, the inventory would pass a marginal NPV test at any discount rate up to 43 percent. By most investment standards this asset performance is handsome.

On the other hand, look at the effect on the inventory turnover ratio. After the new inventory is added the turnover ratio is calculated as:

Cost of goods sold	$1,400,000
Inventory	÷ 400,000
New inventory turnover ratio	3.5
Previous inventory turnover ratio . . .	5.0

Here is a situation where a desirable marginal investment had decreased the turnover ratio. The two performance measures are in conflict and since the rate of return and NPV acceptance criteria relate directly to wealth maximization, one must conclude that the alarm sent out by the turnover ratio is a false one.

The Economic Order Quantity Formula

The economic order quantity, or EOQ formula is used as an evaluative device for certain types of inventory decisions. It particularly relates to inventory which is accumulated for the purpose of reducing costs by eliminating the handling of small shipments or small orders. Purchasing large quantities will reduce the number of shipments or orders but at the same time it will increase the required inventory investment and inventory carrying costs. The formula enables one to find the cost-minimizing purchase size; hence EOQ.

The formula can be made consistent with the NPV methods. One of the variables in the formula is an annual "carrying cost" rate, which should be interpreted as

"Carrying cost" = Discount rate + nonfinancial carrying cost rate,

with the second term expressing such items as spoilage and storage as an annual amount per dollar of inventory. The discount rate provides the linkage to NPV; the formula will set an order quantity to reject marginal inventory investment where NPV < 0 (or equivalently, where IRR < target rate).

Carrying costs vary directly with amount of average inventory. This size varies directly with the size of individual orders. If a new order is placed to replenish inventory just when stockout is to occur, average inventory will vary from a maximum of the amount of an individual order to a minimum of zero, and will average half of the individual order quality. Designating the carrying cost rate as C_1 and order quantity as Q dollars, total carrying cost per year is the equal to:

$$C_1(Q/2).$$

A second cost is also involved: cost of handling each order. This order cost may be designated as C_2. Number of orders placed per year will vary inversely with order size. Where $P =$ annual purchases to be made, number of orders placed will be P/Q and order cost per year will be equal to

$$C_2(P/Q).$$

Total inventory costs then become:

$$\text{Total cost} = C_1(Q/2) + C_2(P/Q).$$

These total costs are minimized under the condition:

$$Q = \sqrt{\frac{2C_2P}{C_1}} \cdot$$

Consider an illustration of its use: A manufacturer makes purchases of a raw material of $100,000 per year. His "carrying cost" rate is 25 percent and his order cost is $50. Applying the formula

$$Q = \sqrt{\frac{2(50)(100,000)}{0.25}} = \$6,324$$

The company should probably try to buy in lots of approximately $6,000. If this policy is followed, average inventory will be $3,000, and the company will place about 17 orders per year. Its total costs will be about $3,000 (0.25) + 17 (50) = $1,600.

This contrasts with costs where orders are at other sizes:

$Q = \$1,000$; Cost $= 500 (0.25) + 100 (50) = \$5,125$
$Q = \$20,000$; Cost $= 10,000 (0.25) + 4 (50) = \$2,750.$

Obviously, the EOQ formula has only limited applicability, where inventory is accumulated with the motive of reducing handling costs. Where it is applicable, the formula has obtained wide understanding and usage.

Safety Stock Simulations

We noted that inventory was sometimes accumulated to protect against stockout costs that may arise because of uncertainties in sales projection, projected rates of production, or projected time required for new orders to be filled. Computerized simulation is often used as a technique for exploring this aspect of inventory accumulation. In principle, the safety stock determination problem is another problem in cost minimization, where the carrying costs associated with enlarging inventory are balanced against the stockout costs which are associated with maintaining a small inventory. These simulations consist of experimenting on the computer with various possible conditions, such as different patterns of market demand and different shipping times. While these simulations cannot offer a neat analytic solution of the type represented by the economic order quantity formula, they offer very valuable insights into the question of setting safety stocks; and have broader and more realistic applicability than EOQ.

CONTROLLING FOR THE RISK OF
INVENTORY PRICE CHANGE

Inventory may lose its economic value, either because of physical deterioration or because of market price change in the commodity being stored. This section will discuss some techniques that are widely employed for protecting a company against this second aspect of the risk in inventory holding—the unpredictability of market prices. Because some of the techniques relate to a particular type of organized marketplace, commodities futures markets, a brief description of these markets will first be presented. Paradoxically, while these markets are associated in the public mind with speculation, they may be used by companies as a means of avoiding risk of price fluctuation.

A Digression on Commodities Futures Markets

Commodities futures markets offer the opportunity for trading in a particular object of value, the commodities *futures contract*. The futures contract is just that—a contract for the delivery of a specified amount of a commodity at a specified future date. For example, it is possible for an individual to go to a futures market and buy a contract for the delivery of 10,000 bushels of wheat at the end of six months. The purchase of such a contract assures its holder of the availability of the grain at a predetermined price.

As in other freely functioning markets, the price of a futures contract is determined by supply and demand conditions. The most important determinant of the price is the expectations that buyers and sellers have about the relative abundance or shortage of the commodity in question at the time of delivery. Not surprisingly, these expectations are frequently revised with resulting price changes. In the example of wheat futures cited previously, information such as the fact of limited rainfall in the Prairie Provinces, or the failure of an Oriental rice crop that will induce the buying of substitute foodstuffs, may cause the price of wheat futures to rise.

On the selling side, the Prairie wheat producer, satisfied with the price prevailing on the futures market, could under take to sell grain for future delivery. In fact he could sell a wheat futures contract with no prospect of actually producing wheat. If he expects the price of wheat to decline, for example, he might sell a 10,000 bushel futures contract for delivery specified six months hence. He would do this in the knowledge that before six months was over he would have to buy wheat to fulfill his obligation under the futures contract. This sale of a futures contract is often called a *short sale,* indicating that the seller of the contract is making an advance sale of a commodity which he does not presently have.

Futures markets exist in many foodstuffs and basic raw materials. Canada's major futures market, the Winnipeg Grain Exchange, is one of the world's important grain markets. However, Canadians wishing to participate in futures markets for other commodities often must arrange transactions outside of their own country: Chicago, New York, and London are particularly important futures trading centres. (The arrangements can be made in Canada.)

A final note: the mechanics of participating in the futures market are quite uncomplicated for the person participating. Most larger cities have commodity brokers who will arrange a futures market transaction. Many of the brokerage firms which handle securities transactions are also commodity brokers.

Hedging Inventories

Futures markets transactions can be extremely useful to companies which hold inventories whose value is subject to deterioration through price change. We may consider an example: suppose an Ontario flour milling firm acquires a large wheat inventory. It does this to assure itself of a supply of grain for its flour manufacturing operations. Of course, if the price of grains should drop after the firm had acquired its inventory, it would be at a competitive disadvantage relative to other firms who did not hold such a large inventory. To protect against this disadvantage it may make use of the futures market in a manner demonstrated by the following example:

1. The company purchases 1 million bushels of wheat at a price of $4 per bushel. This wheat is bought in advance of

current needs; the company expects to use it about eight months later.

2. The company promptly sells futures contracts for 1 million bushels of wheat to be delivered eight months later. For simplification, let us assume that these futures contracts are sold at a price of $4 per bushel.

The company has now protected itself against wheat price fluctuations. Suppose the price of wheat drops to $2 per bushel by the end of the eight-month period. This suggests that the company has been in error in acquiring the wheat inventory; by waiting, and not holding wheat, it could have fulfilled its wheat requirements at half the cost.

On the other hand, the futures market transaction was correspondingly successful. The company received $4 for wheat to be delivered eight months hence. At the time this wheat is to be delivered, the company can relieve itself of its contractual obligations by buying wheat for $2 per bushel on the current market. The result is that wheat sold in advance for $4 million is purchased for $2 million, netting a $2 million profit on the futures market transaction.

Note that the inventory holding loss is offset by the futures contract gain. This has not occurred accidentally. The cause of the loss in the value of the company's inventory (namely, a wheat price decline) is also the cause of the profit on the futures market transaction. This type of sale in the futures market simultaneous with the purchase of inventory is called a *hedging transaction*. When appropriate commodity futures markets are available, futures market hedging can be used to reduce the risk of inventory holding.

It is important to remember that the hedging transaction cuts both ways; the futures market sale will cancel out potential inventory gains as well as losses. In the above example, if the wheat price had appreciated to $6 per bushel, the $2 million appreciation on the inventory would have been offset by a $2 million futures market loss ($6 wheat would have to be purchased to cover the futures contract, originally sold at $4 per bushel).

Commodity futures transactions cannot be executed costlessly; brokerage fees and other costs of maintaining the futures market must be met by the participants in that market. Charges for future market participation differ from commodity to commodity; in general though, these transaction costs are relatively low and often seem a small price to pay for the risk control offered through the hedging transaction.

Alternative to Hedging

Sometimes hedging in the usual sense of the word is not possible because of the lack of an appropriate commodity futures market. For example, a manufacturer of television sets may accumulate a large inventory on the assumption that domestic prices will be sheltered from foreign competition by tariff barriers. To the extent that this removal of the tariff barrier is possible, the inventory may be subject to a potentially precipitous price decline. Yet there is no futures market in television sets available for hedging this transaction.

In this case price protection is left up to the ingenuity of the television set manufacturer. A possible tactic which the manufacturer could consider would be an attempt to sell his production in advance. He might, for example, offer discounts to wholesalers who are willing to place large irrevocable orders for television sets which would be delivered in the future. If he was successful in negotiating such contracts, in the event that tariff barriers were removed the wholesalers who had contracted to buy the now high-priced television sets would absorb the burden of the price decline.

This situation is quite analogous to an ordinary hedging transaction. The selling of the television sets under a fixed price contract for future delivery passes on to wholesalers not only price losses on the inventory but also price gains. If, for example, retail demand for television sets strengthens in an unexpected way so retail prices rise, the manufacturer might have been able to raise the price of the sets in his inventory if he had not contracted them to wholesalers on a fixed price basis.

The analogy may also extend to transaction costs. It is probable when price risk is shifted to others, that the manufacturer will have to sell at a lower price than he otherwise might. This discount for reduction of risk is analogous to the transactions costs in the futures market hedging transaction. It is likely that these discounts will be greater than the costs of ordinary hedging transactions; the holder of the inventory must judge whether or not the reduction of inventory risk is worth the cost of forward-selling.

SUMMARY

Inventory, though classified as a current asset, may represent a relatively permanent commitment. Other activities of the company may be integrated with its inventory policy. This integration may make minimum levels of various inventory items a virtual necessity.

Some inventory may be regarded as nondiscretionary; it is maintained as an effect of another company decision (the technology embodied in plant design may, for example, require a minimum level of work-in-process inventory).

Acquisitions of additional inventory may be made for leveling company production, reducing handling problems, as a marketing tool, or even as a commodity speculation.

Additional amounts of inventory may be held as safety stocks to compensate for uncertainties in the flow of goods into and out of inventory. Various operating costs, as well as capital costs, may be associated with holding inventory. Inventory is subject to risk; the most important component of inventory risk is usually price fluctuation. Protective techniques, principally hedging on commodity markets, are available as devices for reducing inventory risk.

Proposed changes in inventory positions can, and should be, subject to capital budgeting analysis. NPV, rate of return, or other comparisons can identify whether funds are better employed through holding marginal amounts of inventory or in alternative marginal uses.

The inventory turnover ratio is a rough indicator of the efficiency with which a company is using its inventory. The economic order quantity (EOQ) model represents a simplified solution to the issue of how frequently an inventory should be replenished. Simulation may be used to explore for the appropriate level of safety stocks.

QUESTIONS AND PROBLEMS

1. One type of inventory holding has been referred to as non-discretionary, yet obviously all assets are acquired at the discretion of the company. At what point is the decision on "non-discretionary" inventory made?

2. The following data described a company's manufacturing and selling operations.

Time	Cost of Goods Manufactured	Cost of Goods Sold
1st quarter	$10,000	$ 4,000
2d quarter	10,000	6,000
3d quarter	12,000	9,000
4th quarter	12,000	18,000

Assume a beginning finished goods inventory of $3,000. Identify inventory level at the end of each quarter and the company's average inventory holding throughout the year.

3. If a company maintains $1 million of raw materials inventory, it may expect to have its production interrupted about 15 days out of the year because of material shortages. An additional $500,000 in safety stock will reduce production interruption to practically nothing. The only cost of holding the additional $500,000 in inventory is assumed to be financing cost; 15 percent is the approximate discount or target rate. What is the lowest level of stockout cost per day that would justify maintaining the $500,000 safety stock.

4. Can display inventory substitute for sales personnel? For advertising expenditure? Explain.

5. Discuss the risk dimension in holding safety stocks?

6. A company's marginal tax rate is 25 percent and it uses a discount rate of 10 percent in making inventory acquisition decisions. Its comptroller has predicted that an additional $800,-000 of inventory would allow savings of $300,000 per year from production leveling. A spoilage rate of 5 percent is assumed in the inventory. Storage and handling costs are estimated at $5,000 per month extra if this marginal inventory is acquired.

Find the marginal rate of return on the inventory.

Subject this marginal inventory to an NPV test of acceptability.

7. A company maintains an average inventory of $500,000 per year and sustains sales of $3 million with cost of goods sold of $2 million. Calculate the inventory turnover ratio.

8. Explain how a company in the above example might simultaneously reduce its inventory turnover ratio and increase profitability.

9. An office supply store buys about $20,000 per year of a particular type of stationery. It uses a 25 percent carrying cost in analyzing this inventory and estimates the cost of placing an order and receiving an individual shipment of stationery at $35. Calculate economic order quantity.

10. What is a short sale?

11. An Ontario livestock feeder has 100,000 bushels of feed barley in storage. He hedges this barley by selling barley short on the Winnipeg Grain Exchange. During the following month, the price of the barley he has on hand rises from $2.20 per bushel to $2.50 per bushel. The price of barley futures on the Winnipeg Exchange rises from $2.40 to $2.70. Ignoring brokerage commissions and other transactions costs, demonstrate arithmetically what the financial consequences of the hedging transaction has been. Explain, with reference to this example, how a hedge can be desirable ex ante and undesirable ex post.

12. The livestock feeder above, to protect 1 million pounds of beef which is still "on the hoof," desires to place a hedge. He expects to sell this beef on the Canadian market but there is no market for beef futures in Canada. He, therefore, decides to sell short on the Chicago market on the basis of his judgment that price movements in the U.S. and Canadian markets tend to be closely related. During the month after placing the hedge the feeder's "on the hoof" beef has dropped in price by 10 cents per pound, and beef futures at Chicago have dropped 7 cents per pound. Identify the financial effect.

RELATED READINGS

"Commodity Exchanges," and "Commodity Exchange Trading in the Grain Industry," in *Grains and Oilseeds, Handling, and Processing*, 2d ed. Winnipeg: Canadian International Grains Institute, 1975, pp. 194–202, 206–15.

Hadley, G., and Whitin, T. M. *Analysis of Inventory Systems.* Englewood Cliffs, N.J.: Prentice-Hall, 1963.

Hofer, C. F.   "Analysis of Fixed Costs in Inventory." *Management Accounting*, September 1970.

Mehta, D. R.   *Working Capital Management*. Englewood Cliffs, N.J.: Prentice-Hall, 1974, part 2.

Schiff, M.   "Credit and Inventory Management—Separate or Together." *Financial Executive*, November 1972.

Snyder, A.   "Principles of Inventory Management." *Financial Executive*, April 1964.

Thurston, P. H.   "Requirements Planning for Inventory Control." *Harvard Business Review*, March–April 1972.

Wagner, H. M.   *Principles of Operations Research—With Applications to Managerial Decisions*. Englewood Cliffs, N.J.: Prentice-Hall, 1969, chaps. 9 and 19.

7

CREDIT POLICY

The granting of credit implies that goods or services are provided to a customer in advance of his paying for them. The result of granting credit is the accumulation of an asset in the form of a claim for future payment. These assets are usually described as *receivables*. Like other assets, receivables must be financed. They, therefore, should be subjected to the same tests of acceptability as other assets.

Receivables, again like other assets, should be viewed as opportunities for wealth enhancement. The granting of credit and the accumulation of receivables are not necessary evils but positive business opportunities. Credit is always extended voluntarily; even when a sale cannot be made unless credit is extended, the company has the option of foregoing the sale. Indeed, such a situation illustrates the potential of receivable investment; credit may be the key to sales and profit opportunities.

For the student of financial management, receivables differ

from the fixed asset and inventories previously discussed in one important sense. Receivables are financial assets (claims), and are usually subject to day-to-day administration by financial managers. In contrast, financial management is mainly limited to a decision role on physical assets, with actual asset operation and control left to others.

GENERAL CONCEPTS RELATING TO CREDIT EXTENSION

Types of Credit Arrangements

Credit can be granted under a variety of arrangements; the five forms of credit granting described below are the most prevalent, but this list should not be regarded as exhaustive.

Accounts Receivable. This is usually a very informal type of credit arrangement; goods are sold with an oral or written understanding that they will be paid for within a specified period of time. Sometimes there is no explicit financing charge associated with this type of credit; at other times an interest charge is specified. Sometimes a discount is allowed for prompt payment.

For example, a sale on credit terms described as 2/10; n/30 would provide for a 2 percent discount if the account is paid within 10 days; the second part, n/30, indicates that the net or full amount is due within 30 days. Implicitly this arrangement provides for a form of interest charge if payment is not made within ten days.

Accounts Receivable (Revolving Credit). Traditionally, accounts receivable have usually been very short term. Terms longer than 30 days or "end-of-month" (sometimes abbreviated e.o.m.) were infrequent and terms beyond 90 days were rare. A more recently developed type of receivable provides for payment over a longer time period, with payments on a recurrent (usually monthly) basis. Because, under this arrangement, additional credit is often extended before previous credit has been repaid, this form of receivable has become known as revolving credit. The retail credit arrangements offered by Eaton's, The Bay, and other department stores are well-known examples of this type of credit arrangement.

Conditional Sales Contracts.   The pattern of repayment on a conditional sales contract is similar to that of a revolving charge arrangement. A particular purchase is paid for in regular installments, usually monthly but possibly even annually in some types of transactions. These contracts are more formal than the revolving credit arrangements; a written agreement is drawn up in connection with a specific sale. The seller also reserves a specific right to repossess the article sold in the event of nonpayment (in fact, the seller remains the legal owner of the object sold until the final payment is made, though this ownership right is in turn subject to other legal restrictions).

The time payment plans under which automobiles are frequently sold are excellent examples of the conditional sales contract. Nonconsumer durable goods are also often sold under contracts of this type.

Consignments.   A consignment represents another arrangement where legal ownership is retained by the seller until goods are paid for. Otherwise, consignment sales are similar to ordinary accounts receivable.[1] Consignments are not employed in consumer transactions. A typical consignment arrangement would consist of a wholesaler selling goods to a retailer. Ownership in the goods would rest with the wholesaler until he was paid; this might not occur until the goods were in turn sold to a customer of the retailer.

Notes Receivable.   A note receivable is a more formal, and usually a longer term version of an accounts receivable. Again this type of credit arrangement is not typically used in consumer transactions. A manufacturer, for example, might sell a large shipment of supplies to another manufacturer and accept a note in lieu of cash payment. The note would constitute a promise to pay for the goods at the end of a specified period of time, usually with interest.

Why Trade Credit: A Broader View

In coming to grips with credit policy and issues, one needs to confront the question: Why should a company, by extending

---

[1] Accounting usage reflects the legal ownership; goods sold on consignment are counted as part of inventory until paid for, even though they are in effect sold on credit.

credit, involve itself in competition with banks and other firms who are specialized in credit granting? Why not presume that customers can obtain credit elsewhere, and sell for cash?

There are a number of sound economic reasons for the granting of credit by nonfinancial companies, those whose major business activity is not the extending of financing. First, the arranging of credit with a seller saves the buyer the inconvenience of arranging a separate credit transaction. For example, it is simpler for a retail customer to arrange the credit for a new dishwasher at a department store than it is for that customer to make a separate trip to her bank.

The businessman who provides credit has a competitive edge, in another respect, over competing financial specialists. He is often the first person sought out for credit; a customer may discover his need for credit at the same time that he discovers his desire to make a particular purchase. If credit can be offered "on the spot" the customer may accept the credit even though a nearby bank might have been willing to provide it on more favourable terms (had they had the chance).

A third reason, not so evident in consumer transactions as in those between businesses, involves knowledge of the creditworthiness of the customer. A manufacturer of automobiles, for example, may have a great deal of specialized knowledge about the ability of various automobile dealerships to sell cars. The manufacturer may be able to put this knowledge to use in extending wholesale credit to automobile dealers. This knowledge may allow extension of credit in situations which banks would believe to be unsatisfactory. It may also allow the manufacturer to avoid extending credit in situations that might appear acceptable from the viewpoint of an outside financial institution.

Alternatives to Credit Extension

To be sure the above advantages do not imply that nonfinancial corporations can or should be the only source of credit for the customers. Frequently there are situations where credit can be provided more efficiently by specialized financial institutions, such as banks. Between the extremes of either providing credit to customers via receivables, or simply having customers rely on other credit sources, there are a number of ways in which a nonfinancial company can provide credit to its customers and then arrange for a financial institution to actually make the investment in the associated receivable.

One well-known example of the collaboration between a corporation and an outside financial institution is the bank credit card—Chargex or Master Charge. Under these credit card arrangements, a customer can receive credit at point of sale from a retail firm; thus the firm has the opportunity to offer its customers the opportunity to purchase on credit. At the same time, the credit is actually extended by a bank, who will own the resulting receivable and who will undertake the responsibility for its administration. Of course, the bank which has issued the Chargex or Master Charge card may also have the opportunity of collecting interest on the receivable; and the retail firm extending credit on the bank credit card will have to pay a service charge to the bank.

Bank credit card arrangements offer an alternative to carrying receivables for retail customers. There are other arrangements of a similar nature; one of these is *factoring*. Under this plan, a business makes a credit sale and then sells the resulting receivable to an outside financial institution. Again, the firm has the advantage of being able to provide credit without making a receivable investment. Again, also, there is the disadvantage that the earning of interest may be foregone, and that charges may be levied by the financial specialist. Usually the outside financial firm will, along with assuming ownership of the factored receivables, undertake the resulting credit administration and collection—however, usage is not entirely uniform on this.

A variety of other methods for extending credit with someone else's money is also employed. Automobile companies and manufacturers of industrial equipment maintain specialized financial subsidiaries sometimes called *captive financial companies* which will allow sellers of their products to avert receivable ownership. Building contractors frequently develop close associations with trust companies specialized in mortgage lending, so that they can assist their customers with credit arrangements, rather than extending credit directly. The list could go on extensively; there are many situations where mutually beneficial arrangements for handling receivables can be worked out between a corporation wishing to grant credit and a financial institution which is in the business of providing credit.

CREDIT EXTENSION AS AN INVESTMENT

Benefits from Holding Receivables

We have just looked at some alternatives to receivable holding. With these alternatives available, a firm is able to extend credit to its customers and immediately shift the associated receivables to an outside institution. In these situations, where other customer credit sources are at hand, the benefit from acquiring a receivable can be identified rather directly. The company saves the service charges and reaps the interest that would have gone to the outside party.

An example will illustrate the simple nature of the calculation. A retail firm, Ashmore Ltd., is offering credit to its customers and considers the possibility of switching to an arrangement with Chargex. For a retailer of this type, the bank levies a 4 percent service charge on all sales financed with Chargex, and also charges the retail customer 1.5 percent interest per month after the first 30 days. Ashmore Ltd. is currently carrying $300,000 of receivables with an average maturity of 60 days; this investment will be liquidated if Chargex is retained. If Chargex is not retained Ashmore Ltd. believes that it can charge the same rate of interest on accounts due over one month as Chargex does. We also note that the existence of the $300,000 receivable position with an average term of 60 days implies an annual rate of credit sales of $1.8 million. Marginal income tax rate is 45 percent.

Marginal benefits from holding this receivable position, rather than surrendering it to the bank sponsoring Chargex, are detailed as follows:

ASHMORE LTD.
Annual Benefits from Holding Receivables

Saving of service charge		
4% on $1,800,000 credit sales		$72,000.00
Interest obtainable:		
Average maturity of credit	60 days	
Deduct period for which		
no credit charge is made	30 days	
Average period of interest		
charge	30 days	
Average amount of credit		
outstanding	$300,000	
Fraction on which interest		
is charged	30/60	
Receivables drawing		
interest (average)	$150,000	
Annual interest rate		
(1.5% × 12 months)	18%	
Annual interest income		$27,000
Total interest, and service charge saving		$99,000.00
(1 − t)		0.55
Gross benefits from receivables,		
annually		$54,450.00

This calculation demonstrates a substantial gross benefit from extending credit. From this the costs of credit administration would have to be deducted to determine the net benefits.

Actually the issue is not quite this uncomplicated. The use of Chargex or Master Charge might attract customers who would not otherwise patronize the store, so there may be benefits beyond those identified above. On the other hand, a company may be concerned about losing customers by not carrying its own receivables, because customers may be reluctant to deal with a third party or may not have made the necessary credit arrangements to do so. No attempt will be made to quantify these other effects here.

Benefits from Holding Receivables—Alternative Credit Not Available

Identification of benefits where credit alternatives are not available is related to the previous case, but the determination is more complex. Basically the firm must ask itself, how much will the extension of additional credit affect annual income. In turn, this income can be affected in three ways: (1) it may be possible to charge higher prices if credit is provided, (2) sales may be increased if credit is provided, and (3) interest charges may be earned. Obviously, combinations of these effects may occur.

For example, Stephens Beverage, which extends no credit, is currently making sales of $1 million per year. Purchases and direct costs are currently 80 percent of sales, so every $1 of sales is assumed to contribute $0.20 to overhead and profits. The company does not expect to charge interest on its credit, but it predicts, as a result of the use of credit, that it will be able to raise its selling price by 5 percent, and increase its physical volume of sales by 10 percent. If credit is extended, Stephens Beverage expects, on the basis of the experience of other firms, that about 75 percent of its sales will be for credit and that the average account will be outstanding for 45 days. It calculates the effect of the credit extension as follows:

STEPHENS BEVERAGE LTD.
Annual Benefits from Extending Credit

Previous sales	$1,000,000	
Increase of 5% in selling price and 10% in physical volume (1.05) × (1.10) = 1.155	1.155	
Sales if credit is extended	$1,155,000	
Increase in sales if credit is extended		$ 155,000
Previous purchases and direct expenses	$ 800,000	
Increase of 10% in volume	1.10	
Purchases and direct expenses if credit is extended	$ 880,000	
Increase in cost if credit is extended		80,000
Increase in contribution margin by extending credit		$ 75,000
Tax factor (− 0.45)		0.55
After-tax annual gross receipts		$ 41,250
New sales volume		$1,155,000
Fraction of sales on credit		.75
Estimated annual credit sales		$ 866,250
Estimated daily credit sales (above ÷ 365)		$ 2,373.29
45 days credit sales		X 45
Average amount of credit outstanding		$ 106,798

The Stephens Beverage example illustrates the large potential benefits that may be available from credit extension. The ratio of gross benefits to the amount of investment is so high because of the fact that receivable position has a high turnover ratio (recall the discussion from Chapter 6 on "Inventory"). If, as in the above example, a dollar in the receivable position is repaid after 45 days, that dollar can sustain credit sales of 365/45 or $8.11 per year. Only a small profit margin associated with the extension of credit *per dollar of credit sales* can mean a large annual return *per dollar of investment in receivables.*

A cautionary note should follow the example. The increased sales volume could produce secondary effects such as the need for additional overhead and investment. For example, a 10 percent increase in sales volume could require an increase in executive staff or more inventory. Therefore in a real-life situation more detailed analysis may be required.

Costs of Holding Receivables

We have looked at examples of the annual receipts that can be obtained from investments in receivables. These receipts, however, are not net receipts; the owner of a receivable does not, like a bank depositor, passively wait for an interest payment. Receivables if neglected, may never be paid or may be paid only after a long delay. Control of the amount of credit extended and of bad debt losses require active management. The bad debt losses, which escape control and the administrative effort required to exercise control, result in substantial "care and feeding" costs for receivables.

These bad debt and administrative costs are dependent upon the type of receivables held. If a receivable position of a firm consists of many small customer accounts, greater administrative costs can be expected. If the firm has enlarged its receivable position by making credit sales to high-risk customers, this may aggravate both bad debt losses and administrative costs.

(It should perhaps go without saying that these remarks do not imply that small- or high-risk accounts are necessarily bad investments. A firm which deals with "difficult" customers may enjoy a competitive edge and correspondingly large gross benefits on its receivables. So it may be able to well afford the higher carrying costs.)

Returning to Stephens Beverage, let bad debt and administrative costs be 5 percent of credit sales. The following extension of previous calculations, to embrace the costs of granting credit is now appropriate. Credit sales, tax, gross receipts, and average credit outstanding are numbers taken from the previous calculation on Stephens.

On Stephens Beverage the costs of credit extension are comfortably covered by the receipts with the result that net receipts are moderately high relative to investment. Its acceptance of the investment can now be determined by an NPV or IRR test.

STEPHENS BEVERAGE LTD.
Rate of Return on Receivables

Credit sales	$866,250.00
Factor for bad debts and credit administration	.05
Annual costs of bad debt/credit administration	$ 43,312.50
Tax factor	.55
After-tax annual costs	$ 23,821.88
After-tax annual gross receipts (from previous table)	$ 41,250.00
After-tax annual costs	23,821.88
Net annual receipts	$ 17,428.12
Average amount of credit outstanding (from previous table)	$106,798
After-tax annual rate of return	16.3 %

Turnover and Costs

The concept of turnover has its negative aspects as well as positive ones. A cost may seem relatively low when expressed as a percentage of annual sales but loom very high when considered in relationship to a receivable investment. Consider the imposition of a 10 percent cost to an earlier example, where Ashmore Ltd. was considering the accumulation of receivables as an alternative to servicing its customers through Chargex. Here credit sales of $1.8 million were being considered. With 10 percent credit costs, these costs will amount to $180,000 per year, or (using $t = 45$) $99,000 per year after tax. Since gross benefits were only $54,450 per year the weight of the bad debt losses as an administrative cost makes these receivables an unacceptable investment. With receivables turning 12 times per year (30-day credit), a cost ratio of 10 percent *on sales* amounted to a cost ratio (before tax) of 120 percent *on receivables.* Insight into the economics of plans like Chargex is also provided by the example. It may very well be that banks who specialize in credit extension can operate at credit costs far below 10 percent annually; therefore, the banks may be quite satisfied with this receivable investment even though it is unacceptable to Ashmore.

Other Evaluative Criteria

The above examples illustrate that conventional asset analysis is quite applicable to receivable decisions. In addition to this vital analysis, some other evaluative criteria are employed in practice. These supplemental methods are quite analogous to the turnover ratio employed in conjunction with inventory. They may signal possible problems in receivables policy, even though they are subject to theoretical shortcomings.

Average Days' Credit Sales Outstanding. Previous examples have already used an average to summarize the length of time credit is being extended. This average is expressed in formula form as:

$$\text{Average days' credit sales outstanding} = \frac{(\text{Beginning receivables} + \text{ending receivables})/2}{\text{Annual credit sales}/365}$$

This summary of the terms of the credit policy is useful in comparing a company's credit experience with that of other companies. An unusually high figure could indicate excessively "loose" credit management.

As a generalization it is often assumed that the lower the average days' credit sales outstanding, the more efficient the receivables policy. However, this simplification can be erroneous; the marginal benefits associated with accumulating extra receivables through a relaxing of credit policy may be very rewarding. Certainly one would not wish to suggest that the best credit objective always would be the reduction of the average days outstanding figure to close to zero; this would imply de facto abandonment of credit granting.

Aging of Receivables. This method has the same general intent as the preceding one but it goes beyond a simple average and analyzes the current receivables balance according to length of time outstanding. A self-explanatory example is shown:

Aging of Receivables

Period Outstanding	Amounts in Category	Percentage in Category
0–30 days	$400,000	62.5%
30–60 days	100,000	15.6
60–90 days	40,000	6.3
More than 90 days	100,000	15.6
Total receivables outstanding	$640,000	100.0%

This schedule seems to indicate, for example, that if this company was selling on 30-day terms, one might express concern about the fact that nearly one sixth of the receivables have been outstanding longer than 90 days. This suggests some undesirable laxity in credit policy and warrants further examination. (That examination could conceivably reveal, that the tolerance was farsighted; perhaps, for example, the company has discovered that a generous collection policy for promising new firms can result in the development of loyal and profitable customers later.)

CREDIT ADMINISTRATION

So far in this chapter we have been dealing with an overall question of credit policy: Should marginal additions be made to the receivables position? However, those receivables require active management. Indeed, marginal investments in receivables are often rendered attractive or unattractive by the way that individual accounts are managed.

Credit administration can be subdivided into two functions; credit granting and collections. Credit granting refers to the assembling of information and the making of decisions such as which customers should be given credit, how much they should be given, and for how long the credit should be extended. Collection refers to the processes which are developed to ensure that accounts are repaid in an orderly way.

Credit Granting

From a positive viewpoint, good credit-granting decisions help to ensure that credit is extended to those customers likely to carry on credit transactions that are profitable to the company. On the negative side, good credit granting denies credit to those customers who are likely to generate unprofitable receivables. Usually, credit granting has the connotation of screening customers to eliminate potential sources of bad debts. This implies attempting to obtain information about credit applicants and reaching individual decisions about whether their likelihood of default outweighs the other potential profits from extending the credit.

An applicant for credit is almost always asked to fill out a form supplying information about himself. This may range from not much more than name, address, and telephone number to the providing of detailed financial statements and financial and personal histories. In addition to the information given on the application, credit information is often sought from outside sources such as banks, other creditors, employers or business associates, and companies offering specialized credit reporting services. (The most well-known of these companies in the area of business credit is Dun and Bradstreet. Information on consumer and business credit experience is also available from commercial credit reporting centres in most localities.)

On the basis of information assembled, a decision is then made about whether to grant credit. Historically the judgment of the experienced "credit man" was very important at this point. He informally weighed the information, along with such outside factors as local business conditions. This informal weighing process has been characterized as an evaluation based on the "four Cs of credit": Character—the honesty of the applicant; capital—accumulated wealth of the applicant; capacity—the income or annual cash flow of the applicant; and conditions—the degree of prosperity or depression prevailing in the economy. Sometimes a fifth C is added to the list: collateral—the extent to which the property of the applicant could be placed under control of the lender to assure repayment.

Particularly in the area of consumer credit the need to process enormous numbers of applications and the availability of computers have given rise to more formal, less judgmental types of evaluation. One of these approaches is the credit scoring method, where an individual is awarded "points" for various characteristics which are deemed to be indicators of his creditworthiness. For example, he may be awarded more points if he is middle-aged, a high-income earner, has had no legal troubles or criminal record, and has a favourable report from the local credit information service. The points scored for each individual attribute are summed for the individual, and a credit score is obtained. This credit score may then be used to determine whether credit should be extended or the maximum amount of credit that should be allowed.

In principle, whether a judgmental or a more systematized method is employed, the credit-granting decision is closely related to conventional marginal analysis. A threshold of acceptability must be established as an attempt to assure that credit granting is not so restrictive that too many good customers are turned away, nor so liberal that too many "bad risks" are accepted.

The process of credit granting also goes beyond the evaluation of credit applicants. It is appropriate for the credit department to be concerned about soliciting promising credit applications. In this connection, the financial managers of a company may be concerned about activities in the sales division of the company. Selective salesmen or advertising programs can help direct a flow of high-quality credit applications to the company. On the other side of the coin, sales personnel, pursuing customers without reference to credit administration can deluge a company with credit applicants of dubious stature.

Collections

The routine part of the collection process consists of maintaining credit records, billing customers or otherwise keeping them informed of the amount of credit they have outstanding and when repayment is expected. The collection function also includes the handling of accounts which are not paid within a specified repayment period. These methods may vary from tolerance and friendly persuasion to such extreme measures as lawsuits and the use of the services of specialized outside collection agencies.

Again, in principle, the collection process is coloured by a marginal analysis. Collection efforts must be stringent enough so that they deter habitual late payments and defaults; these efforts in turn control credit losses and the size of the receivables position. One should note that allowing the average repayment period on receivables to drift from 20 days to 40 days has exactly the same effect on the total receivables position as if the company had maintained a 20-day collection period but had doubled its volume of credit sales.

Balanced against this pressure for stringency are the disadvantages of strict collection policies. Customers may be lost if collection policies are unnecessarily rigorous and collection efforts may become uneconomically expensive.

Current Public Issues Relating to Credit Administration

In contrast with the purchasing of fixed assets or inventory, the acquisition of receivables involves extensive and quite intimate interaction with individuals and businesses outside the firm. The result of this interaction is that the credit administration practices of companies have become matters of concern to the general public. A number of areas are of particular current interest.

Credit Records. The credit records of companies and of credit reporting firms can have important effects on the personal lives or business success of the credit applicants. Erroneous information or information that is unfairly presented in these records, may cause great harm to individuals or businesses. As a result, these records are increasingly being regarded as something other than the private property of credit granters. At a minimum, the users of credit are gaining the right to inspect these records for possible errors.

Pay Cheque Assignments. Sometimes applicants for consumer credit give to the creditor, in return for being granted the credit, the right to make collections directly from the credit user's employer. These collections "at the source" may inflict considerable personal hardship on the credit user. It seems likely that more consumer rights will be established in this area.

Disclosure of Credit Charges. Consumers and other credit users have already largely gained the right to know the cost of their credit, expressed in the form of an annual rate of return. The seller of goods priced at $10,000 for a $3,000 down payment and three annual installments of $3,000 each must advise the customer that implicit in this transaction there is a financing charge of 14 percent (this percentage is obtained with a conventional rate of return identification).

Holder in Due Course.   To understand this concept consider a hypothetical situation. An individual buys a $150 lawn mower that is guaranteed for three years. Within three months the lawn mower has become inoperable. One obvious recourse which the purchaser might employ would be to withhold payment of the $150.

Suppose, however, that the $150 debt was in the form of a conditional sales contract, and that this conditional sales contract had been sold to a finance company. If the buyer of the lawn mower now refuses to pay the $150 the finance company may, if necessary, collect it through court action. This right of the finance company results from the finance company having acquired the rights of the original holder of the obligation; these rights are called the rights of a holder in due course.

While a holder in due course assumes the rights of the original extender of credit he does not assume the obligations of the original credit seller. Therefore, the finance company can allege that it neither knows or cares about the lawn mower guarantee. If the lawn mower buyer wishes restitution for the defaulted guarantee he cannot obtain this by simply withholding payment; he must undertake separate collection action against the seller of the lawn mower (who might even be out of business at this time).

There is increasing public concern over this transfer of rights without obligations, and a change in public policy may take place on this issue.

RECEIVABLES AS AN INVESTMENT: RISK AND LIQUIDITY

Risk

For any individual receivable a risk dimension is likely to exist; the debtor may not pay part or all of the amount that he has promised to pay, or the payment may occur later than promised. It is very important to understand that high risks in individual receivables do not necessarily sum to high risk in the company's total holdings of receivables. This arises because, over large numbers of debtors, good and bad experiences tend to "average out." An example will serve to illustrate the nature of this phenomenon. A company engaged in automobile financing is at any one time extending credit to about 10,000 customers. When it looks at any individual customer it is difficult for the company to say whether or not that particular individual is going to meet his obligation. However, historically, the company has found that its annual losses from defaulting customers have almost always been at an annual rate of 3 percent to 4 percent of the amount of credit outstanding. Thus bad debt losses for the company as a whole are quite predictable on the basis of past experience, even though little is known about the prospective behaviour of any particular customer.

This does not suggest that a risk dimension in the receivables position can be ignored. Firms with few customers, for example, cannot be confident that their credit experiences will "average out" among customers. Additionally, some external events may simultaneously affect the default positions of all customers in such a way as to cause broad changes in repayment behaviour. For example, the automobile finance company discussed above may find, if the entire Canadian economy experiences a severe bout of unemployment, that the repayment behaviour of large numbers of its customers is affected by the unavailability of regular pay cheques.

It is easy on the basis of causal observation to exaggerate the risk in credit extension. Among assets held by corporations the receivables position is often regarded as a relatively safe component of the asset collection.

Liquidity

In contrast to a tendency to underrate the safety of receivables on the basis of a superficial examination, there is also a tendency to overrate the liquidity of the receivables position. One may look at an individual receivable, conclude that it is likely to be repaid within 30 days, or whatever the terms of the company's credit policy are, and conclude from this that the entire receivables position could be quickly liquidated. In fact, however, this liquidation cannot take place without a basic change in credit policy.

Barring some seasonal pattern in credit sales experience for a company, there is a tendency for the receivable position to remain stable or to grow at a stable rate. This stability results from the fact that as some receivables are being collected the ongoing extension of new credit provides other receivables to replace those which are collected (another case of "recycling"). Only if the making of new credit sales is restricted by change in credit policy, or if there is increased rigour in the collection policy resulting in the shortening of holding times on receivables, can parts of the receivable position be subject to a *net* liquidation.

To be sure the firm's ability to change credit policy could make it possible to realize cash from the receivables position, by curtailing new credit and/or speeding the collection of old credit. However, one must realize that relationships with credit customers are often vital to the success of the company, and an abrupt change in credit policy may seriously damage these relationships. Thus, unless a firm is confronted with a critical need for funds, it probably will not wish to tamper with its credit policy to meet liquidity needs. In other words, for most purposes in the normal life of a company, the liquid appearance of the receivables position can be regarded as illusory.

SUMMARY

Receivables are assets that result from company credit policy. This credit can be extended on a variety of terms, including accounts receivable (both ordinary and revolving), consignments, conditional sale contracts, and notes receivable.

A company offering credit should consider the question, can we offer credit more efficiently than financial institutions? Often this comparison is quite direct; companies have the opportunity to channel their potential credit customers to financial institutions through the use of bank credit cards and factoring. Companies themselves may also develop their own financial subsidiaries, called captive finance companies.

A company may benefit in two ways from holding receivables. It may save fees and earn interest that would otherwise go to financial institutions; or where institutional credit alternatives are not feasible, it may increase price and/or sales volume and possibly obtain interest by extending charge privileges to customers.

The acquisition of receivables through changes in credit policy can be subjected to conventional financial analysis. Benefits, net of the cost of holding receivables, can be compared with the amount of credit extended through rate of return or NPV analysis. Additional evaluation of company credit policy is sometimes done through the use of such measures as "average days' credit sales outstanding" and aging.

Day-to-day operation of fixed assets and inventory is normally done within the company by nonfinancial managers. In contrast, receivables are administered by finance personnel. These personnel are responsible for the individual decisions about extending credit to customers, collections from customers, and other routine administrative matters.

Because the granting of credit often involves direct interaction with consumers, company receivables positions are the object of considerable public policy concern. Public policy appears to be changing, with increasing transfer of rights from the credit grantor to the credit customer.

It is easy to underestimate the risk and overestimate the liquidity of receivables.

QUESTIONS AND PROBLEMS

1. Why are receivables usually classified as current assets?

2. Goods sold on consignment are classified as inventory of the selling company until they are paid for, following conventional accounting procedures. Why do you think that discussion of these assets is included in a chapter dealing with receivables?

3. Note a number of advantages that financial institutions have in the extension of credit. Also note a number of competitive advantages that nonfinancial companies have.

4. Thornton Ltd., a clothing retailer, has been extending charge account credit to its customers. Estimated bad debt and administrative costs are 10 percent of credit outstanding. Receiv-

ables are outstanding for 45 days on an average. Thornton makes no finance charges.

Thornton is approached by a salesman for a type of bank credit card arrangement. He proposes that Thornton discontinue offering charge account credit and instead offer the revolving credit associated with the bank credit card. The credit card company will assume all collection responsibilities, and will charge Thornton a fee of 5 percent on all credit sales. Thornton must telephone for credit card company approval on any sale over $100.

Analyze Thornton's decision.

5. Williston Ltd. believes that if it starts offering charge account credit to its customers, it will rather quickly reach a level where it is selling about $10 million per year on credit. Of these credit sales, $5 million will be made to customers who were previously buying on cash from Williston, and $5 million will be made to new customers attracted by the extention of credit.

Williston considers the following information:
a. Profit margins on additional sales are estimated at 25 percent.
b. Bad debt and administrative costs are estimated at 10 percent of average outstanding receivables annually.
c. Credit will be extended at no charge for 30 days; on accounts due over 30 days a 2 percent month service charge is levied.
d. Estimated average collection time is 60 days.

Williston's marginal tax rate is 20 percent. It used a 15 percent target rate and the rate of return method in approaching receivables acquisition decisions. Evaluate the credit decision.

6. Carefully explain how the following situation could be profitable: A company decides to grant credit at no charge to a class of customers who are predicted to have patterns of slow payment and high probability of default.

Is there any reason to believe that the profit possibility described above would not be regarded as luck, but as consistent with an orderly marketplace for credit?

7. What is a holder in due course?

8. What are the pros and cons of credit scoring versus a more judgmental approach to credit granting? Would you, as a consumer, prefer to be subject to a computerized or a personalized credit-granting decision?

RELATED READINGS

Addison, E. "Factoring: A Case History." *Financial Executive,* November 1963.

Beranek, W. *Analysis for Financial Decisions.* Homewood, Ill.: Richard D. Irwin, Inc., 1963, chapter 10.

Canadian Bankers' Association, "Your Money and Credit. . . ." An elementary pamphlet available through Chartered banks.

Condensed Laws of Business for Credit Managers. Toronto: The Canadian Credit Institute.

Greer, C. "The Optimal Credit Acceptance Policy." *Journal of Financial and Quantitative Analysis,* December 1967.

Johnson, R. W. "More Scope for Credit Managers." *Harvard Business Review,* November–December 1961.

Lane, S. "Submarginal Credit Risk Classification." *Journal of Financial and Quantitative Analysis,* January 1972.

Marrah, F. "Managing Receivables." *Financial Executive,* July 1970.

Mehta, D. "The Formulation of Credit Policy Models." *Management Science,* October 1968.

Myers, J., and Forgy, E. "The Development of Numerical Credit Evaluation Systems." *Journal of the American Statistical Association,* 1963, pp. 799–806.

Wrightsman, D. "Optimal Credit Terms for Accounts Receivable." *Quarterly Review of Economics and Business,* Summer 1969.

8

MANAGEMENT OF CASH

The term cash management is used to include decisions and actions relating to money—cash on hand and bank demand deposits—and also to an array of cashlike assets such as short-term government obligations and short-term bank time deposits. These noncash items which are included under the cash management category are often called *near-cash*, and have the property of being convertible almost frictionlessly into cash itself.

This chapter will examine motives for holding cash and near-cash, and management practices associated with the assets held for each motive. As in the case of receivables, cash and near-cash are financial assets for which financial managers usually bear administrative responsibility.

INCIDENTAL CASH HOLDINGS AND FLOAT

Some cash is often required as the direct result of other operations. It is not held with the intention of increasing the liquidity of the business. An example of this type would be the money that is maintained in cash registers in a retail store for change-making purposes, or that flows into those registers as a result of the day's transactions. A more major type of incidental cash holding would arise in the company's collection process. Cash receipts, often in the form of cheques written by customers, are not received in a place or form where they can be instantly used. Money may have to be transferred within the company, and mailed or carried to a bank for deposit. Even when the cheques are deposited there may be a delay before the money can actually be used because of bank-imposed requirement for the allowance of collection time on the cheques involved.

While holdings of cash may arise incidentally out of other company operations, the holdings are still subject to financial control processes. Consider, for example, money held in retail cash registers. This cash really represents a form of inventory and a company can decide the frequency with which money should be withdrawn from a cash register and the amount of money that should be left in the cash register for subsequent change making.

While few businesses maintain large amounts of cash in cash register drawers, many maintain substantial amounts of cash or potential cash items in transit. This cash provides an attractive target for financial control. For example, a company with $1 million in daily collections may discover that on the average, three days are required before this money becomes usable. Thus, $3 million of cash balances are tied up in unusable form. If the company can increase the velocity of this cash to the point where it flows through to usable form in two days, it has released $1 million of cash for other uses. Thus a company may be willing to spend considerable amounts to hasten the movement of cash. Increased frequency of deposits, the use of banks themselves as collection agents (this practice is very common in the case of utility bills, as an example) and more colourful methods, such as the transfer of funds by special courier or even by chartered plane, all constitute potential techniques for this speed-up process.

Frequently, monies in transit are not even specifically known to the company; cheques are "in the mail." One method employed to make this potential cash more quickly available is a *lockbox* system. This system consists of mailing addresses and post-office boxes at remote points, and an arrangement for local banks to empty these boxes and deposit the cheques in a local company account. Such arrangements are especially useful in international business, where mail delays may be substantial.

One interesting aspect of these incidental cash holdings is the fact of their imperfect liquidity. Though cash and near-cash items are usually thought of as the most liquid of assets, and are in fact, often acquired for purposes of providing sources of liquidity, the incidental cash holdings are bound almost inextricably into the regular affairs of the business. Except to the extent that management can find ways of permanently releasing amounts of this cash from the business through improved handling techniques, along the lines just discussed, the incidental cash cannot be regarded as a source of bill-paying ability for the firm. It would probably be easier for a firm to sell off marginal amounts of just about any other asset holding than it would be to "force" a withdrawal of this incidental cash from the company's ongoing business operations.

Float

Float is defined as an excess of actual cash available above cash shown in the company's accounts. Float arises from outstanding cheques. A company writes a cheque and accordingly reduces the cash balance in its accounting records. Because of transit time, delays in processing by the cheque's payee, and delays in the banking system, days (or on international transactions even weeks) may pass before the cheque reaches the payer's bank and is changed to the payer's deposit account.

For example, a company disburses about $300,000 daily, and finds that average collection time on its cheques is two days. It can, therefore, predict that its "balance per books" will be less than its "balance per bank" by $600,000, on the average.

Not surprisingly, companies (like students) sometimes make use of this float by reducing demand deposit balances "per books" to negative amounts. Float may partially, or even more than offset that part of a company's cash which is in illiquid condition (incidental cash). The relation between the two will largely depend on the nature of cheques received and issued.

(For example, if a company buys mostly in its own locale and sells nationally or internationally, incidental cash will probably overrun float by a considerable margin.) The net effect of incidental cash and float will determine to what extent a company's cash is actually available for disbursement.

CASH FOR PLANNED CASH NEEDS

One salient motive for cash holding lies in provision for expected future cash requirements; this is sometimes called *transactions* cash in economic literature. Cash is kept on hand in anticipation of some known future use. This type of cash accumulation in turn implies cash planning, the systematic attempt to anticipate future cash requirements.

Cash Planning

The basic tool for cash planing is the statement of projected cash flows. This is a statement setting forth the cash a company expects to receive in each of a series of future time periods, along with the cash that will be spent during those time periods. A subtraction of outflows from inflows results in net cash flow projections for each of the ensuing periods, which in turn pinpoints expectations of cash surpluses or shortages.

We have already looked at an analysis similar to the cash flow statement, in considering the evaluation of proposed asset acquisitions. At that time receipts and disbursements arising from the asset were examined. A cash flow statement, on the other hand, assembles predictions of cash flows for an entire company or division of a company. Predictions are made period by period, with net cash flows and cumulative cash flows identified. Cumulative cash flows are sums of a given month and all previous months in the forecast; they indicate the combined effect of all cash flows to date. An example is shown in Illustration 8–1.

The nature of the statements preparation should be virtually self-evident. Cash inflows and outflows, rather than accounting income and expenses, are used; even a dividend (a distribution of profits to shareholders) is counted as a cash outflow from the company's viewpoint.

ILLUSTRATION 8–1

VICTORY JACK COMPANY LTD.
Projected Cash Flows for
Next Six Months

	July	Aug.	Sept.	Oct.	Nov.	Dec.
Cash receipts:						
Projected total sales	$500	$600	$700	$700	$900	$1,400
Cash component of sales (estimated 20%)	100	120	140	140	180	280
Collections (estimated 2 month collection lag) . .	400*	400*	400	480	560	560
Cash sales and collections	$500	$520	$540	$620	$740	$ 840
Other cash receipts:						
Equipment sale			300			
Bank loan negotiated in advance	200					
Total cash receipts	$700	$520	$840	$620	$740	$ 840
Projected total purchases	$400	$400	$400	$500	$500	$ 500
Cash component of purchases (estimated 25%)	$100	$100	$100	$115	$125	$ 125
Payments on credit purchases (estimated 1 month lag)	300*	300	300	300	375	375
Cash purchases and payments on account	400	400	400	425	500	500
Payroll	100	100	100	100	120	120
Other cash expenses	75	75	75	75	75	75
Other cash disbursements:						
Mortgage payment			200			
Loan to supplier				100		
Income tax installments .	20	20	20	20	20	20
Dividend						50
Total cash disbursements	$595	$595	$795	$720	$715	$ 765
Net cash flows	$105	–$ 75	$ 45	–$100	$ 35	$ 75
Cumulative cash flows . . .	$105	$ 30	$ 75	–$ 25	$ 10	$ 85

* Based on previous periods' data not shown.

One may note the advantage of the month-by-month analysis rather than looking at the cash flows for the entire period. During the entire period cash flows are cumulatively positive at $85,000. However, during the month of October an accumulated cash shortage of $25,000 has developed. Without month-by-month analysis, this interim cash shortage would have gone unpredicted.

This problem of interim cash shortages extends to points within months as well as within longer periods. Normally cash flow projections are prepared on a monthly basis, but it is worthwhile considering the possibility of imbalances in cash flows within months on at least a judgmental basis. For example, a $200,000 mortgage payment is included within September's cash outflows. What are the consequences if this payment is due on September 5, before many of the month's cash inflows have had time to materialize?

The above statement has projected cash flows on a month-by-month basis for a six-month period. This was done for illustrative purposes; month-by-month cash projections are normally maintained for at least a year in advance. In addition, many companies do longer term cash projections. These are often done on a year-by-year basis and may extend several years into the future.

Cash Projections and Cash Planning

Once cash projections are made, planning may begin in response to these prognostications. If cumulative net outflows are predicted during some point in the period under which projections are being made, tactics for coping with the shortage must be developed. (In considering these tactics we will initially make no distinction between cash and near-cash.)

Basically cash planning consists of determining whether preliminary cash balances are sufficient to cover projected cash shortages in subsequent periods and what steps must be taken to ameliorate any prospective shortages. Consider the Victory Jack example given above. If the company enters this period with several hundred thousand dollars in cash, it need have no apprehension about meeting its expected cash requirements. For example, even if the September mortgage payment was treated as an August payment, to ensure there was no problem of an intramonth cash imbalance one observes only a maximum cumulative cash outflow of —$170,000. In fact a company with a several hundred thousand dollar cash balance under these circumstances might consider the possibility of diverting some of this cash into alternative investments.

If the company enters this period, on the other hand, with a modest initial cash balance, say $50,000, it may have cause for concern. Again, if the mortgage payment is treated as an August disbursement, the initial cash balance will be insufficient to cover predicted future cash needs, even if all of the cash balance could be employed for this purpose. In fact, some of the cash is most likely an incidental cash balance, which cannot be readily used. In this case, Victory Jack must confront the problem of either getting more cash or taking steps to reduce its cash deficit.

It presently has a loan negotiated in advance available in July for $200,000; perhaps this could be increased by another $100,000 to provide necessary cash buffering. Perhaps a delay in the mortgage payment could be arranged until the end of September to avoid the problems of an interim cash shortage during September. Perhaps collections could be speeded up (though we have discussed the problem of using the receivables position as a source of liquidity). An equipment sale has been contemplated for September, perhaps steps could be taken to ensure that this sale was consummated early in September; this would enable this cash to be used for meeting the mortgage payment on September 5.

We have looked, in the Victory Jack example, at cash planning over a relatively short interval. It is obvious that the company's position would be more comfortable if the possible cash shortages had been anticipated longer in advance. That would have allowed time for the accumulation of a larger cash balance out of the company's operations, for a less hurried renegotiation of loan arrangements or other possible adjustments.

One can observe on the basis of the hypothetical cash flow projection, that cash receipts and disbursements are not perfectly timed. Even a profitable firm may find that at times it has a substantial amount of cash outflow without covering cash inflow. Often, foreward planning can allow the gathering of sufficient cash balances to meet the predicted deficiencies.

CASH FOR THE UNEXPECTED

We have explored two reasons why a company would hold cash balances—some cash is incidentally tied up in connection with the company's operations, and other cash balances are accumulated to meet predicted future cash needs. If these were the only needs for cash, the determination of the company's cash position would be an easy matter. (At least the determination would be easy. The accumulation might not be; for example, cash planning alone cannot ensure the survival of an unprofitable company.) The difficult and judgmental part of cash balance determination arises in providing reserves for unexpected cash needs. Cash held for these needs is sometimes described as *precautionary cash.*

Cash Reserves and the Overall Liquidity Posture

The development of cash reserves cannot be viewed in isolation; it is related to the overall liquidity of the company. To consider a general example, a company may have many rigid payment obligations in connection with its liabilities, and it may hold large amounts of quite illiquid assets, such as specialized manufacturing equipment. Unless such a company was very confident about the regularity with which cash would come into the company (perhaps because of long-term sales contracts with financially unimpeachable customers), it might well decide that the accumulation of sizable cash reserves would deserve an extraordinarily high priority in its asset selection process.

Exploring for the Amount of Cash Reserves

In principle, at least, the determination of the desirable amount of cash balances to meet expected cash requirements follows from the cash flow projection. The establishment of cash reserves for the unexpected is a much more complex and imprecise matter. Practices in similar firms can provide some guidelines. For many firms, the judgment of experienced company officers and directors is of major importance in this determination, even though those judgments are intuitively formulated. Some quantitative procedures also can provide insight into the determination of the appropriate reserve level. One of these methods is the cash flow simulation; another is the quantitative exploration of possible contingencies.

Cash Flow Simulation

The cash flow simulation follows basically the same technique as the simulation of fixed asset net receipts shown in Chapter 5. Simulation consists of systematic experimentation with various quantitative possibilities. A cash flow projection contains best estimates of cash inflows and outflows over a series of future periods. Cash flow simulation explores the possibility of variation around these best estimate figures.

An example will illustrate the basic nature of the cash simulation. In the previous example in this chapter, a cash flow projection was made assuming some sales figures and also assuming a particular collection pattern—a two-month collection period. Suppose the Victory Jack Company wanted to consider the possibilities that sales might be 20 percent less than expected and also that collections might drag to the point where a three-month collection time was normal. These and other possibilities could be explored with a simulation. The effect of these unfavourable assumptions on Victory Jack's cash flows are investigated in Illustration 8–2.

This is a somewhat naïve simulation; a more complex analy-

ILLUSTRATION 8–2

VICTORY JACK COMPANY LTD.
Simulated Cash Flows with 20 Percent Decline below
Expected Sales, and Three-Month Collection Lag
(based on previous example)

Cash Receipts	July	Aug.	Sept.	Oct.	Nov.	Dec.
Total sales	$400	$480	$560	$560	$720	$1,120
Cash component at 20%	$ 80	$ 96	$112	$112	$144	$ 224
Collections	400*	400*	—*	320	384	448
Cash sales and collections	$480	$496	$112	$432	$528	$ 672
Other receipts	200		300			
Total Cash Receipts	$680	$496	$412	$432	$528	$ 672
Total Disbursements . . .	595	595	795	720	715	765
Net Cash Flows	$ 85	–$ 99	–$383	–$288	–$187	–$ 93
Cumulative Cash Flows	$ 85	–$ 14	–$397	–$685	–$872	–$ 965

*Assumes previous receivables are collected in two months and currently accumulated receivables are collected in three months.

sis could have considered the possibility that some disbursements might be adjustable in the light of declining sales; for
example, purchases might be reduced and some other expenses
might be trimmed. Nevertheless, the example illustrates the
search for alternative results that can be effected with simulation. On the basis of the above examination, Victory Jack can
appreciate the possibility that it could conceivably require
nearly $1 million in cash during the next six months to cover
operating cash deficits resulting from unfavourable sales and
collection experience. An analysis of this type, particularly if it
were projected far enough into the future, could be a guideline
for the company in determining the amount of liquid reserves
it should attempt to build up.

A word of caution about simulation is worth repeating at
this point. Elementary simulation can explore a variety of
favourable and unfavourable possibilities, but it does not address their probabilities. Thus simulation analysis could indicate a potentiality of an extremely large cash drain, based on
the confluence of a large number of possible misfortunes. However, the likelihood of these misfortunes occurring simultaneously may be miniscule; cash management policies based on
the extremely large cash outflow would then tend toward excessive conservatism.

Exploration for Contingencies

Cash flow simulation can provide many insights about extraordinary cash flows that may result in connection with a
company's regular operations. The method is less suitable for
dealing with the consequences of major external disturbances
which could impose extraordinary cash requirements on the
company. For example, what would be the consequences of a
prolonged strike in the company itself, or in one of its suppliers
or customers? For a company whose operations are affected by
weather, such as a trucking firm, what are the possible effects
of an especially severe winter? What would happen if a war
were to break out, or if an existing one were to end? What are
the consequences of governmental activity, such as possible
increased stringency in pollution control requirements?

All of these events, and countless more, could threaten the

orderly cash flows of a company and comprise situations where substantial cash reserves could prove useful. On the other hand, the maintenance of cash reserves requires the incurrence of costs for financing of the reserves. The direct return on the reserves tends to be quite low—nothing in the case of money held in the form of actual cash or chequing account balances. Reserves can only pay their own way if they actually offer a valuable liquidity service to the company. If extra reserves are accumulated when a company is already in an adequately liquid position, there is substantial wastefulness in the reserve accumulation.

As noted previously, there is no tidy way of ascertaining the appropriate level of reserves; but there are better solutions than "following hunches" in the face of all the extraordinary cash requirements that might take place. Instead, studies may be conducted to investigate possible contingencies with reference to how much cash would be required if the contingency happened, and what is the likelihood of this occurrence?

For example, a company may be concerned about the consequences of a prolonged strike by its production employees. Suppose the company's inventory position is quite high, that it can easily curtail purchases during the strike (no long-term supply contracts) and that virtually all of the company's production employees are idled by the strike. It is quite possible that such a company could continue to make sales out of inventory for some time. With its reduced purchases and payroll it might actually accumulate substantial amounts of cash during the strike.

Or consider another hypothetical exploration, this time for multiple contingencies. The Blazo Ski Company relies heavily on mail-order sales, and is very concerned about the effects of a postal strike. Blazo also publishes a catalogue, and after such a catalogue is published it regards itself as committed to supply goods at the published prices during the ensuing year. Thus it is quite concerned about unexpected inflation of its costs during the year. As a third consideration, Blazo is intent upon expansion, particularly through vertically integrating its suppliers, and it is concerned about being in a position to act decisively if one of it's suppliers, X Ltd., becomes available for purchase within the next year.

Suppose Blazo Ski's management carefully assesses these situations. It decides that, given two months as a realistic upper limit on the duration of a postal strike, the strike could, at any time during the coming year, result in cumulative cash flow of —$10 million. It also decides that the worst likely inflation that is realistically possible is a 2 percent monthly rate on all its costs except those that are fixed by contract. It estimates that if this galloping inflation were to come about, cumulative cash drains of —$14 million would result. Again, after more study and consultation with an investment banking company, the firm decides that it could acquire X Ltd. with a transaction that would require, at most, $6 million cash.

The company has now surveyed three contingencies and found cash outflow possibilities adding to —$30 million. However, there are two reasons why adding these possible amounts is not appropriate arithmetic. First, some of the numbers may simply not be additive. For example, if the strike and the inflation should both occur, the reduction of sales by the postal strike would mean that fewer purchases of inflated cost items would have to be made; as a result the expected cost of the joint occurrence of a postal strike and a runaway inflation might be not their arithmetic sum of $24 million but some moderated figure such as $18 million.

Second, the simultaneous occurrence of all three events or even of two of them, may be unlikely. To explore this possibility, some basic probability analysis can be called into play. Suppose the best judgment of persons within the company who are studying these contingencies is that during the coming year there is a .1 probability of the inflation occurring, a .05 probability of a postal strike, and .3 probability that the purchase of the supplier company will take place. Suppose that the judgment is made also that all of these occurrences are unrelated to each other; that is, there is no reason to believe that the occurrence of one is likely to be associated with the occurrence of another except by chance.

If the events are unrelated, and probabilities have been assigned to them, a principle of probability analysis can be brought into play; namely, the probability of two or more independent events occurring is the product of the probabilities of individual events. This means, for example, that since there is a

.1 probability of inflation and a .3 probability of the acquisition of the supplier, the probability that an inflation will occur during the next year and also that the supplier will be acquired is .1 × .3 or .03. Using this type of analysis the company can note that the probability of all three of the contingencies occurring is .1 × .05 × .3 = .0015, only one and one half chances out of 1,000. The contingencies and their probabilities are set forth below, ranked in order of cash flow requirements.

Contingencies	Probability	Cash Flow
E (expansion)	.3	−$ 6,000,000
S (strike)	.05	− 10,000,000
I (inflation)	.1	− 14,000,000
SE	.015	− 16,000,000
SI	.005	− 18,000,000*
IE	.003	− 20,000,000
SIE	.0015	− 24,000,000*

*These numbers are based on the joint occurrence of the strike and the inflation causing a cash drain of − $18 million. All other numbers are additive.

Blazo Ski can now consider its reserves in the light of the above numbers. Suppose it couples this consideration with some information about the company's overall liquidity posture—namely, that in the judgment of management, Blazo could (at some cost) meet $10 million of contingencies through sale of assets and through the strength of its credit rating.

Blazo could then devise the following strategy, for example. It would attempt to accumulate $10 million in cash and near-cash. It would then confront contingencies as follows:

E
S   } Use cash reserves.
I

SE
SI   } Use cash reserves plus disposal of
IE   } assets and extra credit.

SIE   Use reserves, asset disposal and extra credit. Forego expansion.

Note that Blazo has had to be a bit philosophical and decide that in the unlikely event that all three contingencies occur it will not be able to make the desired acquisition. In realistic problems companies frequently must confront the fact that it is impossible to protect against a nexus of all possible calamities; that even the soundest of companies must live with some probability that it may end up short of cash.

Managing the Cash Position

We have looked at issues relating to the question of how much cash and near-cash should be held by a company. A second issue remains: What should be done with the cash and near-cash that are maintained? In turn, this divides into two subissues: How should the holdings be split between cash and near-cash, and what type of near-cash assets should be held?

While separated for presentation purposes, the issues of how the company's reserves are managed, and the size of the reserves maintained are not unconnected. To the extent that a company can keep its reserves productive through the earning of interest, capital costs relating to the maintainance of the reserve position are partially offset. This, in turn, means that the safety and flexibility afforded by reserves are available at lower net cost. Hence if one were to think in terms of some ideal or optimal reserve position for a firm, that reserve position would be higher for a firm that was able to put its reserves to more profitable employment.

The Choice between Cash and Near-Cash

Cash, defined as coin and currency on hand and holdings of demand deposits, yields no interest. On the other hand (qualified by the balance of incidental cash holdings and float), this cash can be immediately disbursed. The fact is, however, that much cash accumulated for predicted cash requirements and all cash accumulated for contingencies, does not require immediate disbursement. In other words, a liquid asset is needed but that asset does not have to be in ultimately liquid form. If ultimate liquidity is not required, it is possible to find a wide array of assets that are liquid and safe, and that still bear interest.

For example, a firm may have accumulated cash for purposes of meeting a payroll, due in six days. With a fine-tuned money management program, the company may be able to promptly commit this cash to interest-bearing liquid assets, and convert those assets back to cash on the sixth day, just before the payroll has to be met.

However, these transactions are not frictionless. They require positive action, they may require time, they may require the payment of brokerage commissions or other explicit transaction costs, and they may be subject to size limitations. These impediments all tend to offset the benefits of the interest that can be obtained by converting into and out of near-cash, and limit the use of this type of transaction.

Consider a personal example where a consumer, Marie Johnson, has a noninterest-bearing chequing account and also has a savings account on which 6 percent interest is calculated on a daily basis. She has $300 in her chequing account at the end of the month and receives a $1,000 pay cheque, bringing her balance to $1,300. During the month she expects to spend $30 per day; for simplification, let us assume that this same amount is spent every day. What are some alternative policies available to this consumer for her own cash management? Two extremes may be examined: (A) close the chequing account and use only a savings account, (B) make no further savings account deposits.

If Ms. Johnson followed policy (A), she would promptly deposit $1,270 in her savings account, retaining $30 for spending. Interest on this amount for one day would be ($1,270 × 6%)/365 = $0.21. On the second day, after another $30 was used, daily interest would be ($1,240 × 6%)/365 = $0.20. Over the entire month, as her balance gradually declined to $400 ($1,300 − $30 per day for 30 days), she would earn a little over $4. To earn this $4 she would have made 30 trips to the savings bank, for her daily withdrawals.

On the basis of this limited arithmetic we can assume, if Ms. Johnson is like most of us, that her response to Policy (A) is an emphatic "forget it." She might look around for halfway houses such as making midmonth transfers out of her savings account into her chequing account or she might just decide that, since the maximum possible benefit from this type of cash management (policy A) amounts to only around $50 per year (subject to personal income tax), further calculation just isn't worth the trouble, when compared to policy B. Perhaps she will just decide to settle for a once-a-year transfer of excess funds out of her chequing account into savings.

Now, however, let us retain the basic situation, but imagine instead of Ms. Johnson's situation, we are dealing with Whitmore Mines Ltd. making monthly shipments of ore and receiving payment on these shipments, instead of a personal pay cheque. To change the problem to corporate size, simply multiply all of Ms. Johnson's numbers by 10,000—a $3 million initial cash balance for Whitmore Mines, cash receipts of $10 million per month, and cash disbursements of $300,000 per day. The scale of potential interest earnings also changes, with maximum earnings possible of around $40,000 per month or $500,000 per year. Daily trips to the bank do not look so ridiculous now.

The choice between cash and near-cash has been appropriately characterized as analagous to an inventory problem of the type where the economic order quantity formula can be applied. Instead of holding an inventory of goods to reduce the need for frequent reordering of goods, an inventory of money is held to reduce the need for making frequent transactions from cash to near-cash. Viewed in this way one can, for Ms. Johnson, view the order costs (cost of making daily trips to the bank) as high relative to the amount of money involved. Thus Ms. Johnson finds a solution where she maintains a high inventory of cash to save herself this trouble. With Whitmore Mines order costs are low and the corporation opts for a low inventory of cash on hand.

The view of the problem of shifting between cash and near-cash has been presented here in barebones form. In real-world situations this problem has been addressed with highly sophisticated operations research techniques. However, examination of these would take us into a realm of technical issues which are not appropriate in a general finance text.

Alternative Near-Cash Assets

In the above examples we have treated a single near-cash asset, a savings account. In practice, in addition to choosing between cash and near-cash, a company has a wide variety of near-cash assets from which to select. Some of the more common varieties are catalogued in this subsection. Imaginative company financial officers may reach beyond this list of alternatives, subject to the general restriction that if these assets are to be truly used as reserves they must maintain the properties of liquidity and safety. Here are some of the near-cash assets which are readily available.

TYPES OF NEAR-CASH

Bank and Trust Company Obligations

Chartered banks, credit unions, and trust companies all offer interest-bearing time deposits. These deposits are available with varying maturities. In some cases they are negotiable (they may be sold to third parties). Normally these are regarded as extremely safe obligations. They are not immediately liquid before maturity, unless a buyer can be found for a negotiable deposit, but their short maturity periods makes them useful for cash which is not to be used for a given period of time.

Treasury Bills

The Government of Canada issues its own short-term obligations, as part of its fianancing of the national debt. These bills normally have maturities of from three to six months. They are negotiable so they may be offered for sale to someone else, after they have been acquired and before maturity.

An active secondary market (where securities that have been purchased can be resold to others) exists in these obligations. Because of the unimpeachable safety and short maturity of Treasury bills, there is little fluctuation in prices in this secondary market. Thus, someone holding Treasury bills can dispose of them almost instantaneously and with virtually no risk of serious price fluctuation.

Repurchase Agreements

To eliminate any possibility of price fluctuation as a risk element in the holding of longer term government obligations, it is possible to arrange with an investment brokerage firm for a guaranteed sale of a government obligation at a pre-specified price and time. Through the use of repurchase agreements it is possible for a company to hold Government of Canada obligations of longer maturities than Treasury bills and still regard them as extremely liquid and safe assets.

A word of explanation about this possibility of price fluctuation in a government obligation is appropriate at this point. Price fluctuation in these obligations does not result from any change in the "credit rating" of the Government of Canada; there is no question about its honouring its own obligations (particularly since it has the power to print money). However, if liquidation of a government obligation before maturity is contemplated, the obligation will have to be sold in a secondary market. The price in that secondary market, in turn, will be determined by a discounting process, with the interest rate on newly available government obligations constituting the relevant discount rate.

For example, suppose one purchases a five-year government bond bearing 6 percent interest, payable semiannually. The bond is purchased for $1,000. This bond now represents a claim on the government for a schedule of payments of $30 at the end of every half-year for five years, and a $1,000 principal repayment at the end of the five years. Suppose one bought this bond, held it for a year and then wished to sell it in the secondary market. Suppose at that time the interest rate on comparable new government bonds is 8 percent. Accordingly, the price to the bond in the secondary market would be determined as the combined present value of $30 per half-year for four years and $1,000 at the end of four years, discounted at 8 percent. This discounted value is $937.66. One can now appraise the sad history of the bond purchase:

```
Receipts:
  First year's interest  . . . . . . . . . . . . . .  $    60.00
  Proceeds from sale (ignoring
     brokerage commission)  . . . . . . . . . . .        937.66
        Total  . . . . . . . . . . . . . . . . . .  $   997.66
Disbursements:
  Original cost of bond  . . . . . . . . . . . .   $1,000.00
  Loss on transaction  . . . . . . . . . . . . .   $    −2.34
Interest earnings on bond:
```

$$\frac{2.34}{1,000} = -.2\%.$$

This misfortune could have been avoided with a repurchase agreement.

Commercial Paper

A company may hold some of its near-cash reserves in the form of the short-term obligations of other companies. Many companies issue negotiable short-term obligations and a secondary market also exists in these obligations. Unlike Government of Canada obligations, this company-issued paper is not ultimately safe. However, commercial paper issued by financially strong, large Canadian companies is regarded as of sufficiently high quality to be used as near-cash. The attractiveness of commercial paper to the company money management program lies in the fact that it will normally return a more attractive yield than Government of Canada obligations, and that it enjoys secondary market possibilities, unlike nonnegotiable bank and trust company obligations.

Provincial and Municipal Obligations

Provinces and other governmental units also offer short-term obligations which are suitable for near-cash use. These vary in type and quality and, in general, can be regarded as comparable to commercial paper.

Other Possibilities

The items detailed above represent the major near-cash items available in Canada. Imaginative financial managers frequently go beyond these commonplace obligations and search out unusual short-term investment opportunities, often in international markets. The reward for this aggressive search is the possibility of higher than conventional yields. However, if cash management is carried on with too much "imagination" safety and liquidity may be sacrificed in exchange for yield to the point where the company's reserve position fails to be the buttress that it was originally intended to be. Thus, care and skill are required in going much beyond the list of near-cash items noted above. This care and skill is likely to have its greatest reward when practiced on the cash positions of large companies, where even yield gains of a fraction of a percent translate into many thousands of dollars per year.

SUMMARY

Cash may accumulate in a company incidentally, as a result of other company transactions. Cash balances may also be built up intentionally for the purpose of meeting future cash requirements, and as reserves against unexpected cash needs.

The control and reduction of incidental cash holdings is an essential part of financial management. A company may profit from outstanding float—cheques which have been written but which have not been presented to the company's bank for collection.

It is customary for companies to make detailed forecasts of cash requirements for at least several months in advance and it is common for companies to undertake less detailed cash planning over a period of several years.

In addition to predicting cash requirements, a company can also explore for unexpected cash needs; simulation and other methods may be employed.

Near-cash assets are those that are almost as safe and liquid as cash itself, but which return interest to their owner. Part of the company's cash management will involve the development of policies for choosing when to hold cash and when to hold near-cash. Common types of near-cash include bank and trust company obligations, Government of Canada Treasury bills, repurchase agreements, commercial paper, and provincial and municipal obligations.

QUESTIONS AND PROBLEMS

1. What is float?

2. A company has annual receipts of $2 million per day and disbursements of $1.5 million per day. It estimates that its cash inflows are "in the pipeline" two days on an average before available for use. Its own cheques remain uncollected for three days, on average, after they are written.
   a. What is the amount of the company's incidental cash holding?
   b. What is the amount of its float?

c. Which would you expect to be greater; the company's balance per bank or balance per books?

3. The company above expects a 10 percent after-tax rate of return on safe investments. What is the upper limit of annual cost that the company can incur in efforts to shorten the "in the pipeline" time of its cash receipts by one day?

4. The following facts are available to a company:
December and January sales are $200,000 per month. Sales are expected to rise by $10,000 per month over the following five months. 60 percent of all sales are for cash, the remaining credit sales are normally collected in 30 days.
The cost of goods sold is estimated at 70 percent of sales.

   Payment requirements for cost of goods sold are as follows: 30 percent cash, 50 percent through accounts payable with one-month payment lag, 20 percent with no payment requirement, from decumulation of inventory.

   Selling general and administrative expenses are $15,000 per month.

   The company has an outstanding note of $150,000, payable on March 15. One year's interest at 10 percent is also due at that time.

   The company anticipates disposal of several machines during May, with a total value of $65,000.

   Prepare a projected cash flow statement for January through June. Include predictions of cumulative cash flows for the period. (Income tax is ignored.)

5. The above company's initial bank balance is $30,000 on January 1. Predict its bank balances over the ensuing period.

   What is implied by prediction of a negative cash balance? Is such a balance normally possible, in reality?

6. What is a precautionary cash balance?

7. A company considers two possibilities for extraordinary cash outflow. Because of foreign exchange regulations which may be imposed soon by a foreign country, a $2 million receivable may not be collected as planned.

   The company is being sued for $5 million; it may lose the lawsuit. Should the company provide for $7 million in precautionary cash balances? What other information would be desirable in reaching this decision?

8. A company envisions possible extraordinary cash flows in the

event of three causes: a strike, a flood, and bankruptcy of a major customer. It designates probabilities of .1, .05, and .3, respectively, to these events.

Assuming that the events are independent, identify probabilities for all possible sets of events.

9. What is the significance of the assumption of independence in the above question? Think of a possible reason why two of the events above might not be independent.

10. A company expects to have $1 million available for two days. It estimates a return on near-cash investment at 8 percent per annum and the cost of buying and selling a $1 million near-cash item at $200. Should it hold cash or near-cash?

11. The topic of liquidity has been discussed in conjunction with various types of assets. How does a company's decision about its total amount of cash and near-cash holdings relate to the degree of liquidity possessed by its other assets?

RELATED READINGS

Archer, Stephen H. "A Model for Determination of Firm Cash Balances." *Journal of Financial and Quantitative Analysis,* March 1966, pp. 1–11.

Baumol, William J. "The Transactions Demand for Cash: An Inventory Theoretic Approach." *Quarterly Journal of Economics,* November 1952, pp. 545–56.

Kraus, A.; Janssen, C.; and McAdams, A. "The Lock-Box Location Problem." *Journal of Bank Research,* Autumn 1970.

Mehta, D. *Working Capital Management.* Englewood Cliffs, N.J.: Prentice-Hall, 1974, Part 3.

Miller, M., and Orr, D. "A Model of the Demand for Money by Firms." *Quarterly Journal of Economics,* August 1966.

Orgler, Y. E. *Cash Management.* Belmont, Calif.: Wardsworth, 1970.

Shadrack, F. "Demand and Supply in the Commercial Paper Market." *Journal of Finance,* September 1970.

Sprenkle, C. "The Uselessness of Transactions Demand Models." *Journal of Finance,* December 1969.

Stancill, J. *The Management of Working Capital.* Scranton, Pa.: Intext Educational Publishers, 1971, chaps. 2 and 3.

9

RISK MANAGEMENT

Risk is associated with nearly all assets, and affects capital costs, share, values, and possibly the company's survival. Through the asset selection process and other means, risk is subject to management control. Financial management is intensely involved in this control. This chapter will explore the nature of risk in greater depth, along with approaches toward its control.

RISK CONTROL COMPARED WITH LIQUIDITY CONTROL

A sizable part of the previous chapter was devoted to the problem of maintaining liquid reserves. This, in turn, was related to the whole problem of liquidity, the question of how well a company is able to cope with unexpected needs for money. Cash can be provided not only by using up previously accumulated cash reserves but also by reducing holdings of other assets, especially those that are conveniently salable.

178

Liquidity in a company's assets helps it address the problem of temporary cash requirements. But having assets of a liquid character cannot provide long-term relief for the problem of continuing drains on cash associated with a recurrent lack of profits. If costs have a tendency to overrun revenues, so there is a pattern established in the firm for buying more than it sells, there is a strong tendency toward an inexorable loss of cash which will eventually lead to an exhaustion of the company's resources.

Just as liquidity will enable a company to "ride out" a short-term problem, in effect allowing all-important time for conditions to get better, a liquid position will also provide only basically temporary assistance in enabling the company to take advantage of business opportunities which require cash. For example, a company may use liquid resources to buy up a competitor at a bargain; it cannot usually expect to be able to undertake a series of acquisitions, or a continuing pattern of growth, on the basis of liquidity alone.

We have thus discussed two conditions where liquidity alone is not enough. Usually the second of these situations, the need for money for growth, is not as serious as the first. If the firm is healthy (profitable or with prospects for good profits) it can usually find the means of financing growth by attracting funds from outside sources. The first problem is much more serious; if the company is short of funds because of misfortunes, outside infusions of monies are not likely to be so readily available and the demise of the company may result.

Reasons for Corporate Losses

One of the problems of financial ill health may simply be an ongoing pattern of inadequate management. Revenues may be low and costs high because of disorganization and inefficiency in the company's affairs. There may be no cure for this condition short of a change of management.

A second reason for company failure may be associated not with incompetent general administration of the company, but with what may be loosely described as bad luck. We have already examined a risk dimension associated with the acquisition of assets. A company often buys assets recognizing that, although the prospects for success are favourable on the asset, there is some chance that things will not go as beneficently as hoped for. Weather, consumer tastes, elections, actions of foreign countries, executive personalities, research attempts, and subsurface geological discoveries may be parts of the environment which determine whether ventures succeed or fail; none of these elements are perfectly predictable. One can only make estimates of their yet to be discovered character and even the most assiduously prepared of those ex ante estimates can turn out to be erroneous guesses ex post.

Risk is inherent in business, and therefore, the problem of adverse outcomes, or bad luck, is also inherent. At the same time, risk is subject to control; the probability and intensity of diverse, and especially adverse, outcomes can be limited through positive managerial action. This chapter will discuss various techniques for attempting to control risk and to approach risk-fraught situations in a systematic, rational way.

RISK: A QUANTITATIVE DIMENSION

Expectations and Deviations

In Chapter 1 risk was introduced in the context of a probability distribution. To be sure, the prospects on business ventures are not always described in the form of a probability distribution, although use of this approach appears to be increasing. Nevertheless, in this chapter we will employ the concept of the probability distribution as a basis for analysis of risk. Even if the approach is not always directly applicable to everyday situations, an analysis using the approach will permit a deeper understanding of the nature of risk and associated managerial practices.

A probability distribution can be characterized as a set of pairs of outcomes and probabilities. Each pair can be assigned an identifying subscript using numbers from 1 through n. The notation system can be demonstrated with the following distribution:

Subscript	Outcome	Probability
1	100	.2
2	200	.5
3	300	.3

To illustrate, in this distribution, the number 200 is identified as Outcome$_2$ and the number .5 is Probability$_2$.

Since the *mean*, or *expected value* of the distribution is a weighted average of the distribution, we can describe the expected value as:

Expected value = Probability$_1$(outcome$_1$) + probability$_2$(outcome$_2$)
. . . + probability$_n$(outcome$_n$).

In the above example expected value is calculated as:

Expected value = .2(100) + .5(200) + .3(300) = 210.

Expected value provides a description of the "central tendency" of the distribution. For example, if the outcomes in the above distribution were NPV possibilities, one could say on the basis of the expected value calculation, that there was a general expectation of a $210 NPV. In other words, if one were told to pick a single number to describe the earnings prospects of the above distribution $210 would be the number picked if the expected value approach was used. While expected value is not the only approach to describing central tendency, it is the approach that will be used in the following analysis; it is used in nearly all formal risk analysis.

Once an expected value has been identified, it is possible to describe the various outcomes in the distribution in the form of their differences from the expected value. These differences are called *deviations* and are defined as:

Deviation$_1$ = Outcome$_1$ − expected value.
Deviation$_2$ = Outcome$_2$ − expected value.
Deviation$_n$ = Outcome$_n$ − expected value.

In the above distribution, the deviations are:

Deviation$_1$ = 100 − 210 = −110.
Deviation$_2$ = 200 − 210 = −10.
Deviation$_3$ = 300 − 210 = 90.

Dispersion

If a situation has only one possible outcome, it may be described as riskless. For example, in the previous chapter, Government of Canada Treasury bills were regarded as riskless assets. If the bill has a $1,000 face value upon maturity the government will pay $1,000 to the owner of the bill. There is no possibility that that payment will be anything but $1,000. Thus, the probability distribution describing the prospective outcome from purchasing the bill is:

$$\text{Probability}_1 = 1.0; \text{Outcome}_1 = \$1,000.$$

Following the procedure of the previous section, an expected value can be calculated; it is $1,000. Also, one can observe that there is no possibility of deviation from this outcome. This absence of possible deviation is essential for risklessness; conversely, risk can be generally described as the degree to which deviations may occur.

This concept of risk in turn requires a measure of the degree to which deviation may take place. A widely accepted measure of *dispersion* (the degree of possible deviation) is available in the form of a special type of weighted average, the *standard deviation*. Another closely related measure will also enter the discussion; this measure is called *variance*.

Variance is calculated from the squared deviations of a distribution. The calculation is as follows:

$$\text{Variance} = \text{Probability}_1(\text{deviation}_1)^2 + \text{probability}_2(\text{deviation}_2)^2 \ldots + \text{probability}_n(\text{deviation}_n)^2.$$

Since a riskless situation has no deviation, variance there is 0. Where deviations exist, variance is always a positive number. For example, in the illustration previously used, the calculation of variance is given as:

$$.2(-110)^2 + .5(-10)^2 + .3(90)^2 = .2(12,100)$$
$$+ .5(100) + .3(8,100) = \text{Variance} = 4,900.$$

The second measure of dispersion, standard deviation, is closely related to variance; it is simply variance's square root:

$$\text{Standard deviation} = \sqrt{\text{Variance}}.$$

In the above example, where variance equals 4,900, standard deviation equals 70.

Variance has mathematical meaning but it has no easy intuitive interpretation. Standard deviation, on the other hand, can be viewed as an approximate average of the absolute amounts of the deviations in a distribution (where the minus signs are

ignored), weighted for their probability of occurrence. Recall
in the example that the absolute amounts of the deviations
were 90, 10, and 110. The standard deviation of 70 can be
viewed loosely as a statement about the central tendency of the
deviations.[1]

For purposes of more compact notation we use the following
system of abbreviations:

$$\text{Expected value} = \text{E.V.}$$
$$\text{Standard deviation} = \text{S.D.}$$
$$\text{Variance} = \text{Var.}$$

While they will not be employed in this text, the reader may
also wish to note the mathematical notation that is often employed: using the lower-case Greek letter sigma(σ), standard
deviation $= \sigma$, and variance $= \sigma^2$.

Future Cash Flows as a Random Process

We can now review the concept of the probability distribution as it relates to financial analysis. Financial decisions and
planning affect and involve the future. With rare exceptions
(e.g., the Treasury bill), prospects for the future are uncer-
tainly known. When expectations are formed about some
future event, such as the cash flows that are going to emanate
from an asset, one must recognize that only as time unfolds will
one learn which out of various possible cash flow patterns will
actually occur. Thus, when one stands at the present and attempts to base action or analysis on the prospects for future
cash flows, these cash flows may be characterized as a random
variable, something about which actuality is not yet revealed.

The probability distribution is a description of current belief
about the random variable. It indicates the possible outcomes
that may ensue and the likelihood that any one of the outcomes
(and there will only be one) will actually come to pass. This
distribution then can be summarized with the use of two
parameters: E.V. and S.D.

For example, one may describe a Treasury bill as having an

---

[1] Standard deviation, rather than an average of the deviations, is used
principally because of a mathematical property: squaring converts all deviations
to positive numbers.

E.V. of $1,000 and an S.D. of 0. On the other hand, a bond issued by a small, unstable business firm might also promise its holder $1,000, but one might characterize the cash receipts from such a bond as having an expected value of, say, $950, meaning that when all possibilities are taken into consideration, along with their associated probabilities, there is an average likelihood of some degree of default on the bill.

If the random cash flow from the bond was characterized with an S.D. of $10, one could interpret this as indicating that relatively small deviations are expected; in other words, there is a strong likelihood that partial default will take place. On the other hand, if E.V. were $950 and S.D. were $200, this indication of large possible deviations could well suggest that the bond was more like an "all or nothing" proposition, where no default might occur or otherwise where major or total default might also occur.[2]

RISK CONTROL IN THE COMPANY

When risk analysis is couched in terms of quantitative analysis, one can describe an objective for risk control. In general, this quantitative objective will be to attempt to hold down the standard deviation of the company's overall cash flows. As we shall see later, this is not the only approach to risk management but it is probably the mathematical approach that most closely coincides with existing risk management practice.

The Parts versus the Whole

At first glance controlling risk within the company might seem to be accomplished by attempting to keep S.D. as low as possible in the cash flows from each of the company's assets. A company attempting to curtail its risk might regard a new project as risky unless it had a low S.D. in comparison to its E.V.

---

[2] Most financial analysis deals with probability distributions characterized by two parameters, mean and standard deviation. Two important exceptions should be noted. Some research has suggested that at least one additional parameter, skewness, may also be important in an understanding of risk. Other research suggests that there may be special types of probability distribution relevant in some financial situations, in which variance, or standard deviation, are not identifiable because of the distribution's mathematical properties.

While there is no question that risk adjustment based on such an approach would tend to hold down the company's overall risk, this policy might be excessively stringent, resulting in the unnecessary rejection of many highly profitable assets because of their risk characteristics.

The reason why such stringency may be otiose lies in a fuller understanding of the technicalities of risk. There are actually two determinants of the risk exposure of the entire company: the risk involved in individual projects, and the manner in which these projects enmesh. An agricultural example can be used to illustrate the effect of the manner in which assets "fit together" for risk purposes.

A businessman has decided to buy some farmland. He discovers, studying the market for farmland in his area, that risk differs from farm to farm. In some farms the soil type and topography are of such nature that the farm produces moderately well whether the growing season is characterized as either a wet or a dry year. Other farms produce extremely well in wet years, but dry out severely and are subject to crop failure in dry years. Still others produce extremely well in dry years but are subject to flooding and crop failure in wet years.

On the basis of a study of past production records, and consultation with knowledgeable individuals, the businessman concludes that (in the long run) each of the categories of farmland will average about the same amount of production at about the same amount of cost. Thus, he regards the E.V. of cash flows on each farm category to be approximately the same. On the other hand, risk dimensions are different, especially when one recognizes that a long series of wet years or dry years is possible. Thus the farmland which produces moderately well in both wet and dry years would have a much lower S.D. in its prospective cash flows than the farms which perform extremely well or extremely badly depending on the year.

Complicating the matter, the businessman discovers that the low-risk farmland sells for a higher price than the high-risk farmland. Then, with a flash of intuition (which the reader may have already anticipated) he develops a strategy for the purchase of the farmland. He will buy a mixture of the high-risk land. Then during wet years part of his crop will fail and during dry years part of his crop will fail, but every year he will be assured of moderate results. A blending of high-risk assets has created a composite asset which has a low S.D.

This blending of assets is the essence of risk management. In the above example the individual bought two assets with high S.D. values and ended up with an asset mixture with a low S.D. The reward for this risk management practice was an opportunity to end up with a low-risk composite asset at a bargain price. The characteristics that determine how assets "fit together" for risk management purposes will be discussed in the following section.

Correlation and Standard Deviation Addition

In a technical sense the farmland example above turns on the addition of standard deviations. If standard deviations added by straightforward arithmetic, compiling a mixture of two assets with high S.D. values would lead to a combined asset with a high S.D., too—the sum of the S.D.s on the individual assets. In fact, what occurred in the example was a situation where the high S.D. values on the individual assets added together to produce a low S.D. on the mixture of the assets.

Before proceeding further with the addition of standard deviations, another statistical term must be introduced. This term describes the relationship between outcomes on two assets; the measure employed is the coefficient of correlation, or in abbreviated form, Corr.

The coefficient of correlation assumes numerical values from $+1$ to -1. These values describe the amount and kind of interaction between two random variables, in this case, the cash flows from two assets. Three situations can be examined to obtain understanding of Corr. numerical values. If the returns on two assets always vary in direct proportion, the assets can be described as perfectly correlated, with Corr. $= +1$. For example, two pieces of land which both produce well during dry years could be described as highly, perhaps perfectly, correlated.

If returns always vary in inverse proportion, the assets are said to have perfect negative correlation, described as Corr. $=$

−1. In the farmland case, a piece of land subject to flooding and a piece of land subject to drought can be regarded as behaving oppositely in a particular year and hence, would be represented by Corr. = −1.

For the third case, one can consider a situation where there is no discernible relationship between results on the two assets. For example, a mining company may conduct exploration in two areas. It is possible that the company may succeed in both areas, fail in both areas, or strike it lucky in one area and not in the other. There is no reason to believe that success in one area will be associated with success in the other area or vice versa. In this case, the two exploration projects could be described as being uncorrelated, Corr. = 0. They may also be described as *statistically independent.*

Actual situations may be described within this range from Corr. = + 1 to Corr. = −1 by informal estimation. (Statistical studies may also be applicable; these will not be discussed.) For example, a company considers the development of two new divisions—one will produce and sell television tubes; the second is a motel chain. Some thought suggests that there may be some relationship between success on the two ventures; success on both will be based in part on the general state of the economy. If prosperity reigns, consumer spending on both television sets and motel services is likely to be high on the other hand, there is an element of independence between the two ventures; consumers are fickle, and do not favour all products evenly when they have the ability to purchase. If consumer acceptance is deemed to be the critical factor in determining the success of the ventures, perhaps an estimate of positive but not nearly perfect correlations is in order, say Corr. = + .5.

Adding Standard Deviations

Once a correlation coefficient is estimated, the adding of the standard deviations on two projects becomes a relatively uncomplicated mathematical procedure, following a formula. Because the formula for adding variances is slightly simpler, it will be presented first and then converted to a formula for S.D. addition.

If two random variables are designated by the subscripts a

and b, their individual variances can be designated Var.$_a$ and Var.$_b$, and their combined variance can be designed Var.$_{ab}$. The formula for their addition is:

$$\text{Var.}_{ab} = \text{Var.}_a + \text{Var.}_b + 2(\text{S.D.}_a)(\text{S.D.}_b)\,\text{Corr.}_{ab},$$

where Corr.$_{ab}$ denotes the coefficient of correlation between the two variables.

Similarly, given the relation between S.D. and Var.,

$$\text{S.D.}_{ab} = \sqrt{\text{S.D.}_a{}^2 + \text{S.D.}_b{}^2 + 2\,\text{S.D.}_a\text{S.D.}_b\,\text{Corr.}_{ab}}.$$

An arithmetic example will illustrate the formula's use. One asset has a cash flow distribution with a standard deviation of $100,000. A second has a standard deviation of $200,000. First, presume that the projects are independent; that is, Corr.$_{ab} = 0$. In this case, substitution into the above formula yields:

$$\text{Var.}_{ab} = (\$100{,}000)^2 + (\$200{,}000)^2 + 2(\$100{,}000)(\$200{,}000)(0)$$
$$(\$100{,}000)^2 + (\$200{,}000)^2$$
$$\text{S.D.}_{ab} = \$223{,}607.$$

Now consider the problem with two other assumptions, Corr.$_{ab} = +1$ and Corr.$_{ab} = -1$. Where Corr.$_{ab} = +1$:

$$\text{Var.}_{ab} = (\$100{,}000)^2 + (\$200{,}000)^2 + 2(\$100{,}000)(\$200{,}000)(1.0)$$
$$\text{S.D.}_{ab} = \$300{,}000.$$

Where Corr.$_{ab} = -1$,

$$\text{Var.}_{ab} = (\$100{,}000)^2 + (\$200{,}000)^2 + 2(\$100{,}000)(\$200{,}000)(-1.0)$$
$$\text{S.D.}_{ab} = \$100{,}000.$$

One can now easily observe the effect of the enmeshing of the two projects for risk analysis purposes. Where correlation coefficients on the projects were perfectly correlated, their combined S.D. was simply the sum of the parts. Where they were independent, S.D. was reduced to something less than the simple arithmetic sum; in fact, the standard deviation of the two products is not much greater than that of the larger one alone. In the case of perfect negative correlation, standard deviation of the combined projects drops off markedly. The inverse relationship cancels out much of the risk (had the standard deviations in the projects been equal the cancellation would have been perfect leaving S.D. $_{ab} = 0$).

Control of Risk within the Company

The preceding analysis can be translated back into consideration of practical risk control techniques by thinking of the relationship between risk in any particular asset and the rest of the company's asset holdings. To keep the analysis simple, initially assume that assets are considered one at a time for risk control purposes. One can now think of the company's total risk exposure as being the combined risk in two asset categories—the particular asset and the remaining asset. Following previous procedure, we can then note:

$$
\begin{array}{l}
\begin{matrix} \text{Total company risk} \\ \text{or standard} \\ \text{deviation} \end{matrix}
= \begin{bmatrix} \text{S.D. of} \\ \text{particular} \\ \text{assets} \end{bmatrix}^2 \begin{bmatrix} \text{S.D. of} \\ \text{remaining} \\ \text{assets} \end{bmatrix}^2 \\[2em]
+ 2 \begin{bmatrix} \text{S.D. of} \\ \text{particular} \\ \text{assets} \end{bmatrix} \begin{bmatrix} \text{S.D. of} \\ \text{remaining} \\ \text{assets} \end{bmatrix} \begin{bmatrix} \text{Correlation between} \\ \text{particular assets} \\ \text{and remaining assets} \end{bmatrix}.
\end{array}
$$

Total company risk is thus seen to depend on three variables: S.D. in the particular asset, S.D. in the remaining assets, and the correlation between the particular and the remaining assets. If risk, or S.D., in the remaining assets is taken as given (or not subject to control) there are only two ways of controlling corporate risk:

1. Control Standard Deviation in the Particular Asset. In general this will take the form of keeping S.D. as low as possible. (This generalization is always true where correlation between the assets is not negative, and sometimes true in the rather unusual situation where negative correlation between the assets exists.)

2. Control Correlation. This will always consist of attempting to keep the correlation coefficient between the particular asset and the remaining assets as low as possible. Only in exceptional circumstances will it be possible to reduce this correlation below zero, because of interrelationships between business processes; for example, virtually all business assets will be affected more or less similarly by general economic conditions.

As the company considers new assets or groups of assets which relate to new endeavours, it can regard each asset or group of assets in turn as a particular asset and subject it to analysis for possible risk control. The risk control will in turn take two forms: (1) Standard deviation control, where attempt is made to reduce the dispersion in assets being acquired, or (2) correlation control, where attempts are made to find assets which enmesh well with existing assets through low correlation coefficients.

STANDARD DEVIATION CONTROL ON ASSETS

There are two methods of controlling for risk, or standard deviation, in prospective assets themselves. One of these, which has been discussed previously and will now be reviewed briefly, is the discount rate or target rate of return method. The second method to be discussed will be the certainty equivalent method, a method much less widely used in practice but one with considerable logical appeal.

Discount and Target Rates

This method consists of performing NPV analysis with a higher discount rate, or establishing a higher rate of return target on assets that are perceived to be of higher risk. The effect of this is to insist that high-risk projects be accepted only if they offer compensation in the form of increased net cash flows over and above those portended by less risky projects.

While the rationale for this method can be understood more effectively in the context of the formal risk analysis of this chapter, that formality, or the use of the standard deviation as a risk measure, is not essential to practice of this method. Risk may be assessed judgmentally: we may generally assume that projects assessed as more risky ones by a capable financial analyst would in fact be those with relatively high standard deviations, if that measurement was actually to take place.

The Certainty Equivalent Method

This is a method which has been suggested to correct a deficiency in the method reviewed in the preceding section. The nature of the deficiency is this: the use of a higher discount rate or target rate of return to penalize risky projects results in little penalization for risk on short-lived projects and increasingly severe penalization as the longevity of the project increases.

This is apparent when one recalls the mathematical character of the discount factor, $1/(1+r)^n$. When the formula is used for risk adjustment, the discount rate, r, can be viewed as two components:

$$r = r_p + \text{risk premium},$$

where

r_p = "Pure" rate of interest, applicable where no risk exists;

Risk premium = Addition to discount rate made because of risk.

A riskless project is accordingly discounted at r_p (risk premium $= 0$) while a project with risk is discounted at $r_p +$ risk premium. In other words,

Present value of risky future dollar $= 1/(1 + r_p + \text{risk premium})^n$
Present value of riskless future dollar $= 1/(1 + r_p)$.

The ratio between the above present values represents the amount by which value is reduced in asset analysis because of risk:

$$\frac{\text{PV of risky dollar}}{\text{PV of riskless dollar}} = \frac{1/(1 + r_p + \text{risk premium}^n}{1/(1 + r_p)^n}$$

$$= \left[\frac{1 + r_p}{1 + r_p + \text{risk premium}}\right]^n.$$

It is now apparent that reduction of value because of risk is directly related to time: n in the above formulation.

For an example, the Wilson Company uses the NPV method, with a 10 percent discount rate on projects that it deems to be relatively safe and a 15 percent rate on those which it deems to be risky. Discount factors applied to cash flows expected one year hence are $1/1.15$ or .87 on the riskier project and $1/1.10$ or .91 on the safer project. Since these discount factors will determine present values of the cash flows to be received one year hence, their ratio will indicate the extent to which penalization for risk is taking place. That ratio, .87/.91 or .96 indicates that the risky cash receipts are valued at about 4 percent less than the safer receipts.

Now consider the effect of the Wilson Company's discount rates on cash flows expected ten years hence. The relevant discount factors are now $1/(1.15)^{10}$ or .247 on a risky project and $1/(1.10)^{10}$ or .386 on a safe project. Their ratio $.247/.386 = .64$ indicates a reduction of 36 percent in value will take place because of risk, in contrast to the 4 percent reduction on the cash flows expected one year hence.

The certainty equivalent method avoids this problem by setting penalization rates directly. A firm like the Wilson Company which regarded 10 percent as appropriate for safe projects, would discount all its cash flows, whether risky or safe at 10 percent. This would explicitly take care of the problem of time adjustment. The company then would directly establish a separate adjustment for risk, perhaps neither as high as .96 nor as low as .64 and reduce all cash flows of given risk by this factor. That factor, often referred to as a *certainty equivalence factor*, allows risk adjustment according to the intensity of the perceived risk, and is not affected by the time at which that risk exposure is expected to take place. To repeat, a certainty equivalence factor is one used to adjust value for risk in a manner separated from the process of time adjustment.

One can then identify:

Present value per future dollar (risk adjusted) $= g/(1 + r_p)^n$,

where

$$g = \text{Certainty equivalence factor}; g \leqq 1.$$

Suppose Wilson continued to use $r_p = .10$, and established $g = .8$ for risky projects. (On riskless projects, $g = 1$, always.) Valuation or risky and riskless dollars expected one year hence would then be the products of the discount factor and g. For Wilson, these products would be

Risky, .73; Riskless .91; Value ratio of risky to riskless .8.

For ten years hence

Risky, .309; Riskless, .386; Value ratio of risky to riskless .8.

In the remainder of the book, current practice will be followed. Discount or target rates will be used as a means of adjusting for risk, in the attempt to ensure that high-risk projects are accepted only when they offer compensation in the form of higher cash flows. However, the reader should be aware that future practice could quite possibly change in this matter since the certainty equivalent method appears to be the theoretically superior one.

CORRELATION CONTROL: COMPANY LEVEL

In addition to limiting the standard deviation of its prospective cash flows, the company can also reduce the standard deviation of its overall cash flows by concerning itself with correlation between various projects, or streams of cash flow. A number of existing company risk management practices can be explained through the understanding of their correlation aspects. Particularly, we will discuss three of these procedures, all of which are widely understood and used. They are diversification, hedging, and insurance.

All of these methods have as a common attribute, the intention of introducing new cash flow streams into the company which have low correlation with other company assets. As the title of this section suggests, this type of cash flow selection attempts to reduce the standard deviation of the company's overall asset collection. As we shall see in the subsequent section, correlation control with this objective is subject to criticism. However, there is little point in considering this criticism until current practices themselves are addressed.

Diversification

The virtues of specialization in business endeavours are often extolled. There is obvious benefit from a company concentrating on those things that it knows best, and by this concentration increasing its expertise and competitive advantage in its own field. When a company follows the policy of specialization, it tends to acquire new assets which are closely associated with its existing ones. A steel company buys more steel mills, a home builder hires more crews and undertakes the construction of more houses. Along with the familiarity of these new assets, and their capability for being easily into-grated into existing company operations, comes a potential dis-advantage—high correlation with existing assets.

Because of this, companies may have an incentive to eschew the advantages of specialization and seek new endeavours that are dissimilar to present operations. In capital budgeting, diversification could be favoured by the relaxing of discount or target rates on assets which had low correlation with existing assets. Instead of buying another steel mill, the steel company buys out a plastics manufacturer; or the building contractor opens an insurance office. These moves offer the attractive fea-ture of the fact that the ups and downs of plastics and insur-ance may not coincide too closely with those of steel and home building.

Diversification does not always provide risk reduction with-out cost; the diversifying company gives up the opportunity to concentrate more intensively in its own field. However, it may decide that the associated reduction in its overall risk position justifies this strategy, even if it means acquiring assets which viewed alone, have a risk/return configuration inferior to those available in its line of specialization. The extreme case of diver-sification as a company strategy is represented by the so-called conglomerate firm, which has no identifiable area of specializa-tion. (Recent experience suggests that inefficiencies in manage-ment of a diversified firm may have more than offset any benefits from diversification.) Moderate diversification is clearly a re-spected company practice in Canada.

Hedging

In Chapter 6, the hedging of inventories was discussed. This process can be part of a general company risk control strategy. To briefly review, a hedging operation consisted of undertaking a futures market short sale in the same commodity that com-prised the company inventory. The logic of the process was that if the value of items in the inventory decreased, these losses would be made up by corresponding gain in the futures market transaction.

One may envision the futures market short sale as a form of asset. In selling short, the company is in effect "buying" an opportunity to receive cash flows under a special circumstance—a decline in the commodity market. If the commodity market goes up, no positive cash flows result. Viewed by itself, the short-sale "asset" has cash flows of a high dispersion. The motive for purchasing an asset of this type is its negative correlation with another company asset, inventory. While negative correlations are unusual in business situations, the hedging situation is one of those exceptional circumstances where virtually perfect negative correlation is available.

Especially if inventories represent a large part of a company's asset collection, so the company's future cash flows would be greatly affected by deterioration in the value of items in inventory, the execution of the short sale in the future's market offers the opportunity for an asset that enmeshes well with the company's existing assets. While this type of risk control is not free, since there are transaction costs with the futures market operation, many companies with large inventories are willing to incur these costs in return for risk reduction.

Insurance

Like the futures market transaction used in hedging, the purchase of an insurance policy can be regarded as a form of asset purchase. Consider a fire insurance policy. With the payment of an insurance premium, the company may buy a fire insurance policy on a factory. The terms of the policy are: if the factory does not burn down, the policy returns no cash flow; if the factory burns down the company receives a large amount of cash. The policy may be viewed as an "asset" which will pay a large cash flow in an exceptional circumstance, or else will pay nothing at all (again, high dispersion). On the other hand, if the company's existing cash flows will be substantially affected by the burning down of a plant, the insurance policy is negatively correlated with these existing cash flows. Thus the purchase of the insurance policy, despite its high dispersion, contributes to a reduction of the company's overall risk.

Again this form of risk reduction has a cost, the operating costs and profits of insurance companies require that, *on the average*, payouts on insurance policies must be less than premium collections. This implies that the expected value of the cash flows from an insurance policy must be negative. However, many companies willingly pay this price because the insurance policy enmeshes so well with existing assets.

Companies practicing sophisticated risk management usually do not purchase insurance to protect against minor disruptions in cash flows. For example, a company may decide that the insurance of small buildings is not worthwhile. The loss of any particular small building may be no more severe than any of the other myriad of minor cash flow disturbances that beset a company on a day-to-day basis. (For examples, a sale is missed because a salesman is ill; production costs are higher because a shipment of low-cost raw materials is delayed and some high-cost replacements have to be bought in the local market.)

Several types of insurance are important in the typical corporate risk management strategy. Major buildings and physical facilities are often protected not only against possible loss by fire but also from damage by floods, windstorms, and other causes. Insurance may not only provide for replacement of the physical facility, but some compensation for the interruption in the company's business affairs that takes place because the physical facility cannot be replaced immediately (business interruption insurance). The company may insure itself against the death or disability of key personnel, whose removal from the business would cause an administrative disorder. Liability insurance can protect the company against lawsuits arising from responsibilities to employees, customers, and outside parties. Other specialized types of insurance may also be employed.

CORRELATION CONTROL—INVESTOR LEVEL

A criticism against correlation control in the firm can be made along the following lines. The corporation is expected to act on behalf of its shareholders. The shareholders themselves typically own not just stock in one company, but many stocks. Shareholders are not concerned with minimizing the risk in any one company, but only the risk in their own stock portfolio.

This line of reasoning could cause a rethinking of company

risk strategy. The company, in looking at any particular asset, would evaluate the risk of that asset on the basis of its standard deviation, and the correlation coefficient *between that asset and a typical shareholder's portfolio.* The typical shareholder's portfolio may in turn be approximated by a hypothetical portfolio consisting of a cross section of all the common stocks available. This cross-section portfolio is often called the *market portfolio.* We may then restate the two characteristics of an asset which affect the total risk of the company's shareholders:

a.   Standard deviation of the asset itself.

b.   The correlation between that asset and the market portfolio.

The first of these two determining factors does not differ from previous analysis and is accomplished through the penalization of assets for standard deviation. The second, however, is different, and raises serious questions about risk management based on controlling risk at the company level rather than at the shareholder level.

First, the advantage of company diversification comes into question. Buying into a different type of enterprise may look advantageous from the company viewpoint, but it may not seem particularly advantageous from the point of view of the shareholder. For example, buying a plastic company may look attractive from the point of view of risk control of a steel company; it may look much less attractive to a shareholder of that steel company who already may hold substantial amounts of plastic company stock. Put in a more technical way, the coefficient of correlation between the assets of the plastic company and the assets of the steel company may be much lower than the coefficient of correlation between the assets of the plastic company and the market portfolio. In general the shareholder point of view argues against companies' incurring costs for diversification. If a company can make investments outside of its regular line of endeavour, and earn comparable profits, well and good. But if assets of lower return/risk configuration must be accepted as a consequence of straying from specialization, the diversification may be subject to criticism.

This logic also holds with respect to hedging and insurance. The company may undertake either of these risk management tactics, and their associated costs, to protect major asset hold-ings from possible calamitous loss. This looks sound from the point of view of the company, but if a shareholder holds stocks in many companies he may view a calamity in one company as only a minor disturbance in his entire portfolio. He may even, for example, be holding stock in the very insurance company that will be paying a claim to another company whose stock he also owns. Why should he want any expense incurred for this "robbing Peter to pay Paul" type of transaction?

In spite of these arguments, it appears that, rightly or wrongly, companies act with some thought to their own sur-vival, and attempt control over the overall *company* risk level. Many practice the various forms of company-level correlation control: diversification, hedging, and insurance. At the same time, we must recognize that these practices may not be in full accord with usually presumed corporate objectives. If these company-level correlation control practices do not benefit shareholders and cost money to implement, they violate the precept of wealth maximization.

Beta Coefficients: A Shareholder-Level Risk Measure

If a company operated with concern for shareholder-level risk, rather than company-level risk, the company would, to repeat, attempt to limit the extent of two asset parameters:

a.   S.D.
b.   Correlation between the asset and the market portfolio.

A relatively new risk measure, called the *beta coefficient*, or *beta* is a composite of (*a*) and (*b*) above. Beta is defined as the degree to which outcome deviations of an asset are expected to coincide with deviations of the market portfolio. If the ups and downs of the asset are expected to follow the market portfolio perfectly, a beta coefficient of 1 is assigned.

Other values of beta, as well as 1, are determined as:

Beta = Ratio of deviation of particular asset to deviation of market portfolio.

Examples are given in Illustration 9–1.

ILLUSTRATION 9–1

Example of Beta Values

Beta Value	Description
2	When market portfolio performs 10 percent better than expected, particular asset will perform 20 percent better. If market performs 10 percent worse, asset will perform 20 percent worse.
1	When market deviates from expectation particular asset deviates in same proportion.
5	When market performs 10 percent better than expected, particular asset will perform 5 percent better. If market performs 10 percent worse, asset will be 5 percent worse.
0	No relation between performance of particular asset and the market.
−1	When market performs 10 percent better than expected, particular assets will perform 10 percent worse. If market performs 10 percent worse, asset will be 10 percent better.

If a company opts for a portfolio-oriented, rather than company-oriented version of risk control, beta is an attractive risk measure. It does not require separate estimates of S.D. and Corr. for a particular asset, but only a judgment about how the asset's performance will deviate relative to the ups and downs of the market portfolio. By virtue of the breadth of the market portfolio, this can be restated as a judgment about the relation between the particular asset's performance and the general state of the economy.

High beta assets are then regarded as high-risk assets and penalized accordingly. Low beta assets are less risky, and negative beta assets would be subject to reward rather than a penalty in the company's asset selection process.

This method is not yet used with any generality in current company capital budgeting. However, beta values are now quite widely used by stock market analysts, and it seems reasonable to suppose that this procedure will spread, at least in a supplemental way, into company asset selection practice.

SUMMARY

A company must control for both liquidity and risk. Liquidity problems are associated with insufficient cash; risk is associated with the possibility that expected profit opportunities may not ensue or continue. Risk may be defined mathematically as the dispersion around an expected value; standard deviation is the customary measure.

The future cash flows which may be obtained by the firm are viewed as a random variable. Probability distributions of cash flows can be described with two parameters—expected value and standard deviation.

When two assets are held together, dispersion in their cash flow distributions may be offsetting. Potentiality for this offset is described by the coefficient of correlation between the two assets. Low, including negative, correlations are associated with offset. The offsetting character is often described as diversification and is amenable to mathematical analysis.

A company can control for risk by controlling the standard deviation of its individual assets, and the correlation between the assets.

An important, and unresolved issue, arises over whether risk should be controlled at the level of the company, or at the level of the shareholder portfolio. In the first instance, correlation control within the company is important; in the second it is not. Insurance and hedging are widely used risk control devices that make use of the property of negative correlation.

The beta coefficient is becoming an increasingly recognized measure of the extent to which an individual asset contributes to the risk of a portfolio; this measure is a composite of standard deviation and correlation.

QUESTIONS AND PROBLEMS

1.   Distinguish between cash flows ex ante and cash flows ex post.

2.   You are given the following probability distribution:

Outcome	Probability
$ 5,000	.5
25,000	.4
50,000	.1

Identify expected value and standard deviation.

3.   A profit opportunity is described as consisting of equal chances of obtaining $5,000, $10,000, or $15,000. In describing this profit opportunity, would it be more correct to use the ex-

pression "a risky opportunity to earn $15,000" or "a risky opportunity to earn $10,000"? What is the variance and standard deviation in the distribution?

4. Define coefficient of correlation.

5. Asset A has an expected annual cash flow of $100 with a standard deviation of $30. Asset B has an expected value of $200 per year with a $100 standard deviation.

   If the two assets are statistically independent, what is the value of their coefficient of correlation? Given statistical independence what is the expected value and standard deviation of the combined two assets?

6. Repeat the calculations in the above problem, using perfect positive and perfect negative correlation.

7. A textile manufacturer considers the purchase of a chain of food stores. The manufacturer is concerned about the impact of the acquisition upon its own risk posture. What information is required for the evaluation?

8. A company considers two expected cash flows receivable in year 10—a risky $500,000 and a safe $100,000. Identify present values, using a discount rate of 10 percent for the safe project and 30 percent for the risky one.

9. From the above example, calculate certainty equivalent present values using a certainty equivalence factor of .4 for the high-risk cash flow.

10. Why, when a company considers opportunities for diversification, does it rarely encounter a prospective asset which is negatively correlated with its present assets?

11. Proponents of investor-level, rather than company-level, correlation control will oppose a company hedging its inventory position. Explain.

12. What is the significance of a beta value of 1? 3? Would a company practicing investor-level risk control assign a higher discount rate to high beta or to low beta projects? Explain.

RELATED READINGS

Adler, M. "On Risk-Adjusted Capitalization Rates and Valuation by Individuals." *Journal of Finance,* September 1970.

Arditti, F. D.   "Risk and the Required Return on Equity." *Journal of Finance,* March 1967.

Blume, M. E.   "On the Assessment of Risk." *Journal of Finance,* March 1971.

Breen, J., and Lerner, E. M.   "Corporate Financial Strategies and Market Measures of Risk and Return." *Journal of Finance,* May 1973.

Canada. Studies of the Royal Commission on Taxation.   *Taxation and Investments: A Study of Capital Expenditure Decisions in Large Corporations.* Ottawa: Queen's Printer, 1967.

Fisher, I. M., and Hall, R. G.   "Risk and Corporate Rates of Return." *Quarterly Journal of Economics,* February 1969.

Lessard, D. R., and Bower, R. S.   "Risk-Screening in Capital Budgeting." *Journal of Finance,* May 1973.

Levy, H., and Sarnat, M.   "Diversification, Portfolio Analysis, and the Uneasy Case for Conglomerate Mergers." *Journal of Finance,* September 1970.

Mao, J., and Helliwell, J.   "Investment Decisions under Uncertainty: Theory and Practice." *Journal of Finance,* May 1969.

Markowitz, H.   *Portfolio Selection,* New York: Wiley, 1959.

Paine, N.   "Uncertainty and Capital Budgeting." *Accounting Review,* April 1964.

Robichek, A., and Myers, S.   "Risk Adjusted Discount Rates." *Journal of Finance,* December 1966.

Sharpe, W. F.   *Portfolio Theory and Capital Markets.* New York: McGraw-Hill, 1970.

Van Horne, J. C.   "Capital Budgeting Decisions Using Combinations of Risky Investments." *Management Science,* October 1966.

10

FINANCIAL PLANS AND CONDITIONS

FINANCIAL NEEDS

Up to this point the concentration has been primarily on company assets, the left-hand side of the balance sheet. It is now time to turn to the financing of these assets, the balance sheet's right side. As additions to the asset collection are made, new financing is required. Beyond this, the temporary character of some financing sources requires a process of replacement financing or refinancing. Deficits in the company's operations may also impose financing requirements, just to preserve the magnitude of the company's assets; conversely, of course, the company's earnings provide a spontaneous financing source. This financing process requires an unending series of managerial actions, if the assets of the company are to be adequately maintained or enhanced.

In one sense, these financing transactions are a means to the end of meeting the company's asset needs. In another sense, they can be viewed in a much more positive light. Financial transactions, like other managerial actions, provide opportunities for the firm to gain competitive advantage. Careful, imaginative planning and administration yield positive results in financing as they do in other company endeavours—there is nothing automatic or routine about the financing function.

The next several chapters will examine financing practices and decisions. As a first step, an important tool of analysis for the planning of financing will be introduced; this is the projected sources and applications of funds statement. As a preliminary step, the preparation of projected (or pro forma) accounting statements will first be treated.

Projected Earnings Statements

A projected earnings statement is simply an estimate of what the company earnings statement will look like at some time in the future. It is in turn, based on anticipations of future company activities. Thus it would be quite possible for a company to wish to prepare quite a number of projections. These may be used to explore the financial effect of various policies that it might wish to follow in the future, or various changes in its environment that could possibly ensue. Initially, at least, the projections will usually be made with only broad categories of revenues, expenses, assets, and liabilities. As the company's plans for the future are "firmed up," the level of detail in the projected statements accompanying the planning will increase.

A good starting point for preparation of the projected earnings statement is to look at the earnings statement included in the most recently available company financial statements. Categories in this historical statement can provide a list of the estimates needed for the future, subject to addition or deletion, and also a point of departure for the determination of dollar amounts. From this point one moves ahead, on the basis of assumptions about future policies and quantitative forecasts.

A simple statement, with associated notes can serve to illustrate the process of projecting earnings. This projection is shown in Illustration 10–1. The basis for the statement is a series of "best available" estimates of what will ensue in the next two years. The nature of the individual projections are described in the notes. These notes should serve to provide an impression of the general projection process.

ILLUSTRATION 10–1

CRANDALL HANDLE LTD.
Projected Earnings Statement
(in thousands)

Line No.	Earnings Statement	Recent 1/7/75– 6/30/76	Projected 1/7/76– 6/30/77	Projected 1/7/77– 6/30/78	Pro forma 2-Year Total
1	Net sales	$4,200	$5,200	$6,500	$11,700
2	Cost of goods sold	2,400	2,900	3,500	6,400
3	Selling expenses . . .	300	400	500	900
4	Other expenses	800	1,000	1,200	2,200
5	Net income before tax	700	900	1,300	2,200
6	Net income after tax	400	500	800	1,300
7	Dividend	200	200	200	400
8	Retained earnings	200	300	600	900

Line No.	Notes
1	The company will attempt to increase its physical sales volume by 15 percent this year. It also anticipates annual price increases of 8 percent. Thus it expects sales to grow by the factor of 1.15 × 1.08 = 1.24, or 24 percent annual sales growth.
2	Due to a fixed cost component, cost of goods sold are expected to increase at a lower rate than sales: a 20 percent annual increase is estimated.
3	The major component of selling expense is salesmen's salaries. These are expected to rise by 20 percent per year, based on a view that current salary levels are too low and that some "catching up" is required. In addition, the sales force is expected to grow by 10 percent per year. The compound effect of these two increase factors is 1.10 × 1.20 = 1.32 or a 32 percent annual rate of increase.
4	Other expenses are projected to increase at the same rate as sales, 24 percent annually.
5	Arithmetically determined from above figures.
6	A 40 percent income tax rate is used.
7	Dividends are included with the earnings projection for convenience. The dividend projection is essential in planning the company's financial needs. Because of its expansion plans Crandall Handle is going to attempt to hold the line on dividends.
8	Determined arithmetically.

Projected Balance Sheet

The development of the estimates in the balance sheet is not undertaken in isolation; estimation of the future earnings statement will almost inevitably proceed hand in hand. One cannot, for example, readily estimate the future receivables position without some reference to projected sales. Similarly, one cannot make sales estimates without an estimate of the asset base

ILLUSTRATION 10–2

CRANDALL HANDLE LTD.
Projected Balance Sheet (in thousands)

Line No.	Category		Recent 6/30/76		Projected 6/30/78
9	Cash and near-cash		$ 300		$ 460
10	Accounts receivable		500		1,070
11	Inventory		800		1,320
12	Plant and equipment	3,500		5,500	
13	Less CCA	(600)		(900)	
14	Net		2,900		4,600
	Total		$4,500		$7,450
15	Miscellaneous current payables . . .		600		860
16	Bank notes payable		300		—
17	Mortgages		1,000		700
18	Other liabilities		200		—
19	Retained earnings		900		1,800
20	Common stock		1,500		1,500
21	Additional common stock		—		—
22	Necessary total of blank spaces . . .		$ 0		$2,590
	Total		$4,500		$7,450

Line No.	Notes
9	In the absence of any better way of making this projection, cash is assumed to increase in proportion to the increase in the company's volume of business; that is, it increases at the rate of sales increase of 24 percent per year, or 54 percent for the two-year period. (1.24 × 1.24 = 1.54).
10	Part of the company's tactics for increasing sales will be a more liberal credit policy. At the recent sales rate of $4,200,000/365 or about $11,500 per day, the current receivables position represents about 43 days sales outstanding. The company expects an increase to an average duration of 60 days, for an increase by a factor of 1.38. Coupled with the projected sales increase by a factor of 1.54, receivables are expected to more than double, increasing by an overall factor of 1.38 × 1.54 = 2.13.
11	Half of inventory is assumed to be finished goods. This is expected to increase in proportion to sales. The other half, raw materials and work-in-process, is expected to be affected by the construction of a new plant which will increase the need for these inventories to a projected $700,000. In total then, the inventory projection is:

Finished goods . . . . $400,000 × 1.54 = $ 620,000
Raw materials and work-in-process . . . . <u>700,000</u>
    Total $1,316,000

Line No.	Notes
12	Because of the expected increase in the company's volume of business, a new $2 million plant is contemplated. It is assumed that this plant will be complete by June 30, 1978. (For purposes of this analysis, no capital cost allowance is calculated on the new plant.)
13	Accumulated depreciation on the old plant, per earnings projection.
14	Arithmetically determined.
15	Miscellaneous payables are expected to increase by the cost of goods sold increase, a factor of 20 percent per year, or 44 percent for two years.
16	This line is intentionally left blank in the projection. It will be filled in as the company proceeds with planning for the meeting of its financial needs.
17	Scheduled mortgage payments of $150,000 per year will reduce the balance on the existing mortgage to $700,000.
18	This is also left blank to accommodate financial planning. This caption can be regarded as broad enough to cover the possibility, for example, of new mortgage financing on the new plant.
19	Retained earnings has increased by $900,000 based on the statement of earnings projections for the two years.
20, 21	Additional common stock is intentionally left blank to indicate that the issue of more common stock is another financing alternative which the company may wish to consider for meeting its financial needs.
22	According to the balance sheet projections which have been made, the company will have to secure $2,590,000 from bank borrowing, other liabilities, and additional common stock.

(such as plant and equipment) available for sustaining the sales volume. Both projections must follow from some overall picture of what the company's future policies are going to be.

The actual balance sheet projection can proceed along the same lines as the earnings statement projection. A continuation of the previous example for Crandall Handle Ltd. will illustrate (see Illustration 10–2).

Balance Sheet Comparisons

The next step in moving toward the projected sources and uses statement is an identification of changes that are expected to take place in balance sheet items between the time that planning is taking place and the end of the period for which planning is being done. This can be accomplished by subtraction of recent balance sheet data from projected balance sheet data as illustrated below.

CRANDALL HANDLE LTD.
Balance Sheet Comparisons
(in thousands)

Category	Recent 6/30/76	Projected 6/30/78	Change
Cash and near cash	$ 300	$ 460	+$ 160
Accounts receivable	500	1,070	+ 570
Inventory	800	1,320	+ 520
Plant and equipment	$3,500	$5,500	+$2,000
Less CCA	(600)	(900)	− 300
Net	$2,900	$4,600	+$1,700
Total	$4,500	$7,450	+$2,950
Miscellaneous current payables	$ 600	$ 860	+$ 260
Mortgage	1,000	700	− 300
Retained earnings	900	1,800	+ 900
Total of bank notes payable, other liabilities, and common stock	2,000	4,090	+ 2,090
Total	$4,500	7,450	+ 2,950

Projected Sources and Applications of Funds

Preliminary work is now out of the way and we can proceed toward the preparation of that useful planning tool, the projected sources and applications of funds statement. This statement systematically sets forth a company's needs for financing over the future period (in our example, two years) and the company's plans for procuring financial sources to meet these needs.

Sources of funds include the following items:

1. Increases in Liabilities.   The securing of additional credit is an obvious source of funds.

2. Increases in Net Worth.   These infusions of new funds can be divided into two subcategories:
    a. Sale of common stock, direct capital contributions of proprietors or partners, and other paid-in capital.
    b. Earnings.   Projected excesses of revenues over expenses constitute a buildup of equity, and a source of financing.

3. Disposal of Assets.   This item may also be subdivided:
    a. Direct sale of assets.
    b. Other policies reducing asset positions. For example, tighter credit policies can reduce the receivable position. As another example, cash and near-cash balances can be drawn down to meet financing needs.
    c. Allowances for declines in asset value.   Assets can be reduced by, for example, depreciation (or in tax parlance, capital cost allowance). Because depreciation accounting has been practiced, earnings are stated at a lower level than they otherwise would have been.
        The amount of projected depreciation is therefore included among sources of funds from the company's ongoing business operations.

Applications or uses of funds can also be classified into three major categories.

1. Acquisition of Assets.   This may result from direct purchase of assets, or from buildups in asset positions such as receivables and cash or near-cash.

2. Reduction of Liabilities.   When obligations are repaid, funds are required.

3. Reductions in Net Worth.   Again this can be subdivided:
    a. Retirement or repurchase of common stock.
    b. Dividends, and other distributions of capital such as drawings by proprietors or partners.

ILLUSTRATION 10–3

CRANDALL HANDLE LTD.
Projected Sources and Applications of Funds
January 7, 1976–June 30, 1978
(in thousands)

Line No.	*Sources of Funds*		
1	From operations:		
	Earnings	$1,300	
	Depreciation	300	
	Total sources from operations		$1,600
	Other sources:		
3	Increase in miscellaneous current payables	260	
4	Total increase in bank notes payable, other liabilities, and common stock	2,090	
	Total other sources		2,350
	Total Sources		$3,950
	Uses of Funds:		
	Asset increases (other than cash or near-cash):		
5	Accounts receivable	$ 570	
6	Inventory	520	
7	Plant and equipment	2,000	
	Total increase in noncash assets		$3,090
8	Reduction in liabilities		300
9	Dividends		400
10	Increase in cash and near cash		160
	Total Uses		$3,950

The following notes will explain aspects of the statement that may not be obvious; these are again coded to the numbered lines on the statement:

1   The earnings figure is taken from the earnings projection. A balance sheet comparison only indicated a change in retained earnings. More information is conveyed by following the usual custom of showing earnings, and later, dividends, rather than just a change in the net figure, retained earnings.

2   Determined from the balance sheet comparison this reduction of an asset value would have been subtracted in earnings determination. It is now added back in the operating section to offset this previous charge.

3   From balance sheet comparison.

4   This "catchall" total is still included on the presumption that financial planning has proceeded only to the point where it is believed that necessary funds will have to be accumulated from one or more of these three sources.

5, 6, 7, 8   From balance sheet comparisons.

9   As discussed previously, dividends, taken from the earnings projection, is shown separately.

10   The separation of the accumulation of cash from other assets is done to allow cash to be placed at the bottom of the statement. Sometimes this cash accumulation could be a residual from the other sources and applications. However, in this case, and in most financial planning situations, a desired amount of cash and near cash would be directly projected in the planning process. Thus its placement at the bottom follows convention in the preparation of sources and applications statements, although logically the increase in the cash position might well have been listed along with other asset increases.

c. Projected losses. When expenses overrun revenues, funds are used up in the company's operations.

Making use of this classification of sources and uses of funds, and the data from the Crandall Handle example, a projected sources and uses statement can be prepared.

A projected sources and applications statement provides a picture of how the company plans to generate money over the next two years and what it plans to do with this money. It provides an organized arrangement for considering needs for financing, and how those needs will be covered. If not all needs can be feasibly covered, it may be necessary for Crandall Handle Ltd. to rethink its expansion plans.

FINANCIAL CONDITION

The sources and application of funds statements sets forth the financial needs of the company and provides a format for describing how the needs are to be met. To some extent these needs may be met spontaneously from the company's operations; beyond this decisions must be made about which fund sources should be employed.

In part, decisions about which financing sources to use will be made on the basis of cost considerations. This type of consideration will relate logically to the overall asset selection or capital budgeting process, with cost comparisons taking the place of net benefit evaluation. At a strategic level we recall that asset acquisition decisions were coloured by considerations of liquidity and risk. These same strategic considerations also affect financing choices, making those choices something other than a cost minimization problem. In describing financing decisions, this text will follow custom and discuss these liquidity and risk attributes first. They relate closely to what may be called a *financial condition*, the relationship that exists between the company's assets and the means by which they are financed.

Urgency of Claims and Liquidity

Liquidity in a financing context has the same meaning as when it is discussed in connection with assets; it refers to the degree to which something is convertible into cash. However, because the word is so often used to describe the attributes of assets, or of a combination of assets and liabilities, the term *urgency* will be used to describe the liquidity of claims against assets. The urgency of a claim describes the relative amount of time the company has to discharge that claim through cash payment. Some financing sources are unequivocally demanding of prompt disbursement; on others payment may be postponable, explicitly required far in the future, or not required at all.

For example, just as a Government of Canada Treasury bill is regarded as liquid because of the promptness and certainty with which it will be discharged, a company liability to the government for the payment of income taxes is regarded as urgent because of the requisite prompt and certain conversion into a cash outflow. On the other hand, a company loan payable, on which interest only is due over the next ten years, might be regarded as a claim of low urgency. At the outward end of the continuum common stock as a source of funds may be regarded practically devoid of urgency; with minor exceptions, there is not legal obligation to undertake payment to shareholders at all.

The urgency of a company's financial claims has important effects on its overall liquidity posture. A company with relatively illiquid assets may still have adequate overall liquidity if those assets are financed with nonurgent claims. Delay in payment of claims can release money for emergencies or opportunities in the same way as drawing upon reserves or other liquid assets.

Conversely, urgent claims can aggravate or precipitate liquidity crises. The company is likely to place considerable emphasis on their relative urgency, therefore, in determining which financial sources to use. This may again be regarded as a strategic aspect of a financial decision.

Liquidity Ratios and Other Indicators

The liquidity of a company can be evaluated by careful examination of its balance sheet, and through cash flow projections which take into account receipts that will be coming in and payments that will be going out of the company, including the meeting of its obligations on financing sources. This analysis can be extended further through cash flow simulation, and through analysis of possible contingencies and extraordinary liquidity requirements.

All of these indications of liquidity require analysis in some detail. For quick indices of company liquidity simpler measures are sometimes employed. These measures are subject to serious imperfections, but they may be suggestive of liquidity problems. They are also part of the language of finance, with which the reader should be familiar.

The three measures of liquidity which will be discussed all impend upon the accounting practice of segregating assets and liabilities into current and fixed components. Current assets are those assets which, on an individual basis, are normally converted into cash within a year. Similarly, liabilities are classified as current if payment on an individual liability is required within a year. (This classification extends to that portion of longer term liabilities which must be paid within a year.)

Basically, the three measures equate classification of an asset or a liability as current with classification of it as relatively liquid (or urgent). This equivalence of "current" and liquid is questionable. As we have already seen, current assets, such as inventories and receivables, may not be particularly liquid, because as individual parts of the receivable or inventory position are converted to cash, other cash is devoured in acquiring new inventory items or receivables. Only a change in credit policy or inventory holding policy can normally reduce the entire position in these assets, and this *net* reduction is necessary for the asset to actually generate cash.

In like manner, liabilities which are classified in accounting statements as current may not necessarily be urgent, when viewed in groupings rather than individually. For example, a company may regularly purchase raw materials on a 30-day credit and may maintain a level production process throughout the year. If so the company will always have approximately one month's purchases outstanding, showing on its books as an account payable. Each month the company pays for the past month's purchases and accumulates an account payable on the present month's purchases. This process will delay any net payment of the account payable position indefinitely, as long as the company can continue to obtain 30-day credit from present or potential suppliers.

In spite of these serious differences between "current" and "liquid," measures of financial condition based on current asset and liability classifications are not without some underlying logic. It is true that if the firm continues in production, current assets and liabilities are not necessarily liquid assets and urgent liabilities. However, these items do tend to become liquid automatically if production is interrupted. If the company stops producing and selling, receivables are collected and not replaced, inventories are used up and not replenished, and credit from suppliers is also paid off without replacement. Thus these measures provide some indication of the company's state of liquidity in the event that the company had to stop production. (That is, provided that the production was stopped under orderly conditions, where inventories could be used up and sold without serious loss, and where collections could be made readily.)

So much for the pros and cons of these measures of financial condition; now let us look at the actual measures.

Net Working Capital

This is calculated as:

Net working capital = current assets − current liabilities.

The intent of this measure is to indicate a net dollar amount of company liquidity. For example, on the recent balance sheet of Crandall Handle Ltd. net working capital is calculated as:

Cash and near-cash		$ 300,000
Accounts receivables		500,000
Inventory		800,000
Total Current Assets		$1,600,000
Miscellaneous current payables	$600,000	
Bank notes payable	300,000	
Total Current Liabilities		900,000
Net Working Capital		$ 700,000

Current Ratio

The current ratio uses the same information as net working capital, but expresses the comparison as a ratio rather than an absolute dollar amount. The current ratio is defined as:

$$\text{Current ratio} = \text{Current assets/current liabilities.}$$

For Crandall Handle Ltd. this ratio is calculated as:

$$\text{Current ratio} - \$1,600,000/\$900,000 = 1.78.$$

The advantage of the current ratio over the net working capital figure is its usefulness in making comparisons between companies of different size. While one expects that a large company will have a much larger absolute dollar amount of net working capital, there is no basis for supposing that there will be systematic differences in the current *ratios* of large and small companies.

There are no hard and fast rules for what constitutes a good or bad current ratio. For those who use this measure, a current ratio of 2 or more might under most circumstances be regarded as indicative of adequate liquidity, and a current ratio of 1 or below as an indication of difficulty. However, there are exceptions galore.

"Acid Test" or "Quick" Ratio

This measure is an attempt to correct the current ratio for possible illiquidity in the inventory position. It is calculated as:

$$\text{Acid test ratio} = \frac{\text{Cash} + \text{near cash} + \text{receivables}}{\text{Current liabilities}}.$$

In Crandall Handle Ltd. this ratio would be calculated as:

$$\text{Acid test ratio} = \frac{\$300,000 + \$500,000}{\$900,000} = .89.$$

Those who use this ratio often regard an acid test ratio of approximately 1 as an indicator of adequate liquidity.

Liquidity Ratios in Perspective

Liquidity ratios are used by financial officers of companies, as easy-to-calculate indicators of financial condition. They are also employed by "outsiders," such as financial institutions, credit analysts, and prospective shareholders, who are interested in a company but who do not have ready access to full details about the company's situation. Because these "outsiders" can affect a company's welfare, a company is likely to consider the impact of its actions on its ratios, even though company management does not fully "believe in" the ratio.

RISK AND FINANCIAL CONDITION

Financial condition, the interrelationship between various financing sources and the company's assets, has another highly important strategic facet, beyond liquidity. One important aspect of risk relates to the possibility of company failure. Dangers of failure arising from the risk character of company assets may be aggravated or ameliorated by the manner in which the company undertakes its financing.

Insolvency and Financing

For present purposes failure can be regarded as occurring when a company is in a state of *insolvency;* when it lacks the value of assets necessary to equal its liabilities. The condition is equivalent to the company's net worth falling below zero. The root of insolvency lies in deterioration in asset values. The possibility for deterioration is in turn associated with the dispersion (or standard deviation) in the company's prospective cash flows. The greater the risk in the company's assets, the greater the probability that they may suffer large declines in value.

Beyond the risk in the assets, the potential for insolvency is greater in proportion to the magnitude of the claims of creditors against the assets; that is, the company's liabilities. This relation arises because of the condition for insolvency: Assets < liabilities. With no liabilities, asset values can fall to zero (their minimum) without insolvency. As liabilities are used more extensively, assets need not decline so far in value to fulfill the insolvency condition.

The relationship between danger of insolvency, risk in the assets, and the use of liability financing can be explored through an example. Consider three companies, A, B, and C (see Illustration 10–4). The companies have common elements: two have similar assets and two have similar financing.

Company B uses no debt; A and C use considerable borrowing. Companies A and B have relatively risky assets; C's assets are much safer. Each company values its assets at $1 million on a cost basis; expected value of discounted future cash flows for each company is also $1 million.

Information for each company is given in Illustration 10–4, in the form of a balance sheet and a probability distribution describing the prospects for discounted future cash flows.

On the basis of this information, probabilities of insolvency can be obtained for A, B, and C. Company A owes $500,000 and realizes that there is a .5 probability of its cash flows being

ILLUSTRATION 10–4

COMPANY A
Balance Sheet

Assets $1,000,000	Liabilities . . . $ 500,000
	Net worth . . . 500,000

Probability Distribution of Asset Values

Probability	Present Value of Net Future Cash Inflows from Assets
.5	$ 400,000
.5	$1,600,000

COMPANY B
Balance Sheet

Assets $1,000,000	Net worth . . . $1,000,000

Probability Distribution of Asset Values

Probability	Present Value of Net Future Cash Inflows from Assets
.5	$ 400,000
.5	$1,600,000

COMPANY C
Balance Sheet

Assets $1,000,000	Liabilities . . . $ 500,000
	Net worth . . . 500,000

Probability Distribution of Asset Values

Probability	Present Value of Net Future Inflows from Assets
.5	$ 800,000
.5	$1,200,000

worth only $400,000. If this result ensued, the value of the company's assets (as measured by the present value of the cash flows from its assets) would be $100,000 less than the company's liabilities, and insolvency would exist. Thus there is a .5 probability of insolvency.

In the case of Company B assets are just as risky, but even if the worst result on the assets occurred, where their value dropped to $400,000, the company would be far from insolvent with a net worth of $400,000. Compared with A, Company B, undertaking as much risk in its assets, avoided possible insolvency by using only moderate amounts of borrowing.

Company C assesses its worst possible asset condition as being a decline in value to $800,000. This exceeds its $500,000 in liabilities, so C also contemplates no probability of insolvency. Compared with A, Company C's freedom from possible bankruptcy arises from the safety (low dispersion) of its assets. C used as much debt as A but the debt used was still moderate when compared with the character of C's assets.

The three-company example demonstrates the critical interplay of asset risk and financing sources. This strategic element in financial choice, avoidance of failure, has occupied a great deal of attention on the part of financial managers and scholars. The next subsection will examine a measure of insolvency potential, and this consideration of potential insolvency will colour subsequent discussions which analyze the choice of financing sources.

Measuring Insolvency Potential

Danger of insolvency arises from risk in the company's assets, and in the type of financing the company uses. In other words, an aspect of financing, the extent to which debt is used, is one cause of bankruptcy. Therefore, it is not surprising that one of the important measures of financial condition is a measure of the extent to which a company employs debt. The most widely used measure of this type is the *debt ratio* (or *debt-to-assets* ratio), calculated as:

Debt ratio = Total liabilities/total assets.

To return to Crandall Handle Ltd., this calculation is illustrated as:

Current liabilities	$ 900,000
Mortgage	1,000,000
Other liabilities	200,000
Total liabilities	$2,100,000
Total assets	$4,500,000

Debt ratio = 2,100,000/4,500,000 = .47.

For relatively small companies, such as Crandall Handle, the calculation of the debt ratio based on accounting values is usually regarded as acceptable. In the case of the large, publicly held company, there is a good case for departing from this practice. The reason for this departure lies in the fact that the company's shares have a readily identifiable market price. From this price it is possible to determine a market value of the company's net worth. This market value of the company's net worth represents the value placed on the company's equity by investors. Market evaluation is usually regarded as a sounder and more up-to-date statement of the net worth than *book value*, the value contained in the company's accounting statements.

An example will illustrate; we begin with the accounting balance sheet of S. M. Tinplate Ltd.

Total assets	$25,000,000	Debt	$20,000,000
		Retained earnings	2,000,000
		Common stock*	3,000,000

*2 million shares outstanding.

From this, a debt ratio is calculated at $20,000,000/$25,000,000 = .8.

It is also possible to calculate the value per share placed on the company common shares by accounting balance sheet. Since

$$\text{Book value per share} = \frac{\text{Accounting statement value of net worth position}}{\text{Number of shares outstanding}}$$

we obtain for S. M. Tinplate:

$$\text{Book value per share} = \frac{\$5,000,000}{2,000,000} = \$2.50.$$

Now let us introduce some additional information:

The last available price on this stock was $16 per share. Accordingly, we can calculate that investors are valuing S. M. Tinplate's net worth at 2,000,000 × $16 = $32,000,000. This is in drastic contrast to the $5 million figure on S. M. Tinplate's balance sheet.

It is difficult to argue with this market valuation; investors, in current transactions, are paying hard cash of $16 per share for S. M. Tinplate's shares, even though book value is only $2.50.

A balance sheet may be revised to a security market valuation basis by assuming that the company's assets are worth the sum of the debts of the company and the amount of which the market values the company's net worth. For S. M. Tinplate Ltd., this market value of assets is calculated as:

Total assets (market basis) = Total liabilities
+ net worth (market basis)
= $20,000,000 + $32,000,000.
= $52,000,000.

The market value-based balance sheet becomes:

Total assets (market basis)	$52,000,000	Debt	$20,000,000
		Net worth (market basis)	32,000,000

On a market value basis the debt ratio is calculated at:

Debt ratio = $20,000,000/$52,000,000 = .38.

Obviously the market conversion cuts both ways. In 1976, many Canadian companies were being valued in the market at below their book value. In cases of this type, a market value revision would result in a higher debt ratio than one calculated from book values.

The debt ratio is commonly used as a measure of the extent to which a company uses debt. Again there is no hard and fast rule about what constitutes an appropriate ratio. A sweeping generalization would be that, for manufacturing and extractive businesses, .5 might be regarded as normal. Ratios substantially less than this could indicate inadequate use of debt (for cost reasons we shall discuss later). Ratios greatly in excess of this could indicate a financial condition that is likely to cause insolvency problems.

The most serious limitation of the debt ratio as an indicator of the threat of insolvency is that it says nothing about the character of company's assets or cash flows. For example recall from the A, B, and C examples earlier in this section that Companies A and C had identical debt ratios but A had a substantial risk of insolvency and C did not, because of the different risk dimension in their assets.

Subject to this reservation, the debt ratio is a widely recognized tool. Its use rests on the logical connection between debt use and probable insolvency.

Because the ratio may be calculated on either a book or market basis, it is important when examining a debt ratio prepared by someone else, to ascertain the method used in obtaining it.

PLANNING THE COMPANY'S FINANCING

The extent of debt use and the urgency of financial requirements are important constituents in determining how financial needs should be met. These issues comprise strategic aspects, superimposed on the wealth-maximizing objective of procuring financing at minimum cost. The impact of these strategic considerations can be illustrated through an extension of a previous example, Crandall Handle Ltd. The intent of this example will be to illustrate a charting of financial course.

A company must look ahead in its planning and attempt to foretell the impact of financing proposals on its overall liquidity and risk posture. Its objective must be to simultaneously meet financing needs and, based on measures just considered, maintain an acceptable financial condition.

First, let us recall the projected sources and applications statement of Crandall Handle (Illustration 10–3). The company needed to find $2,590,000 from three potential sources—

bank notes payable, other liabilities, and common stock. Suppose that it begins its financial planning by exploring three simple strategies—selecting any one, but only one of these possible fund sources and raising all its money in that way. The results of these three policies are explored below.

Financing Alternative 1—Bank Borrowing

Crandall Handle first contemplates the possibility of relying on its bankers for its total financing needs. The result is the following projections for June 30, 1978.

CRANDALL HANDLE, LTD.
Projected Balance Sheet—Bank Financing
June 30, 1978

Cash, near-cash and		Miscellaneous current	
receivables	$1,530	payables	$ 860
Inventory	1,320	Bank note payable	2,590
Total current assets	$2,850	Total current liabilities	$3,450
Plant (net)	4,600	Mortgage	700
Total	$7,450	Total liabilities	$4,150
		Net worth	3,300
		Total	$7,450

Current ratio	.83
Acid test ratio	.44
Debt ratio	.56

The difficulty with this course of action is now apparent. The low current and acid test ratios suggest a heavy strain on the company's liquidity. Even if the company were to elect to undergo this strain, the company's banker might be unwilling to tolerate the situation.

Financing with Long-Term Debt

The second alternative Crandall Handle considers is the expansion of its other liabilities by the needed $2,090,000. It might, for example, mortgage its existing plant facilities for a larger amount and also mortgage its new facilities. Through the use of mortgages it would probably be able to attain a long-term loan which would not impose the urgency of the bank credit perused in the previous section.

222   Canadian Business Finance

The projected results of such a policy are as follows:

CRANDALL HANDLE LTD.
Projected Balance Sheet—Mortgage Financing
June 30, 1978

Cash, near-cash and		Total current liabilities	. . . .	$ 860
receivables	$1,530	Mortgages		3,290
Inventory	1,320	Total liabilities		$4,150
Total current assets	$2,850	Net worth		3,300
Plant (net)	4,600	Total		$7,450
Total	$7,450			

Current ratio 3.31
Acid test ratio 1.78
Debt ratio 56

We note that this clears up the liquidity problem, at least insofar as it is manifested in the ratios being used. The debt ratio remains the same, since this alternative was simply a substitution of another form of debt for that used in the first alternative. A ratio of .56 is usually not regarded as, by itself, indicative of serious problems, so this alternative looks like a viable financing strategy.

Financing with Equity

The third alternative considered was to use no more debt, but to issue additional common shares for the necessary funds. The resulting projections are shown:

CRANDALL HANDLE LTD.
Projected Balance Sheet—Equity Financing
June 30, 1978

Cash, near-cash and		Total current liabilities	. . . .	$ 860
receivables	$1,530	Mortgage		700
Inventory	1,320	Total liabilities		$1,560
Total current assets	$2,850	Net worth		5,890
Plant (net)	4,600	Total		$7,450
Total	$7,450			

Current ratio 3.31
Acid test ratio 1.78
Debt ratio 21

This third alternative also shows acceptable liquidity ratios, in fact, the same as the previous ones. In addition, it shows a low debt ratio of .21. Thus this financing option also appears viable. For reasons to be discussed later, there is some tendency for equity to constitute a higher priced source of funds than debt. Thus it is possible that further analysis would exclude this alternative for cost reasons.

A Financing Solution

We have looked at some alternative methods of financing contemplated by Crandall Handle. Obviously, these were not the only options available. Combinations of the various proposed financing alternative could have been employed, and the list of financing sources available might also have been expanded. For example, a more detailed study might have convinced Crandall Handle to actually use the following combination:

1. Additions to current liabilities through bank borrowing of $300,000. This keeps the liquidity ratios at respectable levels: current ratio, 2.46; acid test ratio, 1.32.

2. Use of $1.2 million in mortgage money, secured by the new plant and equipment.

3. Renegotiation of the existing mortgage for the remaining $990,000. These moves would leave the debt ratio at .56, a figure deemed adequate.

SUMMARY

Planning for a future financing requires the projection of company financial statements. A statement of sources and applications of funds can be developed from comparative pro forma balance sheets. This can be used as a planning tool.

Sources of company financing may be more or less urgent. The degree of urgency in its financing contributes to the company's overall liquidity posture. A number of measures, such as the current ratio, are available to provide rough indications of the company's overall liquidity stance.

Risk of failure is related to financing. More specifically the probability of insolvency will be jointly determined by the risk of the company's assets and the extent of the company's debt usage.

In developing a plan for financing, a company will need to consider cost minimization; this is consistent with wealth maximization. However, the objective of wealth maximization is also served by addressing strategic aspects—the effect of financing on liquidity and risk.

QUESTIONS AND PROBLEMS

1. A company's current earnings statement is shown below:

Net sales	$10,000
Cost of goods sold	− 6,000
Margin on sales	$ 4,000
Other expenses	− 2,000
Net earnings before tax	$ 2,000
Income tax at 25%	− 500
Net earnings after tax	$ 1,500

This company projects an increase of 10 percent in its physical volume of sales over the following period, and a 5 percent increase in prices. It predicts that cost of goods sold will show the same rate of physical increase, but will be subject to a 7 percent price increase. Other costs are expected to remain unchanged, as is the tax rate. Develop a projected earnings statement for the following period.

2. Return to the Crandall Handle example, as shown in Illustrations 10–1 and 10–2. Reconstruct the projected balance sheet on the assumption that Crandall Handle would pay no dividends during the two-year projection period.

Trace the effect of this change in dividend policy further, by reconstructing Crandall Handle's balance sheet comparison and its projected sources and applications of funds statement.

3. Describe how the following changes in projections will alter the company's projections of sources and applications of funds:
   a. An upward revision in estimates of executive salaries.
   b. A plan for a purchase of a new plant.
   c. A decision to retire an existing note payable before maturity.
   d. A liberalization of credit terms for customers.
   e. A public sale of shares.

4. Measures of company liquidity distinguish between current and fixed or long-term liabilities. Explain how a current liability may be a less urgent claim than a liability of longer maturity.

5. Distinguish between current and acid test ratios. What is the rationale for the difference?

6. The value of a company's assets one year hence may be described by the following probability distribution:

Asset Value	Probability
0	.1
100,000	.2
200,000	.5
300,000	.2

Prepare a graph which shows the relationship between the company's probability of insolvency and the dollar amount of debt incurred by the company.

7. A company has the following balance sheet.

Assets $2,000,000	Liabilities $1,000,000
	Retained earnings 500,000
	Capital stock 500,000

The company has 100,000 shares of stock outstanding; market value of the stock is $18 per share.
   a. Calculate book value per share.
   b. Revise the balance sheet to a market value basis.
   c. Calculate the company's debt ratio on book value and market value bases.
   d. What is the theoretical advantage of the market value debt ratio over the book value version. Are there any theoretical or practical disadvantages?

RELATED READINGS

Altman, E. "Financial Ratios, Analysis and the Prediction of Corporate Bankruptcy." *Journal of Finance*, September 1968.

Beaver, W. "Financial Ratios as Predictors of Failure." *Emperical Research in Accounting: Selected Studies in Journal of Accounting Research*, 1966.

Jennings, J.   "A Look at Corporate Liquidity." *Financial Executive*, February 1971.

Key Business Ratios in Canada, 1970. Toronto: Dun & Bradstreet.

Lev, Baruch.   *Financial Statement Analysis: A New Approach.* Englewood Cliffs, N.J.: Prentice-Hall, 1974.

Pappas, J. L., and Huber, G. P.   "Probabilistic Short-Term Financial Planning." *Financial Management*, Autumn 1973.

Weston, J. F.   "Forecasting Financial Requirements." *Accounting Review*, July 1958.

11

FINANCING COSTS

Financing is a major ingredient in the production of most Canadian goods and services. Like other company procurement activities—the employment of labour or the purchase of materials—the hire of financing is subject to cost. Cost is not the only important aspect of financing procurement; urgency and risk were discussed in the previous chapter. Nevertheless, cost itself is important. Careless financial management can lead to excessively high financing costs. If these costs are too high relative to other firms, a company's chances of success or survival are impaired.

Unlike many other expenses, financing costs frequently lack obvious "price tags." If these costs are to be controlled, they must first be identified. Therefore, the first order of business for this chapter will be to address the definition and measurement of financing costs. These costs are alternatively called *capital costs*.

Two Versions of Financing Cost

The definition and measurement of financing cost in a company can proceed on two levels. The first of these is with respect to the cost of individual financing sources. For example, credit is offered by a raw materials supplier, what is the cost of using funds from this source?

The cost of obtaining a particular type of financing from a particular source may be called a *specific capital cost*. Specific capital costs are useful in making comparisons between alternative sources of financing available to a company. (Can we obtain money more economically from a mortgage loan offered by an insurance company, or from the public issue of bonds?) Specific costs are also useful in making external comparisons. (Are we getting bank money as cheaply as a comparable company about which we have information?)

While specific capital costs are essential information, this information is not sufficient for financial management. A general statement about financial costs is also required. The funds employed by a company are blended from many sources, and it is necessary to be able to make a statement about the cost of the blended mixture. The problem is analogous to the problem of a coffee company, which is selling coffee of a given quality which is in turn a mixture of lots of coffee purchased by the company from various sources. At some point the company wants a general statement about "the cost of a pound of coffee," rather than the costs of the components of its coffee mixture.

A general statement about a company's financing cost relating to money procured from all sources, is called a statement of *overall capital cost*. The figure is obtained from specific capital cost through an adding, or averaging, process which will be discussed later in the chapter. Overall capital cost is used as a basis for deciding whether assets should be financed. The figure is also useful in making general comparisons with other companies. It is, as well, necessary in making statements about product costs, for such purposes as company cost accounting, labour negotiation, or interaction with regulatory agencies.

Furthermore, we shall see that overall capital cost is important in a choice among various financial sources; these sources may be compared not only in terms of their specific cost, but also in terms of their effect on the overall cost. (The two approaches do not necessarily lead to the same conclusions.)

Specific Cost Identification

The method used almost universally for specific financing cost identification is the internal rate. To review, that means that a discount rate is selected with the characteristic that it will cause the present value of net cash flows to equal zero. In specific capital cost calculation, this usually means that a rate must be selected that will equate the net amount of funds (or *proceeds*) being received from a transaction with a particular financing source, with the present value of all future payments arising from the transaction.

Sometimes the specific capital cost is obvious. For example, money obtained on a promissory note may bear a specified interest rate. If required future payments on the obligation have been calculated using this rate it follows mathematically that the specified rate will be the internal rate. This can be verified with an example. A promissory note requires the payment of annual interest at a rate of 10 percent, and repayment of principal at the end of three years. The note is for $10,000. The following calculation verifies that the specified interest rate, 10 percent, is also the internal rate.

Of course, even transactions which specify an interest rate may not be amenable to such straightforward indentification of capital cost. Any condition of the transaction which departs from the standard interest calculation will necessitate compu-

Time (years from present)	Money Amount	Explanation	10 Percent Discount Factor	Present Value
0 . . .	+$10,000	Received proceeds from loan	1.000	+$10,000
1 . . .	− 1,000	Interest	0.909	− 909
2 . . .	− 1,000	Interest	0.826	− 826
3 . . .	− 11,000	Interest and principal repayment	0.751	− 8,261
		Sum (NPV)		$ 4*

* This value can be regarded as an approximation of zero. The imperfection arises from rounding in the discount factors.

tation for an internal rate. For example, one may leave the terms of the above promissory note the same, but suppose that the loan was accompanied by the payment of a "finder's fee" of $1,000. (Such a fee may occur when a company is unable to obtain the loan at regular financial institutions, and seeks the help of a third party in searching out a loan.) The use of the 10 percent nominal interest rate as a specific capital cost is no longer appropriate, since the payments on the loan were calculated on a $10,000 base but the company actually received proceeds of $9,000 from the loan. Identification of the internal rate, used on asset evaluation, is shown below.

		Possible Capital Cost						
		10%		12%		14%		
Time	Cash Flows	Discount Factor	PV	Discount Factor	PV	Discount Factor	PV
0	+$ 9,000	1.000	$9,000	1.000	$9,000	1.000	$9,000
1	− 1,000	0.909	− 909	0.893	− 893	0.877	− 877
2	− 1,000	0.826	− 826	0.797	− 797	0.769	− 769
3	− 11,000	0.751	− 8,261	0.712	− 7,832	0.675	− 7,431
	NPV		−$ 996		−$ 522		−$ 77

Specific cost of capital is now observed to be slightly over 14 percent in spite of the nominal 10 percent rate.

This method for specific capital cost identification can be applied to all financing sources. It can be used on various types of debt, on debtlike financing arrangements such as leases, and on equity. Specific cost identification on equity will differ from that on debt but only in the manner in which the money amounts are determined.

While that topic will be discussed in detail later, we can now note two approaches for cash flows identification that will be required in the calculation of specific capital cost on equity. For present shareholders of a company, the identification runs along opportunity cost lines: what could those shareholders earn if they invested their money elsewhere? For contemplated sale of new stock, where potential shareholders are involved, the cost identification will relate to the share of expected company earnings that will go to the purchasers of the new common stock.

Tax Matters

So far the identification of specific capital cost has proceeded without reckoning of tax. Just as in asset analysis after-
tax cash flows are necessary in a refined identification of capital
cost. The most vital fact in converting to an after-tax cost-of-
capital identification is this: interest for business purposes is tax
deductible. The effect of this can be noted in the promissory
note example. Using a 40 percent corporate tax rate, all tax deductible outflows are reduced by the factor $(1-t)$, or .6. The
modification of the cash flows is shown in the following calculation:

	(1) Cash Flow Unaffected by Tax	(2) Tax Deductible Cash Outflow	(3) Explana- tion of Deduction	(4) Deductible Cash Flow after Tax (Col. 2 × (1 − t))	(5) After Tax Cash Flow (Col. 1 + Col. 4)
Time					
0	+$10,000	—	—	—	+$10,000
1	—	−$1,000	Interest	−$600	— 600
2	—	− 1,000	Interest	− 600	— 600
3	−$10,000	− 1,000	Interest	− 600	— 10,600

Since the cash flows are exactly the same as if an after-tax
interest rate of 10 percent $(1-t)$ or 6 percent had been used
to obtain them, it is apparent that the internal rate on the
transaction is 6 percent. Therefore, after-tax specific capital
cost here is 6 percent.

If a before-tax capital cost is already known, an adequate
approximation of after-tax cost can be made as:

After-tax specific capital cost = Before-tax cost $(1-t)$.

Note that this formula is directly applicable *only when tax
deductible interest payments are involved.* It does not directly
apply to equity capital sources.

Beyond the general proposition that "only after-tax dollars
matter" there are two particular reasons for always working
with specific capital costs in their after-tax form. First, tax
treatment differs between different sources after taxes have
been netted out. Second, analysis on assets is most rationally
done on an after-tax basis. It is therefore appropriate, when

considering the cost of financing the assets, to have the cost figures on a comparable after-tax basis. Because of these compelling reasons, any reference to specific capital costs in the remainder of the book will presume that the costs are on an after-tax basis unless an exception is explicitly made.

OVERALL CAPITAL COST

The purpose for calculating overall capital cost is to obtain a single figure describing the cost of financing its assets. Overall capital cost is customarily obtained as a weighted arithmetic average of specific costs. Where subscripts from 1 to n are used to denote various financing sources, the formula for overall capital cost is given as:

$$\text{Overall capital cost} = \text{Weight}_1(\text{specific cost}_1)$$
$$+ \text{weight}_2(\text{specific cost}_2) + \ldots \text{weight}_n(\text{specific cost}_n).$$

Weights in turn are determined by the proportions of financing contributed by varying sources. For example,

$$\text{Weight}_1 = \frac{\text{Amount of financing obtained from source}_1}{\text{Total amount of financing used}}$$

or equivalently,

$$\text{Weight}_1 = \frac{\text{Amount of financing obtained from source}_1}{\text{Total assets}}.$$

In determining the weight to be assigned to the shareholder's equity, a market valuation rather than a book valuation procedure is usually regarded as the more correct.

An example will illustrate the obtaining of weighted average capital cost. Roberts Cork Ltd. has the following balance sheet, (Illustration 11-1), with equity adjusted to a market value

ILLUSTRATION 11-1

ROBERTS CORK LTD.
Balance Sheet
(market value on equity basis)

Assets	$10,000,000	Accounts payable	$ 1,000,000
		Notes payable (5%)	1,500,000
		Mortgage (8%)	3,000,000
		Net worth (14%)	4,500,000
		Total	$10,000,000

basis. (Total assets are also adjusted to a market value basis.) Specific capital costs (remember, after tax) are noted with each financing source; accounts payable are presumed to be costless.

Weighted average cost of capital calculation is now shown:

	Weight	Specific Cost	Product
Accounts payable	.10	0	0
Notes payable	.15	.05	.0075
Mortgage	.30	.08	.0240
Net worth	.45	.14	.0630
Sum (overall capital cost)			.0945

The overall capital cost, 9.45 percent, describes Roberts Cork's aggregate cost of obtaining funds.

Some Confusion: Marginal or Average?

As has been noted, one of the uses for the overall cost of capital measure relates to asset acquisition decisions. Overall cost of capital can serve as a guideline for determining the appropriate NPV discount rate or target rate of return in deciding whether to accept or reject marginal assets. The logic of this follows from standard marginal analysis. An asset should be accepted only if its marginal benefit exceeds its marginal cost. The relevant marginal cost here is the marginal cost of financing.

Does this mean that, if the money that is to be used to pay for a new machine is going to be supplied out of the proceeds of a bank note, the specific capital cost on that note should be regarded as the marginal cost of capital for the machine? Or if the machine is to be paid for out of the proceeds of a new issue of common stock, should the specific cost of new equity capital be used? To seek an answer to these questions, suppose that the new machine is expected to provide a marginal internal rate of return of 12 percent after tax, and that the machine is being considered by the company in the preceding example, Roberts Cork Ltd. Following this line of reasoning, the machine would be acceptable if it were to be paid for out of a bank note (specific capital cost, 5 percent) but not acceptable if it were paid for out of money raised with common stock (cost, 14 percent). The problem with the specific cost approach is that these costs represent only parts of whole financing policy.

In fact, the parts of the company's blended financing mixture are closely interrelated. The reason the company can borrow money at 5 percent (after tax) lies in the fact that it maintains an acceptable debt ratio; this ratio requires the use of equity. It is much more appropriate, in making a decision about an individual asset, to think of any asset as being financed with a blended mixture of financing sources rather than by the specific source which, through historical coincidence, happened to generate the particular dollars used to buy the asset.

When one talks about marginal cost of capital, with reference to an asset acceptance decision, the appropriate marginal cost is the change in cost of a blended mixture of capital. This in turn is an average, based on the formula for overall capital cost. And it is a particular type of average—an average *across* the components in a blended mixture.

This cross-section average is different than the average cost concept used in conventional economic analysis. In this analysis, average cost refers to total cost per year (or other time unit) divided by quantity used. In a financial context, the economists' average cost would translate as:

$$\text{Average cost} = \frac{\text{Annual financing cost in dollars}}{\text{Amount of financing used}} .$$

For completeness, the financial version of marginal cost is:

$$\text{Marginal cost} = \frac{\text{Change in annual amount of financing cost in dollars}}{\text{Change in amount of financing used}} .$$

Overall financing cost may be either marginal or average:

$$\text{Average overall financing cost} = \frac{\text{Annual cost of financing from all sources}}{\text{Total assets}} ,$$

$$\text{Marginal overall financing cost} = \frac{\text{Change in annual cost of financing from all sources}}{\text{Change in total assets}} .$$

For financial management the overall cost of capital that is most likely to be used will be marginal in character. This will mean that it will be calculated on the basis of weights determined by the expected blend of financing sources that the company will be using in the near future, and the expected costs of obtaining additional monies from these sources. Current weights, and specific costs currently prevailing at the time planning is taking place, will probably constitute adequate practical estimates of the financial blend and specific costs of various capital sources which will prevail in the near future. Accordingly, an overall capital cost calculation based on current information may be used as the relevant overall cost for use in the company's financial planning.

Overall Capital Cost and Asset Selection

Overall capital cost is an important guideline in the asset selection process. Unless assets collectively provide an internal rate of return equal to the overall cost of capital, the company will fall behind. Put another way, overall cost of capital can be thought of as the discount rate which is used by the marketplace in evaluating a particular company. If internal rates of return on newly acquired assets do not average to overall cost of capital (marginally determined) the result will be that collectively the newly acquired assets will have a negative net present value. This in turn implies that those assets would be detracting from a company objective of wealth maximization.

Because of this important aggregate relationship, overall capital cost serves as a logical guideline for the setting of NPV discount rates or target internal rates of return on marginal assets. This, however, does not imply that overall capital cost will be used as *the* discount rate or target rate on all assets. A set of discount rates or target rates are still appropriate to reflect the risk conditions in the various assets. Overall capital cost provides a guideline for the establishment of this family of individual discount or target rates.

Overall Capital Cost: A Technicality

The determination of overall capital cost by a weighted average method has been subject to some recent criticism. The problem is a mathematical one relating to the propriety of adding or averaging specific capital costs. These capital costs are in the form of time rates which do not average perfectly by conventional arithmetic averaging process.

A simple example will illustrate. Janssen Development Ltd. owes money on two promissory notes of $1,000 each. The notes have the common characteristic that they each call for the annual compounding of interest with payment of all interest and principal at the end of five years. One of the notes is for 6 percent (from a friendly relative) and one is for 14 percent (from a not so friendly finance company). Using weights of .5 for each financing source, overall cost of capital is conventionally calculated as:

$$.5(6\%) + .5(14\%) = 10\%.$$

Now the problem can be converted to dollar amounts based on compounding over a five-year period. Janssen Development Ltd. will have to repay its financing according to this standard future value calculation, on the two notes:

$$P(1+r)^n = F$$
$$\$1,000\,(1.06)^5 = \$1,338.23$$
$$\$1,000\,(1.14)^5 = \$1,925.41$$
$$\text{Total due in 5 years} = \$3,263.64$$

Overall, the two transactions now consist of receiving $2,000 now in exchange for $3,263.64 disbursed five years later. If the overall capital cost of the two transactions is truly 10 percent, a 10 percent NPV calculation should set NPV = 0. This can be checked:

Year	Amount	10 Percent Discount Factor	PV
0	$2,000.00	1.000	$2,000.00
5	−$3,263.64	.621	−$2,026.72
NPV			−$ 26.72

The negative NPV value implies that internal rate on the combined transactions is over 10 percent. In fact, a more precise calculation than possible with the present value tables in this book would identify the true internal rate as 10.3 percent. In other words, the overall cost of capital on the two transactions is not precisely calculated with the conventional weighted average method.

In general the weighted average cost of capital method will produce a small understatement of overall cost of capital. The reader should be aware of this, so that he is not shocked by criticism of the prevailing overall cost of capital calculation. In the opinion of the author the appropriate answer to this criticism is that the error is not a significant one. (The above, 10.3 percent instead of 10 percent, may be regarded as typical of the error that might be introduced.) Since there is no presently available practical way of obtaining a more precise overall cost, the use of the conventional weighted average method seems quite justifiable.

MINIMIZING CAPITAL COSTS

The previous section has concentrated on the measurement and definition of capital costs. This leaves open the question of actually doing something about capital costs. As in the case of other cost items, low capital costs are not only desirable, but often a competitive necessity. Also, as in the case of other costs, rational financing implies an orderly process of funds acquisition; the end is not accomplished by simply "always buying from the cheapest source."

Basically, shopping for financing sources is done subject to not only price but quality ramifications. As discussed in the previous chapter, the financing choice process is coloured by considerations of urgency and risk. Thus, the managerial problem associated with selection of financing sources can be described as minimizing costs, subject to maintaining an acceptable liquidity and risk posture.

Orderly capital cost minimization can be thought of in three stages: (1) minimizing weighted average capital cost within three subcategories—current liabilities, fixed liabilities, and equity; (2) maintaining a cost-minimizing blend of the categories; and (3) moderating this blend of the categories to control for urgency and risk.

Cost Minimization within Categories

To consider cost minimization within a financing category, such as current liabilities, one can conceptualize the choice problem by recalling earlier discussion on asset selection. The relevant portion of the discussion relates to capital rationing, using the rate of return method. In that situation, it is assumed that only a given amount of funds are available for purchase of assets. Available asset alternatives are than ranked by rate of return, and selection proceeds from the highest ranking asset downward to successively lower ranking ones, until the available funds are exhausted.

Cost of financing from various individual capital sources is measured by a rate of return method, specific capital cost. One can therefore think of ranking various financing sources within a category, from the source with the lowest cost to the sources with successively higher costs. One could then go down the list until reaching a total dollar amount equal to the amount funds to be raised in that particular category.

An example can again illustrate. Janssen Development Ltd. tentatively plans to arrange its financing in this manner:

		Percent
Current liabilities	$ 400,000	31%
Fixed liabilities	300,000	23
Equity	600,000	46
Total	$1,300,000	100%

This initial tentative specification of the various financing categories to be used is essential in the planning process, because money available within one category may be conditional upon the relationship between the various categories. To illustrate, a bank might be willing to lend money to Janssen Development with the above 54 percent debt ratio; if that debt ratio was 84 percent, the bank might shun Janssen like the plague.

Suppose Janssen now surveys its available financing alternatives, and finds the following:

1. In its total business operations, it makes purchases of about $80,000 per month. On these purchases, 30-day credit is obtainable with no charge; therefore Janssen can count on one-month purchases or $80,000, being available at no cost.

2. Janssen has discussed the possibility of obtaining additional credit from its suppliers. This credit arrangement would consist of the supplier accepting 60-day promissory notes from Janssen at the expiry of the 30-day free credit period. The interest rate on these notes is 18 percent; Janssen uses a 40 percent marginal tax rate which makes after-tax specific capital cost 10.8 percent.

3. Janssen's banker has told the company that he is prepared to make $200,000 credit available, in the form of notes payable at 12 percent, or 7.2 after tax.

4. The aunt of Janssen Development's principal stockholder has indicated that she would be willing to lend the company $30,000 at 8 percent, or 4.8 percent after tax.

Janssen Development Ltd. can now set forth the following schedule, with these financing sources ranked in ascending order of specific capital cost:

JANSSEN DEVELOPMENT LTD.
Current Liability Sources

	Cost (percent)	Amount	Cumulative Amount
Trade credit (accounts payable)	0	$ 80,000	$ 80,000
Loan from relative	4.8%	30,000	110,000
Bank loan	7.2	200,000	310,000
Trade credit (notes payable)	10.8	160,000	470,000

Accordingly, Janssen Development would reach a cost-minimizing solution within the current liabilities category with the following arrangement:

1. Use all credit available from accounts payable, helpful aunt, and banker.

2. Use $90,000 in notes payable to the supplier.

The same technique, comparative shopping on the basis of specific capital costs, is directly extensible to a choice among longer term liabilities. In principle, the technique also extends to a choice within the equity category. The results of the comparative shopping can be summarized with a weighted average. For Janssen Development's current liabilities, that weighted average is calculated as:

JANSSEN DEVELOPMENT LTD.
Calculation of Weighted Average Current Liability Cost

	Specific Cost (percent)	Weight	Cost X Weight (percent)
Trade credit			
(accounts payable)	0%	$ 80,000/400,000 or .200	0%
Loan from relative	4.8	30,000/400,000 or .075	0.36
Bank loan	7.2	200,000/400,000 or .500	3.60
Trade credit			
(notes payable)	10.8	90,000/400,000 or .225	2.43
Weighted average . . .			5.79%

The cost of financing $400,000 through current liabilities will be a little less than 6 percent after tax.

There is likely to be a regular pattern in these specific cost averages within various source categories. Creditors are most willing to extend credit on the basis of short-term liabilities, because of their liquidity, and as a result costs here tend to be lower. Longer term liabilities, which offer less liquidity to creditors, are usually a somewhat higher cost source of funds. Equity capital, where capital suppliers accept higher risk, will normally have a substantially higher specific cost than debt.

Relationships between Financing Sources

In the previous chapter an important consequence of the relationship between financing source categories was discussed. This relationship affects liquidity ratios and the debt ratio. Current liabilities is the denominator in both of the liquidity ratios, so extensive use of current liability financing will increase the liquidity ratios and signal possible problems in a company's short-term, bill-paying ability. Extensive use of both current and fixed liabilities, or conversely the use of little equity, will produce a high debt ratio and signal a potential for insolvency.

Thus, the financing sources that offer funds at the lowest cost, current liabilities, has the most adverse effect on the company's financial condition, tending to weaken its liquidity ratios and to increase its debt ratio. Longer term liabilities are likely to cost a little more, but apply pressure only on the debt ratio. The use of relatively high-cost equity imposes no liquidity strain and improves the debt ratio.

The effect of the relationship between financing categories on the financial condition of the company can lead to a paradoxical situation. It is possible that a company can lower its overall capital cost by reducing its reliance on a low specific cost financing category and increasing its use of a high specific cost category. This paradox is explained by a feedback from company's financial condition to its cost of raising money.

Suppose a company is using a lot of debt, and decides to issue some additional common stock, using the proceeds to repay some of its debt. The result of this operation may have two effects, beyond the obvious switching from a low specific cost source to a high specific cost source. First, creditors may observe the company's lower debt ratio and interpret it as an indication that the company is less likely to default on obligations to creditors. These creditors perceive themselves as taking less risk, as a result may be willing (or forced by competition) to provide credit to the company on more favourable terms. Second, shareholders considering purchase of the company's common stock also note the improvement in the company's financial condition. There is now less chance that the shareholders' interest in the company will be "wiped out" through bankruptcy. The result is that the full story of the company's financial manoeuvre is described as the simultaneous occurrence of two events:

1. Increased use of a higher specific cost source of funds, equity, and decreased use of a lower cost source, debt.

2. Because of the relative attractiveness of the new debt ratio to both creditors and shareholders, the cost of capital on both equity and debt decline.

An example will illustrate. The Janssen company was considering a balance sheet with a 54 percent debt ratio. Suppose that its overall capital cost, using that balance sheet, was given as follows:

JANSSEN DEVELOPMENT LTD.
Overall Cost of Capital

	Category Cost (percent)	Explanation	Weight	Cost X Weight (percent)
Current liabilities	5.8%	From previous calculation	.31	1.80%
Fixed liabilities	7.0	Assumed	.23	1.61
Equity	12.0	Assumed	.46	5.52
Overall cost				8.93%

Thus, overall capital cost was initially about 9 percent.

Now Janssen Development considers an alternative financing arrangement. It decides to reduce its reliance on fixed liabilities by $100,000 and also on current liabilities by $100,000. This alters the debt ratio from an original $700,000/$1,300,000 or 54 percent, to $500,000/$1,300,000 or 38 percent, and also reduces the urgency of the debt. These changes are expected to induce the following effects on costs:

1. The bank, viewing the company's different financial condition, will lend at 11 percent instead of 12 percent. With only $300,000 in current liability financing needed, the company does not need to rely on notes payable to creditors for any funds. The result is the following revision in the weighted average cost of current liabilities:

	Specific Cost (percent)	Amount	Weight	Cost X Weight (percent)
Trade credit (accounts payable)	0%	$ 80,000	.27	0.00%
Loan from relative	4.8	30,000	.10	.48
Bank loan	6.6	190,000	.63	4.16
				4.64%

2. With only $200,000 of credit needed from fixed liabilities, all of this credit requirement can be handled with a mortgage loan at a rate of 10.5 percent or 6.3 percent after tax.

3. The reduced possibility of bankruptcy reduces cost of equity capital to 11 percent after tax.

A new calculation of weighted average cost of capital can be made for Janssen.

JANSSEN DEVELOPMENT LTD.
Overall Capital Cost

	Category Cost (percent)	Weight	Cost × Weight (percent)
Current liabilities	4.64%	300,000/1,300,000 or .23	1.07%
Fixed liabilities	6.30	200,000/1,300,000 or .15	0.95
Equity	11.00	800,000/1,300,000 or .62	6.82
			8.84%

It is apparent that Janssen Development Ltd. has improved its financial condition through the use of additional equity and at the same time lowered its overall capital cost.

To summarize, specific capital costs are dependent upon the financial condition of the company. The financial condition in turn is affected by the categories of financing sources used by the company. This turns the issue of policy regarding the choice of financing sources into a problem of a simultaneous character. There is no escaping the fact that the choice between financing categories is affected by capital cost within each of the categories, and that capital cost within each of the categories is affected by the relationship between the categories.

Choosing among Financing Categories

The simultaneous aspect of the financing problem does not make that problem insurmountable; it does make the analysis more laborious than it would be if the interrelationship between category choices and category costs did not exist. Basically, the approach required for a practical solution to the problem involves making a series of estimates based on various possible financing patterns. In the Janssen Development example two possible financing schemes were analyzed. In reality a company might want to consider many more. That consideration will involve projecting a possible right-hand side for its balance sheet, and then attempting to estimate costs, *given* this particular balance sheet. The formulation of the required estimates could involve consultation with financial institutions that would be involved in providing financing. A variety of possible balance sheets may be compared by calculating each's estimated overall capital cost.

FINANCING POLICY RECONSIDERED

There is a substantial amount of interrelationship between this chapter and the preceding one. It is worthwhile to review the way the two chapters tie together in describing an approach toward company financing policy. First, a company needs to identify its potential needs for funds and to consider where these funds might come from. It begins this identification with the development of the projected sources and applications of funds statement. It then can explore various alternative methods of meeting these requirements by considering different patterns of potential financing sources. Differing patterns imply different financial conditions for the company, and probably different patterns of overall cost.

SUMMARY

Specific capital cost refers to the cost of obtaining financing from a particular source. Overall capital cost describes the average cost of financing from all sources. Specific cost is determined by an internal rate of return calculation, subject to tax adjustment. Overall cost is calculated as a weighted average of specific costs.

Overall capital cost may be calculated on a marginal basis to identify the change in cost associated with changing the company's scale of asset ownership.

Capital costs are an important component in establishing discount rates or target rates for asset selection decisions; marginal versions are most appropriate.

Financing sources may be grouped in categories—current liabilities, fixed liabilities, and equity. Cost minimization can be thought of in two stages. First, least cost solutions are

effected within categories through a process of bargain hunting. Second, overall capital cost can then be controlled by
altering the relative reliance on the various categories. This
balancing between source categories is a complex process because of interrelationship between costs within categories and
relative reliance on that category. For example, increased reliance on debt is likely to raise both debt costs and equity costs.
At the same time, since debt costs are likely to be lower than
equity costs, increased reliance on debt exerts a diminishing
effect on the overall cost calculation through a change in the
weights with which this average is calculated.

QUESTIONS AND PROBLEMS

1. A company is offered a loan of $1 million repayable in two
   annual installments of $500,000 each, with interest payable
   annually at 16 percent. The company's marginal tax rate is
   45 percent.
   a. Identify specific capital cost, before and after tax, through
      internal rate identification.
   b. Assume that the above loan is not available but the com-
      pany's treasurer believes that money can be obtained on
      those terms if an adequate effort is made. Cost of seeking
      out the money is estimated at $40,000, tax deductible. On
      this assumption, revise the previous calculation of after-tax
      specific capital cost.

2. A company's balance sheet has this right-hand side:

Liabilities	$ 8,000,000
Equity	15,000,000
Total	$23,000,000

   A specific capital cost of 8 percent, after tax, is estimated for
   debt; the corresponding figure for equity is 15 percent. Calculate overall capital cost.

3. The above company considers an expansion increasing its total
   assets to $40 million. The company believes that its current
   financing policy has been optimal. It nevertheless decides that
   current capital market conditions make it advantageous to
   finance its expansion entirely with debt. The effect of this will be
   to increase the company's cost of debt to 9 percent and its cost

of equity to 17 percent. Calculate overall capital cost after expansion has taken place.

4. In the above problem calculate the marginal capital cost of the expansion. What is the relevance of this figure upon the decision to undertake the expansion?

5. Explain why the specific cost of both debt and equity is expected to decline as the debt ratio declines. Why doesn't this simultaneous decline always lead to lower overall capital cost?

6. What effect does the company's choice of financing sources have on its overall liquidity posture?

7. A company has a choice of satisfying its cash needs from three sources:
   a. Paying its bills less promptly, thus allowing its accounts receivable position and accounts payable position to enlarge.
   b. Borrowing from a trust company; this arrangement will require placing a mortgage on the company's plan.
   c. An individual investor has offered to lend the company half of the required money on a relatively informal basis, with liberal repayment terms. His offer of the loan is conditional upon his being able to supply the remaining half of the money as an equity participant.
   Discuss the likely advantages and disadvantages of procuring the money from each of these sources.

RELATED READINGS

Arditti, F. D. "The Weighted Average Cost of Capital: Some Questions on Its Definition, Interpretation and Use." *Journal of Finance*, September 1973.

Barges, A. *The Effect of Capital Structure on the Cost of Capital.* Englewood Cliffs, N.J.: Prentice-Hall, 1963.

Brennan, M. "A New Look at Weighted Average Cost of Capital." *Journal of Business Finance*, Spring 1973.

Lewellen, W. *The Cost of Capital.* Belmont, Calif.: Wadsworth Publishing, 1969.

Malkiel, B. *The Debt-Equity Combination of the Firm and the Cost of Capital: An Introductory Analysis.* New York: General Learning Press, 1971.

Solomon, E. "Measuring a Company's Cost of Capital." *Journal of Business*, October 1955.

12

RAISING MONEY THROUGH SHORT-TERM DEBT

As a rough generalization, Canadian companies derive financing equal to about one fourth of their assets from the use of short-term credit. One of the advantages of short-term credit has been discussed. Because of its attractiveness from the creditor's point of view, particularly in the matter of liquidity, it tends to be a relatively low-cost source of money. One of its disadvantages has also been considered; that same liquidity (urgency) adversely affects the overall liquidity of the debtor company.

Short-term credit takes two principal forms—accounts payable and bank loans. In addition to its tendency toward low cost, this credit has other features which make it attractive to many companies. A discussion of these follows.

MOTIVES FOR USING SHORT-TERM CREDIT

Convenience

Obtaining short-term credit is usually easy and uncomplicated, particularly if it is not used excessively. Trade credit, or accounts payables extended by suppliers of goods that the company purchases, is often available on a virtually spontane-ous basis. When a purchase is negotiated, credit is supplied as part of the purchase. A credit application of some type is ini-tially required but that usually poses little difficulty. The sales-man of the supplier company will often help in completing the application.

Bank credit, too, is broadly accessible. Branches of chartered banks are available virtually everywhere in the country. Fur-thermore, these banks have increasingly begun to regard mar-keting as one of their important functions. They realize that their business is the sale of credit, and accordingly impose as few formalities as possible in the granting of credit. Bank per-sonnel are trained to solicit necessary credit information quickly, and to make funds available promptly. Often money is made available on the basis of an initial interview; more time and deliberation may be required in the case of large loans, or in the case of companies whose creditworthiness is subject to question.

This ease of obtaining credit is in contrast with most other sources of funds that the company may employ. Longer term borrowing and the issuance of common shares typically require much more time and formality. For smaller companies, short-term money may in fact sometimes be too convenient with the result that the company accepts the short-term credit and neglects the making of longer term financial arrangements. This in turn may result in an undesirable strain on the com-pany's liquidity or solvency.

Seasonal Financing

Short-term credit is especially attractive to the firm with peak financing requirements. The reader may recall an ex-ample from Chapter 6 where a snowmobile manufacturer was required to accumulate substantial amounts of seasonal inven-tory if it was to take full advantage of a level production process. Both seasonal inventory accumulation and seasonal re-ceivable accumulation (resulting from high Christmas rush sales, for example) are commonplace.

There are two approaches to the handling of seasonal requirements. One is to finance these requirements permanently, and then make short-term investments with excess funds during the time of the year when they are not needed. The second is to rely on temporary credit during the time of peak need.

Particularly in the case of the growing firm, where the firm's asset acquisitions may have a tendency to outpace its ability to finance them, the idea of using permanent financing for short-term requirements is not very appealing. This lack of appeal is amplified by the fact that the cost of the long-term financing is likely to be greater than that of short-term financing, and much greater than the rate of return available to the company on temporary investments.

Trade credit tends to fill some seasonal credit requirements in a spontaneous way. The company's purchasing activity is likely to be high during the time of year that it is accumulating inventory and/or receivables; a high volume of purchasing activity usually means a high volume of trade credit if credit is being offered by suppliers. In other words part of the burden of carrying the abnormally high inventory or receivables is shifted back to suppliers.

Short-Term Financing for Extraordinary Items

We have already looked at various ways in which a company can meet extraordinary liquidity requirements. It can accumulate cash and near-cash reserves for this purpose, and it can make use of other liquid components of its asset collection by disposing of other assets, if need be.

The company can also look to the right-hand side of its balance sheet for possible help in meeting unexpected payment requirements or taking advantage of surprise opportunities. It may do this because it lacks liquid reserves or other readily disposable assets; or it may rely on short-term financing with the idea of preserving its liquid assets for the possibility of even more extraordinary cash requirements in the future.

The potential use of current liabilities as a source of liquidity during extraordinary circumstances constitutes an argument for moderating their use during "normal" circumstances. If a company regularly maintains a high current liabilities position, with resulting elevation of its liquidity ratios, such a company may be unable to secure additional short-term credit when that credit is really needed.

The argument for maintaining some unused short-term borrowing capacity is quite similar to the argument for maintaining some cash and near-cash reserves. In both cases, an act of current abstinence is required. The yield on cash reserves usually is much less than the rate of return directly available on other assets. Similarly, more use of long-term debt and equity financing instead of regular financing with current liabilities could result in a higher overall cost of capital.

In other words, irrespective of which side of the balance sheet one looks at, liquidity is not available as a free good. But in a longer sighted view, liquidity may be profit-enhancing.

Interim Financing

Short-term bank borrowing is sometimes used as a source of temporary funds while the company is waiting for the arrangement of more permanent financing. For example, a company constructing a building might use short-term bank borrowing for initial phases of its construction; after construction had sufficiently progressed it might arrange a long-term loan to cover most of the cost of the building. It would then use part of the proceeds from this loan to repay the banker who had supplied the original temporary assistance.

As another example, a company might wish to undertake major expansion. Suppose it had decided that it was relying too heavily on debt financing, and that, therefore, most of the money for the expansion should come from the sale of a new issue of common stock. However, the sale of the stock issue might take a number of months. A short-term loan could fill this financing gap and allow the company to proceed immediately with its acquisition; credit of this type is sometimes called *turnaround money*.

Security Arrangements on Short-Term Credit

It is important to distinguish between a general creditor and a creditor with special rights. If a company were to have difficulty meeting its obligations, so that there was some question about the manner in which its assets were to be divided up among creditors who had claims against them, the question of special rights of creditors would arise. A creditor may obtain special rights to assets through a variety of legal arrangements. When the creditor has arranged a special claim on an asset, this claim is said to be *secured*. The asset used to secure the credit agreement is sometimes said to be *pledged* and described as *collateral* or *security*. Without special rights, someone extending trade credit is an *unsecured creditor*, or a *general creditor*. Security arrangements will be discussed in more detail in connection with individual types of credit.

TRADE CREDIT

What is a payable to one firm is a receivable to another, so considerable discussion of trade credit has already taken place in Chapter 7 on receivables. Particularly, that chapter discusses some of the common credit arrangements between supplier and customer, and the economic rationale for the existence of this type of credit arrangement. This section will discuss two other aspects of trade credit that seem particularly germane from the viewpoint of the credit user—contractual arrangements and cost.

The Nature of the Credit Contract

The most common security arrangement on trade credit is to have no security at all. When trade credit is extended without security, it is most likely extended in the form of an *open-book account* or *open account*. This is an informal arrangement where a supplier provides goods for his customer with an understanding that they will be paid for according to prespecified terms of payment. No special document is prepared beyond the *invoice*, a simple statement provided by the supplier which describes the goods supplied and indicates the amount and date of required payment.

There are a number of reasons why open-book credit is so widely used. First, if a customer is financially strong, a security arrangement may be redundant; it only has value in situations where default is a realistic possibility. Second, security arrangements require extra complication and cost. Whether borne by the supplier or the customer, these costs may place the supplier at a competitive disadvantage. Third, the expression of trust implicit in open-book credit may help the supplier in making sales.

The informality of trade credit should not obscure its character as a debt. While there are times when evidence of the liability may be difficult to establish, open-book credit, although based on unwritten agreement, provides the basis for a lawsuit if its repayment conditions are unfulfilled. Even when the supplier does not sue, excessive laxity in discharge of open-book credit can lead not only to curtailment of credit by the neglected supplier, but may also impair the ability of the borrower to obtain trade and other credit elsewhere.

The unsecured promissory note is another form of credit arrangement similar to open-book credit. This arrangement is used much less frequently, is more formal, and is more likely to be used when credit is extended for a period of several months or longer. It is a written promise to pay and usually provides for payment of interest on the amount owing.

A variety of other contractual arrangements are also used. Some examples of more formal practices were presented in the chapter on accounts receivables (Chapter 7); several additional arrangements are briefly described in the following paragraphs. The use of a formal contract may not seem as attractive from the point of view of the debtor company. However, there are situations where such formality is a well-established part of industry trade practice, and there are other situations where a company's individual financial circumstances do not permit it to obtain credit without rather rigid contractual conditions.

Trade credit arrangements are sometimes accomplished with the use of drafts and acceptances. A *draft* is an order to pay; the common bank cheque is a form of draft ordering the bank to make payment to the payee of the cheque. Drafts calling for immediate payment are called *sight drafts* and those which are ordered for payment at some future date are called *time drafts*. For example, Company X, a supplier, draws a time draft on

Company Y before releasing goods. Company Y then formally agrees to pay the amount ordered by *accepting* the draft; at that point the time draft becomes an *acceptance*.

A supplier may ship goods to a customer accompanied by a sight or a time draft. If a sight draft accompanies the goods, the supplier has extended credit only during the time that the goods were in transit and the customer must pay for the goods when he receives them. If the goods are accompanied by a time draft, the customer must accept the draft before he receives the goods. To add an incentive for prompt payment, the acceptance is normally payable at the customer's bank (where payment delay beyond the maturity date will reflect upon his credit standing with his own banker).

Cost of Trade Credit

A great deal of trade credit is obtainable without additional cost, as part of the purchase transaction with the supplier. If there is no incentive for *not* using the credit, it can be regarded as free for purposes of making financing decisions. On the other hand, if there is such an incentive, credit has an implicit cost even though an explicit interest rate is not specified.

There are two types of incentives which may be available in exchange for not using credit. If equivalent goods and services can be obtained from another supplier on a cash basis at a lower price, there is an implicit discount when credit is not used.

An example will illustrate this first type of implicit credit cost. Tyndall Chemicals Ltd. has customarily purchased a particular coal-tar derivative at $100 per barrell from a Canadian supplier, on 60-day terms. These terms, sometimes abbreviated $n/60$ or net/60 mean that the supplier extends open account credit subject to payment at the end of 60 days after the date of the invoice. An aggressive British exporter, Coal Hoskins Ltd., offers to sell Tyndall the equivalent product for $95 per barrel on a cash basis. Tyndall's Canadian supplier is unwilling to alter its price in the face of this competition.

Tyndall, satisfied that the product and all other aspects of the business relationship offered by the British firm are comparable to that of its former Canadian supplier, can now make a straightforward comparison:

$$\$95 \text{ now, or } \$100, 60 \text{ days later.}$$

It is possible to calculate an internal rate on the basis of this information. However, since internal rates are normally calculated with tables, and since most tables are not sufficiently "fine-tuned" for such short-term problems, a short-cut method is commonly employed. This method is given as:

$$\text{Estimated specific capital cost} = \frac{\text{Percentage of cash discount}}{\text{Fraction of year credit extended}}.$$

In the above example, Coal Hoskins is offering a 5 percent discount relative to Tyndall's previous supplier. In return for this discount Tyndall must give up 60 days' credit, or about one sixth of a year. Thus this common-sense formula indicates:

$$\text{Estimated specific capital cost} = \frac{5\%}{1/6} = 30\%.$$

The formula can be verified by extending the example. Suppose that Tyndall Chemical buys 1,000 barrels of coal-oil derivative each month. Using 60-day credit, its normal accounts payable on the coal-oil derivative trade credit will be $200,000. If it gives up the use of this trade credit it will save $5,000 on its purchases every month, for a total of $60,000 per year. Since giving up this $60,000 per year is the consequence of obtaining the $200,000 trade credit, the estimate of a 30 percent annual cost of capital is confirmed.

Sometimes the circumstances of the Tyndall example are reversed. If a company finds itself in difficult financial circumstances, it may be unable to pay cash for purchases. It may then turn to another supplier who offers more generous credit, but who also charges a higher price for his merchandise.

A supplier may also make the use of credit discretionary, with an incentive for not using it by providing a cash discount. Sometimes, the cash discount is just that, and at other times a cash discount is given for prompt, though not immediate payment. For example, with a sale on term of 2/10; n/30, a customer is allowed a 2 percent discount if he pays for the goods within 10 days, although he has the option of using 30-day credit if he wishes. Again, the reward for prompt payment implies absence of reward for delayed payment, or a capital cost. With terms of 2/10; $n/30$, a discount must be given up if the customer wishes to obtain an additional 20 days of credit. (The bill must be paid in 30 days; the discount is available if payment takes place within 10 days.) The estimating formula given above can be employed again:

$$\text{Estimated specific capital cost} = \frac{2\%}{20/365} = 36.5\%.$$

For easier calculation, a 360-day year is frequently used; this would change the estimate to 36 percent.

Terms of Trade Credit

The reader has already sampled some abbreviated expressions of credit terms above: $n/60$ and 2/10; $n/30$. These probably represent the most common usage, with the maturity of the credit expressed as the number of days and with a cash discount allowable within a specified number of days. However, there are quite a number of other expressions also used in practice, including some that indicate that no credit will be extended.

CBD, cash before delivery, and COD, cash on delivery, are self-explanatory. Sometimes terms may be expressed in an end-of-month dating. For example 2/10, E.O.M.; $n/30$ allows a 2 percent discount if goods are paid for within ten days after the end of the month in which they are purchased. In other words goods bought on October 5 would be subject to a cash discount if paid before November 10, and would be due November 30. (Sometimes the expression prox. is substituted for E.O.M.)

Credit terms may occasionally be tailored to the seasonal character of a customer's business. For example, a prairie farmer might be able to buy agricultural chemicals during the winter with credit terms expressed as if the purchase had taken place on April 1. These terms encourage a farmer to accept delivery on his chemicals in advance of his need for them, thus helping both the farmer and the supplier to avoid problems of a "spring rush." An abbreviation for this arrangement could be 2/10; $n/30$ April 1, indicating that although the farmer may have received his chemicals during December, his sale will be treated for trade credit purposes *as if* it had taken place on April 1. He can receive a discount by paying before April 10, with his bill due on April 30.

Floor Plan Financing

A form of credit, used most notably for financing the inventories of retail automobile dealers, is referred to as *floor plan* credit. Under this arrangement, an automobile manufacturer or other financing source extends credit for the purchase of inventory items, and holds ownership of the items until sold. From the purchaser's viewpoint this amounts to a form of consignment sale.

BANK CREDIT

Before we consider the details relating to the use of bank credit, a review problem is in order. Suppose that a company's accounts revealed the following right-hand side on its balance sheet:

Account	Proportion of Total Asset (percent)
Short-term liabilities, the majority of which are payable on demand.	65%
Longer term liabilities (nearly all under 5 years).	30
Net worth	5

At first glance this looks like a desperate situation. The debt ratio is 95 percent, and current liabilities impose an awesome liquidity situation.

But suppose the company was told that it had to live with such a financial structure. What characteristics would the company's assets have to assume if it was to have a fighting chance of survival. First, they would have to be extremely safe since the net worth position is too small to allow a cushion for significant shrinkage in asset value. Second, the assets would have to be extremely liquid to compensate for the urgency of the company's liabilities.

Surprisingly, balance sheets with right-hand sides of the type shown above are standard in one major Canadian industry, an industry which includes some of the country's most prestigious and financially "solid" firms. These businesses are the Canadian chartered banks. Bank lending policies are a direct extension of the character of the bank's own liabilities. The banks must maintain safety and liquidity in their asset collections; they are thus compelled to insist on extending comparatively safe and short-lived credit.

Canadian banks have found their competitive niche as merchants of liquid credit. They obtain funds from depositors on either a demand basis or short-term time deposits; these monies are obtained by the bank at low- or no-interest cost, reflecting the liquidity the bank offers its creditors (depositors). Banks maintain some of these funds in cash (partly because of reserve requirements imposed by the Bank of Canada) and part of the funds in securities. They lend part of them to businesses and consumers at comparative low specific capital cost on urgent repayment terms. While both the banks' self-imposed rules, and those imposed by government regulation do not absolutely restrict banks from making risky or long-term loans, these are the exceptions. The preponderance of Canadian bank lending is credit extended for a short time under fairly safe conditions.

As international comparison is of interest here, particularly since larger Canadian companies frequently deal with foreign banks. Canadian banking at first glance appears much different than banking in the United States. Canada has only a few large chartered banks all of which are big, strong institutions by international standards. Practice in the United States looks different, for there banking is not done only by giant banking companies, but also by myriads of small, independently owned banks. However, this comparison is becoming increasingly illusory, since large U.S. banks with multiple branches much like their Canadian counterparts, now account for the most of the dollar volume of U.S. lending activity.

North American banking practice from the viewpoint of the borrowing businessman is remarkably homogeneous. This can be attributed in large part to the fact that North American banks have in general evolved with balance sheets of the type shown above. North American banks are also restrained by legislation from conducting as venturesome banking practices as their European and Japanese counterparts. These banks outside North America frequently become co-owners of nonfinancial companies, a practice extremely rare in North American banking. In turn, the banks outside of North America are likely to use more equity financing themselves, so they do not need to be as insistent upon safety and liquidity in their loans.

Banking Regulation

Canadian banking practice is subject to detailed governmental regulation in the Bank Act. This act, extensively revised in 1967, specifies extensive rules for the conduct of banking. In addition, the Bank of Canada exercises considerable ongoing control over banking policies. Banking has been regarded as an industry in which the public interest is extremely great; it is widely believed that an unregulated banking system will lead to national economic instability. Furthermore, the government has felt a responsibility to protect the financial positions of banks in order to protect the interests of bank depositors. (Since revisions of the Bank Act take place every decade, new, though probably not drastically changed, banking legislation will be enacted in 1977).

The 1967 revision of the Bank Act added one important element of administrative freedom for banks. In contrast with previous usage no interest rate ceilings are now imposed upon bank loans, though banks are required to disclose the actual interest rate they are charging on money supplied (an internal rate calculation). This freedom to set interest rates allows banks to accept moderate amounts of risk and to charge extra interest to compensate for possible bad debt losses.

(An acceptance of some possibility of bad debt loss with individual customers does not necessarily imply the introduction of much risk into the bank's overall asset collection; recall the discussion about risk and receivables in Chapter 8.)

Cost of Bank Credit

Lending charges of banks change frequently and are reflective of national and international financial conditions. As an example, during periods when retail and wholesale prices are increasing rapidly, businesses and consumers are eager to borrow and "buy now because tomorrow prices will be higher." At the same time depositors are less likely to want to hold their wealth in the form of deposit balances because of the shrinking purchasing power of cash. The result of this interaction of supply and demand conditions is that banks must pay higher interest rates to attract deposits, and are able to charge higher rates on the loans they make.

The most widely used indicator of interest rates that a bank is currently charging is the rate the bank charges to its most favoured loan customers, the *prime rate*. This rate is normally extended to large businesses of well-established credit reputation on relatively short-term borrowing.

The prime rate serves as a basis for other bank rates. For example, a customer who borrows on a smaller scale (and whose loans is hence less profitable to the bank because of fixed cost components in the bank's relationship with its customers) may be charged a rate of 1 percent above prime. A less well-established business or individual could be charged 2 percent or more above prime. Similarly, a large company which would be able to borrow at the prime rate on a short-term basis might be charged 1 percent or more above prime if it borrowed on a longer term basis (usually, over a year).

Demand Notes

The contractual arrangement between a banker and its borrower is usually a promissory note payable on demand. In practice this does not mean that the notes are subject to capricious demand for payment by banks; usually the banker and the borrowing company have at least a general agreement about when repayment is going to take place. However, the use of the demand note does provide the bank with legal power to periodically change the conditions of the lending relationship. This power is used to make adjustments in the interest rate on the note.

For example, at a time when a 10 percent prime rate was in effect, a customer might negotiate a loan with a bank at 11.5 percent, 1.5 percent above prime. Suppose two months later, the prime rate charged by this bank rises to 10.5 percent. The bank would then notify its customer that the rate on his loan was increased to 12 percent, maintaining the 1.5 percent premium over prime. Suppose that further down the road the prime rate were to fall to 9.75 percent; in that case the customer would again be advised of a change, that his interest rate was now 11.25 percent.

There are pros and cons to this flexible interest rate implicit in the demand note. To be sure, the borrowing businessman is never quite sure of what the actual interest on his note is going to be. On the other hand, the flexibility does tend to keep his costs competitive. The businessman who borrows at a prime rate of 10 percent knows that, if the prime rate should later drop to 7 percent; he will obtain funds on as favourable a basis as other comparable companies who are currently negotiating loans. Another less apparent advantage of the flexible rate arrangement is that this shifting of risk of changing capital market conditions back to the borrower probably enables banks to offer loans at lower rates than they would otherwise be able to.

Legally a bank can insist on payment on a demand note at any time. There are two reasons why banks will exercise that power to *call* a demand note with great care. First, the bank is in the business of making loans, and is reluctant to discontinue a business relationship with a customer. Second, excessive use of the right to call loans can give the bank a harsh reputation. Usually that would be just opposite to the image that the bank is trying to maintain with its marketing endeavours.

Term Loans and Installment Loans

While demand loans are very common, banks undertake other types of lending agreements. Some loans, called term loans, are negotiated for a definite period of time, and have a predetermined interest rate which is not subject to change. Others, particularly at the consumer and small business level, are negotiated on an installment basis, with a specified series of payments to discharge the loan. Installment loans are also negotiated on the basis of a fixed interest rate.

Term and installment loans are more frequently used when a

bank is extending credit to a business for a protracted period of time. A description of lending policies for longer periods will be deferred until the following chapter. Though banks have a strong preference for liquidity in their assets, profit possibilities on longer term lending encourage them to undertake this activity in a controlled way.

Credit Cost Disclosure

The Bank Act requires that banks disclose the true interest rate on loans that they make; this is often called a *truth-in-lending* provision. The attractiveness of this requirement for uniform use of the internal rate method of interest calculation is illustrated by showing some alternate modes for reckoning interest. At best, a variety of methods would make comparative shopping more difficult. At worst, variations of interest rate determinations may be vehicles for misrepresentation.

The add-on method has been used frequently. With this method, if a consumer was financing a car over a three-year period, interest might be expressed as 7 percent add-on. If the car was to be paid for in equal installments over three years, three-years interest on the full amount financed would be added onto the amount of the loan. If the loan was for $1,000 the amount of this loan would make the amount to be repaid $1,000 + $1,000(7\%) \ (3) = $1,210. If the loan was to be repaid in monthly installments, the installments would then be calculated by dividing by the number of installments on the above loan with 36 installments. Monthly payments would be $1,210/36 = $33.61 per month.

In contrast, internal rate identification requires finding an interest rate which will set NPV of all these cash flows—an original $1,000 proceeds followed by a $33.61 payment every month for 36 months—equal to zero. An interest rate of slightly over 1 percent a month is identified with this calculation: over 12 percent per year in contrast to the stated 7 percent based on add-on computation.

The second example involves the use of a compensating balance. A *compensating balance* is a minimum demand deposit balance required by a bank in conjunction with a loan agreement. The effect of the compensating balance requirement is for the left hand to take away part of what the right hand has given. Suppose a company negotiated a loan with an interest rate of 9 percent, accompanied by a 20 percent compensating balance requirement. In the absence of a disclosure requirement, nothing further would be said about the interest rate beyond the nominal rate of 9 percent. In fact, however, the borrower would receive as net proceeds from his loan only 80 percent of every dollar on which interest was being charged; the remaining 20 percent would stay in the bank as the compensating deposit. The effect of this is to make the actual interest rate $0.09/0.8 = 11.25\%$.

This can be illustrated by assuming that a company wishes to buy some industrial equipment costing $100,000. With a 20 percent balance requirement, the company must actually borrow $125,000 and leave 20 percent of this, $25,000, on deposit with its bank if it is to have $100,000 available for machine purchase. At 9 percent, the annual interest charged on the loan will be $0.09 \times \$125,000 = \$11,250$, or 11.25% on the money actually being received by the company.

A compensating balance may be used as a device for circumventing laws setting interest rate ceilings, if the ceiling is based on the nominal rate charged and ignores the compensating balance requirement. This could enable the bank and its customer to negotiate mutually acceptable transactions at a true interest rate above the legal ceiling. Since the 1967 revision of the Bank Act, which removed rate ceilings, there is little incentive for the use of the compensating balance requirements in Canada. Where it is used, it must be made an explicit part of the loan contract, and the actual, rather than nominal, interest rate must be dislosed.

One discrepancy still exists between stated bank interest rates and the customary method of identifying specific capital cost. The difference is small but still material. It arises out of the common bank practice of quoting interest as an annual charge and then collecting interest by monthly deductions on the borrower's current account. A given annual interest charge, payable in monthly installments, is not equivalent for purposes of financial analysis to the same interest charge being paid at the end of the year.

Consider an example to illustrate the difference. The Waterhouse Company needs $1 million at the beginning of the year, and wishes to discharge its loan at the end of the year. If interest were payable annually this would be a simple matter. Assuming, for example, interest at 12 percent, $1,120,000 would be due at the end of the year.

If the Waterhouse Company is financially unable to make payment on its loan until the end of the year, and if monthly interest payments are required instead of an annual payment, Waterhouse will have to revert to additional borrowing. At the end of January, it will meet its first month's interest charge by borrowing an additional $10,000 from the bank. The result of this additional borrowing necessary each month will be to increase the total end-of-the-year payment required to the bank to cover the interest of the interim borrowing (and monthly interest on that accumulated interest). The actual effect of this is the imposition of monthly interest compounding at a rate of 1 percent. Using the compound interest formula, with n denoting number of months,

$$F = P(1 + r)^n = \$1,000,000 \, (1.01)^{12} = \$1,126,825.$$

Thus on an annual basis the interest charged on this loan can be described as $126,825/\$1,000,000$ or about 12.7 percent. Note that the logic of this calculation does not require the assumption, used for illustrative purposes, that borrowing was necessary for monthly interest payments, but only a general proposition that the timing of money amounts matters.

The Banking Relationship

A company's banking connections can be a useful part of its overall liquidity posture. Although it is possible for a company to shop around each time it plans to use bank credit, a more normal pattern is for a company to settle on one bank (perhaps after several trials) and continue to borrow from that bank recurrently. The relationship is likely to develop on a quite personal basis; normal bank practice will allow the same bank officer or officers interacting with a company on each of its transactions.

One advantage of maintaining a relationship with a bank is the possibility of developing a *line of credit*. With this arrangement the bank assures the company in advance that it can borrow up to a given amount. For example, a canning company might negotiate a $1 million credit line with its bank to handle its seasonal borrowing requirements. Once the agreement is made, the company can obtain a series of individual loans without further negotiation. It might, for example, borrow $100,000, wait for a week and borrow another $100,000 and continue this process as its seasonal inventory accumulated. The advantage of the credit line to the company is that the company need not borrow all of its anticipated credit needs at once (and pay interest on the full amount) in order to assure itself that its peak needs will be met.

Sometimes credit lines are simply oral understandings between a company executive and the company's banker. At other times written contracts are used. If a company wishes to maintain a large line of credit for use under extraordinary conditions, without actually doing much borrowing from the bank, the bank may ask the company to pay a *stand-by* fee for the maintenance of the credit line. With this type of arrangement, the company is explicitly purchasing liquidity.

Beyond lines of credit, which seldom extend for more than a year, another type of mutual understanding can develop between a company and its banker. As they continue to do business together, and continue to treat each other with fairness and absolute honesty, a type of loyalty is likely to develop. The bank comes to expect a company's business, including its holding of the company deposits. The bank is also likely to manifest trust in its "regular customer" by providing it with loans when money is "tight" or when the company is experiencing difficulties.

In addition to providing credit, a bank provides its clients with a variety of other services. It offers assistance in financial planning, including counsel from personnel specialized in the financial problems of particular industries. The bank can provide assistance to the company in the transfer of money from one part of the country to another or in the collection of money. A Canadian bank typically maintains extensive banking connections in other countries so it can be particularly helpful in the transacting of international business. It also provides safe storage facilities for company securities and other valuables, and may offer other miscellaneous services, such as computer time-sharing or the performance of some company bookkeeping functions.

Bank Security Arrangements

Bank loans are made extensively on both a secured and unsecured basis. The relative advantages and disadvantages of using security are essentially the same for banks as they are for the providers of trade credit. Security provides safety to the lender, but at a cost in inconvenience, expense, and psychological remoteness.

Banks may secure loans in a number of ways using various types of collateral. Short-term loans may be secured by the pledging of assets through mortgages. This could be done through the use of *chattel mortgages,* which give the bank the right to take possession of specified movable property in the event that a loan is defaulted. Real estate mortgages may also be used.

More commonly, mortgages are reserved for the securing of longer term credit and current assets are used to secure short-term credit. Receivables may be assigned to a bank, or the bank may take actual physical control of inventory. This control will be manifested by the bank's holding of a warehouse receipt, or under exceptional circumstances, by field warehousing, where a bank or its agent actually holds the key to a warehouse or a segregated storage area on the company's property.

One widely used type of inventory loan is the "Section 88" loan, a reference to a part of the Bank Act which authorizes it. Under such an arrangement, a company can pledge inventory to a bank by a simple listing of inventory items. To ensure that inventory is not used as collateral with two or more lenders simultaneously, and to advise other lenders of the bank's secured relationship, a central registry of Section 88 loans is maintained.

COMMERCIAL PAPER

A number of attractive features of carrying on business with banks have been discussed. There is one aspect of the banking relationship which is troublesome, especially to large companies. The banks are financial intermediaries or "middlemen" who in effect buy funds wholesale from depositors and resell them retail to business customers, at a profit. Particularly where it can be done on a large scale, there is an attractiveness to the company to attempt to "deal direct" with savers and thus avoid middleman's charges. Where the company elects to by-pass banks or other financial intermediaries it is often said to be engaged in *disintermediation.*

The most important type of short-term disintermediation is a company's issuance of its own commercial paper. The company issues negotiable promises to pay and sells these directly to other companies and the public. To a limited extent, an intermediary is still used, since commercial paper will be marketed through an investment dealer, but an incentive still remains for issuing commercial paper. For large, well-established companies its cost is likely to be lower than the prime rate. (Fixed costs are apt to make the issuance of commercial paper unattractive from the viewpoint of smaller firms.)

It is common practice for a firm to issue commercial paper and also to transact sufficient business with a bank to maintain a satisfactory bank-relationship. One of the problems with too extensive disintermediation is the loss of the banking relationship. There is nothing equivalent to a line of credit or "loyalty" in the commercial market. If a firm develops financial problems, a bank, out of loyalty (and concern for its image of loyalty) may continue to lend in an attempt to help the company out of its financial difficulties. At the same time, the company's commercial paper may have lost its marketability.

As noted in Chapter 9, an organized market exists for commercial paper. This money market helps make commercial paper marketable, by assuring buyers of the paper that facilities for the orderly secondary sale of the paper are available.

SUMMARY

Current liabilities represent a major source of financing for Canadian firms. They are convenient, flexible, and relatively low cost. Though often unsecured, they may be subject to security arrangements.

Trade credit is received from suppliers. It may be costless, but often costs attach—either through overt interest charges, or through cash differences and other differences between cash and credit prices. A variety of repayment terms are available.

Bank credit is also widely used; banks tend to specialize in the making of short-term and fairly conservative loans. The prime rate is an interest charge levied by banks on short-term loans to customers who borrow large amounts and inflict little risk on the bank. Charges above prime are associated with lending on a smaller scale, for a longer term, or under conditions of greater risk. Short-term bank loans are typically in the form of demand notes on which interest rates are revised to reflect current market conditions.

A close informal relationship is likely to exist between a company and its bank. In addition, the bank may give formal assurance of its willingness to lend to a customer by providing a line of credit for a predetermined amount.

Companies sometimes supplement or bypass financial institution lending sources, by issuing commercial paper.

QUESTIONS AND PROBLEMS

1. Company X pays cash for all raw materials purchased, even though liberal trade credit is available. The company is now contemplating purchase of a new plant site. The company comptroller suggests that trade credit might be used to provide funds for acquiring the site. Another financial officer counters with the contention that trade credit can only be used for raw material purchases.

   Resolve the dispute.

2. What motivates a supplier to offer interest-free trade credit arrangements? Presumably the supplier does not provide this without cost to himself.

3. A company uses 100,000 feet of steel cable per month in its manufacturing operations. This cable is available from one supplier on a cash before delivery basis at 84 cents per foot. A second supplier offers identical cable for 86.4 cents per foot on terms of 2/10; net 30.

   Identify the dollar amount, and cost, of the two levels of trade credit available. Use the "short-cut" method.

4. Using internal rate method, find the specific capital cost implied by the credit terms: 2 percent cash discount; accounts due in 30 days.

5. The prime rate is 9 percent in February, when a company negotiates a bank loan at an interest rate of prime plus 2.5 percent. In April the prime rate drops by 0.25 percent. What rate will the company then be paying on its demand loan?

   Suppose the following January, the company and its bank negotiate a change in lending terms to 3 percent plus prime. Meanwhile no further change in the prime rate has taken place. What will the company's interest rate be? What reasons do you think would prompt the bank to renegotiate the loan to a prime plus 3 percent basis? What reason can you think of for the company's being willing to accept this upward adjustment?

6. A company borrows money from a bank at 13 percent with interest collected monthly. It has a chance to obtain funds from another source at 14 percent with interest payable on an end-of-year basis. Which source is costlier? Explain.

7. Why would a company be willing to pay a stand-by fee?

8. What is a Section 88 loan?

9. What is the "money market"?

RELATED READINGS

Agemian, C. A. "Maintaining an Effective Bank Relationship." *Financial Executive,* January 1954.

Anstie, R. "The Historical Development of Pledge Lending in Canada." *The Canadian Banker,* Summer 1967, pp. 81–90.

Bond, D. E., and Shearer, R. A. *The Economics of the Canadian Financial System.* Scarborough, Ontario: Prentice-Hall, 1972, chaps. 9–11.

Brosky, J. J. *The Implicit Cost of Trade Credit and Theory of Optimal Term of Sale.* New York: Credit Research Foundation, 1969.

Canada. *1964 Report of the Royal Commission on Banking and Finance.* Ottawa: Queen's Printer, 1964.

Canadian Bankers Association. "The Chartered Banks of Canada." An elementary pamphlet available through Chartered banks.

Canadian Bankers Association. *Factbook '75.* Available through Chartered banks.

Greer, D. F. "Rate Ceilings and Loan Turndowns." *Journal of Finance*, December 1975.

Nadler, P. "Banking after the Penn Central Collapse." *The Canadian Banker*, March–April 1971.

Neufeld, E. P. *The Financial System of Canada*. Toronto: Macmillan, 1972.

Robinson, Roland. *The Management of Bank Funds*. New York: McGraw-Hill, 1962.

Rose, P. S. "Two Banking Systems Enter a Crucial Period." *The Canadian Banker and ICB Review*, 4th quarter, 1975.

Wood Gundy Securities Ltd. *The Canadian Money Market*, 1969.

13

LONGER TERM BORROWING: INSTITUTIONAL SOURCES

Noncurrent debt in use in Canada is, like current liabilities also equal to about one fourth of Canadian business assets. This debt is often subdivided into two categories. Intermediate term is often used to describe debt maturing from one to roughly five years, while long-term debt describes longer maturities. There is no sharp distinction.

Both short-term and longer term debt represent relatively permanent sources of funds for most Canadian companies. They are permanent in the sense that the borrowing positions typically recycle. As individual debt obligations are repaid, they are replaced. Longer term debt, however, is likely to have more stability than short-term debt. Short-term debt use fluctuates because of seasonal needs and other temporary financing requirements. By the very nature of the borrowing contracts involved, longer term debt tends to change in infrequent increments.

The incurrence of a longer term obligation is usually associated with some particular purpose, such as purchasing equipment, real estate, or another company. Other major direct purposes are *funding*—replacement (or *refinancing*) of shorter term debt—or *refunding*—the refinancing of a longer term debt. At other times, however, issues of common stock are used for these same purposes. Thus it is more appropriate to think of long-term borrowing not so much as being for a particular purpose as comprising part of the aggregate financing strategy of the company. Longer term borrowing is introduced at times and in amounts appropriate to the maintenance of the company's desired blend of financing sources.

Beyond its subdivision into intermediate- and long-term debt, longer term borrowing can be subdivided in another way, the manner in which funds are raised. Funds can be borrowed from financial institutions or they may be obtained from other sources, usually through public sale of securities. Much intermediate-term borrowing is done through institutions. Public bond issues, a form of disintermediation with a long tradition, are the mode for a substantial part of long term corporate financing. This chapter is devoted to longer term debt procured from institutional sources. Because of the debtlike character of many leases, lease financing is also discussed here.

CONTRACTUAL CONDITIONS

A number of different lending arrangements are in practice when funds are secured from lending institutions. Major types are detailed below.

Term and Installment Loans

These loans, calling for repayment at a specific time or series of times, may be on an unsecured basis, or they may be supported by a pledge of assets. Current assets are not well suited for longer term collateral, since their frequent turnover creates legal problems in identifying specific assets as the collateral. Thus these longer term loans are likely to be secured by chattel or real estate mortgages, if security is used.

Hypothecation is a less formal type of security arrangement. With this method a lender is given physical control over securities or certificates of title to real estate. During the time the secured loan is outstanding, the hypothecated property cannot be sold or pledged without the lender's consent. The advantage of the use of the hypothecation is its simplicity and low cost.

Equipment Purchase Contracts

These contracts are virtually identical to the conditional sales contracts used in consumer transactions. A seller of equipment or a third party extends credit for the purchase of equipment, usually requires installment payments, and retains legal title to the equipment until the payment schedule is completed. The payment schedule is normally devised to provide for a discharge of the obligation at a more rapid rate than the rate of deterioration in the value of the equipment.

On equipment purchase contracts and also on term and installment loans, lenders are likely to insist that a loan be of a "self-liquidating" character. By this they mean that the asset purchased with the proceeds of the loan or financed with the equipment purchase contract should generate cash flows in an amount sufficient to discharge the associated obligation. Unless the repayment period is unusually short relative to the asset's useful life, this requirement should pose no serious problem, since an asset which was not self-liquidating would also be rejected by the borrower's capital budgeting asset acceptance tests. (In one respect, if NPV or the rate of return method is used, those tests are likely to be more rigorous because they will use as a discount rate not the loan's rate of interest but instead a higher rate based on overall capital cost and appropriate reflection of risk.

Long-Term Real Estate Mortgages

Land, the minerals under it and the forests on it, the buildings and other improvements that have been added to it, all comprise real estate. Real estate has three important aspects which make it particularly attractive as security for long-term loans. It is subject to formal, legal title, maintained in a central government registry. It cannot be readily moved, so the borrower cannot literally run away with it. Third, it does not normally deteriorate in usefulness over a short period of time, unlike the wearing out of equipment.

The last two of these characteristics are subject to notable exceptions—minerals and timber can be removed from land. Improvements on land can deteriorate physically. Land itself may remain physically stable but deteriorate in economic value, as when abandonment of a planned highway causes drastic falls in the value of land intended for commercial use. Notwithstanding these limitations, real estate has a long history of being regarded as excellent collateral.

The execution of a mortgage creates a property interest for the lender, or *mortgagee*. In return for receiving a loan, the borrower, or *mortgagor*, enters a contract whereby he transfers his property to the mortgagee unless the associated loan is discharged as promised. We should note that reading the contractual terms of a mortgage does not tell the whole story of the enforceable agreement between borrower and lender. Common-law and many provincial statutes may restrict the nature of the creditor's rights. For example, it is almost inconceivable that a mortgagee could seize a piece of real estate on the basis of a few days' tardiness in an installment payment, even though a mortgage contract may appear to give him that right. Because of their legal complexity, mortgages are almost always arranged with the advice of legal counsel for both mortgagee and mortgagor.

An *agreement-for-sale* is a financing instrument closely resembling a mortgage. An agreement-for-sale is often used when a company is purchasing real estate which is to be financed by the property's seller. The legal form of the agreement-for-sale provides that the buyer of real estate, like the buyer of equipment under an equipment purchase contract, does not receive full ownership of the property until his purchase obligation is discharged. In practice, the rights of the buyer and seller under an agreement-for-sale are similar to the respective rights of a mortgagor and a mortgagee.

Mortgages are usually repaid in installments—annually, semiannually, quarterly, or monthly. There are exceptions—on a *balloon mortgage* repayment of all principal on the mortgage is deferred until the final maturity date, even though interest is paid on a periodic basis. In a normal case, where principal installments are used, periodic payments are determined by two common methods: (1) equalized payments of principal and (2) equalized blended payments.

Equalized Payments of Principal.   Under this method the period over which repayment is expected to take place, or *amortization period,* is determined. The principal amount of the mortgage is then divided by the number of time periods (whether months, years, or whatever is chosen) within the amortization period. Periodic payments then consist of the amount of the principal payment, the same for each period, and the amount of current interest, which decreases from period to period as principal is repaid. An example will illustrate.

A mortgage loan is consummated with a ten-year amortization period, and annual payments at 11 percent annual interest. The principal amount is $200,000. Each year's payment consists of one tenth of the principal, or $20,000 plus the appropriate annual interest amount. In the first year the payment will be $20,000 principal plus $22,000 interest, or $42,000. During the second year the payment will be $39,800 ($20,000 principal plus $19,800 interest on the $180,000 left unpaid after the previous year's installment).

Equalized Blended Payments.   With this method the total amount of each installment payment is made equal. This involves lower payments of principal during early periods, when interest requirements are great, and correspondingly greater payments of principal during later periods after previous retirement of principal has reduced the interest required. Identification of periodic payments is customarily based on mortgage tables, which are forms of annuity tables. These tables differ slightly, depending upon the assumptions that underly them. For example, one mortgage payable in monthly payments may specify that interest is to be calculated every month; another may specify an annual calculation (presuming that payments during the first part of the year are interest and during the last are principal). These differences are small and for purposes of a company's financial analysis, mortgage payments can be adequately approximated with the use of an annuity table, or more precisely with the formula given below.

For example a company may consider borrowing $500,000 using a 20-year amortization, 8 percent interest, and monthly installments. Using a conventional annuity table, the problem can first be solved in terms of annual installments; these installments can then be divided by 12 to approximate monthly installments. Using previously introduced notation, the problem sets up as:

$$P = \$500,000$$
$$r = 8\%$$
$$n = 20$$
$$A = \text{unknown}$$

Looking at the table, the annuity factor for $n = 20$, $r = 8\%$ is 9.818. The annuity factor is a ratio, P/A. Using its reciprocal, $A/P = .102$, one calculates $A = \$500,000\,(.102) = \$51,000$ annual payments. Monthly payments are estimated at $51,000/12 or about $4,250.

A formula is available for a more precise calculation though as noted earlier the formula results will not coincide with all mortgage tables. The formula is given as:

$$A = \frac{Pr}{1 - \dfrac{1}{(1 + r)^n}}$$

The formula can be applied in the above example by using a monthly interest rate of $8\%/12 = 0.667\%$. On a monthly basis the number of periods must be expressed in comparable units: 20 years $\times$ 12 = 240 months. Now, substituting into the formula:

$$A = \frac{\$500,000\,(.00667)}{1 - \dfrac{1}{(1.00667)^{240}}}$$

$$A = \$4,183.45.$$

Note that the difference between the easier approximation using the annuity table, and the detailed formula calculation, is slight.

Mortgages typically have one feature in common with the demand note; they provide for interest renegotiation. In a demand note this may be done at frequent intervals, conceivably more than once within a month. On a mortgage the negotiations are much more infrequent, often at five-year intervals. The initial interval before renegotiation takes place is called the *term* of the mortgage.

Technically, repayment of the mortgage is required at the end of its term. In practice, institutions issuing mortgages are not likely to exercise their right to insist on repayment on a mortgage, in the same way that banks do not call their demand loans. Instead, a renewal of the mortgage is effected for a term comparable to the initial one but at a rate reflecting current capital market supply and demand conditions. The financial institutions' motives for not exercising their full legal rights are similar to the banks. Both derive their profits from lending money, and both wish to avoid the damage to corporate image by causing customers unnecessary financial inconvenience or embarrassment.

Not only the interest rate, but installment payments, are affected by the interest renegotiation. To continue the previous example which used an equalized blended payment, a mortgage table would indicate that after five years of payments at $4,183.45 per month the principal of the mortgage would have been reduced to about $438,000.[1] Suppose that at the end of the term, mortgage rates have risen to 10 percent. Accordingly the mortgage would be renegotiated using a 15-year amortization period (the original 20 years minus the 5 years that have elapsed) and a 10 percent interest rate. Using the formula, the new monthly payment would be calculated as:

$$A = \frac{Pr}{1 - \dfrac{1}{(1+r)^n}}$$

$$A = \frac{\$438,000(.003)}{1 - \dfrac{1}{(1.0083)}180}$$

$$A = \text{about } \$4,700.$$

---

[1] The fraction of the loan repaid at the end of the term can be approximated by a ratio of annuity factors. For example, with an original amortization period of 20 years, a 5-year term, and an interest rate of 8 percent, the fraction of the principal repaid during 5 years will be given by the ratio of discount factors for 8 percent, 15 years, and 8 percent, 20 years. This ratio is 8.559/9.818 = 0.872. Applying this to the above example, $500,000 (0.872) = $436,000, about the same as the table result in the example.

Note that as a result of the renegotiation the monthly mortgage payment has risen by over $500.

LENDING INSTITUTIONS

There is some overlap between institutions providing short- and longer term credit. Chartered banks offer intermediate-term credit, and suppliers of industrial equipment provide what amounts to a longer term version of trade credit. However, much intermediate-, and nearly all long-term money supplied by institutions emanates from specialists in the handling of long-term funds.

Banks and Banklike Institutions

Banks, as noted previously, must maintain safe, liquid asset collections. However, partly because a portion of the banks' own deposit liabilities are intermediate term in maturity, they participate in intermediate-term lending themselves. In return for this departure from liquid loans, banks typically charge somewhat higher interest rates on intermediate financing. One can also expect a considerable element of conservatism in lending policies from banks, since they can tolerate only limited amounts of risk in their asset collections.

In addition to offering intermediate loans, banks purvey limited amounts of long-term mortgage money. They also may assist in the procurement of other long-term funds. For example, the Canadian Imperial Bank of Commerce acts as agent for Kinross Mortgage Corporation, and United Dominion Corporation, a British-controlled financial concern. Through these agencies, the Bank of Commerce offers longer term and higher risk financing than the bank itself would normally undertake.

Co-operative lending institutions, though small in total *volume* of business, have been growing more rapidly than chartered banks. These institutions are financed in a manner similar to banks and thus have roughly similar constraints with respect to risk and liquidity. These institutions are more likely to make loans to consumers than to business, but they do make some business loans on terms roughly comparable to those offered by banks. Since co-operatives—the credit unions and caisses populaire—tend to be small and locally organized, they are not suitable bankers for large companies. However, they can be a financing source for small businesses and may have some appeal for a locally orientated business which wishes to deal with a local credit source, rather than a branch office of a chartered bank. They also frequently act as bankers for other co-operative enterprises.

Looking ahead, a number of impending policy developments, tending to amalgamate the activities of cooperative lenders, may adapt these institutions to compete more effectively as large scale bankers.

Supplier Financing

Sellers of industrial equipment often provide credit in the form of equipment purchase contracts. The economic basis for this type of credit has been discussed in Chapter 7 on accounts receivable. Credit may be extended directly by a supplier, or by a finance company owned by the supplier. These *captive finance companies* (GMAC, or General Motors Acceptance Corporation, is perhaps the most well-known example) are separate corporate entities which serve to segregate the supplier's financing activity from the rest of his operations. The extension of intermediate credit through a captive finance company, rather than directly, is now normal practice.

Compared to bank credit, credit from captive finance companies is often high cost. On the other hand it is conveniently negotiated. Since the suppliers have the double incentive of profiting from the equipment sale as well as receiving interest on the purchase contract, this type of credit may be obtainable under conditions where banks would reject a loan application because of excessive risk.

The Nature of Trust Companies

Trust companies are like banks in that they solicit deposits from the public, and offer loans to customers and businesses. There are, however, important differences in both form and substance. While a bank is characterized as a buyer and seller of money, the trust company is normally acting as a *trustee*, an agency entrusted with the administration of other people's money.

One can best understand a trust company by understanding the four sources from which it derives the financial resources under its management:

1. Company Money.   These funds consist of the shareholders' equity and liabilities incurred directly by the company. (This is a relative small source of trust company funds.)
2. Guaranteed Trust Accounts.   These funds are obtained from deposits and investment certificates (in effect, term deposits). Assets purchased with these funds are not owned by the trust company but directly by the depositors. The deposits and certificates are not liabilities of the trust company in a direct way. Indirectly, they are liabilities, because the trust company guarantees them in the event that assets bought on behalf of the depositors and certificate holders are insufficient to discharge the principal and interest on the deposits and certificates.
3. Other Trust Accounts Not Guaranteed.   These include money from estates, funds owned by wealthy persons who do not wish to manage their own money, and other personal and corporate monies entrusted to the trust for management. The trust company, as trustee, does not guarantee any results to these persons or companies (*trustors*) whose funds it is managing. It is normally, however, legally responsible for careful management, under a well-established principle of common law called the *prudent man rule.*

    Pension funds are becoming an increasingly important element in trust company operation. One trust company, Royal Trust, now claims responsibility for over $5 billion of pension money (equal to about 6 percent of *all* chartered bank assets, for comparison). These funds are accumulated by periodic contributions from employees and employers for use later in providing old-age or other pension benefits.
4. "Mutual Funds."   Trust companies often operate and/or manage investment trusts, in which shares or certificates are sold to the public. These funds may be designed for

various types of investments; they again represent massive amounts of money under trust company administration.

Trust Company Lending

Trust company lending policies are fundamentally different from banks in one respect—they are principally providers of longer term monies. Safety and security are important to trust companies because of the safety requirements of many of their trustors and because of guarantees made to depositors. This tolerance of longevity, coupled with a tendency toward insistence on safety, have made trust companies major suppliers of intermediate- and long-term mortgage financing. They are also major purchasers of corporate securities.

In addition to lending, trust companies provide many of the ancillary services, which are offered by banks. It is not a gross departure from fact to describe the trust companies as bankers for long-term money. Indeed, a major public policy issue at the time this book is being written is the extent to which trust companies should be regulated under the Bank Act.

Insurance Companies

Insurance companies, too, derive their bread and butter from financial transactions. Besides acting as insurers, these companies hold large amounts of assets as reserves for the meeting of future insurance claims. Regulation and the fact that insurance companies again tend to have thin equity positions, require that the reserves be invested in safe assets. However, particularly in the case of life insurance companies, illiquidity is quite tolerable in these assets. Therefore insurance companies have become major mortgage lenders. Because of their large financial resources, and also because of their lack of "retail" credit granting outlets such as the trust companies and banks, they are more likely to make large loans. It should be noted that in addition to activity as mortgage lenders, insurance companies are also major purchasers of corporate bonds.

Insurance companies have been leaders in the development of an increasingly popular type of lender compensation, the "equity kicker." If an insurance company's bargaining power as a lender is substantial, as it may be in a case where large amounts of money are involved and where some risk is being undertaken, the insurance company might be in a position to negotiate a high-interest rate. However, if the insurance company is providing most of the funds for the venture, such as the development of a shopping centre, an onerous interest rate could be too burdensome and cause a default in the event that the venture being financed is only moderately successful. One way of getting around this problem is for the insurance company to make the loan at a more moderate rate (still substantially above prime) and receive a participation in profits as additional compensation. In that way, if the venture proves especially successful, the effective "interest rate" may be very high.

Obviously there is no simple way to estimate capital costs in the event that an equity kicker is required by a lender. One possibility is the making of a number of assumptions about the degree of success of the venture and their probabilities, and then calculating an expected value of the total cash outflows that will go to the creditor. Specific capital cost can then be identified by finding the internal rate which equates the expected outflows with the proceeds from the loan.

For example, an insurance company may lend $50 million to finance a shopping centre amortized over 20 years at 10 percent. In addition, the loan agreement provides that the insurance company will receive 15 percent of gross rental income over $15 million per year. The following calculation illustrates a possible capital cost estimation:

```
Proceeds . . . . . . . . . . . . . . . . . . . . . . . . . . . . . . . . . . .  $50,000,000
Annual payment to amortize proceeds at 10% over
   20 years (based on annuity table)  . . . . . . . . . . . . . . .  $ 5,900,000
```

Assumptions about Annual Rentals and 15 Percent "Kicker" Payments
(in millions)

Probability	Rentals	Kicker	Probability X Outcome
.3	Under 15	0	0
.2	20	.75	.15
.2	30	2.25	.45
.2	40	3.75	.75
.1	50	5.25	.53
Expected value			1.88

Expected annual payment:

Amortization	. . . .	$5,900,000
Kicker	. . . .	1,880,000
Total	. . . .	$7,780,000

Annuity factor implied $50,000,000/$7,780,000 = 6.43.
By interpolation in annuity table, where n = 20, r = about 13%, before tax.

Government Lending Institutions

In an attempt to help small businesses and to promote industrial development, the federal government and each of the provinces have developed industrial development banks. The
federal version is called the Federal Business Development
Bank; the provincial versions go by various other names. The
purpose of these organizations is to fill an apparent gap in the
country's financial system.

By the nature of its own financing, the chartered banking
system is not well suited to the extensive assumption of risk.
Long-term mortgage lenders may be somewhat more venturesome but they typically require real estate or other readily
marketable assets as collateral.

Beginning businesses as a class are unquestionably risky and
often lack acceptable collateral. For example, a company developing a new product may require specialized equipment; if
the product is not accepted by the market, the equipment may
be worthless. Money may also be needed for inventory accumulation; again consumer rejection of the product renders
this worthless. One can understand why conventional lending
sources, with heavy responsibilities to depositors, trustors,
pensioners, or policyholders, cannot effectively provide funding for many new ventures. One possible avenue for funding of
new ventures is the sale of common stock, but as we shall see,
this is seldom feasible on a small scale.

Industrial development banks are expected to provide funds
in cases where other avenues of financing are not readily available, but where a venture is still deemed to be a basically
sound venture. Industrial development banks will protect
themselves as well as possible by using the collateral available.
The intent of these industrial development bank is that they
expose themselves to a higher probability of default than conventional financing sources. Their principal role is not profit-

making, but the long-run abetment of the national or provincial productivity.

Loans for Risky Conditions from Private Sources

In addition to the government industrial development banks, there are a number of private risk capital sources available. Equipment purchase contracts, already discussed, provide one instance where financing may be available from private sources. For the new company, finance companies, largely consumer-oriented, may offer some credit. One large organization, Roynat Limited, was formed by the Royal Bank and a group of trust companies with the intention of offering more flexibility with respect to risk taking. In addition, wealthy individuals are sometimes willing to provide money for high-risk small businesses providing their compensation is commensurate to the risk.

To some extent, however, the credit gap for new businesses is likely to remain at least partly unfilled. Even where the prospective borrower is known to be honest and well intentioned, the probability of partial or total default may be just too high. An example will illustrate the nature of the problem. Suppose the lender wishes to make three $100,000 loans to emerging businesses and is reasonably confident that one of the three businesses will fail and default totally. Suppose, furthermore, the company believes, as a reasonable compensation for risk, that it should expect to make 20 percent after covering expected bad debt losses.

Now credit terms can be established. For easy calculation suppose that each of the loans is to be of one year's duration. The lender wants to recover $360,000 after one year, his original $300,000 plus 20 percent interest. Since he expects that one of the three loans will fail, he must plan to recover $180,000 apiece from the remaining two. In other words, to earn an expected 20 percent on his money, he must set his interest rate at 80 percent. Even though such a rate might be a perfectly fair one, it is so far above rates to which borrowers are accustomed that it is likely to appear usurious and unacceptable.[2]

---

[2] The example is illustrative; the relationships shown may be altered by tax considerations.

LEASE FINANCING

Leasing refers to hiring the use of an asset, usually on the basis of a formal contract, and usually over an extended period of time. Less formal and shorter lived arrangements of this type are usually referred to as rentals, although there is no precise distinction between the two.

A dichotomy is made between a *commercial lease* and a *financial lease*. In a commercial lease, such as a long-term agreement for the use of office space in a building, physical services are the central theme of the contractual relation between lessor and lessee. The lessor is typically in the business of owning and maintaining property which he offers for hire under a lease contract. In the financial lease, the main thrust of the agreement is the provision of financing. The lessee desires the use of an asset, which he will physically maintain himself. He approaches the lessor as a source of money, and the lease becomes similar in intent (though not in legal form) to a security arrangement between borrower and lender.

This chapter applies principally to financial leases, which are more expressly sources of financing than their commercial counterparts. However, the separation is a blurry one. The company obtaining office space under a commercial lease is, by avoiding the building of its own office building, conserving funds for other purposes. If the commercial lease cannot be called a source of financing, it must at least be called a potential substitute for a financing source.

To understand the actual nature of the lease, acquisition of the use of an asset through a lease can be compared with buying an asset under an equipment purchase agreement. In both cases, the company receives the use of an asset in exchange for committing itself to a series of future payments. In both cases, repossession is not the only recourse of the creditor or lessor; the company can be sued for the missing payments. About the only difference in substance lies in the fact that if the asset is leased, the lessor retains an interest in the asset after the payment schedule is discharged. In the case of equipment leases, however, this residual interest is likely to be small and perhaps negligible.

It is apparent from the above that there is little difference between the acquisition of an asset through a lease; and acquisition of an asset through purchase, financed by borrowing. Even the difference of possible residual interest is only one of degree; in that case the lessor purchases part of the property rights in an asset, the right to use of the asset for a specified period of time. Leasing has increased rapidly in popularity as a method of financing. Beyond the long-standing practice of commercial leasing of land and buildings, businesses now can lease a wide variety of industrial and commercial equipment.

Motives for Leasing

There are two possible motives for acquiring assets through lease rather than purchase. One of these may be regarded as minor and the other as major. The minor one relates to accounting practice with respect to lease financing. If an asset is acquired through a lease, the asset, and the correspondingly obligation, does not have to be shown on the regular body of the company's balance sheet, but only described in a footnote. This practice may have the effect of changing the company's debt ratio. An example will illustrate.

A company currently has the following balance sheet:

Assets	$6,000,000	Liabilities	$3,000,000
		Net Worth	$3,000,000

It contemplates the purchase of $2 million in additional assets, through borrowing. If the assets are acquired in this way, the balance will become:

Assets	$8,000,000	Liabilities	$5,000,000
		Net Worth	$3,000,000

On the other hand if it were acquired through lease, the balance sheet could remain unchanged. If it does remain unchanged, the company's debt ratio will stay at .5; if the assets are acquired through purchase, the debt ratio will increase to $5,000,000/$8,000,000 or 0.625.

This accounting practice is subject to increasing question; proposed changes in accounting usage would require the inclusion in the balance sheet of an asset called a leasehold, and a corresponding liability. Even now, it is questionable whether the distortion of the debt ratio in this way could fool many analysts, even if a company wished to practice deception, since footnote disclosure of lease obligations is required.

Tax Aspects of Lease Financing

The tax advantage of leasing arises for the tax deductibility of lease payments. If the asset was bought and financed by borrowing instead of being leased, tax relief arising from the asset would emanate from its capital cost allowance tax shelter. Since the CCA rate is fixed by tax law, that component of tax relief is subject to an externally determined time-shape.

In contrast, since lessee and lessor can jointly control the time-shape of lease payments, they can control the time-shape of the tax relief on a leased asset. An example will illustrate.

Kennedy Ltd. is negotiating purchase of a $500,000 machine from Paton Ltd. The expected usuable life of the machine is ten years. The relevant CCA rate is 20 percent. Both Kennedy and Paton are subject to 40 percent corporate income tax. Paton is willing to extend credit amortized over approximately five years at an 18 percent interest rate. They jointly examine a conventional credit sale and an approximately equivalent lease arrangement.

Under an equipment purchase contract, required annual payments over five years would be about $160,000 per year. In designing an equivalent lease they must modify the terms to conform to two conditions:

a.   At the end of five years, the machine will still have a remaining five years of useful life. To be equivalent to a purchase, the lease must allow Kennedy use of the machine during this second five years.

b.   To comply with tax law, the lease agreement must be kept distinguishable from a sale. Providing Kennedy with an option to purchase the machine for a nominal sum after five years would be ruled out on this ground. (This is illustrative, and does not purport to be a general statement of lease tax.)

In view of these facts, the transactors consider the following lease. Annual payments of $180,000 per year for four years. Assured renewal of the lease after four years with annual payments of $9,000 for the next six years. (An internal rate identification on this lease yields an implied before-tax-interest rate of 18 percent.)

Now the tax aspects may be compared. Kennedy, as lessee, gave up the tax deduction of a capital cost allowance to obtain the full tax deductibility of the lease payments. Suppose Kennedy uses an after-tax discount rate of 10 percent. A comparison follows:

Tax shelter from CCA:

$$\text{Cost } \frac{d}{d+r} t = \$500,000 \frac{.20}{.20+.10} \, .4 = \$133,000.$$

Tax shelter from lease payments:

(Present value of lease payments discounted at 10%)$t = \$239,950.$

Clearly, Kennedy benefits by the tax treatment offered with the lease.

How about Paton? Had Paton sold the machine, profit on the sale would have been immediately taxable; interest charged on credit extended would have been taxable later. Under the lease arrangement, taxation of profit on the machine is delayed until lease payments are received. So the lease arrangement benefits the lessor as well, and is jointly advantageous in this case.

Specific Capital Cost on a Lease

To identify specific capital cost calculation on an after-tax basis, one assumption must first be made. The assumption is that the asset on which a lease is being considered could pass an acceptance test if bought on a cash basis; that is, if it were financed in some other method than leasing. The significance of this assumption will become more apparent in a following section. It allows us to regard lease financing available with the asset as a pure question of source-of-financing, comparable to other forms of debt.

Financing by lease induces two tax effects: loss of capital cost allowance, and deductibility of lease payments. For financial evaluation, proceeds from the lease are the cash price of the asset less the value of its tax shelter. Cash outflows are the lease payments, reduced to an after-tax basis. An example follows.

An Example of Leasing Cost

Speed Goods Company Ltd. has decided to purchase a large hydraulic press at a cost of $100,000. In lieu of a cash purchase, the supplier offers lease financing on the following basis:

1. End-of-year lease payments of $35,000 per year for four years are required.
2. As additional information, Speed Goods' marginal tax rate is 40 percent. The company uses a 10 percent discount rate on safe projects, and the appropriate capital cost allowance rate for the press is 20 percent.
   The calculation is shown as follows:

Amount of Financing Received

Cash price	$100,000
Value of tax shelter lost:	
Cost $(d/d + r)t = \$100{,}000\ (.20/.30).40$	$ 26,667
Total amount of financing received from	
lease, net after tax	$ 73,333

Future Payments (years 1–4)

Gross payment	$ 35,000
$(1 - t)$	.6
After-tax payment	$ 21,000

Specific Capital Cost Identification
via Internal Rate

		Trial Internal Rates					
		10%		8%		6%	
Year	Cash Flow	Annuity Factor	PV	Annuity Factor	PV	Annuity Factor	PV
0 . . .	+$73,333	1.000	+$73,333	1.000	+$73,333	1.000	+$73,333
1-4 . .	− 21,000	3.170	− 66,570	3.312	− 69,552	3.465	− 72,765
NPV			$ 6,763		$ 3,781		$ 568

One observes that the specific capital cost on this lease is slightly less than 6 percent.

The possible tax-created efficiency of lease financing is again illustrated in this example. Lease payments offered to Speed Goods were calculated to yield an annual rate of return before tax of about 15 percent to the lessor. (An IRR comparison of $100,000 and four yearly payments of $35,000 will verify this.) Had the lessor instead offered financing on the same terms through an equipment purchase contract, Speed Good's after-tax capital cost would have been $15 (1 - t)$ or 9 percent, instead of under 6 percent on the lease.

Nonseparable Lease Decisions

It is conceivable that an asset is only available on a lease basis. In this case, the asset and its financing are inextricably bound together. Similarly, it is possible that an asset is desirable *only* because it carries extraordinarily favourable financing in the form of a lease opportunity. (The asset, viewed without the available lease financing, has an NPV < 0.)

These situations are exceptions, which will seldom be encountered. If they are (the situations are easily recognized), the previous analysis does not apply. Ideas for coping with these oddities may be found in the Readings listed at the end of the chapter.

In conjunction with this type of asset, it is appropriate to stress a *don't* of asset-*cum*-lease analysis. The fact that an asset generates cash flows sufficient to cover all its lease payments is not sufficient justification for acquiring the asset. The lease obligation is debtlike, and must be discharged even if the expected cash flows on the asset fail to materialize. The asset is justifiable only if its expected cash flows relate favourably to overall cost of capital, suitably modified for risk.

Convenience of Lease Financing

Lease financing may sometimes be used where it offers no advantage over other types of debt in terms of specific capital cost (or even where it is at some cost disadvantage). This phenomenon arises out of the leasing's convenience and availability. If the vendor of a piece of capital equipment offers accompanying lease financing, it may be attractive for a company to accept this needed financing rather than to enter negotiations elsewhere.

Another use of the lease lies in the obtaining of real estate. It may be possible to negotiate a lease with an option to buy. With a situation of this type, lease financing can be used until other financial arrangements, such as a mortgage or a stock issue, are completed.

SUMMARY

Longer term borrowing is available from a number of institutional sources, including banks. Contractual arrangements include term bank loans, equipment purchase contracts and real estate, and other long-term mortgages.

Typically, mortgage payments may be of two forms. A given proportion of the original principal may be repaid in each period, along with current interest, or equalized blended payments may be used. Blended payments, calculated through a variant of present value analysis, equalize the sum of principal and interest for each period.

Trust companies, insurance companies, and various government agencies specialize in longer term lending. Some government institutions and private concerns are specialized in offering funds under conditions of relatively high risk.

Funds may be obtained under financial leases; these are largely similar to loans in financial effect, except for the possibility of significant income tax advantages. Specific capital cost determination on leases follows an internal rate of return procedure.

QUESTIONS AND PROBLEMS

1. Distinguish between funding and refunding.

2. What effect will funding tend to have on a company's general financial condition?

3. What is a hypothecation and what is the advantage of this mode of security?

4. A $500,000 mortgage is repayable as follows:
   Ten equal annual installments of principal, and interest payable annually at 10 percent. Identify the mortgage payment for the first year and for the tenth year.

5. A $500,000 mortgage is repayable in ten equal blended payments of principal and interest, with interest reckoned at 10 percent per annum. Identify the first year's and tenth year's payments.

6. A tract of land is to be sold for $100,000, with a $20,000 down payment. The balance of $80,000 is to be financed by a mortgage at 12 percent interest. As part of the purchase agreement the buyer has insisted on $15,000 annual blended payments of principal and interest. How long will it take for the mortgage to be discharged?

7. How does a credit union differ from a bank, in form of organization and in type of financial services provided?

8. What is the prudent man rule?

9. Banks obtain most of their funds from depositors; where do trust companies obtain their money?

10. Describe the reason why life insurance companies have specialized in long-term lending.

11. An insurance company provides $3 million for constructing a new apartment block. The loan agreement specifies payment in 20 equal annual blended installments with interest at 9 percent. In addition the insurance company is to receive 10 percent of all rents in excess of $1 million. The expected value of annual rents is $1,750,000. Estimate specific cost of capital before tax.

12. A venture capital company considers offering one year loans to a number of small risky businesses. It estimates that three fourths of the businesses will survive and repay their loans and the other one fourth will fail and default completely. The venture capital company desires to set an interest charge that will allow it to receive an expected return of 25 percent before tax on its investment. What interest rate must the company charge?

13. Consider the following assertion:

   "I would rather lease an asset because my entire lease payment is tax deductible. If I buy the asset and make loan payments as a result of it, only the interest portion of the loan payment will be tax deductible."

Identify the oversimplification in this assertion.

14. A company has a marginal tax rate of 40 percent; the relevant CCA rate used in this problem is 10 percent and the relevant discount rate is 12 percent after tax.

   An asset can be purchased for $5,000. Alternatively it can be leased for ten years (its expected life) for $900 per year. What is the specific capital cost on the lease after tax?

15. Explain how the tax aspects of lease financing may be jointly beneficial for the lessor and the lessee.

RELATED READINGS

Axelson, K. S. "Needed: A Generally Accepted Method for Measuring Lease Commitments." *Financial Executive,* July 1971.

Beechy, T. H.   "Quasi-Debt Analysis of Financial Leases." *Accounting Review,* April 1969.

Jenkins, D. O.   "Purchase or Cancellable Lease." *Financial Executive,* April 1970.

Johnson, R. W., and Lewellen, Wilbur G.   "Analysis of the Lease-or-Buy Decision." *Journal of Finance,* September 1972.

Middleton, J. W. "Term Lending—Practical and Profitable." *Journal of Commercial Bank Lending,* August 1968.

Nelson, A. T.   "Capitalized Leases—The Effect on Financial Ratios." *Journal of Accountancy,* July 1963.

Roenfeldt, R. L., and Osteryoung, J. S. "Analysis of financial Leases." *Financial Management,* Spring 1973.

"Term Financing? Equipment Leasing?" A brief advertising brochure available from Roynat.

14

BORROWING WITH BOND ISSUES

Essentially, a bond is a loan sliced in pieces for broad distribution. It may be intermediate or long term, though most bonds run ten years or more. The *bonds* themselves are certificates representing participation in a loan, or *bond issue;* bondholders have rights of creditors comparable to those rights residing in institutions which have loans outstanding. In fact the major financial institutions—chartered banks, trust companies, and insurance companies—are all important bond purchasers.

A bond issue will be subdivided into bonds of various denominations or dollar amounts based on marketing considerations. The denominations customarily range from as low as $1,000 to as high as $1 million. Once issued the bonds are negotiable. Thus the composition of the lenders on the bond issue may change while it is outstanding. This makes the relationship between the company and its bondholding creditors characteristically a remote one, a disintermediated situation of the type discussed under commercial paper issuance.

CONTRACTUAL CONDITIONS

The Formal Agreement

Underlying the bond issue will be a detailed agreement, called a *trust indenture* or *trust deed*, or often simply *indenture*. That agreement is administered by a *trustee*, usually a trust company, charged with representing the bondholders' interests and taking collective action on their behalf. For example, if it becomes necessary to proceed against a borrowing company because of default on terms of the trust indenture, each bondholder need not take individual action; the trustee will act instead.

The indenture will, of course, specify required interest and time(s) of principal repayment. In addition it may provide a variety of other conditions and restrictions. For example, it may specify limits on other borrowing the company undertakes. It may limit the scope of the borrowing company's management, by requiring the maintenance of minimum current ratio. It may allow a representative of the bondholders to have an active voice in management under conditions where the bondholders' investment is in jeopardy. It may provide an escalator clause, where default on a single required payment of principal and interest may render all of the principal immediately due. The indenture is a mutual agreement, and the possibility for provisions within it are virtually unbounded.

Bond Security

Bonds may be secured by the pledge of assets. *First-mortgage bonds* are secured by real estate, in the same way as other first mortgages. A *second-mortgage* (or a *general mortgage*) bond issue may also be issued. This represents a secondary claim against real estate already encumbered with a first mortgage. In the event of liquidation, holders of second-mortgage bonds have a claim against remaining value in the asset after claims of first-mortgage bondholders have been fully satisfied. This coincides with the use of second mortgages at the consumer level, or as security for business credit from institutional lenders.

Bonds may be secured by pledges of other assets as well. Those secured by pledges of equipment, closely comparable to credit extended under equipment purchase contracts, are called *equipment bonds* or *equipment trust certificates*. Bonds may also be secured by stocks and bonds. X Company may hold common stocks or bonds issued by Y Company, and may surrender control of these to a trustee in support of its own issue of X Company bonds. Such bonds are called *collateral trust bonds*.

Debentures

In addition companies may issue unsecured bonds, called *debentures*. Some debentures are issued under conditions where none of the borrower's assets have been previously pledged. In situations of this type, the borrower may provide formal assurance to the prospective debenture holders that the borrower will not subsequently pledge assets to secure other loans, except to an extent specified in the indenture covering the debenture issue. This type of agreement is referred to as a *negative pledge* and provides protection for debenture holders. Otherwise, it would be conceivable that a company could borrow on a debenture issue, obtaining this credit on favourable terms because it had solid assets and earnings, and few other obligations. The company might subsequently mortgage its assets, thereby creating claims of higher priority than those of its debenture holders. These subsequently issued claims could seriously prejudice the financial position of the debenture holders.

In addition debentures may be issued with the understanding that some assets are already pledged, with the result that some creditors enjoy higher priority claims than the debenture holders. This can be carried a step further. Debentures can be issued with the explicit condition that they are of lower priority than some of the company's other debt obligations. These debentures are known as *subordinated debentures*.

Debentures may be issued under a variety of circumstances.

They may be used by a company so financially sound that its debt requires no pledge of assets. Or, at the other extreme, they may be issued by companies whose assets are so encumbered that debentures are a last recourse. In short, their weakness or strength turns entirely on the financial condition and reputation of the issuer.

In general, security is offered on a bond issue to make it more marketable, and to allow it to be sold at a lower interest cost. A company with a strong financial position may be able to market a debenture issue accompanied by a negative pledge, on quite favourable terms. Such a company might be particularly inclined to issue debentures if it held little real estate suitable for securing a mortgage bond issue.

A company with extensive real estate would probably be inclined to issue a first-mortgage bond issue rather than debentures, because of their broader marketability. These bonds would be salable to certain trusts and institutions who were restricted from unsecured lending. This extra source of demand for the issue might enable it to be marketed at a slightly lower cost. Other things being equal, one can expect lower marketability (higher interest charges) on more junior obligations, such as second-mortgage bonds or debenture issues subordinated to previously issued debentures or mortgages.

COSTS AND PAYMENTS

Specific Cost of Bond Borrowing

An interest rate is expressed in a bond issue; this interest rate determines the amount of interest payment that must be made to the bondholders. The bond issue will express a *face amount* which represents the principal of the bond issue which must be repaid to bondholders. The interest rate expressed on the bond (sometimes called the *coupon rate*) relates to this face amount. For example, an 8 percent bond issued by Char-Bown Ltd. with a face amount of $1 million pays $80,000 per year.

The stated interest rate, however, is almost never the specific cost of capital on a bond issue. The difference arises for two reasons:

a. The bonds may actually be sold to the bondholders at a premium or a discount rather than at the face value amount.
b. Costs of marketing the bond issue will have to be deducted from the amount paid for by the bonds by bondholders, in determining the proceeds of the bond issue.

Suppose the Char-Bown bond, $1 million at 8 percent, is a 20-year balloon payment bond, with interest payable in annual installments. Cash outflows on the bond will then consist of $80,000 per year for 19 years and $1,080,000 during the 20th year.

Now suppose that bond was originally sold at a discount, for a price of 93½. Bond price is a percentage of face value, so the actual amount that bondholders paid for the bond was $935,000. Suppose also that $15,000 in marketing costs were associated with the sale of the bond. In this case, Char-Bown actually receives $920,000 for its bond. Internal rate calculation would disclose that on this bond the internal rate is something more than 8 percent. The calculation is shown below:

Cash Flows		Trial Rates			
		8%		10%	
Year	Amount	Discount or Annuity Factor	PV	Discount or Annuity Factor	PV
0	−$ 920,000	1.000	+$920,000	1.000	$920,000
1–19 . . . −	80,000	9.604	− 768,000	8.365	− 669,000
20 . . . . +	1,808,000	.215	− 232,000	.149	− 161,000
NPV			−$ 80,000		+$ 90,000

By interpolation, specific cost is about 9 percent.

Detailed bond tables, similar to mortgage tables are used for refined calculations. Capability for generating these tables are sometimes programmed into computers or portable calculators.

Provision for Interest Payment

Interest is usually paid semiannually on bond issues. This payment may consist of mailing cheques to a list of registered bondholders. When secondary sales of bonds have been made, amendments to this list of registered holders must also be made, based on notification of the secondary transaction. Bonds of this type are referred to as being *registered as to principal and interest.*

A *coupon bond* is also a possibility. A bond of this type has attached to it interest coupons which are, in effect, drafts against the issuing company for interest. Coupons are dated, and as each interest payment becomes due, the bondholder removes or "clips" his coupon and presents it for payment. Coupon bonds are not registered as to interest, but a list of registered holders may still be maintained to protect bondholders from theft. Such bonds are registered as to principal only. Where no registry is maintained, no notification is required in secondary market transactions. The coupon bonds are then also referred to as *bearer bonds.*

Bond Retirement

There is one common method of bond retirement and several less common varieties. The first of these is retirement under a *sinking-fund* arrangement. Under this system the bond issuer makes regular installment payments to a sinking-fund trustee, again usually a trust company or investment dealer. Through these regular sinking-fund payments, a fund is accumulated for the discharge of the bond at maturity.

The sinking fund constitutes a form of installment payment. Another type of installment repayment can be effected with the use of serial bonds. Under a method of this type, maturities of the various bonds in a bond issue are distributed over time in such a way that some of the bonds are retired after a short time, while on others retirement is deferred until the full length of life of the bond issue.

In addition to these installment methods, bonds can be retired with a balloon payment. Although rare, it is also possible for bonds to be issued with no provision for retirement of principal. A bond of this type is called a *perpetual bond,* or a *consol.* If the holder wishes to liquidate his bond, he must then rely solely on the secondary market, where the bond will sell at the discounted value of a perpetual stream of interest payments:

$$\text{Price} = \frac{\text{Perpetual annual payment}}{\text{Appropriate discount rate}}$$

PREMATURE RETIREMENT

There may be a number of reasons why a company may not wish to wait the legally permissible length of time before discharging its principal obligation on all or part of a bond issue. One reason for retiring an old issue might be to take advantage of a decline in interest rates, where the old issue could be replaced with a new lower cost issue. The second reason would be attributable to a company's wishing to decrease the liquidity of its obligations. The company may feel that, for example, a balloon bond issue a few years from maturity is uncomfortably current and may wish to replace this with a longer term obligation. Finally, a company may wish to effect a change in its financial condition by lowering its debt ratio, and may wish to accomplish this by bond retirement.

Call Privilege

There are three methods in which retirement can be effected. The first of these is by including a formal right of retirement, described as a *call privilege*, into a bond issue's indenture. A call privilege is an option allowing the company to retire bonds by paying a specified price to bondholders; usually this *call price* is substantially above the price at which the bonds were originally issued.

If a call privilege exists, it is possible for the company to readily take advantage of declines in interest rates. An internal rate can be calculated using the remaining payments of interest and principal on the bond issue as cash outflows, and the value of the bonds at the call price as the cash inflow. (This is the amount of cash that the company is currently "receiving" from the bond issue, since this is the amount of money the company will have to give up to discharge it.) Suppose for example, in the Char-Bown bond issue, five years have elapsed from the time of issue and that the call price is 120. Remaining payments on a $1 million bond and the price of calling it now, are detailed below:

Year (commencing 5 years after original date of issue)	Cash Flow	Explanation
0	−$1,200,000	Call price.
1–14	+ 80,000	Interest saving if call is exercised.
15	− 1,080,000	Interest and principal saving.

The internal rate that equates these payments is about 6 percent before tax. Therefore, if the interest rate on comparable bond issues were to fall below 6 percent, Char-Bown could profitably refund its bond issue.[3]

A call privilege, with a call price as low as possible, is desirable from the point of view of the bond issuer, at least in a superficial way. It gives him an opportunity to take advantage of possibly more favourable future capital market conditions. On the other hand, it is undesirable from the point of view of bondholders, since a low call price can force them to reinvest money under unfavourable conditions. Accordingly, a low call price will detract from the initial marketability of the bond issue, and may raise the issue's specific capital cost. Thus a call privilege is not something to be regarded as a gift from the bondholders, but a privilege extended by them at a price. It becomes a matter of judgment for a company's financial managers as to the extent to which they should be willing to trade initial marketability of a bond issue for a favourable call privilege.

A second possibility for retiring bonds lies in negotiation. The bond indenture may empower the trustee to conduct this negotiation on behalf of the bondholders. It is not likely that the borrower will be able to effect an interest rate saving from negotiation of this type, since a negotiation implies that terms must be mutually acceptable, but it is quite possible that a negotiation could lead to an exchange of bonds of longer matu-

[3] This analysis could be slightly affected by income tax aspects not discussed.

rity for those that were nearing retirement age. Such an arrangement might be desirable both from the viewpoint of the borrower, who wishes to improve his liquidity position, and from the point of view of creditors who want longer term commitment of their funds.

Bond Repurchase

A third method of premature retirement is through repurchase. A company may attempt to repurchase part or all of its outstanding bond issues through secondary market transactions. It is unlikely that bond repurchase can lead to significant interest cost saving, since if current interest rates have declined since the time of the bond issue, the secondary market price of the company's outstanding bonds will be correspondingly high. (Their price will be determined in the secondary market by discounting at the current interest rate. A low-interest rate will yield a high present value and hence a high price.) Repurchases can be used, however, to allow the replacement of some short maturity bonds with longer ones, or to reduce the amount of the outstanding debt.

A major disadvantage of repurchase lies in the difficulty of repurchasing an entire bond issue. If an entire issue can be discharged, as may be possible through call or negotiation, all collateral pledged to support the bond issue is released, and any restrictions included in the indenture become nonexistent. With only piecemeal retirement by repurchase, the still existent indenture may impose conditions which interfere with the obtaining of replacement financing if it should be needed.

INVESTMENT DEALERS

A company wishing to market a bond issue will engage the services of an investment dealer. While the term dealer is widely used, dealer-broker would be more technically correct. A *dealer* buys and sells for his own account, and a *broker* is an agent who buys and sells on behalf of others. "Investment dealers" often perform both functions, and typically handle a wide variety of financial transactions. Transactions handled by major Canadian investment companies include:

a. Marketing new issues of bonds and common stock.
b. Guaranteeing the successful sale of new security issues—the underwriting function.
c. Acting as brokers in the secondary sale of securities.
d. Acting as buyers and sellers of securities.
e. Providing research, counselling, and other assistance for both issuers and purchasers of securities.

Financial officers of large companies maintain regular contact with investment dealers. The investment dealer may even be represented on the company's board of directors. In this way the dealer provides ongoing financial counsel to the company, particularly regarding security issuance. At the same time, board membership enables the dealer to maintain intimate familiarity with the operations of his client company.

Marketing Services of the Investment Dealer

Beyond advice, there are a variety of services offered by the investment dealer for the marketing of bond issues. In the first of these, the investment firm commits itself to act only as a broker. This first method, referred to as a "best effort" basis, is an undertaking by the investment dealer to use the contacts, branch offices, and other marketing facilities of his organization to sell the bond issue at the best possible price. The investment dealer may attempt this through a *private placement*, where he sells the entire issue to one or few financial institutions, such as trust companies or insurance companies. Or he may undertake a public offering of the securities, usually with assistance from other investment firms.

The investment firm may also act as an *underwriter* of this security issue. In this case the investment dealer not only undertakes the services provided under "best effort" marketing but also guarantees that a specified price will be received for the bonds. For example, if an underwriting agreement provides that a price of 98 is guaranteed on a bond issue, the investment dealer and other collaborating dealers will buy securities not sold to the public at this price. In turn they will resell them to the public later, even if this may entail a sizable loss to the participating dealers.

The underwriting service may be quite vital to a company that is counting on the proceeds of its bond issue for immediate use and which may suffer financial difficulty if a bond issue expected to sell at 100 actually cannot be placed at above 80.

In addition to the services of an underwriter or a broker, the investment firm may perform a dealership function. This is sometimes done in connection with the firm's "best effort" marketing. The investment dealer will attempt to bolster the demand for the security issue by purchasing some of the securities for later resale. In some instances, a dealer may purchase an entire security issue, and then resell it to investors; however this practice is usually reserved for government security offerings.

In return for their services investment dealers will charge varying fees. On a best effort marketing, the fee will be a relatively low brokerage commission. Underwriting fees will be substantially higher, depending upon the amount of risk the investment dealer believes he is assuming. Depending on services offered, issue size and reputation and financial condition of the borrowing company, these charges could range from a low of 0.5 percent to a possible charge as high as 10 percent.

Investment dealers normally collaborate in the exercise of underwriting and selling functions. Particularly in underwriting, where heavy financial responsibilities may be involved, a group of many investment firms may be assembled by the original investment dealer to share the risk and profit in guaranteeing an issue. On larger Canadian issues, American investment bankers may be heavily involved in the underwriting efforts.

In addition to the underwriting group, a second group of collaborating firms, called a selling group, is also likely to be assembled. While underwriting groups are organized to enlist financial strength, selling groups are formed to gather marketing power. Investment dealers with many branch offices are particularly attractive as marketing group participants. Marketing is also likely to be international in scope, particularly on larger issues. In fact, major Canadian investment dealers themselves usually maintain offices in New York and London, and often in other world financial centres (e.g., Chicago, Tokyo, Paris, Frankfurt, and so on).

Public Regulation

Where public issue, rather than a private placement, is to be undertaken rigorous rules of disclosure must be met. These rules vary from province to province and are administered by provincial bodies, called securities commissions, or equivalent terms. Since the hub of Canadian financial activity is Toronto, the Ontario Securities Commission and Ontario securities legislation are usually regarded as the most significant. Ontario legislation also is often a pattern for legislation in other provinces.

A formal document describing the bond issue, called a *prospectus,* must be prepared before bonds are offered for sale. This is customarily prepared by a law firm, in consultation with the company and its investment dealer. The prospectus describes not only the provisions of the bond issue but also the nature of the issuing company. It may certify that the securities are suitable for life insurance company investment, a generally accepted indicator of high quality. It must also call explicit attention to potential problems in the security issue or the issuing company. Failure to comply meticulously with these disclosure requirements may result in a security commission's refusal to allow marketing of the issue.

SECONDARY BOND MARKETS

The set of transactions and related institutions which accomplish the initial sale of a security issue are called a *primary market.* Securities issued by companies are negotiable (they may be resold by their holders). The institutions and transactions achieving the transfer of previously issued securities are called the *secondary market.* The facilities for secondary disposal of a company's bonds are important to the issuer because if the bonds have ready resale potential their original marketability is enforced.

There is nothing to prevent the original holder of any company security from reselling it to one of his acquaintances. However, usually it is difficult for prospective buyers and sellers to contact each other spontaneously. To provide this contact a well-organized market has developed for secondary security sales.

Security Exchanges

The secondary security market consists of three major segments—security exchanges, dealership operations, and brokerage outside of security exchanges. Canadian security exchanges, which will be discussed later in connection with common stocks, do not trade bonds. However, a few major Canadian bond issues are traded on the New York Stock Exchange. Interaction with this marketplace may be carried on through Canadian investment dealers.

Over-the-Counter Market

The major secondary market for Canadian bonds is maintained by the bond trading departments of Canadian investment dealers. These departments buy and sell bonds for profit, and in the process maintain a valuable liquidity service. The dealer will buy bonds even with no immediate resale prospect, accumulating the bonds in a securities inventory. Holding of the inventory allows the dealer to have bonds immediately available for investors who wish to buy securities in the secondary market. A dealer who stands ready to buy or sell a particular bond at specified prices is said to *"make a market"* in that bond.

For example, a dealer may make a market of the bonds of Barber-Cooke, Ltd. He may believe that a price of approximately 105 is appropriate for the bonds. Accordingly, he may offer to buy the bonds at 104½ and to sell them at 105½. The buying price is called a *bid,* the selling price an *ask,* and the difference between the two a *spread.* If all goes well the spread should enable the dealer to cover his expenses and make a profit, but if he misjudges the market, he may overaccumulate inventory and be forced to dispose of Barber-Cooke bonds at a loss.

Larger security dealers maintain inventories in the hundreds of millions of dollars, financed almost entirely by short-term bank credit. Each dealer does not attempt to bid (make a market) on all bonds. Instead specialization and collaboration takes place. For example, if dealer A is offered a particular bond by a prospective he may act as an agent for a dealer who makes a market in that bond. This network of collaborating dealers is often called the *over-the-counter market,* or OTC.

Bond Brokerage

Particularly where large blocks of bonds are being bought or sold, security dealers may arrange transactions directly between investors, without going through either a security exchange or an OTC dealer. For example, the security firm may match up a Canadian mutual fund wishing to sell a large block of bonds with an American insurance company which wants to purchase them. This is typically done on an informal, telephone call basis, although U.S. firms are pioneering more systematic methods, involving computerized matching of buyers and sellers. Transactions which by-pass OTC dealers and security exchanges are often called *"third market"* transactions. Their obvious attraction is the avoidance of OTC spread or security exchange commissions. In method they closely parallel private placements of primary issues.

BOND TRANSACTIONS

Yield

The rate of return received by bondholders is called bond *yield.* The term is sometimes subdivided as follows:

1. *Yield to maturity.* The discount rate which sets the present value of future bond interest and principal repayment equal to the bond's selling price. From the bond investor's point of view, yield to maturity (or YTM) is the bond's internal rate of return. When the term bond yield is used without further description, it should be interpreted as meaning yield to maturity.
2. *Current yield:* The ratio of annual bond interest payments to selling price. This description is used much less frequently than yield to maturity. It is of interest to persons concerned with the current cash flows derived from bonds they hold; the measure is of particular interest to retired investors living off their security holdings. The measure ignores potential appreciation or depreciation as the bond approaches maturity, an inevitable process if the bond was not bought at a price of 100.

Bond issues are identified among investors by three attributes: issuing company, coupon rate, and maturity date. Bonds issued by Labatts, bearing a 9 percent coupon rate and due in 1994 would be described as Labatt 9s of 94.

If these bonds sold at a price of 86 in 1975, yield to maturity is determined as:

Interest remaining (1977 to 1994):
$9 per 100 of face value annually for 17 years
Principal repayment:
$100 (face) after 17 years
Price:
$86 per $100 face value
Yield to maturity, obtained by experimental discounting
11%

Current yield would be calculated as:

$$\frac{\text{Coupon rate}}{\text{Price}} = \frac{9}{86} = 10.5\%.$$

The difference reflects the incomplete character of the current yield calculation, which disregards the fact that the bond, though priced at 86 now, will appreciate to 100 at maturity, when repayment of face value will occur.

Yield versus Expected Rate of Return

Bond yield calculations are based on the assumption that default will not occur, that interest payments are all promptly discharged, and that full repayment is received at maturity. The probability of default may colour the picture painted by the yield calculation. To think about a bond clearly one should regard bond yield as the *maximum* rate of return it will afford the investor. If a probability > 0 is assigned to any degree of result, expected rate of return to the investor will be less than calculated yield.

BOND YIELD VARIATION

Bond yields are closely akin to interest rates on other loans, and vary in a similar pattern. One can expect rates to reflect market preferences for both liquidity and safety.

The Yield Curve

In one sense, most long-term bonds are highly liquid, because of the existence of secondary markets. Through these markets they can normally be converted into cash almost instantly. However, because of their tendency for price volatility (see Chapter 8) they are imperfect instruments for personal or company liquid reserve holdings. Thus even where company bonds have little chance of default, one can expect some decrease in their marketability (increase in their required interest rate) because of their longevity.

The relation between interest rate and longevity is often referred to as the *yield curve*. Typically this curve, if graphed, has a positive slope. For example, at a time when 90-day commercial paper is being discounted at 5 percent, it may be necessary to offer 6 or 7 percent on a 20-year bond if it is to sell for face value. It should be noted that upward slope is only a general tendency. Sometimes the curve displays no discernible slope, and occasionally it "inverts" to negative slope.

Riding the Yield Curve

The tendency toward positive slope in the yield curve has prompted financial analysts to identify an interesting arithmetic result—effective yield on securities bought or sold before maturity are likely to be higher than if the securities are held or left outstanding until the maturity date.

An example will illustrate. The Laval Company buys a 10 percent, five-year balloon bond in 1973 and sells it three years later in 1976. The yield curve during the period may be simplistically summarized by the following schedule:

Market interest rates:
More than two years to maturity 10%
Two years or less to maturity 6%

The original purchase takes place at a price of 100, since the coupon rate of 10 percent coinceded with the going market rate. At the time of resale, the bond has two years to run. Its remaining payment schedule, assuming annual interest payments, is:

Year	Cash Flow per $1,000 Bond	Explanation
1 (1977)	+$ 100	Interest
2 (1978)	+$1,100	Interest

From the yield schedule we observe that the appropriate discount rate in the secondary market for this bond, which now has two years or less to maturity, is 6 percent. Therefore, the bond is priced to yield 6 percent and sells for $1,073.

We now turn to a cash flow schedule describing Laval's total experience with its bonds.

Year	Cash Flow per $1,000 Bond	Explanation
0 (1973)	−$1,000	Cost
1 (1974)	+$ 100	Interest
2 (1975)	+$ 100	Interest
3 (1976)	+$1,173	Interest and resale

An internal rate analysis will disclose that Laval's 10 percent bond, bought at 100, has in fact yielded over 12 percent (ignoring taxes and transaction costs).

The reasoning that explains this apparent anomaly is not complicated. The 10 percent on long-maturity bonds was based on the fact that during the last years of their life, these bonds would be very liquid instruments, suitable, for example, for use as corporate liquid reserves. Laval received an extra reward for holding the bonds *only* during that part of their life when they were relatively illiquid.

This technique has its reverse side. A company which issues long-term bonds and wishes to repurchase or refund them before they mature can expect a specific capital cost somewhat above the cost calculated on the basis for retiring the bonds at maturity. The benefit derived from this extra cost lies in the discharge of a liability before it becomes too urgent.

Risk Premiums

The yield curve, albeit erratically, may explain some difference in corporate bond yields. Much greater differences are attributable to risk. The financial condition of the issuing corporation and the security offered on a bond contribute to the safety it affords investors. It is not uncommon for bonds of comparable maturity to be issued by one company to yield 8 percent while those of another may be offered simultaneously at a yield of 15 percent. Risk premium differences may exist not only between companies but also between bond issues where a company has more than one issue outstanding. For example, a company's first-mortgage bonds may be yielding 8 percent while a new subordinated debenture issue may require a rate of 12 percent if they are to be marketed.

Risk Premiums: A Philosophical Note

The existence of risk premiums need not suggest that the marketplace is "working against" companies which issue high-risk bonds. These companies may be undertaking risky but potentially lucrative ventures; bondholders are simply participating to some extent in the fortunes, good or ill (with possible default losses on bonds) of the venturesome company.

From another viewpoint, too, the risk premium does not seem categorically onerous to the borrower. Consider a company choosing between a first-mortgage bond issue at 9 percent or a debenture issue, with a rather liberal indenture, at 12 percent. The high priority claim of the first-mortgage bondholders might make it difficult for the company to borrow additional money, while the lower priority status of the debenture holders will not constitute such a deterrent to other creditors.

In other words, if an enterprise wishes to undertake a risk, this risk must be absorbed by someone. If bondholders can obtain absolute safety, all risk must be borne by stockholders and other creditors. If bondholders will shoulder some of the burden of the company's risk, paying extra hire for this service may be sound financial practice.

THE "BURDEN" OF DEBT

Meeting the obligations of a bond issue imposes cash flow requirements on a company. Interest payments must be regularly met as well as required retirements of principal. If the retirement is of an installment type, sinking-fund payments, or serial bond payments impose recurrent cash outflows; if the bond is of a balloon form, part of the liquidity problem is deferred until maturity date of the bond. Certain indicators are customarily used to measure a company's ability to meet its debt obligations, as they come due. They are usually used in conjunction with the debt ratio.

The debt ratio indicates the proportion of the company's assets that are being financed by borrowing, and complementarily the cushion of equity that protects the bondholder's investment. The other measures, all variations on the same theme, measure another aspect of the company's ability to discharge its debt obligations, by comparing the cash inflows of the company available for debt repayment with the magnitude of the company's repayment obligations. Several of these measures are listed.

Times Interest Earned. To express this ratio and subsequent ones the expression EBIT is introduced. This is an abbreviation for "earnings before interest and taxes"; it is calculated by adding back a company's interest payments to its net earnings before income taxes. The ratio itself is:

$$\text{Times interest earned} = \frac{\text{EBIT}}{\text{Annual interest payments}}.$$

A decline in this ratio, or an absolute level of the ratio approaching 1, would suggest inability to meet interest payments.

Fixed Charge Coverage. An obvious deficiency in the above ratio is failure to recognize that the company's long-term debt obligations can include installment principal payments as well as interest. A naïve version of the ratio is:

$$\text{Fixed charge coverage} = \frac{\text{EBIT}}{\text{Interest} + \text{principal installments}}.$$

More sophisticated versions recognize that principal installments are particularly burdensome because they are not tax deductible. They may consider that depreciation charges, deducted in determining EBIT, is a noncash expense and hence represents cash flows available for debt service. One revised version of the coverage rates becomes:

$$\text{Fixed charge coverage} = \frac{\text{EBIT} + \text{depreciation}/(1-t)}{\text{Interest} + \text{required principal}\ \text{repayment}/(1-t)}.$$

Note that the after-tax character of both depreciation and principal repayment are recognized. To the extent that a company has significant amounts of lease payments, it is appropriate to add those into the above denominator as well.

These ratios may be historical in character, or they may compare historic EBIT with a denominator embodying anticipated charges of prospective bond issues. They typically do not include repayment obligations on current liabilities (this is taken care of through liquidity ratios), nor do they typically consider balloon payment obligations.

The ratios have obvious logic. To the extent that EBIT is an indicator of the company's cash flows available for debt service, they indicate something about the likelihood of repayment difficulties. While it is true that these repayment difficulties may be handled through refinancing, or through the company's other liquidity sources, both bondholders and corporate financial officers would prefer to see the company throw off operating cash flows sufficient to comfortably meet its debt obligations.

Several problems exist in the use of the ratios. First, EBIT and the company's cash flows available for debt service may not coincide. For example, in a growing company, some of the earnings are likely to be based on increases in credit sales. Part of EBIT then in fact represents a receivable accumulation rather than cash flow.

Probably more importantly, the use of a historic EBIT figure based on a previous year or an average of previous years tells little about the risk dimension in the company's cash flows. A historically based coverage ratio of 2, where previous and prospective earnings are very stable, may afford more protection to creditors than a coverage ratio of 4, based on historical earnings which may evaporate without notice.

In spite of the deficiencies, there is a great deal of common sense in the coverage ratios and they are widely used. Even if a company believes it has better means of evaluating its ability to repay debt, and thus lacks direct interest in the ratios, it may be concerned with them because of their credibility to prospective financing sources. The company may then wish to attempt to control the ratios by moderating the urgency of its debt commitment, to avoid impairing the marketability of its bonds.

SUMMARY

Larger companies typically obtain much of their longer term debt money from the issuance of bonds. A contract, or indenture, exists between borrower and bondholders; this may be secured or, in the case of debenture issues, unsecured.

Interest payments may be made directly to bondholders, or through the use of coupons attached to the bonds. Repayment arrangements for principal may be through a sinking fund, through the use of serial bonds, or by balloon payment.

Bonds often contain a call privilege which allows the borrower to retire the bonds prematurely. Bonds may also be retired through negotiation with bondholders, and through repurchase in the securities market.

Bonds are typically issued with the assistance of an investment dealer. Investment dealer, usually in conjunction with other dealers, will market the bonds, and may underwrite them to guarantee their salability. Public issues of bonds are subject to public regulation.

An orderly secondary market exists for most bonds; the principal vehicle for secondary bond transaction is the over-the-counter market.

As bonds often sell at a premium or discount, the interest rate specified on the bond (coupon rate) will usually not correspond to the yield which the bond provides to its owner. This yield is determined by rate of return calculation.

A yield curve describes the relationship between bond yields and bond maturity.

A number of measures are available for describing the relationship between required cash flows on bond issues and the earning power or cash flow of the borrowing company. These are said to measure the burden of debt.

QUESTIONS AND PROBLEMS

1. Why does a bond issue require a trustee?

2. What is the purpose of a negative pledge?

3. The company issues a 10-year bond requiring annual interest payments, at 9 percent, and repayment of principal at maturity. The bonds are issued at a net price of $94. Identify specific cost of capital.

4. In a market where bonds of a certain type are being priced to yield 12 percent, what is the difference between the expected market price on a 20-year, 8 percent bond and of an 8 percent consol?

5. A company issues bonds described as 12s of 92 during 1977. The bonds have a call price of 120. By 1980, interest rates on comparable bonds have declined to 9 percent. Analyze, on a before-tax basis, whether it is rational to call the bond issue.

6. While the functions are often performed by the same firm, distinguish between the roles of a broker, a dealer, and an underwriter.

7. What is the difference between an over-the-counter transaction and a third-market transaction?

8. Bonds out of an issue of 8s of 84 are, in 1979, selling in the over-the-counter market at bid 88, ask 89. Identify the yield to maturity and current yield for the prospective purchaser.

9. Repeat the above calculation on an after-tax basis, assuming that the prospective purchaser has a marginal personal income tax rate of 50 percent and that the difference between maturity value and purchase price will be taxed as a capital gain at maturity.

10. A yield curve is described in an oversimplified way as:
    a. All bonds over five years yield 10 percent.
    b. All bonds under five years yield 5 percent.
        A company considers the possibility of issuing ten-year bonds, and repurchasing them four years before maturity. On a before-tax basis, estimate full cost.

11. Describe how a bond issue may be "designed" in ways that will shift more or less risk to the prospective bond purchasers.
        Indicate how the shifting of risk to the bondholders may help relieve the risk borne by other claimants.

12. List the advantages and disadvantages of measures of "burden of debt" which compare company cash flows with debt obligations.

RELATED READINGS

Boot, John C. G., and Frankfurter, G. M.   "The Dynamics of Corporate Debt Management, Decision Rules and Some Empirical Evidence." *Journal of Financial and Quantitative Analysis,* September 1972.

Bowlin, O. D.   "The Refunding Decision: Another Special Case in Capital Budgeting." *Journal of Finance,* March 1966.

Dobell, R., and Sargent, T.   "The Term Structure of Interest Rates in Canada." *Canadian Journal of Economics,* February 1969.

Fullerton, D.   *The Bond Market in Canada,* Toronto: Carswell, 1962.

Jen, F. C., and Wert, J. E.   "The Deferred Call Provision and Corporate Bond Yields." *Journal of Financial and Quantitative Analysis,* June 1968.

Johnson, R. W.   "Subordinated Debentures: Debt That Serves as Equity." *Journal of Finance,* March 1955.

Litzenberger, R. H., and Rutenberg, D. P.   "Size and Timing of Corporate Bond Flotations." *Journal of Financial and Quantitative Analysis,* January 1972.

Peters, R.   *Economics of the Canadian Corporate Bond Market.* Montreal: McGill-Queens University Press, 1971.

Van Horne, J.   "A Linear-Programming Approach to Evaluating Restrictions under a Bond Indenture or Loan Agreement." *Journal of Financial and Quantitative Analysis,* June 1966.

————.   *The Function and Analysis of Capital Market Rates.* Englewood Cliffs, N.J.: Prentice-Hall, 1970.

Weingartner, H. M.   "Optimal Timing of Bond Refunding." *Management Science,* March 1967.

Winn, W. J., and Hess, A.   "The Value of the Call Privilege." *Journal of Finance,* May 1959.

15

FINANCING SOURCES BETWEEN DEBT AND COMMON STOCK

Conventional debt obligations, whether in the form of loans from institutional sources or in the form of commercial paper and bonds, are quite rigid financial arrangements. Irrespective of the contemporary fortunes of the borrower required interest and principal payments must be met, or the company's life may be forfeited. One of the ways in which a company can avoid this rigidity is to issue common shares instead of undertaking additional borrowing. In this way the company takes in new owners, who own a share of the company's earnings only if and when those earnings materialize.

While common stock financing may offer a company a total lack of rigidity, this avenue too has its problems. As new shares are sold, each new common shareholder becomes a full-fledged participant in the ownership of the company's common equity and has a right to claim his full proportionate share of *all* earnings that the common shareholders receive, as long as the company continues to exist. This problem of the need to share with new owners is often called *dilution*.

There are a number of financing possibilities that allow a compromise between the rigidities of debt and the full extent of equity participation involved in common stock issuance. These may take the form of debt which confers certain ownership rights or equity which has some debtlike characteristics. One type of debt with equity features has already been discussed—the "equity kicker" that may be included in a mortgage contract; several types of bond issues with equity features will be discussed in this chapter. In addition, a special class of equity will be discussed, a class which establishes a set of shareholders who may be close kin to creditors.

CONVERTIBLE BONDS

The most popular of the bonds *cum* equity participation are *convertible bonds*. A convertible bond (often shortened to convertible) carries with it as part of its indenture a contractual specification called a *conversion privilege*. A conversion privilege is a right of exchange, a right of a bondholder to trade his bond for a specified number of shares of the borrowing company's common stock. The bondholder thus gets something of both worlds. If the company's fortunes prove to be modest, the convertible bondholder can insist on his rights as a creditor and sue if necessary for promised payments of interest and principal. On the other hand, if the issuing company flourishes, he may exercise his conversion privilege and participate in the company's good fortune by becoming a shareholder.

At a naive glance this situation seems too good to be true from the viewpoint of the convertible bondholder. Why does the bond issuer confer this dual set of benefits? A simple answer is that both benefits are modulated. The company expects to borrow at a lower interest rate because it offers an accompanying conversion privilege. Other benefits to the borrower will be observed as the discussion progresses.

The Conversion Privilege

A convertible bond, like any other bond, has a face value which constitutes the principal amount of the bond and is equivalent to a price of 100. The conversion privilege is expressed in the form of a *conversion price*. This determines the exchange ratio or *conversion ratio* offered in a conversion from a bond to common shares. If the face value of the bond is $1,000 and the conversion price is $25, the bond is convertible into 40 shares of common stock.

The conversion privilege can extend over the entire life of the bond, or may be in effect for a limited time. It is also possible to express a conversion privilege in stages, with successively higher conversion prices; such a feature tends to encourage early conversion.

Forcing Conversion

A company may desire to exert pressure on the holders of its convertible bonds to convert them into common stock. This is particularly true if a substantial number of the bonds have already been converted and the company wishes to "clean up" the remainder of the outstanding bonds. The device used for inducing conversion is the call privilege.

Convertible bonds like other bonds can be issued subject to a call privilege. With a conventional bond, the exercise of a call privilege will require a disbursement of cash to cover the call price of the bonds being retired. However, if the bond is convertible and if stock prices are sufficiently favourable, the exercise of the call privilege will result in conversion.

An example will illustrate. Gardiner Mines Ltd. issues bonds with a conversion price of 50 and a call price of 120. The market price of the shares rises to 70. Thus, a bond with a face value of $1,000 can be converted into shares worth $1,400. If the company now gives required notice that it will exercise a call, the bondholder has the choice of converting to shares worth $1,400 or receiving the $1,200 call value. As long as there is enough spread between conversion value and the call value to overcome a little bondholder inertia, the company can confidently predict that the call will not be accompanied by cash redemptions but by the desired conversion.

Besides cleaning up the remainder of a convertible issue that has already been mostly converted, forced conversion can serve another purpose as well. A company's shares may have risen in price to a point where conversion represents an attractive alternative to the bondholders. However, the company may be following a policy of paying low dividends on its common shares, retaining its earnings for company growth. In a situation of this type it is tempting for bondholders to delay conversion as long as possible. They know that eventually they will be able to convert and obtain the rights of shareholders, including a share of the retained earnings. At the same time, by delaying conversion, they continue to receive interest payments as bondholders. In such a situation, forcing conversion allows the company to avoid the interest payments on the convertible debt.

Specific Cost of Convertible Bond Financing

Cost identification on convertible bonds is in principle the same as the identification discussed in connection with "equity kickers." Bondholders are getting a promise of interest payments and principal payments. However, that promise only establishes a floor on the potential receipts of the bondholders; if a company's share prices perform favourably, the bondholders may obtain shares worth much more than the face value of the bond. The critical aspect in the calculation is estimation of the future price of a company's stock, a notoriously difficult undertaking.

Obviously the future share price is a random variable. Accordingly, specific capital cost on a convertible is also a random variable, which can be characterized by a probability distribution. For simplification, we can identify specific capital cost on the basis of a single assumption about future stock price; a more searching analysis would require consideration of a number of possible future stock prices, and their probabilities. Our simplified example follows:

Coal Lake Land and Steam Navigation Ltd. considers the possibility of issuing convertible bonds, which mature in ten years. The bonds will be convertible at a conversion price of 50 and it is estimated that conversion will not take place until the end of the ten-year period because of Coal Lake's modest dividend policies. The bonds pay 7 percent interest, and are expected to sell at par. Coal Lake's share price at the end of ten years is estimated at $100 per share. Coal Lake's marginal tax rate is 40 percent.

On a $1,000 bond, Coal Lake's interest payments will be $42 per year after tax, running for ten years. Conversion is expected at the end of the tenth year; at this time bondholders will receive Coal Lake shares, which the company could have otherwise sold to new shareholders for $2,000. (The conversion price of 50 makes the bond convertible into 20 shares; price is projected at $100 per share). Given these assumptions, specific capital cost is obtained with the following internal rate trials:

		Trial Rates						
		4%		8%		10%		
Time	Cash Flow	Discount or Annuity Factor	PV	Discount or Annuity Factor	PV	Discount or Annuity Factor	PV	
0 . . .	+$1,000	1.000	$1,000	1.000	$1,000	1.000	$1,000	
1–10 .	– 42	8.111	– 340	6.710	– 281	6.145	– 258	
10 . .	– 2,000	0.676	– 1,352	0.463	– 926	0.386	– 772	
NPV . . .			–$ 692		–$ 207		–$ 30	

This calculation indicates an after-tax capital cost of slightly over 10 percent, *if* future share price is $100.

Pros and Cons from the Purchaser's Viewpoint

The combination of enjoying the protection of a creditor and the opportunities of a potential shareholder are attractive. One can isolate the valuation of the convertible bond into two parts: its "theoretical" bond value, and its conversion value. The bond value is obtained by discounting the bond's promises to pay interest and repay principal, on the assumption that conversion will not take place. The going market rate for non-convertible securities is used as the discount rate in this calculation. For example, a 20-year 7 percent convertible bond, in a marketplace where comparable nonconvertible bonds are yielding 10 percent, would have a discounted value or bond value based on a $70 per year, 20-year annuity and a $1,000, 20-year future payment. As the reader can verify, this bond value is $745.

In addition, the convertible has a value based on its potential common stock content. For example, if the above bond has a conversion price of $40, and the company's common shares are selling at $35, the 25 shares into which the bond can be converted are worth $875.

One can expect that this convertible bond will be worth *at least* the higher of its bond value and its conversion value. Beyond this, convertible bonds usually sell at a premium above the higher of bond or conversion value. This premium can be explained by the fact that even though the bond value is the higher of the two values there is usually some hope that stock price may rise in the future. Similarly, if the conversion value is the higher of the two, investors are willing to pay more than the price of the obtainable shares because of the protection afforded by the *"floor,"* the lower limit imposed on the security's value by the bond value, in the event that share prices decline.

There are two other features of the convertible that are attractive to investors. One of these is an appeal to investors who are subjected to regulations or the conditions of a trust, which restrict the extent to which investment in common stock can take place. By holding convertible bonds, the investor is able to obtain some of the "action" of the stock market since high stock prices will cause the price of convertible bonds to appreciate, without actually holding common shares.

The second advantage lies in the fact that convertible bonds allow investors the potential for substantial rewards, without imposing an onerous debt burden on the issuing company. Maintaining a company in a constant state of liquidity crisis does not serve the welfare of creditors. Their wealth is likely to be protected more effectively in a healthy company where management is left with some effective freedom of action. Furthermore, creditors do not want to impose credit terms which are likely to cause bankruptcy, because of the attendant delays and legal complications and also because of possible losses which may accompany this process.

Convertibles, like the other financing instruments to be discussed later in the chapter, have this distinctive feature; a substantial part of the benefits expected by creditors are conditional upon the success of the borrowing company. Such an arrangement may be preferable to a completely rigid payment requirement that is more likely to be defaulted.

At the same time convertibles do not appeal to everyone. Many investors prefer a fully defined series of payments in connection with their bonds. Where a company has the financial strength to credibly define a rigid series of payments with little chance of default, there would seem to be little advantage in offering the feature of convertibility. But where significant risk compensation of creditors is required, the lighter debt burden associated with convertibles may be mutually beneficial to borrower and lender.

Pros and Cons for the Borrower

The mutual advantage that can be obtained from using a convertible bond rather than a more rigid form of debt obligation has been noted above. A continuation of the previous example will reinforce this point. Let us suppose that Coal Lake's hypothetical share value of $100 at the end of ten years was in fact an expected value of the future share price, with substantial dispersion around that price, and that this expectation is shared by both borrowers and lenders. If $100 is the expected share price we observe that a contract has been consummated with an expected specific capital cost, after tax, of 10 percent. Had the same bargain been consummated in the form of a nonconvertible obligation, where all compensation to creditors had to be reflected in the interest rate, annual interest payments after tax would have been $100 for a $1,000 bond instead of $42. This would represent a substantially greater interest burden, with corresponding strain on such ratios as "times interest earned."

The issuing company must compare the issuance of convertibles not only with more rigid debt alternatives, but also with the issuance of common shares. When shareholders supply funds their compensation is entirely conditional on the success of the company, and there is no marginal debt burden at all. On the other hand, there will be dilution, which could be diminished by using convertible bonds. This diminution occurs because the conversion price is usually set substantially above the current market price at the time of issue. The result is that, per dollar of funds supplied, the company will have to issue fewer shares when the conversion privilege is exercised than it would have in a direct sale of shares.

An example can again illustrate. Forsythe Feeds has 200,000 shares of common stock currently outstanding, selling at approximately $60 per share. The company wishes to raise $6 million, and plans to do this either through the issuance of common stock or convertibles. If convertibles are issued, they will be issued at a conversion price of $100.

Ignoring transaction costs, raising $6 million through new common stock will require the issuance of 100,000 shares. The company ends up with 300,000 shares outstanding, one third of which are owned by suppliers of the $6 million. On the other hand, with a conversion price of $100, the $6 million in convertible debt would convert to $6,000,000/$100 or 60,000 shares. That leaves the company with 260,000 shares outstanding if all of the bonds are converted; the new shareholders then own a fractional interest of 60,000/260,000, or about 23 percent.

In other words, where the company believes that it can stand *some* debt burden, a convertible issue may in the end prove less costly to the company's present shareholders than an issue of common stock. At the same time the burdens of a straight debt issue are also partly avoided.

BONDS WITH WARRANTS ATTACHED

This financing arrangement is similar to convertible bonds. Instead of a conversion privilege, the bondholders are given warrants, which are options for the purchase of the company's stock at a specified price. The warrants are separately negotiable; that is, bondholders may sell their warrants and keep their bonds. Secondary markets exist for their resale.

As an example of warrant valuation, a warrant is attached to a $1,000 Koenker-Bullard, Ltd. bond, giving the owner of the warrant the right to purchase five shares of stock at $50 per share. To the extent that the Koenker-Bullard's stock has a potential for exceeding a $50 price, the warrant has value, in the same way that a conversion privilege does. If the company's share price should go to $70, the warrant would be worth *at least* the difference between the option price and the market price of the five shares. Therefore, a Koenker-Bullard warrant should sell for at least $100. In fact, warrants often sell above this theoretical minimum because they offer as much appreciation possibility as the common stock itself, without requiring as much investment.

Advantages and disadvantages of attachment of warrants are quite similar to those associated with offering the conversion privilege. There are two differences that may be important in some situations. With convertible bonds, debt is removed from the company's balance sheet as conversion takes place. Through forced conversion, the debt can be eliminated, thus effecting a possible substantial change in the company debt ratio. When warrants are used, new equity is sold at the option price when the warrant's option is exercised, but the associated debt remains.

While the above may be a disadvantage of warrants, they also have one distinctive advantage—flexibility. With a convertible bond the extent of a creditor's equity participation can be controlled in only one way—by the amount of the conversion price. If only a modest equity participation for creditors is desired, the conversion price must be set very high. In this way, creditors obtain equity participation only in the form of a "long shot" based upon a small probability that share prices will rise above the conversion price.

With warrants two variables can be manipulated—the option price and the number of shares per warrant. The result is that a modest equity participation for bondholders can be devised either by setting a high option price, the equivalent of a high conversion price; or by setting the option price relatively low but limiting the number of shares over which the option can be exercised. If the second technique is used, bondholders can be offered a modest, but rather sure, equity participation. This results from the fairly high probability that the share price will exceed the option price.

The principle is illustrated in the following way. Suppose that on the expiration date of either a conversion privilege or a warrant, the following distribution of company share prices is expected:

Probability	Market Price
.2	$75
.5	45
.3	30

Using this distribution, the company attempts to design an equity participation with an expected value of $100. One of the ways it can do this is by establishing a conversion price of $50. With that price, the conversion privilege would only be exercised in the event that share price is over $50. In our example, the only possible price where conversion will take place is $75. On a $1,000 bond, which converts into 20 shares, the value of the conversion privilege at a share price of $75 is 20 shares × $25 or $500. There is a .2 chance of this ensuing so the expected value of the conversion privilege is .2($500) or $100.

This situation can be duplicated by attaching a warrant with an option to purchase 20 shares at a price of $50. Consider another alternative warrant, an option for the purchase of six shares at a price of $30. Using the same distribution of terminal share prices, the expected value of this warrant is calculated as:

Probability	Share Price	Warrant Value (Share Price − $30) × 6 Shares	Product
.2	$75	$270	$54
.5	45	90	45
.3	30	—	0
Expected value of warrant			$99

It is obvious that this warrant offers its expected value of approximately $100 with much less dispersion than that possible for the same expected value under a convertible bond. These warrants have some value throughout 70 percent of expected share price conditions; the conversion privilege is worth something in only 20 percent of expected cases (though its rewards will be handsome then).

INCOME BONDS

An income bond is distinguished from a conventional bond by the provision that contractual interest payments are deferred or cancelled in years when the issuer cannot meet them out of current income. While these bonds create no potential equity interest for creditors, in a legal sense, creditors do undertake to share some of the vicissitudes of the company. Again this is a device for avoiding some of the rigidity of a conventional bond's payment schedule.

A serious problem associated with income bonds is their equation of the issuer's income with his "ability to pay." A company may show income in its financial statements, and still lack the cash flows necessary for meeting its interest obligation without serious strain. It should be noted here that the interest obligation is likely to be quite high, since creditors must exact all of their compensation in the form of interest payments which are receivable only in years when income is earned. The strain of interest payment may be compounded because, under current income tax rules, income bond interest may not be tax deductible. (It is too similar to a dividend payment).

PREFERRED SHARES

Preferred shares represents an equity interest in the firm which is distinguished from common shares by one or more special features. These special features may offer benefits to the preferred shareholder which the common shareholders do not enjoy; on the other hand the conditions may also deny rights on preferred shares which are available on the common.

The conditions that usually distinguish preferred shares tend to make them similar to debt obligation, although these shares are distinctly not a debt in a legal sense. We shall see that in a financial sense preferred may fill a role similar to that of convertible bonds or bonds with warrants. It should be noted that preferred shares are a form of financing that has recently been on the upswing. While this financing method has been subject to a tax disadvantage, recent tax legislation tends to alleviate this disadvantage. Before considering the tax issue, which relates to specific capital cost, the special features which may characterize preferred stock will be discussed.

Preference in Liquidation

If a company encounters financial difficulties, claims against a company's earnings (by then perhaps nonexistent) may not be as important as claims against its assets. In the event that a company must be liquidated to discharge its obligations, preferred shareholders are given priority in this liquidation over common shareholders.[1] Without such a preference, all shareholders would share proportionately in any equity interest in the company's assets remaining after creditors were paid. With preference in liquidation, preferred stockholders receive priority in the dividing up of the equity interest. Of course, preferred shareholders will still have lower priority than the lowliest of creditors; even subordinated debt claims would be fully discharged before preferred shareholders received a penny.

An example will illustrate. Lenker Lumber Ltd. was forced to liquidate its assets. Claims against the assets are as follows:

First mortgage on land (the major asset remaining for liquidation)	$2,000,000
Second mortgage on land	1,000,000
Claims of general creditors	5,000,000
Priority established for preferred shareholders	1,000,000

We can observe from the assets on the list that unless the assets are liquidated for more than $8 million, shareholders will receive nothing. If they are liquidated for more than $8 million preferred shareholders receive any remaining amount up to $1 million. Only after these higher priority items have been met will anything go to the common shareholders.

Preference in Dividends

Preferred stockholders are almost always given preference with respect to the distribution of dividends. This preference creates a claim which has some similarity to a debt interest obligation. Before any dividends can be paid to common shareholders, a specified dividend must be paid to preferred shareholders. For example, if a preferred share has a face value, or *par value* of $100 and carries an 8 percent dividend preference, no dividend may be paid to common shareholders in a particular year unless preferred shareholders have received $8 per share.

---

[1] In the event that asset preference is not given, shares which would otherwise be called preferred are described as special classes of common, such as Class A or Class B.

There is an important dissimilarity between the requirement for payment of a preferred dividend and the requirement to pay interest. As long as a company does not pay a dividend on its common shares, it has no legal obligation to pay a dividend on its preferred. Even if the company earns substantial income, the preferred shareholders may not sue to receive any payment. Thus the incentive for paying preferred dividends rests on the company's desire to pay common dividends, and its sense of moral obligation or concern over financial image.

Dividend preference is normally made *cumulative*. This means that if a company misses a preferred dividend one year, the dividend preference accumulates. If the dividend on the 8 percent preferred mentioned above was missed in 1975 and 1976, then in 1977 a preferred dividend of $24 per share would have to be paid before any payment to common shareholders could take place.

Participation in Earnings

In addition to their dividend preference, preferred shares may be made *participating*, carrying a right to additional distributions of company earnings. With unrestricted participation preferred shareholders participate proportionately with common shareholders in all dividends. One may think of such an arrangement sequentially; first, the dividend preference is satisfied, then common stockholders are given an amount proportionate to this, and finally, any further dividends are shared proportionately.

Full participation is usually not given to preferred shareholders. When participation is given it is usually in a restricted form. For example, the 8 percent preferred issue described above might provide for participation to an upper limit of 12 percent.

Other Preferred Stock Conditions

Preference in liquidation and earnings distribution, and limits on participation all tend to make preferred stock debtlike in character even though it is legally equity. Another condition which normally separates preferred shareholders from the common shareholders lies in the control of the company's management. Preferred stockholders are usually not given regular voting rights and hence do not share in the selection of the company's directors and officers.

Preferred shares often have a call feature similar to that on bond issues. This feature is particularly valuable on preferred, because unlike bonds preferred shares have no maturity date. Therefore, they could potentially remain outstanding for the life of the company, with no option available for thier sure removal. Preferred shares may also be made convertible, in virtually the same way as a bond issue. A combination of the call privilege and convertibility again provides an opportunity for forcing conversion.

Preferred shareholders' interests may be terminated by conversion, or by exercise of the call privilege. At present, a company's repurchase of its own preferred shares is restricted by the legislation of some provinces. However recent relaxation of this prohibition by Ontario may portend a general legalization of preferred share repurchase.

Specific Capital Cost

If preferred stock is nonparticipating and nonconvertible, and if (the usual case) the company expects to pay the preferred dividends regularly, capital cost identification is straightforward. Since the cash flows from preferred dividends can be treated as a perpetuity, internal rate is identified as:

$$\text{Specific capital cost} = \frac{\text{Annual preferred dividend per share}}{\text{Proceeds from sale of one share}}.$$

If 7 percent, $100 par preferred is sold at a price of $100 less $5 underwriting costs, the capital cost is $7/$95 or 7.4 percent.

Complications arise when participation and/or conversion rights exist. In principle, these identifications are probabilistic in character along lines which have been discussed previously when considering debt instruments.

If the preferred is callable, and the company expects to exercise its call privilege at a specific future date, the calculation is changed to a standard internal rate identification. Following the calculation used on debt, the preferred dividends substitute for annual interest payments, and the call price substitutes for the bond's maturity value.

Preferred share dividends are just that, dividends, for tax purposes. They are treated as a distribution of earnings, not as an expense; hence, a tax deduction does not arise from the payment of a preferred dividend. Therefore, the calculations discussed above may be regarded as after-tax capital cost identifications.

In the event that one wished to compare the cost of preferred stock with the cost of debt on a before-tax basis, the appropriate comparison would be to identify the amount of before-tax earnings the company would need to cover the expected cash disbursements on the preferred. In general the relationship would arise:

$$\text{Before-tax specific capital cost on preferred} = \frac{\text{After-tax specific capital cost}}{1-t}.$$

Converted to a before-tax basis, the 7.4 percent after-tax identified above would, in a company with a 40 percent marginal tax bracket, amount to 12.3 percent.

The "Tax Disadvantage"

The above analysis suggests that preferred shares fare badly in comparison with debt, insofar as corporate income tax is concerned. This is unquestionably true, but that tax effect may be substantially mitigated by another tax consideration. Dividends, as opposed to interest, are treated with relative favour in the hands of their recipients. If preferred dividends are received either by a corporation or by an individual, accompanying corporate or personal tax obligation is less onerous than it is on receipts from debt. This serves to enhance the marketability of preferred shares.

If preferred shares are held by an individual, their dividends are subject to the same tax rules as common dividends. These rules are as follows:

1. The taxable income from the dividend is determined as $\frac{4}{3}$ of the actual amount of the dividend.

2. A tax credit of about 27 percent[2] of this gross amount is allowed to the stockholder. (To review, a tax *credit* does not reduce the amount of taxable income, but the tax itself.)

These conditions can be distilled algebraically to the following expression:

Tax rate on dividends = ⅓ (personal tax rate) − 36%.

For example if an individual's marginal personal tax bracket is 50 percent, the tax rate applied to dividends received by that individual is:

Tax rate on dividends = ⅓(50%) − 36% = about 31%.

With more algebraic manipulation one can observe that if an individual's personal tax rate is below 27 percent he actually obtains a reduction in his tax bill through the receipt of dividends.

If dividends are received by another corporation, they will probably be regarded as intercorporate dividends. As a general rule these dividends are tax exempt. Note that these personal and corporate tax treatments contrast with the treatment of interest receipts, which in both cases are taxable at ordinary tax rates.

An example will illustrate the impact of the joint effect of tax treatment on capital costs. Suppose that a corporation in a 25 percent marginal tax bracket hopes to sell securities to private investors whom it characterizes as being in a 50 percent marginal personal tax bracket. It wants to design a security issue that will allow these investors to receive 6 percent annual return on their investment after they have discharged their personal tax obligations. We may start by identifying the amount of before-tax dividend or interest that must be given to an individual in a 50 percent tax bracket to allow him 6 percent after tax. The calculation can be made with the following equation:

$$\text{Required before-tax return} = \frac{\text{Required after-tax of return}}{1 - \text{Marginal tax rate}}.$$

On the preferred dividend the marginal tax rate will be 31 percent (from the previous calculation) while on the interest it

_____
[2] The precise amount depends on the province.

will be 50 percent. Therefore, to net 6 percent after tax an investor must receive a preferred dividend return of $6\%/(1 - .31)$, or 8.7 percent. To receive 6 percent after tax from interest he requires $6\%/(1 - .50)$, or 12 percent. In other words, if all other conditions are equal, an investor in a 50 percent personal tax bracket ought to be as content with 8.7 percent on a holding of preferred shares as he is with a 12 percent return on bonds.

The example can now be carried forward to the corporate level. If a company issues preferred shares with return to the investor, or cost to the company, of 8.7 percent, the nondeductibility of the preferred dividend make its after-tax specific capital cost 8.7 percent. On the other hand, if a bond were issued at 12 percent, specific capital cost would be tax deductible and therefore reducible by the factor $(1 - t)$. With a 25 percent corporate income tax bracket, the after-tax cost of a 12 percent bond is 9 percent.

One can, therefore, observe that the inefficiency of preferred shares at the corporate level may be largely offset at the personal level. It seems reasonable to believe that investors will tolerate sufficiently lower returns on preferred shares (*other things being equal*) to largely negate the preferred's corporate tax disadvantage. Of course, these personal level tax calculations are not directly required in identifying the specific cost of preferred. They were introduced to illustrate that rejection of preferred shares out-of-hand, because of apparent tax disadvantage, is inappropriate under current tax legislation.

Pros and Cons of Preferred

The case for preferred shares as a financing source is similar to the case for other "compromise" instruments such as convertible bonds. Preferred shares can offer the investor a relatively high return under conditions of favourable personal income tax treatment in return for the absorption of considerable risk. He must expect to participate in the ups and downs of the company; he has no recourse to the courts just because an anticipated preferred dividend does not materialize. He may also be offered participation and conversion privileges as added inducement.

From the company's viewpoint preferred is especially attractive because of its moderate liquidity requirements. It usually requires no sinking-fund payments or other provision for discharge of principal, and even the preferred dividend can be passed if necessary. (It should be reiterated however, that the preferred dividends are not passed lightly; such an action could jeopardize the company's credit reputation.) In addition, unless the preferred shares are made fully participating, the dilution effects of common stock issurance are avoided through the use of preferred.

In comparison with convertible bonds or bonds with warrants attached, preferred stock must be regarded as somewhat closer to the equity end of the debt: equity continuum, in fact as well as legality. The company obtains more freedom from liquidity requirements through the use of preferred; and usually preferred stockholders absorb more of the risk of the company. In turn, the company should expect to pay extra for the risk-taking role undertaken by preferred shareholders.

The stability of the company's cash flows, the burden of existing debt, and cost comparisons can determine which, if any, of the financing halfway houses between conventional debt and common shares should be employed.

SUMMARY

On long-term financing a company has a choice between debt and common shares. There are also halfway houses between these alternatives, which avoid some of the rigidities of liability claims at the expense of some sharing of potential company successes.

Convertible bonds offer their holders an obligation for principal repayment and interest; in addition the holders have the option of converting their bonds into common shares on the basis of a prespecified formula. From the borrower's viewpoint, offering the conversion privilege allows the negotiation of less stringent terms with respect to interest and principal payments. It is sometimes in a company's best interests to force conversion; this may be done through the use of a call privilege.

A cost-of-capital determination on convertibles must appraise not only the promises of interest and principal payment, but also a probabilistic assessment of the value that will be surrendered to bondholders if conversion takes place.

A financial arrangement similar to convertible bonds is found in the use of bonds with warrants attached. These bonds are issued with accompanying options for purchase of specified amounts of company shares.

An income bond will typically provide generous interest to creditors, but the use of the bond avoids some cash flow rigidity for the borrower. On the income bond, interest payment is required only to the extent that the company has earnings in the current year.

While preferred shares are not debt, they share many attributes of debt. Dividends of a prespecified amount are required on a preferred share before common dividends may be paid. Preferred shareholders also rank above common shareholders in any distribution of the company's assets through bankruptcy or liquidation. These, and often other special provisions, tend to make preferred shares debtlike. At the same time the obligation to pay preferred dividends is clearly not as onerous as the obligations a company incurs under a bond issue.

Preferred shares unlike financial instruments that are legally debt, are not deductible as expenses for corporate income tax purposes. This disadvantage, however, may be largely offset by the fact that preferred share dividends are treated more favourably than interest at the personal tax level.

QUESTIONS AND PROBLEMS

1. Convertible bondholders seem to have everything—assured interest and principal payment, and a chance to participate in common share appreciation. Comment.

2. A convertible bond has a conversion price of $80. Into how many shares will convertible bonds of $10,000 face value convert?

3. Suppose the shares of the company in Question 2 are selling for $100 and the convertible bonds are callable at $110. Will a call force conversion?

4. In 1977 Company C has outstanding an issue of 8s of 92, convertible. Bonds of similar quality without *conversion privileges* are currently being priced to yield 10 percent.

C's bonds have a conversion price of $40. Company C's common shares are currently selling for $32 per share.

What is the minimum value for which Company C's convertibles will sell?

5. What are the major differences in financial effect between conversion of a convertible bond and exercise of the option contained in a warrant?

6. Define the following terms which apply to preferred stock.
   a. Preference in liquidation.
   b. Preference in dividends.
   c. Participation.
   d. Cumulative.

7. A company has 100,000 shares of preferred outstanding, with a $7 per share annual preferred dividend, nonparticipating. During 1977, the company earns $10 million, but pays no common dividend. What is its obligation to preferred shareholders with respect to dividend payment in 1977?

   In 1978, the same company earns nothing, but, because of pressure from influential shareholders, undertakes to pay a common dividend. What is its obligation with respect to preferred dividend in 1978, assuming that the preferred dividend is noncumulative?

8. An investor has a 60 percent marginal tax rate. What rate of interest must he earn to obtain a 6 percent after-tax return on his money? What rate of preferred share dividend will satisfy this 6 percent target.

9. A company has a 40 percent marginal corporate income tax rate. Consider your answers in the above question. If an investor is to be afforded a 6 percent after-tax return, would it be more advantageous for this company to provide that return through a preferred share dividend, or through the payment of interest?

RELATED READINGS

Brown, B.   "Why Corporations Should Consider Income Bonds." *Financial Executive,* October 1967.

Donaldson, G.   "In Defense of Preferred Stock." *Harvard Business Review,* July–August 1962.

Hayes, S. L., III, and Reiling, Henry B.   "Sophisticated Financing Tool: The Warrant." *Harvard Business Review,* January–February 1969.

Miller, A. B. "How to Call Your Convertible." *Harvard Business Review*, May–June 1971.

Shelton, J. P. "The Relation of the Price of a Warrant to the Price of Its Associated Stock." *Financial Analysts Journal*, May–June and July–August 1967.

Stevenson, R. "Retirement of Non-Callable Preferred Stock." *Journal of Finance*, December 1970.

Stevenson, R. A., and Lavely, J. "Why a Bond Warrant Issue." *Financial Executive*, June 1970.

Walter, J. E., and Que, A. V. "The Valuation of Convertible Bonds." *Journal of Finance*, June 1973.

16

FINANCING TI IROUGH COMMON STOCK

SOURCES OF EQUITY

Borrowing arrangements may contain elements giving lenders some of the risks and opportunities associated with equity. However, under typical circumstances the chances for unusual losses and unusual gains, resulting from the vagaries of corporate fortune, reside in the hands of that class of capital suppliers called the common shareholders.

On a book value basis, about half of the financial interest in Canadian companies is represented by the equity of common shareholders. However, as we noted in the discussion of the debt ratio, the proportion of financing supplied by creditors—or shareholders—is more appropriately measured by market value. At present, the shares of Canadian companies are selling below book value on average, resulting in less-than-half financial participation by common shareholders on a market value basis. In past periods when share prices have been substantially above book, the common equity ratio has been well above half. Therefore, while half may be a reasonable approximation of equity ratios on a market value basis, this statement is conditional upon the ups and downs of the stock market.

There are three significant sources from which a company can obtain additional common equity capital. Two of these may be called external sources, like debt financing, in that they involve the procurement of funds from outside the company itself. These sources are from the sale of common shares by the already established company or by the company that is being formed, and the paying in of supplemental capital by a company's shareholders. (For larger companies this latter source may be regarded as trivial.)

The most important source of equity capital is internally generated through the company's retention of its own earnings. When a company earns net income and has discharged its income tax responsibilities, equity is established in the business. Unless this equity is disbursed through the payment of dividends it remains in the company, displayed on the right-hand side of the company balance sheet as "retained earnings" or some other descriptive term. With the exception of possible claims of preferred shareholders having cumulative dividend rights, these retained earnings represent the interest of the company's common shareholders. They may not belong entirely to the company's existing shareholders, in the sense that conversion privileges and options may give parties who are not currently shareholders an opportunity to claim some interest in them. However, they are the property of the common shareholders in the sense that claimants who are not present shareholders must become shareholders before their claims are exercisable.

Though the accumulation of equity capital through retained earnings is more important in magnitude, in this text we will begin the study of equity financing by considering the sale of common shares. This offers the opportunity to explore characteristics of the common share itself, and hence the opportunities and hazards of the common shareholder. It is also logically sequential, since there is considerable commonality between selling common shares and a recently discussed topic, selling bonds.

Two additional substantive points should be noted in closing this introductory section. First, forming equity by sale of common shares and by retaining earnings are closely related. Often a company faces a choice of using one or the other: paying a dividend and selling new shares, or getting its equity by abstaining from the dividend.

The second point is that while the dollar volume of new common share sales varies greatly from year to year, it is usually much less than the volume of new borrowing. For example, in a given year the amount of new borrowing may exceed the sale of common shares by a ratio of 10 to 1. This does not imply that if such a pattern continues over time, company funds derived from external equity sources will come to assume the same ratio. The explanation lies in the fact that much borrowing is short term and virtually none exceeds procurement of funds for more than 30 years, while common stocks are perpetual lived. Following the example, if the average life of companies was 100 years (this would be the expected life of "perpetual-lived" shares) and the average life of a debt instrument was 10 years, a 10-to-1 ratio between new borrowing and new sales of common shares would be necessary to maintain approximate equality in the company funds derived from these two sources.

CHARACTERISTICS OF COMMON SHARES

Residual Claimancy

The fundamental strength and weakness of the common shareholder's position lies in his claim to company "leftovers." Claims of creditors and preferred shareholders contain elements of rigidity ranging from the absolute claims of many creditors for fixed schedules of repayment of interest and principal to modified versions, where some participation in company fortunes is acquired by those who are not common shareholders. In general, the common shareholders own all of the company's cash flows and properties that are not subject to the finite claims of others. Since there is usually no obvious upper bound on the values that a company's assets may assume, there is also no obvious upper limit on the wealth that may accrete to shareholders. At the same time if things go badly, common shareholders always stand in last place in the claimant line, and if the value of the company's assets has fallen to a level at or below the other claims against them, common shareholders depart empty-handed.

As a matter of convenience, with a good deal of factual if not legal basis, subsequent discussion of "equity" in this chapter will refer to common equity and exclude preferred shareholders.

Negotiability

Company shares are fully negotiable under usual circumstances. No consent from the public company is required for the disposal of its shares by a shareholder. However, a registry of shareholders is maintained so notification is usually necessary if negotiation takes place.[1] Otherwise the new shareholder would not receive dividends, corporate reports, or other emoluments to which he is entitled.

Voting Rights

A limited company is typically not a democracy in the sense of one-man, one-vote. It can be more closely described as plutocracy where governance is based on wealth, since the ruling principle is one-share, one-vote. It follows that if a corporation has 10,000 shareholders and one of those shareholders owns 51 percent of the shares, that shareholder is a majority unto himself.

Corporate voting takes place at annual shareholder meetings, or under unusual circumstances at special meetings. A shareholder need not be present to cast the votes available to him; he may delegate this right to someone else through a legal instrument called a *proxy*. At the meeting voting will take place for the selection of company directors, who in turn are charged with the practical governance of the company. Votes may also be taken on various aspects of company policy covered by corporate rules of operation, called *bylaws*.

---

[1] An exception is shares held in *street name;* that is, where formal ownership is held by a securities dealer. These shares may be sold by the dealer, and resold by their buyers, with records of ownership, and so on, provided by the dealer, rather than the issuing company.

Company Governance

A corporation is a creation not of nature but of law and has no identity other than that given it by legal prescription. At the time of corporate formation, a *charter* (or similar document) is established which specifies the objectives of the company and the manner in which it is governed. Part of the development of the charter is discretionary for the initial shareholders organizing the company; part of it is determined by the law of the land. Ultimate authority for the affairs of the corporation are given to its shareholders, who may even terminate its existence. These shareholders delegate much of their decision-making power to a board of directors, who in turn select company officers responsible for the day-to-day affairs of the company. A set of *bylaws*, or rules of company operation, are established by shareholders as a general control on company affairs.

In small corporations these three levels of company rulers—shareholders, directors, and officers—may be partly or wholly the same set of persons. In larger companies, with many shareholders, obviously only a few shareholders may have board membership if the board is to be kept within feasible size. Some company officers are often given board membership. In large companies with myriads of shareholders, it may be possible for the directors (who may also be corporate officers), even with relatively modest personal shareholdings, to hold proxies for sufficient shares to perpetuate the board of directors and to call the tune at shareholders' meetings.

Without violating the basic spirit of the one-share, one-vote rule, an attempt may be made to inject an element of greater democratic representation. This may arise from a choice of the voting process that will be specified in the company bylaws. Traditionally separate votes are taken for each director. By this method a group of shareholders holding over half of the company votes, either through ownership of shares or the holding of proxies, can elect all the directors. They simply cast their majority vote, no matter how slim, and each director is elected; holders of 51 percent of the votes can choose 100 percent of the directors.

The alternative method available is cumulative voting. Under this method the general effect is that directors are elected in aggregate, in such a way that groups of shareholders can obtain representation on a board in approximate proportion to the votes that they control. Under this system the group controlling 51 percent of the shares could elect a majority of board members, but not all of them.

It should be noted that the cumulative voting rule is hardly a radical concession to democracy, since majority rule governs at board of directors' meetings. In a 12-man board of directors, the directors' decision is just as binding on company activity if it is determined by 7-to-5 vote as by 12-to-0 vote. However, the cumulative method does at least allow for increased possibility of dissenting argument at the board level. Since company directors are often independent thinkers, rather than simply puppets of the group responsible for their election, the presence of dissent could potentially affect company policy.

Implicit Powers of Governance

In practice, most shareholders do not attend annual shareholder meetings. Typically, the meetings are dominated by a few major shareholders, or by the managing officers of the company who have solicited a sufficient number of shareholder proxies to dominate the meeting. Of course, even shareholders with as little as one share of stock have a right to attend, and sometimes do, out of curiosity or to raise a voice of protest on an issue about which they feel strongly. Still, the meeting is typically a formality with predetermined results.

And yet there is reason to doubt the frequently advanced proposition that shareholders have little power in the widely held company. If management acts in such a way that a company's shareholders become dissatisfied, typical shareholders are not likely to combat this perceived mismanagement by formal action at an annual meeting; they are much more likely simply to dispose of their shares. Added together these individual share sales can depress a company's share price to the point that the company becomes an attractive target for an attempted takeover by an outside investment group.

This takeover attempt may come through the gradual purchase of the shares of dissatisfied shareholders or it may come as a formal *tender*. A tender is an offer made to all the company's shareholders, usually above the current market price, and generally couched in terms that make the offer effective only if it is accepted by a majority of shareholders—in other words only if it leads to control of the company.

Threat of takeover implicitly reminds company management to keep shareholders satisfied and to attempt to anticipate their desires—even if those desires are not formally imposed. This tendency to represent shareholders' interests is, of course, reinforced by a sense of professional responsibility on the part of many company officers, who believe it is their role to represent the interests of shareholders whether forced to or not.

Minority Shareholder Suits

Controlling shareholders, directors, and managing officers of a company may comport the firm's affairs in such a way that the interest of shareholders not in the majority are prejudiced. Consider a simplified, but not unprecedented example. Mr. Anderson owns 51 percent of Basket Ltd. and 100 percent of Landform Ltd. Basket is a grocery firm and Landform is a real estate development firm. Anderson, dominating the affairs of Basket, causes Basket to lease store buildings from Landform at exorbitant rental payments.

Suppose that these rental payments amount ot $1 million per year over and above lease arrangements available from other realty companies. The effect of this is to decrease Basket's profits by $1 million causing (ignoring tax considerations) an annual $510,000 decrease in the wealth of Anderson and $490,000 decrease in the wealth of the remaining shareholders. Landform reaps an extra $1 million in profits, thus contributing a positive $1 million to its sole owner, Anderson. The net result of the combined transactions has been a transfer of $490,000 from the minority shareholders in Basket to Mr. Anderson.

Basket's minority shareholders have another recourse besides the sale of their shares. In fact, if the transaction of the type exemplified above was massive enough, and carried on without advance warning, Basket's shares might be salable only at a severe loss. A minority shareholders' alternative is the courts. They may initiate a lawsuit alleging that their interests have been abused by the actions of the majority shareholder(s). If the court agrees with their allegation they may receive money damage payments or other legal remedies.

Other Shareholder Rights

Another shareholder right not formally contained in company charters is being increasingly amplified by the action of the courts. This right may be called a right of disclosure. Shareholders (and here the term is usually broad enough to include not only existing holders of the company's shares but prospective purchasers of those shares) are entitled to be told of developments that could affect the value of their shares.

For example, a mining company may discover a new ore body. It is possible at first, that only a few persons within the company will know of this discovery. Those persons might use this information to attempt a stock market profit, by buying shares before the information about the new ore body becomes generally available. Increasingly courts are restricting the opportunities of individuals to take advantage of "inside information" and insisting that shareholders (or in effect the public at large) be promptly apprised of such information through appropriate press releases or other modes of communication.

Other possible shareholder rights with respect to the receipt of dividends and the participation in the purchase of newly issued company shares will be discussed subsequently.

ISSUING COMMON SHARES

Issuance of Shares to "Outsiders"

Common shares may be issued in two ways. They may be sold, like bonds, to anyone, including existing shareholders who wish to buy them. For convenience, let us call this a sale to "outsiders." They may also be initially offered only to the company's present shareholders.

The primary sale of common shares typically proceeds like the primary issuance of bonds. A securities firm may offer counselling and research services and may, usually in conjunction with other firms, undertake sale of the stock on a "best effort" basis or with an underwriting agreement. Underwriting costs are normally higher on shares than on bonds because of greater price instability characteristic of the stock market.

Common shares may be sold through private placement; more likely there will be a public offering if the issue is a large one. With a public offering, securities legislation and the jurisdiction of securities commissions applies. A formal prospectus is required for the offering, again along the lines of that used for bond issue.

Sales to Shareholders

There are two ways in which the primary issuance of stock is likely to differ from a primary bond marketing. The first of these relates to providing an opportunity for existing shareholders to participate in the new issue of common shares. A second relates to conformity with "listing requirements" of stock exchanges.

One conventional prerogative of the common shareholder has been the *pre emptive right*. This right gives existing shareholders first opportunity to purchase a proportion of any new issue of common shares equal to the proportion of the company's shares each presently holds. The purpose of the pre-emptive right is to assure existing shareholders that their proportion of ownership, or extent of voting control, may be maintained.

The pre-emptive right is not now a necessary part of company charters. It is a discretionary feature; some companies provide for pre-emptive rights and others do not. If a company's charter provides for the pre-emptive right, a new issue of shares must be offered first in its entirety to the existing shareholders in proportion to their shareholdings. This will be done by the use of *rights*, which are options to purchase new shares at a specified price; they are not substantially different than the warrants discussed previously in connection with bond issues.

For example, L. F. Nelson Ltd. has 100,000 shares of common stock outstanding and plans to issue another 10,000 shares. The market value for Nelson shares is approximately $50. Nancy Johnson currently holds 20,000 Nelson shares. With a pre-emptive right, she will be mailed rights to purchase 2,000 shares of the new offering at a specified price, say $48. In other words she receives rights to purchase .1 share of new stock for each share of stock that she presently owns. Rights have a termination date, and she must act before that date if she wishes to exercise her rights.

Whether shareholders hold the pre-emptive right or not, the issuance of rights has proved to be an effective marketing device for shares. Rights can be issued below the going market price, and are normally made negotiable. With this arrangement an existing shareholder can either purchase addition stock at a "bargain price" or sell his rights to others.

When rights are issued at below market value, as they customarily are, shareholders are induced to take positive action to protect their share of the company's wealth. The rights become objects of value, and if they are not exercised or sold, value is lost by the existing shareholders. An example will illustrate.

Suppose, to make the example extreme, the Nelson company issued rights for 20,000 shares at an option price of $25 per share, and the current market price on the existing shares is $50. This existing price of $50, coupled with the information that Nelson has 100,000 shares currently outstanding, indicates that Nelson's equity is currently being valued in the market at $5 million. The price of a share after rights are exercised can be predicted as follows:

Existing equity		$5,000,000
Number of new shares to be sold	20,000	
Price	$25	
Addition to equity (20,000 × $25)		500,000
Total value of equity after new shares are issued		$5,500,000
Total shares outstanding after new shares are issued (previous 100,000 + 20,000)		120,000
Predicted new value per share ($5,500,000/120,000)		$ 45.83

If a shareholder fails to exercise his rights, we have predicted that he will lose wealth as his shares fall from $50 to $45.83. This arises because of a dilution effect when new shares are issued at bargain prices.

This line of reasoning can be extended to calculate a predicted market value of rights themselves, the price at which one expects them to be salable by shareholders who do not choose to exercise them. That valuation will be the difference between the option price on the right, and the predicted share price after the rights have been exercised. In the above case rights needed to buy one share would have been valued at $45.83 — $25.00, or an estimated $20.83, and each right at $20.83/5 = $4.17.

These calculations can be generalized into a set of formulas:

Current company market value = Current number of shares × current market price.

Predicted company market value after rights issue = Current company market value + (number of new shares) (Option price)

Predicted share price after rights issue = $$\frac{\text{Predicted company market value after rights issue}}{\text{Current number of shares and number of new shares}}$$

Predicted price of 1 right = $$\frac{(\text{Predicted share price after rights issue}) - (\text{Option price})}{\text{Number of rights needed to buy 1 share}}$$

Rights will be extended to the current shareholders of the company, and this set of shareholders will be defined as those persons holding the shares of the company on a particular date. Before that date stock is sold *rights on*; after that date, subsequent purchasers are not entitled to the rights, and the stock is said to sell *ex rights*.

The Pros and Cons of Rights Offerings

The attraction of the use of a rights offering lies in the fact that, while the offering may be made with the assistance and consultation of an investment dealer, usual investment dealer marketing services do not have to be paid for. On the other hand, legal services are required to establish the rights issue, and rights must be sent out to the company's shareholders; this is not done without some cost.

Furthermore, the success of a rights offering is going to be related to the option price; if that price is set quite low almost all of the rights are likely to be exercised. If it is set high, and the price of the company's stock should decline (for who knows what reason) prior to the termination date of the right, virtually none of the rights might be exercised. Following further, if the option price on the rights is set low, the interests of shareholders who inadvertently failed to exercise their rights could be seriously degraded.

One way around the problem is to set the price of the rights moderately high so there is a high probability that they will be exercised, and then work out a special form of underwriting agreement with a group of investment dealers which in effect guarantees that all rights will be exercised. Again, however, this adds to the cost of the issue.

Of course, where the charter of a company provides for pre-emptive rights, a company has no choice but to make a rights offering in connection with the issuance of common stock. Where the pre-emptive right does not exist there does not appear to be a clear-cut answer on whether or not a rights offering is the best marketing strategy for the sale of additional company stock.

Listing Requirements

Just as in the case of bonds, or for that matter just about anything else, a company selling new shares of stock is interested in marketing them at as high a price as possible. One of the ways of making them attractive to prospective buyers may be by enhancing their negotiability in secondary transactions. Traditionally, stock exchanges have been the principal vehicle for secondary transactions in shares. Stock exchanges, however, do not provide secondary market facilities for all shares, but only for those that they have approved for trading on their exchange. When a stock exchange approves a stock for trading, it is said to *list* the shares. Two stock exchanges account for most of the trading in Canadian common shares—those at Montreal and Toronto. Of these, the Toronto Stock Exchange is dominant, accounting for over two thirds of the dollar volume of Canadian share transactions.

A company planning to market its stock for the first time (more about this in a later chapter) or to market additional shares not already listed may want to consider having them listed. This will require a fee (modest) and conformity to the listing requirements of the exchange. The exchange will not only require the company to have a minimum net worth position (in 1976, the Toronto Stock Exchange required $1 million for many companies) but may also impose other requirements. One common requirement is that there be a wide distribution of the company shares; the security exchanges presume that there will be unprofitably few transactions in companies that are *closely held* (have few stockholders). Conformity to a listing requirement may influence the amount of shares that a company offers for sale or the form of the offering. For example, if a closely held company wanted to conform to a listing requirement requiring greater breadth of share ownership, it would probably not attempt to market its new shares through a rights offering (provided it had a choice in its charter).

Secondary Markets for Stock

Over-the-counter and third markets operate the same for common shares as for bonds. In an over-the-counter market, an investment dealer makes a market in the stock by quoting bid and ask prices on that stock. Third market transactions are arranged informally in the manner of private placements. As noted earlier, however, the prominent method of secondary share sales is through stock exchanges.

A stock exchange provides a meeting place where prospective buyers of stocks can encounter prospective sellers and vice versa. The public at large does not participate directly on the exchange, but uses the facilities of the exchange through the agency of exchange members. Major investment dealers usually hold memberships on both Toronto and Montreal exchanges and often also hold memberships on the minor Vancouver and Alberta exchanges.

Someone wishing to buy or sell shares of a particular stock gets in touch with the local office of his investment dealer and indicates his desire to dispose of the stock. In return for a commission, the investment dealer will act as his broker and execute an order for the transaction. The order may be in the form of a *market order,* where the broker is instructed to buy or sell at the best price he can obtain. It may also be in the form of a *limit order* to sell at or above, or buy at or below, a specified price.

This order will be transmitted to a representative of the investment dealer on the trading floor of the stock exchange. In a busy stock exchange, such as Toronto, orders to buy and sell will be pouring in from all over the country and from other countries. It is the job of the dramatis personae on the trading floor to match the orders to buy with the orders to sell in an efficient manner.

Operation of the Toronto Stock Exchange

Various security exchanges use different procedures for accomplishing their appointed task of marrying buyers and sellers. We can briefly examine this process on the Toronto Stock Exchange (TSE), the most significant national example. At the same time we may observe that other Canadian exchanges and the major exchanges outside of Canada do not follow exactly the same procedures. Membership of the TSE is confined to securities firms who delegate employees to act as their representative on the trading floor. The exchange has international flavour, inasmuch as affiliates of foreign, especially U.S., investment dealers hold some of the exchange memberships. Orders from clients of the member firms are communicated to the trading floor by telephone; the firms may also, under some conditions, buy for their own account.

The TSE uses the *trading post* system. The trading post is a point on the exchange floor where trading in a particular set of stocks takes place, and where information on offers to buy and sell those stocks is maintained. When a representative (or trader) of the investment dealer receives an order to buy or sell a particular share, he literally shouts the number of shares he wishes to buy or sell, along with the best price at which he thinks he can consummate the transaction. The offer may be accepted, or a counteroffer may be made.

A price is not always agreed upon. For example, a client may have instructed his investment dealer to buy a stock, provided it can be purchased at a price no higher than $48 per share. If there is no one willing to sell at this price, the order cannot be executed.

The most impressive aspect of trading on the TSE is the physical character of the transactions. Prospective buyers and sellers are not matched automatically, though electronic sign boards are used on the trading floor for purposes of recording information about offers that have been made for purchases and sales. Actual sales are made by the interaction of persons, not machines, in a bargaining process that is similar to that employed when the exchange opened (as an informal association) well before Confederation.

Criticisms of the Stock Exchange System

There is now considerable argument that the stock exchange system has outlived its usefulness. The argument runs that modern electronic devices, which allow instantaneous communication, obviate the need for the gathering of a group of traders at a particular point. It is contended that the exchange, and the associated commissions charged on its transactions, are too costly a method for performing the stock brokerage function. Particularly in the United States, stock exchanges are being increasingly bypassed by alternative modes of economic matchmaking.

Proponents of the exchange system argue that electronic systems cannot match the decision-making capabilities of the "man on the spot" in consummating transactions. At the same time, these proponents are often members of the exchanges, who have a vested interest in their maintenance. At the time this manuscript is being prepared, it is too early to pass judgment about whether the exchange system of secondary share trading will survive, but it is appropriate to point out that this issue is now taken seriously.

Secondary Offerings

Occasionally a large block of shares will be offered for sale in the secondary market. An agent of the estate of a dominant shareholder, for example, may wish to liquidate a large fraction of the shares of a major company. In a case like this, a marketing effort is often mounted comparable to that employed in the primary marketing of a new issue of common stock.

Some Stock Exchange Usage

A few terms are widely used in discussions of the securities market, and should be familiar to the student of finance. It is often possible to arrange to commit oneself to selling securities without actually owning them at the time. Such a sale, called a *short sale* as it is on the commodity market, is based on the expectation of market decline. If the market rises, the short seller loses, because he must buy high-priced stock to cover his sales commitment. The problems of the short seller in a rising market is summarized by a jingle from older (and harsher) times: "He who sells what isn't his'n, either pays or goes to prison."

It is possible to sell shares that you do not have; it is also possible to buy shares with money that you do not have. Investment dealers offer credit arrangements in connection with their sales of securities so the buyer can purchase securities by providing cash equal to only a specified fraction of the securities price. This practice is referred to as buying *on margin*. If, for example, the purchaser is allowed to buy shares on 20 percent margin, he receives a loan from the investment dealer for 80 percent of the purchase price. Therefore, with a given amount of his own money he can buy five times as many shares as he would have been able to obtain on a cash basis. In a rising market rewards from such margin buying are handsome. A fivefold increase in volume of share ownership results in a fivefold increase in capital appreciation (less interest charges on the margin loan). However, if the market goes down, the multiplicative effect turns malignant. A margin buyer can expect a call from his broker advising him that unless he posts more money to compensate for his diminished equity in his shareholdings, the broker will exercise a proviso contained in the margin loan agreement and sell the financed shares. A request for more funds from the investment broker is referred to as a *margin call*.

SPECIFIC COST OF CAPITAL

Unlike the incurrence of a debt obligation, when new common shares are sold no formal promises of payment are made to the new common shareholders. On the other hand we can be assured that most of these new shareholders have not bought their new holdings for eleemosynary reasons; they expect compensation. That compensation comes in the form of a right to share in the wealth of the company. Although there are un-

usual situations where company's shares are bought in anticipation of the liquidation of the company's existing properties,
as a general rule new shareholders expect to see the company
continue as a going and hopefully profitable concern. The
wealth they expect is their proportionate share of the company's earnings, whether distributed as dividends, or retained
for reinvestment within the company.

Compensation, a share in company earnings, is not a cost in
the usual accounting sense, since after the new shares have
been sold, the new shareholders are full fledged co-owners.
Nevertheless, unless the persons to whom the new shares are
sold are actually the old shareholders, all buying exactly the
same fraction of the new shares as they held of the old shares,
the purchasers of the new shares constitute a different set of
persons, at least in a financial sense, than the existing shareholders. Again, from a financial standpoint, this makes the
potential purchasers of new shares external suppliers of funds.
As in the case of any other external source of funds, it is appropriate for company's financial managers, as representatives of
existing shareholders, to analyze the procurement of these new
funds in terms of the proceeds expected from the new stock
issue, and the after-tax compensation that will be required in
return for those proceeds.

An Example of the Cost of New Common Shares

An example will illustrate the economic cost that can be
inflicted upon existing shareholders by the issuance of new
shares of stock. Suppose Barefield Ltd. is regularly earning
around $1 million per year, and has 100,000 common shares
outstanding, with earnings per share (EPS) of $10. Now it
issues an additional 100,000 shares, at a price of $100 per share
and (neglecting for the moment issuance cost) receives proceeds of $10 million. Now stretch your imagination a bit and
imagine that this $10 million is unproductively used, so that it
adds nothing to Barefield's previously existing $1 million in
annual earnings. The result, of course, is that with the previous
level of earnings, and 200,00 shares instead of 100,000 shares
outstanding, EPS drops to $5 per share.

It is now obvious that there was a cost for the use of the new funds. Existing Barefield shareholders lost earnings because the new shares were issued. This does not imply that new share issues are categorically unproductive. Suppose that the $10 million from the new Barefield issue enabled the company to modernize its plant, and as a result annual earnings increased from their previous $1 million per year to $3 million per year. Now the situation is different. With earnings of $3 million, and 200,000 shares outstanding, EPS has increased to $15 per share, and existing shareholders have profited by the issuance of new shares. It is again apparent, that even though funds from the sale of new common stock have a cost, that cost may be a profitable purchase of financial input, so far as existing shareholders are concerned.

Specific Cost Identification in Principle

In principle specific cost of new common shares is obtained as an internal rate. As usual, it is the discount rate which sets NPV equal to zero for the proceeds received from a source of funds and the compensation given to that source of funds. The proceeds from a common stock issue are easily defined. They are the monies received from the sale of new shares after deducting the fees of the investment dealer, possible stock exchange listing fees, legal expenses, and other costs that may have been incurred in selling the shares.

At the time that the planning of the stock issue is taking place, its proceeds may be difficult to predict. The stock market is notoriously fickle, and shares which are expected to sell at $50 may in fact sell at $35. The uncertainty may be removed by shifting the risk of market instability through an investment dealer's underwriting agreement.

The compensation accorded to new shareholders is a share of expected company earnings. In this sense, capital cost analysis must depart from the usual practice of identifying compensation of the capital source in the form of a stream of cash outflows and instead deal in terms of potential outflows. The new shareholders will receive cash outflows from the company if dividends are paid but the proportion of earnings retained within the company will also belong to those new shareholders. Therefore, expected compensation of new shareholders is their portion of all expected after-tax earnings of the company.

Technically, this portion could be calculated by projecting company earnings far into the future, including earnings arising from assets procured with the sale of the new stock. Then an appropriate fraction of projected earnings (the proportion of the number of new shares to the total number of company shares) could be allocated as compensation for the new shareholders. Ingredients for an internal rate calculation would now be available.

To recall the Barefield example, if after the issuance of the new stock, earnings were expected to continue indefinitely at $3 million per year, and if the new stockholders had a claim upon half of these earnings (100,000 shares/200,000 shares) their expected compensation would be $1.5 million per year in perpetuity. Proceeds from the new stock issue were assumed to be $10 million, so the specific cost of capital is 15 percent.

This cost calculation can be verified by continuing with the Barefield example, where company's earnings were increased from $1 million to $3 million per year. This implies a marginal return on the new assets purchased with the proceeds of the share issue as $2,000,000 per year/$10,000,000 or 20 percent per annum. With a marginal capital cost of 15 percent for the new funds, new assets yield a marginal profit of $500,000 per year to the old shareholders. This is reflected in their increase in EPS by $5 ($500,000/100,000 shares) from $10 to $15.

SPECIFIC CAPITAL COST ESTIMATION

In practice, making detailed projections of new shareholders far into the future may be too burdensome, or too devoid of credibility because of the "ifs and ands" in the predictions. Because of these problems, estimating techniques are often employed based on two commonly used formulas for the valuation of common shares. These formulas will be presented, and then adapted to capital cost estimation.

The Discounted Earnings Valuation Formula

We have previously discussed the pricing of a bond in a marketplace, with that price being determined by the present value of existing future payments from the bond, discounted at a discount rate commensurate with current capital market conditions and the risk of the bond. The same approach can be applied to a common share. Current EPS may be treated as equivalent to the level of cash flows from a perpetual bond (actual flows if paid as a dividend; potential if not). The recent record of EPS is then, in the absence of other information, regarded as the best available estimate of the company's continuing future performance. It follows that current EPS is then treated as a perpetual stream of earnings and discounted at a rate deemed appropriate by the market. Let us call that discount rate k_i, where the subscript i refers to the degree of riskiness of the stock. We can then express a simple valuation formula:

$$\text{Share price} = \frac{\text{EPS}}{k_i}.$$

At first glance this formula looks naïve; it seems to presume that earnings will always be maintained at the current level when in fact it is common for company earnings to grow. In fact, in companies that traditionally disburse only a small fraction of their earnings to the stockholders as dividends, it would be surprising if earnings growth did not take place. Each year shareholders, by collectively choosing not to withdraw earnings from the company, are in effect increasing their investment within that company. Unless the marginal investment is unproductive, EPS must rise.

However, there is more sophistication in the approach of "Share price $= \text{EPS}/k_i$" than initially meets the eye. This will become apparent in a following subsection.

The Dividend Growth Valuation Formula

The previous formula was based on a discounting of current earnings to obtain a valuation of a stock. A second approach also widely used is to subdivide a shareholder's benefits from his stock into two parts—dividends, and possible growth in the value of the share itself. For example, a shareholder holds a share which is valued at the beginning of the year at $100. During the year he receives a $5 dividend on the share, and at the end of the year the share is worth $110. He can count his benefits on the share as $5 in dividends and $10 in appreciation or growth for a total return of 15 percent on his original $100.

From this subdivision a valuation formula may be developed where D refers to the current level of dividend and g to the expected growth rate in the value of the company's shares per year. This formula[2] is:

$$\text{Share price} = \frac{D}{k_i - g}.$$

A simple example will compare the results of the two formulas. Suppose Schrech Enterprises Ltd. has an EPS of $5, of which $3 is paid as a dividend. Suppose, furthermore, that Schrech's earnings, dividends, and share prices are expected to grow at an annual rate of 5 percent, according to the best estimates available. Further assume that the appropriate discount rate for a company in Schrech's risk category is deemed to be 15 percent. The results of the two formulas follow:

$$\text{Share price} = \frac{\text{EPS}}{k_i} = \frac{\$5}{0.15} = \$33.33.$$

$$\text{Share price} = \frac{D}{k_i - g} = \frac{\$3}{0.15 - 0.05} = \$30.$$

The Common Ground of EPS/k_i; and $D/(k_i - g)$

The proximity of these two results does not occur entirely by coincidence. A major explanation of the growth of a company may lie in the reinvestment of company earnings. Thus growth in EPS may be caused simply by the company's dividend policy. With low dividends as a proportion of earnings (low *payout ratio*), growth can be expected by the simple fact of the enlargement of the company's investment base. It may even occur if retained earnings are reinvested within the company at a rate lower than that prevailing under conditions of comparable risk in the marketplace, namely k_i.

The relationship where growth is explained by reinvestment of retained earnings can be explored further. Let d = the company dividend payout ratio, and by complementarity $(1 - d)$, the company's proportion of earnings retention. Now let these

---

[2] This formula is developed in a straightforward way, on the basis of summing a geometric progression. The dividend increasing annually by the factor $(1 + g)$; a discount rate of $(1 + k_i)^n$ is applied where n refers to number of years.

retained earnings be committed to assets which yield a marginal rate of return, m. We can now explain a company's growth in terms of its reinvestment of retained earnings as:

$$g = (1 - d)m.$$

For example, if a company earns $3 per share in 1975, and pays a $1.20 dividend, it has retained 60 percent of its earnings, or $1.80. Let us assume that this $1.80 is invested in assets yielding a marginal 10 percent return after tax. In this case, without any other change in the company's operations, we expect that if the company has increased its shareholder's investment by $1.80 per share and this investment is yielding 10 percent, EPS will rise by $0.18 during the next year. This represents an annual growth rate of 6 percent in earnings ($0.18/$3); if the same dividend payout ratio is maintained, the annual growth rate for dividends will be 6 percent, too.

This example coincides with the formula given above:

$$m = 0.10$$
$$d = .4$$
$$g = (1 - d)m = (1 - .4).0.10 = 0.06.$$

Now let us make another assumption, namely, that a company's retained earnings are reinvested in assets which yield a rate of return equal to that available on common stock of comparable risk; that is, $m = k_i$. This is not a totally arbitrary speculation but instead one consistent with the concept of rigorous competition among companies for assets. One must recall that a company must compete for assets with other companies who can raise money in the stock market under conditions of comparable risk at a cost of k_i; so it would not be surprising if marginal company investments earned approximately k_i.

The setting of $m = k_i$ leads to an interesting result. Consider first the redefinition of g:

$$g = (1 - d)m = (1 - d)k_i.$$

Now let us substitute this redefined g into the share valuation formula based on dividend growth:

$$\text{Share price} = \frac{D}{k_i - g} = \frac{D}{k_i - (1 - d)k_i}.$$

The formula can be manipulated further by recalling that d, the dividend payout rate, is a ratio relating dividends per share to earnings per share, so $D = d(\text{EPS})$. This expression can also be substituted into the previous formula to yield:

$$\text{Share price} = \frac{d(\text{EPS})}{k_i - (1 - d)k_i}.$$

Now, by straightforward algebra, this formula is reduced to:

$$\text{Share price} = \frac{\text{EPS}}{k_i}.$$

Thus the two valuation formulas—discounted EPS or the dividend growth method—yield equivalent results so long as $m - k_i$. To the extent that a company's marginal investments yield more than the going rate on equivalent common stock investments ($m > k_i$), the discounted EPS method will give a lower valuation. Because of the tendency for similarity between m and k_i, the differences are not likely to be great.

Therefore because of its simplicity, the EPS formula is often the best way of estimating share price. The EPS formula, although it might first appear to do so, does not ignore growth. Instead, even though current EPS is used, the formula implies EPS increase based on reinvestment of some or all earnings at competitive rates.

FROM VALUATION FORMULA TO SPECIFIC EQUITY COST

These valuation formulas can be easily used to obtain an estimate of the company's cost of capital. This assumption presumes that the issuance of the new common stock will not cause major change in the nature of the company; and accordingly, its stock will continue to be valued at approximately the same discount rate that it was previously, k_i. One can easily calculate k_i from available facts in the marketplace; namely, the company's share price and the company's EPS. In other words, if

$$\text{Share price} = \frac{\text{EPS}}{k_i},$$

it follows that:

$$k_i = \frac{\text{EPS}}{\text{Share price}}.$$

For example, if Company X's earnings are $10 per share and its stock is selling at $60 per share in the market, we can estimate that the market is discounting stock at a k_i given as:

$$k_i = \frac{\text{EPS}}{\text{Share price}} = \frac{\$10}{\$60} = 16\tfrac{2}{3}\%.$$

The same manipulation holds if the dividend growth formula is used. Following the logic above, applied to this second formula:

$$k_i = \frac{D}{\text{Share price}} + g.$$

For example, if X's current annual dividend payment is $4, and its dividends and earnings have been growing at a rate of approximately 8 percent per year we obtain:

$$k_i = \frac{D}{\text{Share price}} + g = \frac{\$6}{\$60} + 0.08 = 18\%.$$

To estimate cost on a proposed new share issue, one can use the net selling price of the shares after selling costs. To complete the definition in algebraic form, simply define:

Proceeds per share = Share price − selling costs.

Proceeds per share can then be used to obtain a more refined version of estimated specific cost of new common shares. For example, if X Company elects the EPS method, and also estimates that selling costs on the new shares would be $5, its specific capital cost estimate becomes

$$\text{Estimated capital cost} = \frac{\text{EPS}}{\text{Proceeds per share}} = \frac{\$10}{\$55} = 18.2\%.$$

Estimation in the "Growth" Company

Shares of some companies command substantial market value even though the company has no or negligible history of earnings or dividends. Share price is, in this case, based on the company's future prospects rather than its history. (Actually, of course, this is always the case, but recent earnings and dividends history may often be regarded as an adequate predictor of the future.) In a situation where meaningful EPS and dividend figures are not available, the estimating methods described above simply do not work. In this case the firm is forced to fall back on direct estimation of its future earnings prospects. If it is to rationally obtain a specific capital cost figure for its new common equity, it must make estimates, even if they are crude ones, about what the company's future prospects are and what proportion of these are going to go to new shareholders. On the basis of "best available guesses" the company must attempt to decide whether the cost of marginal equity will make the acquisition of new assets prohibitively expensive, and whether the company should try harder to procure funds from alternative sources.

SUMMARY

Common shareholders are residual claimants of the company, absorbing most of the misfortunes and profiting from the successes. When funds are obtained by the sale of new common shares, the burden of debt is avoided in exchange for dilution of ownership.

Common shareholders participate in governance of the company through their voting rights. They elect directors and vote on company by-laws. Even minority shareholders are entitled to a stewardship from company management, and they may enforce this right in the courts.

Public issuance of shares follows the mechanics of bond issue. Since security exchanges play a large role in the secondary distribution of common shares, conformity to security exchange listing requirements is an additional consideration for common shares. Existing shareholders frequently are entitled to pro rata participation in new share issues.

Major Canadian security exchanges are located at Toronto and Montreal; Toronto is larger.

Funds obtained from the sale of new common shares have a cost, the anticipated stream of future company earnings that is diverted to the new shareholders. Specific costs of capital can be inferred through the use of evaluation formulas. A first method identifies cost of capital as a ratio of current earnings to current share price. A second method estimates cost of capital as the current dividend/share price ratio plus a growth rate. Both have practical applications, and are subject to some conceptual reservations.

QUESTIONS AND PROBLEMS

1. A company has 1 million shares outstanding. The "majority group" owns or holds proxies to 700,000 shares; a "minority group" holds the remainder. What will be the composition of the company's ten-man board of directors, assuming both traditional voting and cumulative voting?

2. A company's shares are currently selling on the market at $60. The company, in marketing additional shares, provides rights for the purchase of one tenth of an additional share for each share currently outstanding. The share price specified in the rights is $50.

   What is the predicted value of one right?

   What is the predicted amount of loss for a holder of 10,000 shares who neither exercises nor sells his rights?

3. Identify two major motives for the use of rights in company financing.

4. Why do security exchanges not wish to list closely held companies?

5. Distinguish between a market order and a limit order.

6. The New York Stock Exchange uses a "specialist" trading system. Through this system dealers on the floors of the exchange act as buyers and sellers of specified lists of securities. Other exchange members who wish to buy or sell a particular security do so through the specialist.

   How does this system differ from the one used on the Toronto Stock Exchange?

7. Discuss the proposition that security exchanges are, or will soon become, obsolete.

8. An individual buys 100 shares of Widget Corporation at a price of $60, and in two months sells for a price of $70. Broker-

age fees are estimated at 1.5 percent on the purchase and 1.5 percent on the sale. The transaction is financed with a 40 percent margin; 10 percent interest is charged on the borrowed 60 percent.

Identify the amount of cash required to initiate the transaction and the net amount recovered at the end of two months.

9. A company is considering issuing some additional common shares, to be offered to the public at $80 per share. Underwriting and other issuance costs are $5 per share. Historically, this company's earnings have been around $8 per share after tax and the company has been paying a $3 per share dividend.

The company has recently been awarded a series of favourable long-term production contracts, and on the basis of these projects future earnings per share are $12, sustainable into the indefinite future. Dividends are expected to rise to $5 per share.

Estimate specific cost of equity on the new share issue.

Is this a before- or after-tax estimate?

10. A company's recent earnings per share are $4 annually. Riskiness of the company's share leads one to expect that the market would discount their future earnings at a rate of 15 percent. Estimate the selling price of the shares, using the discounted earnings valuation formula.

11. Suppose the above company follows a practice of paying out half its earnings in dividends. Retained earnings are reinvested in the company at an estimated 20 percent rate of return.

Estimate the growth rate in the company's dividends.

Using a 15 percent discount rate again, and the dividend growth valuation formula, estimate the value of the company's shares.

Explain the relationship between this valuation and the one previously obtained using the discounted earnings valuation formula.

12. A company's recent earnings are 50 cents per share and the shares have recently been selling for around $3.

Estimate specific cost of equity capital.

Refine the above calculation on the assumption that underwriting and other issuance costs for new shares would absorb 20 percent of the proceeds from any new issue.

RELATED READINGS

The Canadian Security Dealers' Institute. *The Canadian Securities Course*, 1973.

O'Neal, F. H. "Minority Owners Can Avoid Squeeze-outs." *Harvard Business Review*, March–April 1963.

Shaw, D. "The Allocational Efficiency of Canada's Market for New Equity Issues." *Canadian Journal of Economics*, November 1969.

Stevenson, Harold W. *Common Stock Financing*. Ann Arbor: University of Michigan, 1957.

Toronto Stock Exchange. "Regulations Applicable to Listed Companies," 1974.

17

FINANCING THROUGH
RETAINED EARNINGS

The preponderance of equity capital in Canadian companies is formed through retention of earnings. Using book values, retained earnings account for nearly two and a half times the equity supplied by sale of common shares. (Market values of balance sheet items cannot be used for the comparison since the marketplace values all of a company's equity rather than individual components.)

The decision to form capital by retention of earnings is, conversely, a question of dividend policy. Should a company finance its assets by withholding dividend payments from shareholders, or should it rely more heavily on external sources of funds, whether debt or equity? The question will turn, among other things, on cost considerations.

TECHNICAL ASPECTS OF DIVIDEND POLICY

Dividend Declaration

Although a company may regard itself as morally committed to the payment of a regular dividend, in a legal sense no such commitment exists. Common dividends are declared at the discretion of the company's board of directors. Once a dividend is formally approved by the directors, however, it is irrevocable and constitutes a liability of the company.

The declaration of a dividend will establish a *date of record* for the dividend. Dividend cheques will be sent to shareholders who are listed on the company's shareholder registry at that date. A shareholder who has sold his shares after the date of record but before the dividend is paid will still be legally entitled to his dividend cheque. Shares sold after the date of record are described as being sold *ex dividends*.

As a general rule, the board of directors may declare dividends not only to the extent of current earnings, but also of any accumulated retained earnings on the company's books. This right, in turn, may be abridged by agreement with creditors. For example, one of the terms in a bond indenture may be some restriction on the debtor company's discretion over its dividend policy.

On the negative side, dividends cannot be freely declared beyond the extent of the company's retained earnings. Creditors, without any formal agreement, are entitled to some limitation on the company's declaration of dividends. Without this limitation it would be possible for a company to withdraw virtually all of its equity capital *after* debt funds had been procured, and leave the company's creditors bearing all of the risk of the company's activities.

Exceptions to this rule are permitted if appropriate legal procedures are observed. When dividends are paid beyond the extent of the company's accumulated retained earnings they are normally called *liquidating dividends*.

Companies that wish to preserve a reputation for a stable dividend policy may attempt to change their dividend rates only gradually in accordance with long-run earnings trends. Some companies pride themselves on long histories of uninterrupted dividend payments. A company wishing to maintain an image of dividend stability may wish to make a distinction between its *regular* dividend and *special* dividends. If the company has an extraordinarily favourable earnings picture for one year, or if the company wishes to limit its accumulation of common equity capital for some reason, it may choose to declare a dividend beyond its usual dividend practice. In such a case, the company will label this extraordinary dividend a *special dividend* to indicate to shareholders that they should not expect this dividend to constitute a change in the company's ongoing policy. Suppose a company which has regularly paid a $3 per year dividend suddenly pays $6 per year without explanation. Shareholders might believe that this represented a permanent policy change; by labelling $3 per share as special, this expectation is allayed.

Stock Dividends and Stock Splits

It is not unusual for a company to declare a stock dividend, rather than the conventional cash dividend. With a stock dividend additional shares of company stock are issued and distributed pro rata to the company's shareholders. For example, if a shareholder owns 100 shares of stock in a company which declares a 10 percent stock dividend, he will receive an additional ten shares of stock.

Because a stock dividend is a distribution of additional shares in exactly the same proportion as existing shareholdings, a stock dividend does not change the shareholder's fractional interest in the company. If he owns 2 percent of the company's common shares already, the declaration of a stock dividend of any size will still leave him in possession of 2 percent of the company's shares. Furthermore, even if the stock dividend were to double or triple the number of shares that he held, there is no obvious reason to believe that the total value of his shareholdings would have changed an iota.

When a cash dividend is paid, money already owned by the shareholders is transferred out of the company and directly into the hands of the shareholders. When a stock dividend is declared, not even movement of money takes place. Furthermore, a stock dividend procedure is not costless. New stock certificates must be printed and distributed to shareholders. With an increase in the number of common shares outstanding, additional charges may be levied by the stock exchange on which the shares are listed.

Why then is a stock dividend declared? One argument runs

to the effect that either the payment of a cash dividend or a stock dividend is an expression of managerial confidence; a signal of company success beyond that given in the company's earnings statement. Beyond that rather dubious proposition there are two real effects of the payment of a stock dividend.

First, with an increase in the number of shares outstanding, the market price per share will be reduced by the declaration of a stock dividend. If a shareholder previously owned 10 shares of a company and after a 10 percent stock dividend owns 11 shares which represent exactly the same claim on the company the shareholder held previously, it is reasonable to believe that the company's shares will fall in price *per share* to 10/11 of their old price. Some writers and financial officers have alleged that the marketability of a company's shares is enhanced if their value per share is kept within reasonable bounds. While this argument does not seem particularly convincing it occasionally is used to justify stock dividends.

A second, and more convincing, case lies in a legal effect of the stock dividend declaration. When the dividend is declared, the effect on the company's balance sheet is to transfer accounting value out of the retained earnings account and into the capital shares account. Since a company's power to declare dividends is limited by the retained earnings that it has accumulated, the payment of a stock dividend constitutes a voluntary abridgment of the company's dividend-paying power. At first glance this may seem to work to the detriment of the shareholders. On reflection one can see that shareholders may benefit through easier credit availability if the company limits its discretion to withdraw equity. In other words, for every $1 of stock dividend declared, prospective creditors are assured that $1 of cash dividend cannot be declared.

The stock split is closely related to the stock dividend, but it lacks this latter feature—the abridgment of dividend-paying power. When a company makes a stock split, it issues additional shares to its existing shareholders, again in direct proportion to existing shareholdings, without making a dividend declaration and the associated bookkeeping transfers from its retained earnings account to its capital stock account. If, for example, a company splits its stock on a 3-to-1 ratio, a holder of

10 shares of the company's stock ends up with 30 shares. Again, his fractional holding of the company is unaffected. It may be expected that, with three times as many shares outstanding, the value of each share will fall to one third of its original value. A stock split again is not accomplished without cost, and its only apparent purpose is to affect the market value *per share* of its stock with the intent of enhancing the marketability of the shares.

This method of adjusting price per share can work two ways; a reverse stock split can be used to reduce the number of shares outstanding. For example, with a reverse split of 1 to 3, a holder of 300 shares of company stock would hold 100 shares after the reverse split, with value per share expected to be three times as high as its previous level. Some investors are believed to regard stocks with a low price per share (often called *penny stocks*) as by their nature speculative in character; a reverse split can attempt to eradicate this image.

SPECIFIC COST OF RETAINED EARNINGS

In the sale of common stock, one considers the garnering of equity money from a set of potential owners which does not exactly coincide with the set of existing owners, and therefore is regarded as external. Retained earnings on the other hand are funds withheld from the company's existing owners, to whom management bears direct responsibility. In the sale of new common stock, it is the responsibility of financial management to drive as hard a bargain as possible—selling new shares for "all the traffic will bear," or providing shareholders with rights which allow them to do this. On the other hand, when management considers availing itself of monies through dividend abstention, the best interests of its capital suppliers must be the governing consideration. These particular capital suppliers, the existing shareholders, are sovereign in the company.

The question of best interests of the shareholders can be summed up as "will the shareholders be better off if they withdraw their earnings from the company or if they allow them to remain for reinvestment within the company?" One can approach this problem first by characterizing shareholders as persons who are net savers, and who are therefore steadily seeking out investment opportunities. This is not the only characterization possible, but it provides a good starting point for analysis. For most companies, furthermore, it is probably a characterization that fits the holders of the majority of the company's shares, though not necessarily the majority of the company's shareholders. Since one-share, one-vote, rather than one-man, one-vote, governs in the determination of company policy, it is more appropriate to seek a characterization for the holders of the majority of shares.

With the characterization of the shareholder as a saver, the question of earnings retention or dividend policy reduces to a fairly straightforward issue of opportunity cost. If we reintroduce the term k_i to denote the market discount rate on shares with risk comparable to a particular company, the fact that this rate is generally available in the marketplace under conditions of comparable risk establishes it as an opportunity cost for the withholding of dividends. If the shareholders received the dividends, they could invest them in the marketplace to obtain a return of k_i.

From this point on, the analysis becomes coloured by tax considerations. Before shareholders can take advantage of alternative investments yielding k_i, they will first have to receive a dividend, and dividends are taxable. The taxation on common dividends is the same as that on preferred dividends, with rate:

Tax rate on dividends = ⅓ marginal personal tax rate − 36%.

However, for the common shareholder, retention of earnings cannot be regarded as a full escape route from personal taxation. Sometime the shareholder may wish to sell his shares. If so, the probable accretion in value arising from earnings retention will be taxed at the capital gains rate: 0.5 (personal tax rate). There is no easy answer as to how this should be taken into account, but for purposes of drafting a working rule, the following method is suggested. Presume that payment of a marginal dollar of dividend has two personal tax effects:

1. Dividend tax at a rate of ⅓ (marginal personal tax rate) − 36%.

2. Capital gain tax *saving* at a rate of ½ (marginal personal tax rate).

When these two effects are summed, the *net* tax effect of dividend payment is:

$$\text{Dividend tax rate, with capital gain offset} = \tfrac{5}{6}\,(\text{Marginal personal tax rate}) - 36\%$$

These tax effects are calculated for shareholders in various marginal tax brackets (Illustration 17–1):

Marginal Personal Tax (percent)	Dividend Tax Rate with Capital Gains Offset (percent)
30%	−11%
40	− 3
50	6
60	18
70	22

Now let us turn to an example of a shareholder in Black Ltd. whose family income is $30,000 per year and whose marginal personal tax rate is about 50 percent (federal and provincial). If he is paid a dividend, he is subject to net personal tax of 6 percent, from the above chart. This leaves him with 94 cents out of every dollar paid, for reinvestment in alternative investment at k_i. Accordingly, we could regard Black's opportunity cost of retaining earnings, in full cognizance of this shareholder's personal tax situation, as $.94\,k_i$.

Because of shareholders' income differences, provincial tax differences, and questions about the propriety of assuming that retained earnings will be taxed at the present capital gains rate (the shares might be subject to disposal in an estate; the shareholder's personal income bracket might be different when he sold the shares, and so on), there is little point in trying to be precise about specific cost of retained earnings.

Maybe it is sufficient to say, under present tax laws, that the cost of retained earnings should be regarded as "a little less than k_i"; on an opportunity cost basis. To go out on a limb, how about $.9\,k_i$ as a crude approximation?

There is one conclusion that can be drawn from the above analysis. Unless there are other than opportunity cost considerations involved, it is almost certain that retained earnings will constitute a cheaper source of common equity funds than sale of new common shares. Issuance costs which reduce the proceeds on new common share issues will leave the cost of selling new common stock at slightly above k_i. But perhaps opportunity cost analysis does not tell the whole story.

Cost Considerations Other Than Opportunity Cost

A taxpayer may not think of the alternative to earnings retention as being other investment at k_i. Instead, he may think of the alternative to dividend payment as the need to provide for his consumption purchases elsewhere. This situation is quite likely in the case of the shareholder who has accumulated shares to provide for his retirement. Could this strengthen the case for a dividend above that provided on the viewpoint of the net saver's opportunity cost?

Probably not. Unless a "net-consumer" shareholder is concerned with questions of his relative voting power in a company (not very likely), he can retrieve money from a company in two ways: by receiving a dividend or by selling part of his shareholdings. If he sells his shareholdings, he will only be subject to capital gains tax on appreciation that has taken place since January 1, 1972 (when the capital gains tax went into effect); or in any event he will only be taxed on appreciation above the price he paid for the shares.

Therefore, he can probably liquidate shares with only modest personal tax effect. To be sure, when he sells shares, he must pay a brokerage commission, but this is not likely to exceed 3 percent and may be considerably less. Thus capital gains tax and commission probably will not offset potential dividend tax unless the shareholder has a rather low income (which the holders of most shares do not).

The Traditional Cost for Dividends

In addition to the cost calculations, another argument has been advanced in advocacy of dividend distribution. This argument is that the marketplace looks at dividends in a different light than it looks at company earnings. Earnings are abstract, a creature of accounting principles and accountant's judgments. Dividends are "tangible benefits" for the shareholder, actual disbursements of cash.

One now harks back to the concept that the basic objective of the company's financial affairs was presumed to be maximization of shareholder's wealth. If dividends are treated with special regard in the marketplace, even if not necessarily by the company's own shareholders (though there is probably no reason to regard them as atypical), the payment of dividends may enhance share value. In this sense, the abstinence from the dividend would have a double cost: the loss of alternative investment opportunities for shareholders and the inducement of a decrease in share price.

The argument extends not only to a case for dividends but to one for an orderly dividend policy. It is argued that dividends will be particularly value enhancing if they emit from the company on a regular, predictable basis.

The scientific evidence is conflicting on this extra valuation effect, alleged to derive from dividend payment and especially from regular dividend payment. Similarly, logical deduction does not offer a clear-cut answer with respect to the validity of the case. It is true that the distribution to a shareholder of something that already belongs to him, when a dividend is declared from company earnings, should not enhance the wealth of the shareholder. On the other hand, it is also true that the measurement of earnings by conventional accounting practice (or any other conceivable practice, for that matter) is imprecise and abstract, and the payment of a dividend may more closely reflect the directors' judgment about the success of the business' current operations.

This last argument has an additional troublesome aspect. If directors could express confidence via dividend payment, and affect market values, could they not declare dividends to deceive instead of to inform. Since this possibility exists, how can dividends be regarded as conveying credible information?

The issue of dividend policy is an unsettled one; many scholars and businessmen of respected judgment advocate the extraordinary valuation effect in spite of the arguments above. These persons contend that a company should declare regular dividends, even if this means that necessary equity capital must be derived from the simultaneous sale of new common stock.

Specific Cost Summarized

For purposes of subsequent analysis in this book, let us end with a compromise. We will presume that for a well-established company with reasonably regular earnings, some regular dividend *will* be paid. Perhaps one could arbitrarily treat a 30 percent payout ratio as nondiscretionary. Beyond this arbitrary point one could then let retention of earnings be regarded as wholly discretionary source of funds, with a cost of capital equal to somewhat less than k_i ($.9 \, k_i$ was suggested).

This approach can be exemplified as follows. Suppose that a company earns $1 million in a given year, or $1 per share. Its shares are selling in the market for $10. This $1 million earnings figure is consistent with recurrent company experience, and the company regards a 30 percent dividend payout ratio as nondiscretionary. In this case, the company would take a $300,000 dividend as given, and decide from there whether to retain part or all of the remaining $700,000 in current earnings within the company. It would do this on the basis of the specific capital cost of the earnings.

Using the discounted EPS method, k_i would be estimated at 20 percent. Cost of retained earnings would then be less than 20 percent, perhaps around 18 percent. Since there is no income tax effect at the corporate level, whether dividends are paid or not, this cost may be regarded as the after-tax specific capital cost of funds obtained from retained earnings.

CURRENT DIVIDEND PRACTICE

Consistent with the ambiguity in the current state of theory on dividend policy, dividend usage varies substantially from industry to industry, and from firm to firm. If one wanted a working generalization, however, it would be that there is a tendency for payout ratios to average between 40 percent and 50 percent. Because of a tendency for companies to maintain regularity in their dividend policy, a payout ratio is likely to be higher in years of low earnings and lower in periods of high earnings.

OVERRELIANCE ON RETAINED EARNINGS
FOR COMMON EQUITY

Particularly for small companies, retained earnings constitute a convenient source of equity capital. The formality of common stock issue and its attendant costs are avoided. As we have seen previously, common equity derived from retained earnings is almost certainly going to have a lower specific cost than equity procured through the sale of new shares. Furthermore, funds from retained earnings are virtually a perfect substitute for funds from common equity, the only difference being the availability of retained earnings for subsequent dividend payments. (This difference can be removed by a stock dividend declaration or other legal action of the company if it is important for purposes of credit procurement.) It is possible for these attractions to lead a company to excessive reliance on retained earnings. This statement applies particularly to the rapidly growing company. In fact it may follow inexorably from a simple mathematical relationship.

Profit Rates and Growth Rate

The formation of equity through retaining earnings, of course, requires earnings themselves. In other words, current earnings impose an upper limit on the amount of equity that can be currently formed through earnings retention, even if a company declares no dividend.

It is possible to identify a ratio between a company's current earnings and the value of its outstanding equity. This ratio is commonly described as the rate of return on equity. It can be calculated on a book value basis, a ratio of current annual earnings to previously accumulated retained earnings plus other equity capital; or on a market value basis, a ratio of current earnings to the market value of outstanding shares.

This rate of return on equity has an important interpretation; it represents the upper limit of the growth rate of the company's common equity through earnings retention. In other words if a company's rate of return on its equity is 20 percent, its maximum growth rate in its equity capital can be predicted at 20 percent. As usual these calculations are made on an after-tax basis, since Revenue Canada's share of the company's earnings are not available for retention.

It is possible for a company to be enjoying good corporate health in terms of its rate of return on equity, but also to be enlarging its scale of company activities at an even greater rate than its return on equity. Suppose, for example, that Mirus Ltd. earns 20 percent on its equity and is growing so rapidly that its annual sales increase is 50 percent per year. Unless the increased sales are made with increasing efficiency with respect to asset use, a 50 percent increase in annual sales is probably going to require a 50 percent increase in the Mirus's investment in receivables, inventory, and other assets; there is a strong tendency for asset growth to parallel sales growth.

To continue the example, it is quite possible that this successful company, enjoying a rate of growth in sales and assets at 50 percent per year, and earning 20 percent on its equity, may find itself in financial difficulties. These difficulties will arise out of the differences between the two rates, a rate of increase in the company's asset requirements over time, and the rate of growth in its equity.

Financial Strain through Growth

The effect of asset growth in excess of a company's rate of return on equity follows with straightforward mathematics. Each year, if assets increase faster than the maximum rate by which equity can be built up through earnings retention, the ratio of equity to assets must decline. Correspondingly, a company must increasingly rely on debt financing, unless it is prepared to embellish its equity position through the issuance of additional common stock. Where companies grow rapidly and attempt to finance their growth in equity by retained earnings only, the result may mean that a company, otherwise healthy, becomes so laden with debt that the slightest reversal in the company's fortunes can reduce it to insolvency.

Let us follow the Mirus Ltd. example somewhat further. The company starts business in 1975 with $100,000 of assets, $50,000 from common stock accumulated from the personal savings of its owners, and $50,000 from creditors. This leaves it with a debt ratio of .5 on a book value basis. (This is the usual basis for calculating debt ratios in small companies, since they have no well-established market value.) Now, using the above growth rates, let us look at the Mirus's positions in subsequent years, assuming that *all* company earnings are retained.

MIRUS LTD.

Year	Assets	Equity	Debt (Assets — Equity)	Debt Ratio
1975	$100,000	$ 50,000	$ 50,000	.50
Growth factors	1.5	1.2		
1976	150,000	60,000	90,000	.60
Growth factors	1.5	1.2		
1977	225,000	72,000	153,000	.68
Growth factors	1.5	1.2		
1978	337,500	86,400	251,100	.74
Growth factors	1.5	1.2		
1979	506,250	103,680	402,570	.80
Growth factors	1.5	1.2		
1980	759,375	124,416	634,959	.84

To repeat, there is nothing unhealthy about a 20 percent annual increase in the shareholders' equity through retention of after-tax earnings. Nor is there anything unhealthy in itself about 50 percent annual growth in the company's assets. Aggressively managed companies will frequently seek out sales growth, and this growth requires supporting assets.

But it is apparent, in spite of their attractiveness as a source of funds, that retained earnings have their limitations. The growth can sometimes not keep pace with the needs of the growing company. In such a case, even if all dividends are eschewed, external equity financing will probably have to be sought if the company's growth rate is to be sustained. Failure to do this, because of difficulty or high cost in getting external equity, must eventually lead to a ponderous debt ratio. With such a ratio either failure may ensue (perhaps from a short-term type of misfortune), or else reluctance of creditors may eventually set a boundary on the company's aspirations.

The next chapter will deal in much more detail with the question of what constitutes an appropriate debt ratio. However, to anticipate a subsequent conclusion, there is a rather convincing case against extremely high debt ratios. The Mirus example has shown the point to which reliance on earnings retention for equity can easily lead the aggressive, and otherwise healthy, firm.

CO-OPERATIVES AND THEIR FINANCING

Though co-operative companies do not loom particularly large in the national scene, they have considerable regional importance, particularly on the prairies. They dominate one major Canadian industry, the purchase and handling of grain, and are very important in some other agricultural markets. They are also significant in retail and wholesale mercantile trade, and in banking (credit unions, and so forth).

Co-operatives have many features in common with other companies; they are corporations with identities apart from their owners. They enjoy limited liability, generate equity through the sale of common stock and earnings retention, and are subject to corporate income tax.

They also differ in a number of important ways: they are governed by one-man, one-vote, rather than voting in proportion to value of shareholdings. Their shareholders are typically also their customers. They also differ greatly in their mode of dividend payment, including its tax aspects.

Treatment of co-operatives is included in this chapter on earnings retention because of their extensive reliance on a form of that financing source to generate their equity.

Patronage Dividends

Co-operatives are owned principally by their clientele (or patrons as they are often referred to by co-operative organizations). Thus they are likely to equate the concept of maximizing the wealth of their owners with that of maximizing the welfare of their patrons. If, for example, a co-operative company carries on business in the form of purchasing grain from farmers and reselling it, one would expect it to buy grain from its customers at as high a price as it can pay, consistent with due allowance for its own costs. This is the opposite of the behaviour one would predict from conventional companies, which are usually expected to minimize input prices.

Actually rather than pay high prices to its patrons for the

grain initially, the co-operative is likely to pay relatively conservative prices and await the outcome of its own operations in disposal of the grain. If these operations prove successful, so that a large "profit" has accumulated on the transactions, this "profit" (or savings, as the co-operatives may call it) will be rebated to patrons by some formula dependent on the amount of business done with each particular patron.

Virtually all patrons are likely to be shareholders, since substantial benefits may obtain from the ownership of a single share, and the common shares are typically priced at a nominal amount (usually under $10). Thus the rebate to customers is technically a form of dividend, because of the coincidence of patrons and shareholders. By the nature of its distribution formula it is called a *patronage dividend* or *patronage refund*.

The patronage dividend has a tax treatment which differs from conventional company dividends. Because it can be viewed in one sense as a customer rebate, it is treated for tax purposes as an after-the-fact adjustment of the original price paid to or received from the customer. Following this line of reasoning, the patronage dividend is deductible for corporate income tax purposes by the co-operative company. If the dividend arose from a business transaction, it is taxable as ordinary business income in the hands of its recipient. If the dividend emanated from a consumer transaction, no personal tax is levied.

Earnings Retention through Patronage Dividends

Although patronage dividends on business transactions are taxed as if they were price rebates to patrons, dividends need not be disbursed in cash. In this way the co-operative obtains an unusual form of earnings retention power. Its directors, elected by its shareholder patrons, can elect to retain company "income" without paying corporation tax on it. They do this by declaring a noncash dividend (in form much like a company stock dividend) which shifts tax liability directly to the patrons. Particularly if a co-operative should believe that its patrons were in relatively low personal income tax brackets, it could retain "profits" for purposes of expanding company equity and supporting the company's growth, under favourable tax conditions.

Typically, patronage dividends are disbursed only fractionally in cash (perhaps enough to cover the associated personal income tax for at least relatively low-income patrons). The bulk of the dividend is noncash. This noncash component, while it remains with the company, is accumulated in an equity account for each shareholder-patron.

Not only is it convenient, and possibly tax-advantageous, for co-operatives to form equity in this way, but in fact they have no other feasible alternative for forming common equity. The principle of one-man, one-vote, and the principle of dividend declaration in proportion to patronage rather than the value of equity owned by the individual shareholder, preclude public offerings of conventional common stock by the co-operative company.

Co-operative Debt Financing

One usually expects companies to provide credit to their customers (co-operatives share this practice); it is much less usual for companies to solicit credit from their customers. Occasionally conventional companies obtain financial support from their customers, but co-operatives have followed this practice much more extensively. Probably their success in this endeavour lies in their double relationship with their customers, who are both patrons and shareholders. In any event it has been common practice for co-operatives to market their own bonds to their customers, sometimes carrying out their sales efforts with their regular operating personnel.

This is not to suggest that co-operatives obtain all of their financing from customers, either through patronage dividend retention or sale of debt securities to customers. They, like other companies, make extensive use of short-term credit obtained from suppliers, banks, and other debt-financing sources. The co-operative form of organization extends to financial institutions (for example, credit unions), and often preference is given to these other co-operatives when a nonfinancial co-operative is searching for external debt funds.

SUMMARY

Most Canadian equity capital is generated through earnings retention. Therefore, dividend policy is a major factor in determining company equity formation.

It is common for a company to try to maintain a regular cash dividend, which it adjusts over time only gradually, and then to identify additional amounts of dividend as special.

Distributions to shareholders in the form of stock dividends and stock splits leave the company's total equity position unchanged.

The specific cost of capital from retained earnings is an opportunity cost; when earnings are retained, dividends are not available to shareholders for other uses. In the absence of personal tax considerations, this opportunity cost can be approximated by the discount rate applied to the company's equity in the market. Following this method, cost of retained earnings is approximately the same as cost of new issued equity.

Personal tax situations vary between shareholders, but as a generalization it is reasonable to suppose that retained earnings are a slightly cheaper source of equity than newly issued shares after personal taxes are taken into account.

It is widely believed, though not proved, that "some" dividend payout enhances share value. In recent years, Canadian dividend payout has been at 40–50 percent of earnings.

The growing companies face a special type of financial problem; their rate of asset growth may exceed the rate at which they are able to retain earnings. Companies of this type must choose between increasing debt ratios or forming equity through sale of new shares.

Cooperative companies are organized on a one-man, one-vote system of governance. They typically pay dividends on the basis of patronage rather than share ownership. It is possible for cooperatives to declare noncash patronage dividends; these shift income tax responsibility directly to the share holder. The result is that earnings may be retained without income tax at the company level.

QUESTIONS AND PROBLEMS

1. What is a liquidating dividend?

2. Compare the effects on a company's equity accounts of a 2 for 1 stock split and a 100 percent stock dividend.

3. A company shareholder has a marginal personal tax rate of 55 percent. He receives $10,000 in dividends.
   How much income tax does he pay?

4. How much income tax would the above shareholder pay on $10,000 of capital gains?

5. What relevance does the personal tax situations of shareholders have on company financing decisions?

6. A company has the following balance sheet:

| Assets . . . . . | $1,000,000 | Liabilities . . . . . | $500,000 |
| Net worth . . . . . | | | 500,000 |

The company anticipates growth in sales and assets of 40 percent per year over the next five years. It estimates that it will earn 20 percent after tax on equity during the five-year period (both rates of increase compound annually). If no earnings are declared as dividends project the company's balance sheet at the end of five years, assuming no infusions of equity.

What is the effect on the projection if one fourth of earnings are declared as dividends?

Calculate the debt ratio at the end of five years under the assumption of no dividends and of 25 percent divident payout.

7. Officials of co-operatives, and current tax policies, regard co-operative patronage dividends as different from conventional dividends.

Explain the rationale for this differentiation.

Explain the effect of this differentiation on income tax at both the company and personal levels.

Express a counterargument with respect to making a distinction between a patronage dividend and a conventional common share dividend.

RELATED READINGS

Barker, C. A. "Evaluation of Stock Dividends." *Harvard Business Review,* July–August 1958.

Elton, E., and Gruber, M. "Marginal Stockholder Tax Rates and the Clientele Effect." *Review of Economics and Statistics,* February 1970.

Fama, E., and Babiak, H. "Dividend Policy: An Empirical Analysis." *Journal of the American Statistical Association,* December 1968.

Friend, I., and Puckett, M. "Dividends and Stock Prices." *American Economic Review,* September 1964.

Gordon, M. *The Investment, Financing, and Valuation of the Corporation.* Homewood, Ill.: Richard D. Irwin, Inc., 1962.

Gordon, M. "Optimal Investment and Financing Policy." *Journal of Finance,* May 1963.

Lintner, J. "Dividend, Earnings, Leverages, Stock Prices and the Supply of Capital to Corporations." *Review of Economics and Statistics,* August 1962.

Millar, J. A., and Fielitz, B. D. "Stock-Split and Stock Dividend Decisions." *Financial Management,* Winter 1973.

Miller, M., and Modigliani, F. "Dividend Policy, Growth, and the Valuation of Shares." *Journal of Business,* October 1961.

Wallingford, B. "An Inter-Temporal Approach to the Optimization of Dividend Policy with Predetermined Investments." *Journal of Finance,* June 1972.

Walter, J. *Dividend Policy and Enterprise Valuation.* Belmont, Calif.: Wadsworth, 1967.

18

FINANCING STRATEGY

This chapter will deal with two basic issues. The first of these relates to the question of whether some patterns of financing are likely to be superior to others. Particularly this issue has resolved to the question of whether one can find general reasons for asserting that some debt ratios are likely to be more wealth-maximizing than others.

The second issue taken up in the chapter relates to timing in the financing process. One often reads or hears the advice that if the stock market is in a depressed condition, a perspicacious company will postpone the issuance of common stock and wait for more fortuitous conditions, when stock prices will be higher; or reciprocally, when (EPS/share price) or k_i will be lower. This and other issues relating to the timing of securities will also be discussed.

TRADITIONAL VIEWS ON THE DEBT RATIO

It is true that the ratio of debt to total assets is not the only element of concern in developing the best financing strategy for a company. (For purposes of this discussion we will include preferred shares and those debt instruments that provide some claim on equity in the debt category.) The type of debt instruments used, including both their maturity date and the rigour of the claims they impose on the company, are also important issues and have already been given considerable discussion. However, there seems little question that the most fundamental strategic issue is in determining the debt ratio. To what extent should a company rely on borrowed money and to what extent should it attempt to employ common equity, whether elicited through earnings retention or through the issuance of new common shares?

The Concept of Leverage

One way of approaching the issue of debt versus equity is to start from an extreme position, and assume that a company is financed solely with equity. It can then consider the possibility of acquiring additional assets through the use of debt financing. *Financial leverage* refers to the fact that the rate of earnings on equity capital can be enhanced if equity is augmented by borrowed money, provided that the marginal investments made with the borrowed money yield more than the cost of that money. The term leverage is borrowed from physics to convey the concept of increasing the "power" of the equity by associated debt usage.[1]

An example will illustrate. (Assume all values are on an after-tax basis.) A company has access to assets yielding 12 percent, and currently is financed solely with equity capital with a book value of $1 million. Accordingly its rate of return on the equity is 12 percent, since that is the yield on the assets purchased with the equity. Now consider the possibility of doubling the company size through the use of borrowing and assume that the borrowed money is available at 6 percent. If one assumes that marginal assets yielding 12 percent are still

---

[1] Another variant of leverage is sometimes employed in asset analysis. Just as success in financial leverage depends on matching favourable asset earnings against the fixed financing charges of liabilities, operating leverage is used to describe the situation where a production process embodying fixed cost components is employed in the hope that favourable sales or production volumes will reduce costs per unit. Like its financial variant, operating leverage is two-sided.

available, the effect of this manoeuvre is to increase the company's asset collection to $2 million, and its earnings (before interest payments) to $240,000. The effect of the leverage is illustrated by the following calculation:

Earnings before interest
   $2,000,000 at 12% $240,000
Interest $1,000,000 at 6%   60,000
Earnings available to common
   shareholders $180,000
Rate of return on shareholder's equity
   $180,000/$1,000,000 . . . .   18%

Through the use of borrowing the company has been able to increase the return on shareholders' money from 12 percent to 18 percent.

Of course, if returns on assets do not materialize as planned, the effect of leverage is reversed. Suppose we continue with the above example, but assume that, even though assets were expected to earn 12 percent, plans went awry and the return on assets turned out to be 3 percent. Now we can repeat the calculation of the effect of leverage.

Earnings before interest
   $2,000,000 at 3% $60,000
Interest ($1,000,000 at 6%)   60,000
Earnings available to common shareholders . . . . $ 0

With the use of leverage when misfortunes occurred, the shareholders managed to parlay the 3 percent return they would have obtained if they had not borrowed down to a return of 0.

The term leverage is widely used; it is extended into such nomenclature as "the highly levered firm," which refers to a company with a high debt ratio. The problem with the concept is its failure to tell the full story. The notion of attempting to borrow at 6 percent to invest at 12 percent is, by itself, no more sophisticated than the banal proposition, "buy low, sell high." What is left out of the idea of leverage is explicit consideration of the extent to which the risk borne by the common shareholders is amplified through the use of borrowing. The above examples have illustrated this amplification but the issues here are so critical to company financing strategy that they deserve much more careful analysis.

Overall Capital Costs and the Debt Ratio

The concept of leverage points out the opportunities and pitfalls of debt in a world of uncertainty. A company can never be sure whether, as events reveal themselves, it will regret or rejoice over its incurrence of contractual obligations to creditors. This uncertainty, however, does not lead to the conclusion that a company's choice of financing is just a matter of luck. Instead, a company can improve its expected outlook for gain by attempting to effect a least cost financing solution. That is, along the lines and subject to the qualifications discussed in Chapter 11, it will try to design a financing strategy that minimizes overall capital cost.

One aspect of minimizing capital cost may seem bothersome to the reader. There can be little objection (if one accepts the objective of shareholder wealth maximization) of trying to hold the cost of borrowed money down to as low a cost rate as possible. Similarly, since persons buying new shares of stock can be regarded as a different set than the company's existing shareholders, there can similarly be little objection to attempting to procure financing through the sale of new common shares at the least cost possible. But how can a company think in terms of cost minimization with respect to the portion of company funds supplied by its existing shareholders? That portion also constitutes part of the company's overall financing mix with a specific cost and weight built into overall cost of capital calculation.

Minimizing the cost of existing shareholder equity can be seen to be consistent with maximization of the wealth of shareholders if one first recalls that the appropriate cost for the equity of existing shareholders is an opportunity cost based on what they could earn on investments of comparable risk. This opportunity cost is determined by earnings available on common shares of equivalent risk; it is lowered when the risk on the company's own common shares declines (because of the market's tendency to capitalize low-risk shares at lower discount rates). But if the opportunity cost, k_i, is lowered this is equivalent to saying that the company's shares too, will be discounted at a lower rate. Expressed alternatively, the market price associated with the company's EPS will increase.

To summarize, holding down the cost of equity is equivalent to holding down k_i. Lower k_i, in turn, has two effects. If the company attempts to sell common stock, it will do so at a lower cost. At the same time a lower k_i will mean a higher value for the company's existing shares, and this maximization of the value of existing shares is directly consistent with the principle of wealth maximization.

Again, as noted previously, minimum overall capital cost is not necessarily achieved by holding all specific capital costs to their minimum possible level. Overall capital cost is built on two components, specific capital costs and their associated weights. For example, the concept of leverage applied in a more sophisticated way, might suggest that the company could gain from the use of relatively high debt ratio, even if that ratio resulted in the company paying high interest to creditors (due to its high debt financial condition) and experiencing a high cost of equity (again because of the riskiness in the equity introduced by the high debt ratio).

The debt costs and equity costs are both made higher by the debt ratio, but if at the same time debt cost is still considerably lower than equity cost, what the company loses in specific cost increases may be made up for by the increased weight of debt.

An example illustrates: in effect this is still a review of a discussion previously advanced in Chapter 11.

Company	Debt Ratio	Specific Debt Cost	Specific Equity Cost	Overall Capital Cost
A 3		6%	12%	10.2%
B 7		8%	14	9.8

We still cannot say, until after the fact, which company's policies will have proved most successful. If misfortunes occur, the shareholders of A are probably going to be better off and if extraordinary good fortune occurs B's shareholders will be all smiles. But we do not know what the future will bring, and based on current information, with due allowance for risk as reflected both in the charges of creditors and the capitalization rate k_i reckoned on the equity, B's rather than A's expectations of costs are lower, and thus B's position is more favourable ex ante.

The Cost of Capital Curve

The relationship between overall capital cost and the debt ratio can be expressed in the form of a widely used curve, which may be called the cost of capital curve. The reader is cautioned to note the difference between this curve and other cost curves that are often used in economic analysis. The typical economic cost curve relates costs to quantity or example; even capital costs could be related to the amount (scale) of capital employed by the company. The cost of capital curve used here is different. It relates cost of capital to the *proportion* of debt (debt ratio) used by a company. Examples will follow in the ensuing sections.

The U-Shaped Cost of Capital Curve

At the level of analysis of simple leverage, many proponents of its use assert that leverage is a good thing if not carried to extreme. They contend that moderate increases in the debt ratio are examples of astute use of "other people's money" but that an extremely high debt ratio would result in inordinately high borrowing costs, and in an unacceptable level of risk for the shareholders.

Another version of leverage is embodied in the so-called U-shaped cost of capital curve. The traditional line of reasoning justifying it is that so long as borrowing is carried to a judicious (moderate, temperate, or what have you) extent, borrowing costs will not be affected very much. For example, the firm which can borrow at the prime rate with a 10 percent debt ratio may also be able to borrow at prime rate with a 40 percent debt ratio. At the same time, proponents of the U-shaped capital curve contend that if debt ratios are kept moderate, the capitalization rate accorded by the market to the company's stock (k_i, the basis for cost of equity) will also be unaffected by debt use.

With k_i greater than the interest rate, if the weight of borrowing in the overall cost of capital calculation can be increased, with no change in either k_i or interest rates, overall capital cost is bound to fall. Eventually, though, if the debt ratio becomes "immoderate," creditors and the stock market are alerted and the marginal benefits from borrowing cease to obtain; in fact the company may be penalized for its immoderate use with a rising overall capital cost. This traditional U-shaped cost of capital curve is shown in Illustration 18–1.

ILLUSTRATION 18–1
U-Shaped Capital Cost Curve

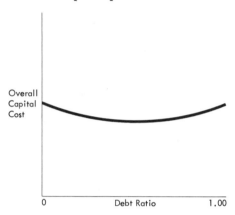

The advocacy of the U-shaped capital curve just presented may seem a trifle fuzzy; the arguments presented are what Professor J. K. Galbraith might call "conventional wisdom." However, we should note that the U-shaped cost of capital curve is consistent with present usage.

One expects, if companies are to succeed or survive in a competitive marketplace, that they cannot conduct many of their activities in violation of the precepts of profit maximization, including seeking least cost solutions to problems whenever possible. The fact that the vast majority of Canadian companies use debt ratios within a moderate range of 30 to 60 percent suggests that least cost financing solutions lie within this range and not at extremes of debt or equity use. Intuitive promulgations of the U-shaped capital cost curve, in spite of sometimes nebulous logic, may have turned out to be right. We can now turn to a more modern and rigorous examination of this critical problem of financing strategy.

Modigliani-Miller and Proposition 1

In a landmark article written about two decades ago, Professors Modigliani and Miller attempted to inject some harder thinking into analysis of the cost of capital curve. In their celebrated paper they advanced an argument which they called Proposition 1. The gist of this proposition is:

a. The value of a company is determined by its current earnings before the payment of interest (sometimes called net operating income or NOI), discounted at the overall cost of capital. In other words, creditors discount their claim on the company at the interest rate (cost of debt) and shareholders discount their claim on the company at k_i to determine the market values of their holdings. The sum of these two values is the overall market value of the company.

b. The market is sufficiently perceptive that a company with given levels of NOI and risk will not be able to change the total market value of the claims to this income flow (all its securities) irrespective of the proportion in which it finances with debt or with equity. In other words, no matter how the company is financed, the collective value of all the company's securities should be the same.

c. If the value placed on a company's earnings cannot be affected by the proportion in which the company issues securities against them, it follows, since overall cost of capital is a ratio between NOI and the total value of the company's securities, that overall cost of capital cannot be affected by a company's choice of mode of financing.

The Modigliani-Miller position implies the following cost of capital curve (Illustration 18–2).

Besides the basic general logic presented above, Modigliani and Miller (or M-and-M) advanced an argument to show, in detail, *why* a company can obtain no benefit for its shareholders by manipulating its debt ratio. This concept is referred to as "homemade leverage."

Homemade Leverage and Other Rationale for M-and-M

Homemade leverage argument is based on the idea that there is nothing exclusive about a company's ability to finance with debt; shareholders themselves can also borrow.

ILLUSTRATION 18–2
Modigliani-Miller Cost of Capital Curve

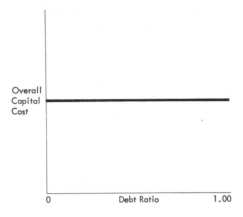

If a shareholder can borrow on the same terms he is able to replicate personally any advantage of borrowing at the corporate level. Suppose Company A borrows and passes the profits and risk of leverage on to its shareholders, while Company B does not. An individual can buy B's shares on margin and obtain the same results of levering obtained by A's shareholders. Given this personal-level opportunity, it is quite plausible to expect that A will reap no benefits for its borrowing, nor will B be penalized for abstaining.

Varying other arguments have been advanced in support of M-and-M's flat cost of capital curve. Perhaps the most important may be described as the risk/valuation contention. Basically this holds that the risk character of the company's assets is fully reflected in the total collection of claims against those assets. If so, the risk borne by the company's creditors and shareholders in toto is unaffected by the debt ratio. If the total risk in all securities (debt + equity) is left collectively unchanged, their value should also be. If changing the debt ratio cannot affect the total value of a company's securities, it cannot affect overall capital cost.

M-and-M Reviewed

M-and-M's Proposition 1 may be paraphrased as "no matter how you slice it. . . ." The logical appeal is plain. One should not, in an orderly market, expect that the value of a company can be changed simply by seeking out some widely known, readily accessible debt use optimum. This is not to suggest that financing strategy is trivial. Individually companies seek optimal financial structures, and no doubt there are winners and losers in the competition for least cost financing solutions.

The issue posed by M-and-M is not whether there are or are not least cost financing solutions available to business on an individualized, ad hoc basis. Their analysis addresses the question of whether there is a pattern in these least cost solutions, whether some ranges of debt ratio are a better hunting ground than others for least cost solutions. Their answer, via Proposition 1, is No. However, M-and-M and others have, building on the logic of Proposition I, found some amendment necessary. One of these amendments, which may predict a zone of efficiency on the cost of capital curve, arises from the tax environment.

TAX CONSIDERATIONS

To understand the tax issues in connection with financing strategy, it is necessary to think of a corporation as a vehicle for carrying on business operations on behalf of its shareholders. Personal and corporate income taxes, even though levied for legitimate social purposes, divert earnings of the company to nonshareholders, thus reduce the efficiency of a company's ultimate endeavour, the maximization of the wealth of its shareholders. (We take this objective as an existing condition, without attempting to pass judgment on whether it is ethically superior to a more altruistic view toward taxes.)

In determining financing strategy, a company must be aware of tax considerations in three places. Two are obvious: the company will manage its affairs in such a way that corporate income taxes, and personal income taxes of shareholders, will be kept as low as possible. In addition, it must be concerned about the personal tax consequences of its payments to other financing sources (namely, creditors) since the marketability of the company's debt instruments, the terms on which it can borrow, are likely to be conditional upon the amount of *after-tax* benefits that can be conferred to creditors.

As a general rule, it is consistent with the search for a least cost financing solution for a company to minimize the joint impact of taxes on the company itself, and on its payments, actual or potential, to all financing sources. These joint taxes, from the company's viewpoint, constitute a friction or a wastage, and control of this wastage is important in devising a company's financing strategy.

A Tax Efficiency Rule

Pretax operating income (EBIT) may become either interest income to creditors or net income remaining for shareholders; the split will depend on the debt ratio. To measure the extent to which EBIT directed toward either creditors or shareholders is eroded by taxes, a tax efficiency ratio may be devised. Where t_c and t_p refer to income tax rates at corporate and personal levels, the tax efficiency ratio becomes:

$$\frac{\text{After-tax personal income}}{\text{EBIT}} = (1 - t_c)(1 - t_p).$$

An example will explore the use of this ratio.

A Simplified Example

Let us consider a simplified situation first and then move toward greater reality. Begin with the assumption that a 40 percent corporation income tax exists, that interest paid to creditors is deductible for corporate tax purposes, and that interest received by creditors is treated exactly the same for personal income tax purposes as shareholder earnings (whether disbursed as dividends or retained). Marginal personal tax rates are 50 percent.

It is apparent, under such a tax regime, that the use of debt has an advantage. Money disbursed to creditors is only taxed once at the personal level while money earned by shareholders is taxed twice, first at the company level with the corporate income tax, and then at the personal level. Such a tax regime leads to a bias in favour of borrowing.

The bias is identified precisely through the use of tax efficiency ratios. Where EBIT flows through to creditors subject to no corporate tax, the efficiency ratio for creditors' share of EBIT is

$$t_c = 0$$
$$t_p = .5$$
$$(1 - t_c)(1 - t_p) = .5.$$

On the shareholders' portion of EBIT

$$t_c = .4$$
$$t_p = .5$$
$$(1 - t_c)(1 - t_p) = .3.$$

We observe that EBIT directed to creditors is subject to income taxes of 50 percent, while that destined for shareholders is taxed at 70 percent.

The tax efficiency of debt can be illustrated in another way, assuming the above conditions:

> An ingenious solicitor devises a company structured along the following lines: The company would be financed entirely with debt, except for one share of stock. That share of stock would be owned jointly by the creditors of the company. The debt is in the form of bonds, with an interest rate set as high as the maximum NOI possible on the company's assets.

What our solicitor has done is to create a situation where there can be no possible returns on the stock; the bondholders receive all the NOI of the company and bear all of its risks. The bondholders, of course, would really be shareholders, but the company would pay no corporation tax. Because of this feature the total value of its bonds would have to be greater than the total value of a similar company that was financed entirely with common stock. Reciprocally, its capital cost would be lower.[2]

The Simplified Tax Example and M-and-M

The original M-and-M analysis, with its horizontal cost of capital curve, was based on a neutrality of tax effects. One may now consider the effect of the tax environment pointed out in the previous example, with income taxes falling more heavily

---

[2] In fact, a consortium of courts, Revenue Canada, and legislation would unquestionably undo the work of our imaginative solicitor.

on the shareholders than on the creditors. If the cost of capital curve was flat under tax neutrality, and if taxes now favour debt, the curve cannot remain flat.

Increasing the debt ratio generates tax savings. The effect of these savings is an offset to capital costs that would otherwise be incurred if all equity was used and none of the marginal benefits of debt's tax efficiency were obtained. The effect of the tax saving on the cost of capital curve is illustrated in Illustration 18–3.

ILLUSTRATION 18–3

M-and-M Cost of Capital Curve (simplified tax revision)

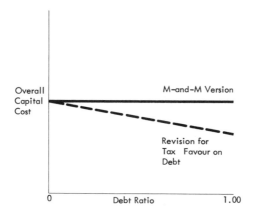

Actual Tax Conditions

In fact the real tax environment is not as simple as the above example. While borrowed money gets a break at the corporate level, shareholder money gets better treatment at the personal level. When creditors receive interest, that payment is fully taxable at ordinary personal tax rates (or corporate tax rates if the creditor is another corporation).[3]

There are several reasons why one can only explore tax efficiency of varying debt ratios, rather than make a definitive statement.

1. Corporate tax rates vary (through a range of 46 percent to 23 percent at the time of writing).

---

[3] Recent tax rules exempt $1,000 of interest income from personal taxation under some conditions. This does not affect the marginal analysis of any but quite small-scale creditors, and is excluded in this analysis.

2. Dividend payout rates vary.
3. Marginal personal tax rates vary, depending on the status of the person (from a high of over 67 percent to a low of zero in 1976).

In exploring the question, the tax efficiency ratio must be refined, to recognize that shareholder income is, in fact, subject to two personal tax rates:

$$t_{pg} = \text{Capital gains tax} = \tfrac{1}{2}t_p,$$

$$t_{pd} = \text{Dividend tax} = \tfrac{4}{3}t_p - 0.36.$$

The relative applicability of these two rates is determined by the dividend payout ratio, d. If shareholder earnings are declared as dividends, t_{pd} applies; if not t_{pg} rules. In general, personal tax rate on shareholders' imputed income is a composite:

$$t_{ps} = dt_{pd} + (1 - d)t_{pg}.$$

Substituting from the above equations:

$$t_{ps} = d(\tfrac{4}{3}t_p - .36) + (1 - d)(\tfrac{1}{2}t_p)$$
$$= .833\ dt_p + .5t_p - .36d.$$

Given this special personal tax treatment for shareholders, shareholder tax efficiency is now expressed as

$$(1 - t_c)\ (1 - t_{ps}).$$

which in turn becomes

Shareholder tax efficiency $= (1 - t_c)\ (1 - .833dt_p - .5t_p + .36d)$.

On the other hand, creditor tax efficiency is left unrevised, since all creditor income avoids corporate tax and is taxed fully at the personal level. The resulting tax efficiency ratio is

Creditor tax efficiency $= (1 - t_p)$.

An efficiency comparison is now seen to be dependent on three variables: d, t_p, and t_c.

To make the analysis more manageable, let us assume that dividend payout is either half or nothing $(d - .5, 0)$. This explores a range from rather typical dividend usage down to the zero usage which most firms would employ if they were motivated only by tax efficiency in their dividend policy. Now let us consider some representative combinations of personal and corporate tax rates.

Corporate rates to be explored are:

t_c = .46, maximum.
t_c = .40, manufacturing companies.
t_c = .25, oil and many other resource companies.

Personal tax rates to be examined are simply a rather broad selection:

t_p = .61, maximum in Ontario.
t_p = .50, approximate marginal rate at $30,000 gross income.
t_p = .35, approximate marginal rate at $10,000 gross income.

The comparison can be expressed as another ratio, constructed for convenience in this presentation:

$$\text{Relative shareholder tax efficiency} = \frac{\text{Shareholder tax efficiency}}{\text{Creditor tax efficiency}}.$$

Values of the ratio above one indicate the tax climate favours shareholder financing; below, creditor financing and high debt ratios. These values are displayed in Illustration 18–4.

ILLUSTRATION 18–4
Relative Shareholder Tax Efficiency

Corporate Income Tax Rates	Personal Income Tax Rates		
	0.61	0.50	0.35
0.46	0.96*	0.81*	0.69*
0.40	1.07*	0.90*	0.76*
0.25	1.34*	1.13*	0.95*
0.46	0.86†	0.78†	0.71†
0.40	0.95†	0.87†	0.79†
0.25	1.19†	1.08†	0.99†

*Dividend payment of 0.0 assumed.
†Dividend payout of 0.5 assumed.

These results do not conclusively favour debt or equity. Since most shares tend to be owned by high-income individuals, the personal tax rates of 0.5 and 0.61 seem most likely to dominate. The 12 situations examined within these personal tax categories provide results ranging from equity enjoying 1.34 superiority to 0.78 inferiority, and average to 1.00 (1.04 with no dividends, 0.96 with).

If one assumes the existence of "typical" dividend usage ($d = 0.5$), a "typical" shareholder ($t_p = 0.5$ or 0.61) and a "typical" manufacturing company ($t_c = 0.40$), debt use enjoys a small edge; averaging over the two values of t_p, the relative shareholder tax efficiency is 0.91.

On balance, one may be left with an impression of a slight bias toward debt financing. However, under existing tax laws, information available does not support substantial amendment of M-and-M's cost of capital views. Perhaps a slight downward inclination in the cost of capital curve could be justified—but only slight.

The reader should recall that the tax laws on which these calculations are based are a substantial departure from tax laws that prevailed a few years earlier. At that time, the tax efficiency of debt was much greater. Thus if one encounters writings based on tax laws of, let us say 1970, or writings based on U.S. tax law, one is likely to find the conclusion that the use of debt is highly tax efficient. Under present conditions in this country however, such a strong statement cannot be made.

OTHER FINANCING EFFICIENCIES

Procurement Costs

Some debt and some equity can be obtained at a fairly low cost of procurement. While the floating of bonds or common stock issues require the payment of fees to investment dealers and other expenses, no administrative cost is associated with the retention of earnings. Similarly, credit from suppliers can also be procured almost frictionlessly; and in fact may be obtainable at "zero cost" simply because of the unavailability of purchasing arrangements which reward nonusers of supplier credit. Additionally, both supplier credit and bank credit can be allowed to fluctuate for seasonal or sporadic financing needs with little inconvenience and expense. Again, a case is being made for the efficiency of *some* debt (namely, trade and bank credit), and *some* equity (namely, retained earnings). Again, conversely, this is a case against extreme solutions, an argument for the U-shape in the cost of capital curve.

It would be easy to inadvertently extend this argument to a comparison between the costs of floating issues of bonds and common stock and observe that bond flotation costs are usually somewhat lower. That would not be a fair comparison, because typically bonds are issued under conditions of lower risk in current usage; so one would expect that, in particular, underwriting fees on bond issues would be lower because of this characteristic. If the cost of underwriting risky bond issues was compared with the underwriting of issues of common shares with comparable risk, it is questionable whether any significant efficiency would be revealed.

For the company that needs financing in excess of that provided through earnings retention and conventional trade and bank credit, there seems little basis for a preference between the issuance of new common stock or the issuance of other types of securities on the basis of procurement cost. Again thinking about the modification of the original M-and-M curve, if a company refuses to use funds that it can easily generate through trade and bank credit or retained earnings, these foregone efficiencies will tend to impart upturns to the extreme ends of the capital cost curve. The lack of difference in flotation efficiency of the stock and bonds does not alter previously drawn conclusions about the shape of the function. Modifications in the original M-and-M function can now be summarized in Illustration 18–5:

ILLUSTRATION 18–5
Cost of Capital Curve, Showing Procurement Efficiencies

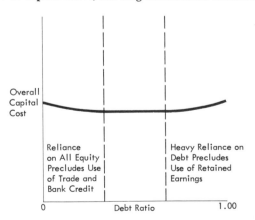

Bankruptcy Costs

Discussion of financing efficiency is rightly centred on means of attempting to get as much of the company's net operating income to its financing sources without diversion into the hands of "outsiders." For most companies, the principal outsider is Revenue Canada. We have seen that the foresight of existing tax legislation makes it difficult to escape this tax drain on EBIT by choice of financing strategy. We have also looked at another set of outsiders, investment dealers (not to exclude other financing agents and intermediaries) and suggested efficiency from taking advantage of those fund sources with low administrative or flotation costs. Now we turn to a third class of outsiders, the recipients of costs associated with a company's going bankrupt.

To appreciate the cost of bankruptcy, first consider the possibility of a costless bankruptcy. Suppose a company finances with a great deal of debt. The company's cash flows turn sour, and it is unable to meet its obligations to creditors. One could conceive of a situation where the company's insolvency became apparent on Thursday afternoon, and on Friday morning creditors had equitably and contentedly divided up the remaining assets of the company, or left the company intact with the former creditors now the owners.

If the world were like this, most shareholders in a high debt company might be disappointed because company fortunes had necessitated the transfer of ownership, but there would be no wastage associated with the process. Shareholders had consented in advance to the use of debt, knowing that such an ownership transfer was a possibility. They played the leverage game and lost.

In fact, the real world operates differently. A company which fails to meet its obligations on Thursday afternoon might be in the throes of complex legal procedures a year from the following Friday morning or even later. The solicitors and others involved in the process of equitably resolving the affairs of the insolvent company do not provide their services gratuitously; so they constitute another set of potential outsiders to whom corporate wealth may be diverted.

A company which uses no debt financing never is exposed to

the possibility of going bankrupt. A series of operating losses may eventually exhaust the original capital of the company, in which case all its assets will have been dissipated and it will no longer have a factual existence. However, when it ceases to factually exist, there is nothing left to divide up and hence no reason to incur costs for a dividing-up process.

On the other hand, when a company is financed with a substantial amount of debt, the equity of the shareholders may be eradicated but significant amounts of assets may be left for division among creditors. The greater the extent that debt is used, the higher the probability that bankruptcy will take place; and because of the "thinness" of the shareholder's interest, the higher the probability that assets of substantial value will remain for division among creditors. Therefore, since bankruptcy involves disbursements of company wealth to outsiders, and since the probability of costly bankruptcy proceedings increases as the debt ratio increases, it follows that an inefficiency—the expected value of payments for bankruptcy administration—rises with debt usage. This constitutes another amendment to the M-and-M point of departure, tending to raise the cost of capital as the proportion of company debt increases.

Explicit bankruptcy costs may not be the only wastage associated with a company's experiencing bankruptcy, or even exposing itself to a substantial probability of bankruptcy. A company which uses a large amount of debt, with the resulting possibility of bankruptcy, may have trouble attracting capable managerial personnel because of their apprehension about possible association with a failing company.

COST OF CAPITAL CURVE REVIEWED

This completes the analysis of the cost of capital curve. One is reminded of the statement, "the ancients have stolen our secrets." Starting with M-and-M and correcting for various inefficiencies has led us back to a U-shaped capital cost curve. This whole set of revisions are summarized in Illustration 18–6.

This unquantified approximation of the cost of capital curve's shape is consistent with Canadian practice. One would not expect the use of extremes of debt or equity in financing

ILLUSTRATION 18–6
Amendments to M-and-M Cost of Capital Curve

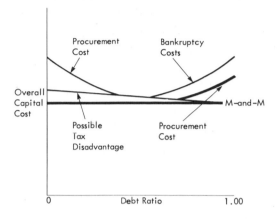

strategies given the existence of a curve shaped roughly like the one above, and in fact one only infrequently finds such extremes in practice. It should be noted, incidentally, that recent tax legislation has tended to reverse a bias which previously imparted efficiency to debt financing. So if one were to venture prognostications about the future, it could well be that one would see companies placing increased reliance, though certainly not sole reliance, on equity financing.

Another conclusion that one is led to, on the basis of theoretical examination and observation of practical usage, is that, while there are good reasons for avoiding extremes of financing, there is probably a broad intermediate range of usage where there is no compelling reason for preferring one debt ratio strategy over another. This existence of a wide range of relatively efficient debt ratios has some interesting aspects which will be explored in the next section.

THE TIMING OF FINANCING

The Attraction of Ideal Timing

Supply and demand conditions change frequently in capital markets. Interest rates move up and down, and share prices fluctuate with even greater amplitude. From time to time these differences in interest rates and share prices reflect broad market movements, quite apart from differences that may exist between the interest rates paid by individual companies because of differences in their risk, et cetera; or differences that may exist between the share prices of various companies for similar reasons. Buying in the securities market has always attracted a good deal of attention from persons with speculative inclinations, who try to buy bonds when interest rates are high (or when bonds are priced low) and sell them in a low-interest rate market; and more notoriously those who try to buy low and sell high in the stock market. The intriguing potential of successful security market speculation is not confined to buyers of securities; potentially the same type of speculation can be and is practiced by issuers of securities.

Let us consider two possible speculative aspirations of security issuers. The first relates to the timing of debt issues. If a company wants to raise money through the issuance of debt, and it expects that interest rates are going to decline in the future, it may attempt a tactic of undertaking its necessary borrowing on a short maturity basis. In this way it hopes to avoid a long-term commitment, and to wait until market conditions are more propitious before issuing long-term debt such as bonds. If the tactic works, it is certainly better to pay 7 percent for 1 year and 5 percent over the next 20 years instead of jumping into an immediate commitment for 7 percent over 20 years.[4]

A second, and even more alluring dream, is to fine tune the timing of new issues of common stock. Suppose a company believes that it is ready to float a new issue of common stock but that the current condition of the stock market is a depressed one, with share prices likely to rise within a couple of years. With this belief, the company will try to postpone its share issue and rely temporarily on borrowed money. For example, a company wishes to avoid selling its shares when prices are depressed to the point where $k_i = 25$ percent. Instead it decides to borrow money for a couple of years, in the hope of then finding a stock market where k_i will, because of a general rise in the level of security prices, be 15 percent.

---

[4] A horizontal yield curve is implicit in this example; that, however, is apart from the argument being presented.

These tactics are postulated on the ability to forecast securities markets. If the forecasts are wrong, these speculative ventures turn to misadventures. If the company abstains from long-term borrowing at 7 percent, and a year down the road finds that the general level of long-term rates has risen to 9 percent, it is left with cause for lamentation. Similarly, the company may find that, bad as the stock market seemed, it worsened in the following years, with the comapny eventually having to raise equity money at $k_i = 35$ percent instead of 25 percent. So, to repeat, timing tactics of this speculative variety rely on ability to forecast interest rates or share prices.

The Random-Walk Hypothesis

Nearly anyone familiar with securities markets is aware that forecasting them is not a problem with easy or obvious solutions. Bernard Baruch, a famous American financier (perhaps better known in history as an adviser to presidents) in all seriousness described his prodigious success as a stock market speculator almost entirely to good luck.

This difficulty of forecasting should not be particularly surprising when one gives the matter a little thought. Suppose, for example, that it is very easy to forecast that share prices are going to rise by at least 30 percent next year. Since there are a great many sophisticated buyers in the stock market, one would expect these buyers to immediately act on this information and as a result, create a heavy demand for shares in the market. At the same time persons holding shares, also privy to this well-known forecast, would wish to hold their shares rather than to sell them. The result would be an immediate demand-supply imbalance in the market, and an immediate price rise. In other words, if there were readily available information about a future price rise, that future price rise would be transported in time to the present, and be reflected immediately in share prices.

In general form, this view of the market says that current share prices already reflect all readily available information about the future prospects for the market. This applies to individual shares (the price of a mining stock does not wait for an actual ore discovery to take place; price adjusts every day as probabilities of a successful discovery change) and it also applies to the market as a whole.

With certain technical exceptions, which do not detract from the general point being made, this common-sense notion that market prices will reflect all readily available current information has an interesting implication. If all known information about the future is reflected in current security prices, the only information about the future that is not reflected is currently *unknown* information. By the very fact that this information is unknown, there is no basis for predicting whether it will be favourable or unfavourable when it does become known.

To complete this deduction about stock market behaviour we may recapitulate:

a. Current stock prices reflect all known information about the future.

b. As additional information becomes available, that information may be either good or bad.

c. As the future information becomes available, it will cause stock prices to go up or down, depending upon whether it is favourable or unfavourable information.

d. Because the character of the information is now unknown, there is no basis for predicting whether tomorrow (or next year) will bring a rise or a decline in security prices.

This line of reasoning, that any or all security prices have as much chance of going up as going down in the future, is known as the *random-walk* hypothesis.

Consider, for example, forecasting attempts which try to employ trends in the security market. Suppose stock prices have been falling more or less continuously for the last three years and are now at a low point in terms of recent history. Should one project this downtrend further, or should one decide that stocks are at a historic low, and therefore they are likely to rise in price. In fact there appears to be no basis for making a rational choice between the two interpretations.

The random-walk hypothesis has been borne out by two lines of investigation. First, the behaviour of stock prices has been subjected to intensive statistical analysis. Various methods of attempting to identify trends and patterns in the market have been "tried on" with past stock market data; these attempts to discern patterns of market behaviour that can be developed into profitable trading rules have not been successful.

Second, extensive studies have been conducted relating to the success of professional investment managers, who are presumed to have expertise in the business of stock market prediction. The results of these studies suggest that professional money managers have been no more successful at choosing stocks (that is, making predictions about their future behaviour) than "unenlightened" individuals. The "professional" might as well have been using that time-honoured method of attaching the stock market pages from his *Financial Post* to his recreation room wall and making his selections by throwing darts from a distance of 15 feet.[5]

These statistical analyses and empirical studies of the performance of money managers are not absolutely conclusive. Perhaps there are ways, yet unknown, for maintaining a consistent batting average on stock market predictions. (Maybe E. P. Taylor knows and won't tell.) Nevertheless, there is enough evidence available to suggest that the prospect of easily reducing the company's cost of capital by "astute" speculative timing of security issuance is naïve. If there is a way of doing this, that way is certainly not obvious.

Timing to Minimize Issuance Cost

There is another, and a very defensible, basis for developing timing tactics for security issuance. This lies in the possibility of economies of scale in the flotation of common stock or bond issues. Suppose, for example, that a company has decided on a financial strategy where it will maintain a debt ratio of about 50 percent. Such a policy could be so strictly interpreted that, every year, if the company's debt ratio was even slightly over 50 percent, the company would hurry to put an issue of common stock on the market of the precise amount necessary to bring the debt ratio back to the 50 percent target. Such a

---

[5] There are exceptions; the statements refer to average performance of groups of professionals. And the underlying studies are mostly based on U.S. data; maybe Canadian "pros" can do better.

policy could result in annual, or even more frequent, flotations of common stock issues, probably all in relatively small dollar amounts.

If one recalls the previous discussion of the probable shape of the cost of capital curve, there is reason to believe, both on the basis of theory and of observed company usage, that while the curve is U-shaped, it is in the shape of a broad-bottomed U. There is probably little difference for most companies, in terms of financing efficiency, in whether they use a 35 percent or a 55 percent debt ratio, as long as they maintain their debt ratio within a "moderate" range.

This condition implies that a company need not be particularly concerned about maintaining a precise level of debt ratio. Instead it may let its debt ratio gradually rise, perhaps by use of increasing trade and bank credit, and then when the debt ratio starts getting near the upper end of the range which the company deems acceptable, it can float a large common stock issue, and abruptly lower its debt ratio by 10 percent, or 15 percent, or even more. In general the debt ratio may be allowed to fluctuate in order to allow the use of large security issues, and with this largeness attain scale economies in their issuance.

SUMMARY

Traditional analysis with respect to company debt usage was related to the concept of financial leverage. Borrowing was regarded as profitable if proceeds could be invested in assets yielding above the interest cost. The extent of borrowing practice was limited by the need to maintain a perceived "moderate" debt ratio.

The more modern viewpoint tends to separate investment and financing, and considers the optimal use of debt to be that debt ratio which results in minimum capital cost.

Modigliani and Miller (M-and-M) have argued, subject to a number of assumptions, that capital cost will be invariant with respect to the debt ratio. Capital cost is related to risk exposure, and since the company's overall risk exposure is determined by the risk of its assets, it is contended that the value placed on a company by financial markets (and reciprocally, cost of capital) cannot be changed through alterations in the mixture of claims issued against those underlying assets.

Consideration of corporate and personal income taxes requires modification of the M-and-M conclusion. The combined impact of personal and company taxes tends to be less on interest than on shareholder earnings. This modification suggests a cost advantage to be obtained by use of debt.

Since increased use of debt increases the probability of company bankruptcy, and since bankruptcy is a costly process, high levels of debt may be associated with increasingly high probabilistic assessments of bankruptcy cost.

The result of tax, bankruptcy, and other modifications of M-and-M is to predict, instead of a horizontal cost of capital curve, one that is moderately U-shaped. In turn, this implies that companies are likely to find least cost financing solutions in the region of "moderate" debt ratios. Interestingly, this conclusion tends to coincide with the traditional viewpoint.

Companies may attempt to time security issues in an attempt to capitalize on trends in the financial market. For example, an issue of common shares may be delayed during the period of "low" share prices in an attempt to sell the shares in a higher market, and thus reduce specific cost of the new equity.

Studies of the workings of financial markets have led to formulation of a random-walk hypothesis. This hypothesis contends that past trends and patterns in financial markets cannot be used to predict future trends and patterns.

There is often a conflict between company beliefs that they can speculatively time their issuance of securities, and the random-walk hypothesis.

Security issues may also be timed to minimize issuance costs. This technique involves delaying security issues until relatively large issues can be placed. This aspect of timing is not in conflict with random walk.

QUESTIONS AND PROBLEMS

1. A company's assets and net worth are currently $100,000 each. The company contemplates the purchase of an additional $100,000 of assets. The company has currently been earning 10 percent on its assets, and it expects that this rate of return is sustainable on the new assets. Rate of return on shareholder equity is also 10 percent, since the shareholders are financing all of the assets.

If additional equity money can be obtained by sale of a half interest in the company for $100,000, what will return on shareholder investment be after the $100,000 in new assets are purchased and financed?

Assume that the $100,000 can be raised in another way, by borrowing at 6 percent. What will be the effect on shareholder rate of return if the new assets are financed by debt instead of by equity?

Consider the possibility of a misfortune; that the marginal $100,000 of new assets provide no return instead of a 10 percent return. Under this assumption, again contrast the impact on having financed the new assets with equity and with debt on the rate of return afforded to company shareholders.

2. A company considers increasing its debt ratio. Indicate the expected effect of this increase upon
   a. Specific cost of debt.
   b. Specific cost of equity.
   c. Overall capital cost.
   Explain why you can be more confident on your answers to (a) and (b) than on your answer to (c).

3. A company considers the following financing alternatives:

Debt Ratio	Specific Debt Cost (percent)	Specific Equity Cost (percent)
.2	6%	12%
.4	7	13
.6	9	15
.8	12	17

   Plot the cost of capital curve.

4. Is the above cost of capital curve consistent with the Modigliani and Miller position? Explain.

5. What is homemade leverage, and how does it relate to the Modigliani-Miller argument?

6. A company retains no earnings. All of its shareholder income is subject to tax at both corporate and personal levels. Assuming a marginal corporate tax rate of 40 percent and a marginal personal tax rate of 50 percent, calculate the tax efficiency ratio.

   How would the equity tax efficiency ratio be affected if the company expected to pay no dividends, with shareholders retrieving all of their earnings through share disposition and resulting payment of capital gains tax?

7. A company decides to rely almost exclusively on debt financing and as a result retains almost no earnings. Identify the financing inefficiency associated with this policy.

8. Describe bankruptcy cost, and how it may be expected to affect cost of capital.

9. A company's shares are currently priced at $40 per share; company earnings are currently $6 per share. The company feels its equity position is strained; but it decides that the stock market is "too low" at present, that its share prices should climb back to $60, a value they had held in a previous period.

    If the company's prediction should prove true, what will be the impact on a specific cost of the new equity?

    What are the consequences of a wrong prediction?

10. The random-walk hypothesis assumes that all currently available information is reflected in current market prices. Explain in detail why this assumption implies that patterns in past market prices cannot be used to predict future market prices.

RELATED READINGS

Baxter, N. D. "Leverage, Risk of Ruin and the Cost of Capital." *Journal of Finance,* September 1967.

Durand, D. "The Cost of Debt and Equity Funds for Business: Trends, Problems of Measurement." In *Conference on Research in Business Finance.* New York: National Bureau of Economic Research, 1952.

———. "The Cost of Capital, Corporation Finance, and the Theory of Investment: Comment." *American Economic Review,* September 1959.

Hamada, R. S. "The Effect of the Firm's Capital Structure on the Systematic Risk of Common Stocks." *Journal of Finance,* May 1972.

Modigliani, F., and Miller, M. "The Cost of Capital, Corporation Finance and the Theory of Investment." *American Economic Review,* June 1958.

———. "Corporate Income Taxes and the Cost of Capital: A Correction." *American Economic Review,* June 1966.

Mumey, G. A. *Theory of Financial Structure.* New York: Holt, Rinehart & Winston, 1969.

Robichek, A., and Myers, S. *Optimal Financing Decisions.* Englewood Cliffs, N.J.: Prentice-Hall, 1965.

Weston, J. F. "A Test of Cost of Capital Propositions." *Southern Economic Journal,* October 1963.

————. "A Test of Cost of Capital Propositions." *Southern Economic Journal,* October 1963.

19

INCIDENTS IN THE LIFE
OF A COMPANY

For the most part the previous chapters have dealt with the affairs of the company carrying out its regular business activities. In a financial sense these activities have been the purchasing and financing of business assets. Most financial managers devote most of their time to these issues. Occasionally, though, financial managers are likely to be involved either directly, or indirectly through transactions with other companies, in some irregular financial issues. This chapter will be devoted to a number of these exceptional incidents. They include: initial formation of businesses (especially those organized as corporations); the conversion of a company from one whose shares are closely held to one of a more public nature; the joining of once separate companies through acquisition and mergers; and problems associated with company insolvency.

FORMING A NEW BUSINESS

The essential element in any new business is an idea, conceived by an individual or group, for the carrying on of some business activity. The idea may be an invention to be manufactured, a new selling technique to be exploited, or an almost

413

414   Canadian Business Finance

infinite array of other plans, schemes, and dreams, including simply attempting to duplicate the operations of another already successful business. Typically, or at least ideally, the idea is refined into a feasibility study, an assessment of the idea's profit potential. If the idea appears adequately lucrative and if its initiators have not lost interest by that time, consummation of the idea will require financing. Even businesses which appear to need little in the way of physical facilities usually require inventory, perhaps receivables, and a little cash. It is easy for prospective businessmen to overlook these requirements. The inventory accumulation may be quite subtle and informal—the buying of materials and paying of employees for perhaps months before goods are in condition to be marketed, for example. In fact, many new businesses founder because of failure to anticipate and cover these elemental financial needs— let alone the possibility of contingencies.

Once initial asset requirements are identified, planning of the necessary financing can proceed. In principle this is a little different than the planning and obtaining of finances for the going concern, with one very important exception. The beginning business must start from scratch on its equity capital. There are instances where this is not a problem. Financial needs of the new business may be small relative to the personal wealth of its founder(s); or the business, though new, may be of sufficiently large scale and appear sufficiently sound, to allow a prompt sale of common stock in a manner similar to that done by an already established company. The problem area lies in between—new businesses too big to secure their equity from their owners' personal resources and not yet ready for a conventional issue of common shares. Such companies are in need of *venture capital*. (Other terms are in use; miners seek "grubstakes," theatrical producers look for "angels.") There is little in the way of an organized market for venture capital; success in obtaining it is often contingent upon the resourcefulness of the new company's financial management.

Sources of Venture Capital

Someone in search of venture capital is usually looking for more than a few thousand dollars, which he could normally borrow on the basis of his future earnings power or existing assets if he does not have it already. An upper limit might be around $1 million, a point where it is likely to be economical to undertake a conventional issue of common shares. The form of venture capital may vary—it may be called either debt or equity in a legal sense—but all venture capital will share the essential fact that the capital supplier will be bearing a considerable part of the risk of the new company.

Some potential sources of venture capital can be found among conventional debt suppliers. Trade creditors have been known to relax their usual credit requirements to assist the small promising firm (which has a potential for becoming a major customer). Even banks occasionally support a new venture, particularly if they can be convinced that its earnings prospects and the integrity of its developers are sufficient to offset the deficiency of initial equity capital. As noted previously, government development banks and finance companies constitute other possible sources.

Beyond this, though there is no orderly national market, almost every community of any size has a company or individual —somewhere—with wealth available for commitment as venture capital. These sources will usually expect handsome compensation if the venture succeeds. In exchange for absorbing some of its risk they may require participation both as creditors, to allow them to claim any remaining assets if the venture fails, and positions as equity participants so that they may share in the fruits of the venture if success ensues. If success ensues, the result of the use of these sources of venture capital will be an extremely high capital cost, *calculated after the fact*. Nevertheless, because of the risk involved, the terms exacted by these sources may represent fair bargains. (In fact it is difficult to establish any standard of unfairness on ethical grounds in a transaction that is voluntarily entered into by well-informed contracting parties.)

In any event, tapping the venture capital market is much like developing a new product. There are no easy rules to follow. Here financial management must be at its most imaginative; with a sound business idea, some good financial salesmanship, tenacity, and a little luck, venture capital is frequently found.

Financial Aspects of Choice of Organization

There are three major financial reasons for considering the formation of a company, instead of allowing a business to operate as a proprietorship or a partnership. The first of these, particularly appropriate for larger ventures, is the infeasibility of the broadly held partnership. Questions of possible liability, difficulty of creating new interests in a partnership, and the lack of negotiability of partnership interests all tend to render a partnership form of organization unworkable if very many equity participants are going to be involved. It follows that a public offering of equity interests in a partnership is now virtually inconceivable.

Limited liability of a company contributes to the marketability of its equity shares, since persons buying these shares need only be concerned about the loss of money they have paid for the shares, and not about further personal liability.

There is a minor exception. If shares—either common or preferred—are designated as having a par value and if the shares should be initially sold below this par value, shareholders are liable for the difference. The rationale for this rule lies in the fact that, if a par value is expressed for the company's equity position on its balance sheet, creditors should have the right to expect that money of that amount has actually been made available to the company. In practice, this issue is quite unimportant because many companies issue shares with no par value designated, and those that do designate a par value are normally careful to set that value low enough so that the shares can be marketed at or above par.

For the small closely held company the apparent financial advantage of limited liability often turns out to be illusory. Even though a limited company is organized, unless that company has a strong equity position creditors of the company are likely to ask the owners of the equity to personally guarantee the company's obligations. With this endorsement the common shareholders of the company are deprived of the protection of limited liability.

Tax Aspects of Company Formation

At present, a provision of tax law makes organization of a small company quite attractive. This provision, subject to some qualifications, specifies that until a company has earned a total of $500,000 over its lifetime as a company, it is entitled to a 25 percent corporate tax rate on the first $100,000 of its earnings per year. Unless a taxpayer is in an extraordinarily low personal tax bracket, this low corporate tax rate allows more rapid equity accumulation through formation of a company than through leaving a business in the form of a proprietorship or partnership.

An example will illustrate. John Brown forms a company and expects to devote full time to the management of its affairs. He anticipates that the company will earn about $40,000 per year before income tax. He hopes to limit his consumption expenses to $1,000 per month, and to allow the remaining money to accumulate as equity. His choices are for this money to accumulate as company retained earnings or as personal savings (which still add financial strength to his business venture). Let us consider two alternatives open to Mr. Brown:

a. Form a company, pay himself a $17,000 per year salary, which allows him an estimated $12,000 per year after he accounts for his personal tax responsibilities. The remaining $23,000 will then be subject to corporate taxation at a rate of 25 percent. Retained earnings can accumulate at an annual rate of $23,000 (1 − 0.25) or about $17,000 per year.

b. Leave the business in an unincorporated condition. He can still designate $17,000 as a salary and from this obtain his $1,000 per month living allowance. The remaining $23,-000 will be subject to ordinary personal taxation, which one could approximate at 50 percent in this tax bracket. This would leave $11,500 as after-tax personal savings available as business equity.

Obviously, in this not atypical case, the formation of a company has a distinctive tax advantage when one looks at the objective of the rapid accumulation of business equity. The analysis becomes more complex if one looks ahead to some point in time when the shareholder may wish to make withdrawals from this company equity, either through sale of shares (subject to capital gains tax) or through dividends (subject to dividends taxation). However, in most situations under current tax law, as the reader can verify from previous discussions, the company form of organization will turn out to be wealth maximizing in this long-run sense too. And short-run considerations may be critical; the survival of a company may turn on its ability to form an equity base as rapidly as possible.

FORMATION OF A COMPANY

Usually about the only advantage to not doing business in company form is the mystery or cost associated with the formation of a company. A company, as an artificial legal being, must be created by a specified legal procedure. At one time this legal procedure was very complicated, often requiring a special act of Parliament or some other means of granting an individual company charter by the Crown. Nowadays, the formation of a company has been made so routine that it can sometimes even be accomplished without the assistance of a solicitor. Where the services of a solicitor are used (which may be worthwhile because of the learning time required to avoid their use) costs and fees associated with the formation of a simple company are likely to be a three-figure amount.

The form of company formation varies in different parts of the country. In Ontario, Quebec, and several other provinces the corporation is formed under a system called *letters patent*. In the remaining provinces, incorporation takes place under a *registration system*. In general the systems work the same way, but some legal niceties separate the two; these niceties are more properly discussed in a textbook on business law.

In addition to the formal system of incorporation, provinces differ with respect to a distinction between a public and a private company. In some jurisdictions provision is made for the establishment of *private companies*.

A private company is one which has a limited number of shareholders (50 is a common cutoff) and does not offer shares to the public. A possible motive for maintaining private company status lies in secrecy—private companies (Eaton's is the classic example) may keep financial information secret.

Breach of a requirement for a private company causes transmutation into a public company, whose financial statements may become common knowledge. In any case, when a company undertakes a public sale of shares, it must conform to the securities legislation that has been discussed previously.

GOING PUBLIC

Whether or not a legal distinction is made between a private and public company there is a factual distinction. At some point in its life a company's management may decide that the company cannot grow adequately on the basis of retained earnings or the capital contributions from a small number of shareholders. It may then wish to make a public offering of the company's shares. Aside from the legal and marketing problems associated with such share issuance, which have already been discussed in one context or another, the principal consideration involved in the first-time marketing of a public share issue will be valuation. How should the shares be priced? If they are initially offered at too high a price, no buyers will be found. If they are offered at too low a price, the cost of capital on the new share issue will be unnecessarily high.

For the going concern which already has shares outstanding and is thinking of issuing more, pricing of additional shares is a relatively easy problem. They must bear some reasonable relationship to the value of shares already on the market. To ensure the success of the issue of additional shares, some discount below existing market price may be offered; still it is established market price that is the prime determinant. When the company initially is going public (issuing common shares to the general public for the first time) the market price guideline is not available. Accordingly an estimate must be formed on what will constitute the shares potential market price.

If the company has an earnings history, the share price $=$ EPS/k_i formula may be employed as an estimating technique, with k_i being approximated by observation of other companies whose shares already have an established market value and which are deemed to be of comparable risk. Similarly, though this is much less likely, if a private company has established a credible dividends' history the dividend growth valuation formula may be of some assistance.

Where a company has neither earnings or dividends history a price must be determined by the use of other valuation bases. Book value of prospective shares may be an important consideration; this can be estimated from current book value per share:

$$\text{Current book value per share} = \frac{\text{Current net worth (book value basis)}}{\text{Current number of shares outstanding}}.$$

The logic of using book value rests on asking new shareholders to contribute as much capital per share as the previous shareholders have contributed, either through share purchase and other forms of paid-in capital, or earnings retention. Its limitations are the same as those that are always associated with book values; new shareholders are more interested in prospects than in a record of previous capital contributions.

Other methods may also be employed. An appraisal company may be asked to appraise the value of the company's properties. This would be particularly important in the case of a company with little earnings history but with potentially valuable tangible assets, such as a company holding mining properties or other real estate. Another valuation basis may be transactions that have taken place in the company's shares already, particularly if there have been a number of such sales and the sales have taken place at *arm's length*. (Usually an arm's-length transaction is one where the transacting parties are not close relatives.)

Again it is apparent that there is no easy way of pricing an issue of new shares. The problem is in some ways similar to that of raising other forms of venture capital. The company's financial management, in consultation with the company's investment dealer, and conforming to legal and personal ethical strictures relating to accurate representation, must assemble as good a case as possible in support of high share value. To do less is to impair the marketability of the shares and possibly subject the company to an unnecessarily high cost of additional equity capital.

THE JOINING OF COMPANIES

The Case for Joining Two Firms

Before discussing ways and means by which two or more firms join into one, it is appropriate to stop and ask why they should desire such a juncture. Like other financial changes, the amalgamation of companies does not occur frictionlessly. Laborious planning and negotiation, and substantial legal costs are often involved. There may also be tax ramifications (though these will not be discussed in this text). Before firms join there should be some positive case for the process of getting them together.

One of these may be operating economies of scale. Two or more firms may enhance their competitive posture by joining into a bigger firm, which will sustain a more efficient assembly line, do research and development that the firms individually could not afford, and so on. Joining may be advantageous even where these anticipated economies of scale could be achieved by separate companies.

For example, if companies A and B are producing a common product, Company A could produce subassemblies of the product on a large scale and sell these to Company B for final assembly on a large scale. There are instances where companies actually join their plants physically to achieve operating economies, though each is maintaining a separate company identity. However, the two companies may well decide that, to avoid either constant bickering over what price A should pay B for its subassemblies, or the rigidities of a long-term contract for subassembly supply, the companies should sit down for a once-and-for-all negotiation and join together. In other words, while the joining of companies may not be the only way of obtaining scale economies, it may be the path of least resistance for the attainment of these economies.

Economies of scale are not limited to such tangible areas as plant efficiency. The joining of companies may allow them to concentrate on a single marketing image for more efficient marketing organization. It may turn out to be a more satisfactory arrangement than licensing or royalty agreements if one company wishes to use patents or copyrights that presently belong to another. The list could go on; among other things it includes possible financing economies.

Suppose, for example, that a company currently has a net worth of $100,000. To finance available investment opportunities adequately without becoming excessively debt laden, it should really have a net worth of $300,000. In other words, it needs the infusion of some additional equity. The owners of the company may have already exhausted their own resources; retention of additional earnings may take too much time. The marginal $200,000 is too small to justify the fixed costs of a public issue of shares. That leaves the possibility of an ad hoc search for venture capital and suppose the company has not had much luck there. Where can it turn, when it is in this stage of financial adolescence? One of the answers may be to join with another company. It may find another company which is long on net worth and short on investment opportunities. Or it may find another company which is also short of equity, and the two of them may be able to jointly have sufficient equity requirements to justify an efficient public issue of common shares.

Eventually, at least in the aspect of finance, these scale economies run out. It is highly questionable whether the joining of one $100 million company with another will, by itself, have much effect on their joint capital cost since they are both already big enough to exploit about all the efficiencies there are to exploit in financing. But for smaller companies, financial conditions may be a compelling reason for amalgamation.

There are two other reasons why companies may wish to join forces beyond the obtaining of scale economies. The first of these is often illegal but it is still sometimes tried. The companies may wish to join to reduce the competition between them. It is beyond the purview of this book to discuss the extent to which anti-combines legislation and the courts will suppress or condone such endeavours. Often the issues are very complex, because the attainment of economies of scale and the possible suppression of competition may go hand in hand. In fact, it is one of the hard choices of national economic policy to decide the extent to which big firms should be tolerated.

The third justification for joining two companies has been discussed previously in Chapter 9. We already have looked at this issue at two levels of intensity; there is also a third level to be considered. It is true that two companies may decrease their joint riskiness by joining together if their expected cash flows are not closely correlated. It is also true that this lack of correlation may be exploited by shareholders themselves through their holding of the common shares of the imperfectly correlated companies. These two issues were covered in Chapter 9 under the section headings of "Correlation Control—Company Level" and "Correlation Control—Investor Level."

It is now time to introduce a further argument in favour of risk control at the company level:

1. Companies which join together and which have operations that are not closely correlated will unquestionably have less dispersion in their joint cash flows than the sum of the dispersion in the individual cash flows.

2. It is usually not economical for a company to rely solely on equity capital, but to employ some creditor money.

3. It follows that the reduction of risk at the company level may reduce the probability of company bankruptcy.

4. To recall an argument presented in Chapter 18, bankruptcy itself costs money.

5. Thus, unless there are other disadvantages associated with a joining of two companies, this juncture may become economical by reducing the probability that bankruptcy expenses will be incurred.

Where now do we stand on this issue? The case for company risk control, whether by merger or by other risk control devices such as the purchase of insurance, is not as dramatic as it would be if one considered only a company level of analysis, and ignored the shareholder level. On the other hand, particularly where company risk levels coupled with their debt ratios expose them to a probability of bankruptcy, at least some case exists for risk control at the company level.

How strong this case is will vary so much with individual circumstances that it is difficult to come forth with any rules. While there may be some merit to the risk-reducing aspect associated with the joining of companies, this risk control measure, like similar measures, must be viewed with great circumspection. If it looks like a risk control is going to be obtainable only at substantial cost, it is probably not worth the effort. For one thing, reduction of the debt ratio may be relatively inexpensive, and that, too, is a way of reducing bankruptcy exposure.

Disadvantages of Joining Companies

The organizational frictions of putting two companies together have already been mentioned; they may be regarded as inevitable impediments to the joining of companies. A more major detriment of company amalgamation could arise from possible scale diseconomies. These may take two forms. First, there is the contention, which dates back at least to Adam Smith, that bigness in a company makes the company difficult to manage and control. It is hard to think of this as a very important general principle affecting possible marriages of Canadian companies, when one views their yet fairly small size (even looking at the largest Canadian industrial organizations) relative to their counterparts in the United States, Japan, and Europe.

A more realistic form of scale diseconomy is likely to show up in the form of disturbance of a working system of management. The joining of companies may result either in a management team being built jointly from existing staffs of the two companies, or a situation where the management staff of one company undertakes the supervision of the affairs of both. In one case, personality conflicts and the disruption of established patterns of authority, responsibility, and participation could result. In the other case, management successful in the operation of one company could be amateurs in the operation of the second. Again, the record of the conglomerate companies which were assembled with such flamboyance in the 1960s suggests that sometimes the managerial difficulties of joined companies may more than offset other efficiencies.

One should note quickly that this contention about management slices both ways. Managerial problems are only a potential danger; sometimes under either of the patterns mentioned above, management of the joined companies is substantially improved. The participants in a joint managerial team may complement each other, or the joining of companies may result in a strong management group from one company displacing a weaker one in another.

Methods of Joining Companies

There are a wide variety of ways of bringing the operations of two separate companies under a common corporate enclosure. If Pandora Ltd. wants to join with Box Ltd. it can undertake any of the following methods:

1. Pandora may buy the assets of Box paying for them with cash. Box now still has a separate identity but its operating assets are all in the hands of Pandora, so the operations of the companies have been effectively joined.

2. Pandora may purchase all or a majority portion of the shares of Box. The companies maintain separate corporate identities, but are under common control with Box designated as a subsidiary.

3. A third company remote from Pandora and Box may buy the assets or shares of both, again placing them under common control.

4. Merger of the companies may take place. In this case a single company results. It may operate under the corporate charter of one of the previous companies, or under a new charter with a new corporate identity. In the consummation of a merger an exchange of securities will take place. If Pandora's corporate identity is maintained, shareholders in Box will receive Pandora shares (or perhaps other Pandora securities as well) in exchange for their own shares. If a new company is formed, shareholders of both Pandora and Box exchange their existing shares for securities of the new company.

This is not intended to be an exhaustive list. There may be other ways of bringing the affairs of two companies under common control. However, the intent, advantages, and disadvantages are similar irrespective of the method actually chosen. The method itself may be regarded as a technical issue.

The Problem of Valuation

Unless Pandora or an outside group simply buys control of Box Ltd. in the marketplace by piecemeal purchase of its shares, at going stock exchange prices, negotiation of the terms under which companies should be joined is likely to be complicated and protracted. Even when companies have common shares with well-established market values, these market values may not represent a satisfactory valuation of the company's net worth from the viewpoint of the majority of the shareholders of one or both of the joining companies. These may believe that the current market price does not represent the "true worth" of their holdings; the fact that the shareholders have not in fact sold their shares at the going market price lends credence to their assertions that they place a higher value on their shares than that price currently obtainable in the market.

The problem is complicated even further if current share transaction prices are not available for one or both of the joining companies. In that case one is back to valuation problems very similar to those associated with a company which first offers its common shares for public sale. Which value should govern? The value based on past earnings and/or dividend history? A value based on predictions of future earnings from data other than past history? Appraisals? Book values?

To add to the confusion here are additional approaches:

a. *Breakdown Value.*   What would the assets of the company be worth if they were liquidated part by part? For example, a manufacturing company might establish a minimum value on its assets by considering how much money it could obtain if it sold its machinery "secondhand," its buildings and land to other manufacturers or real estate firms, its inventories of raw materials to other manufacturers or back to its original suppliers and its inventories of finished goods to wholesale firms; and if it anticipated collection of its receivables. (This method would probably be used as part of but not the sole basis for establishment of a value by a professional appraisal firm.)

b. A rather curious method which has use in some industries is the sales multiplier method. For example, a rule of thumb once expressed in the communications business was that the the value of a radio station was about two and a half times its current sales. This is a peculiar case, of course, where a station may have value not only because of physical assets that it owns but also because of earning power conferred by its license to operate (which may offer some protection from competition). The logic of the sales multiplier is that it may provide a guideline to what a well-managed company *could* earn as opposed to what it has actually been earning.

In principle valuation often seems simple—one discounts future earnings at an appropriate rate. The variety of practical usage in valuation arises from the fact that there is usually a lack of agreement about what future earnings prospects are, and about the discount rate that is appropriate.

An example of evaluation problems will illustrate the difficulties of joining companies. Orange Ltd. holds mining properties, acquired at a cost of $1 million. It is a closely held company and the majority of its shareholders have agreed that promising explorations indicate that the present value of their ore bodies, net of extraction costs, is at least $3 million and may be as high as $10 million. They are considering a merger under which they would exchange shares in their company for the shares of a larger manufacturing company, Green Ltd., whose shares are currently selling at $50 per share in the market. Green is a widely held company. The directors of Green believe that Green's value is underestimated by the market. They believe that the "true worth" of Green shares is closer to $75; they are also inclined to accept only the minimum $3 million valuation placed on Orange properties by Orange's shareholders.

In negotiations Orange's representatives start out by proposing that shareholders of Orange collectively receive 200,000 shares of Green in exchange for their own shares. They arrive at this value based on their upper appraisal of their own net worth at $10 million, and the current market value of B's shares of $50 per share; $10,000,000/$50 = 200,000 shares. Green, asserting that Orange's net worth should be valued at $3 million and its own shares at $75, proposes that Orange shareholders receive 40,000 shares of Green ($3,000,000/$75). Thus negotiations begin from the point of departure of a difference of opinion over whether Orange shareholders should receive 200,000 shares or 40,000 shares, a fivefold variation. Whether the parties ever solve this negotiating problem will depend partly on their fair-mindedness and goodwill; do they jointly want to attempt to establish a fair ratio of the values of the two companies? However an important consideration is going to lie in the question of whether or not the merger itself makes economic sense. If the joining of the companies is mutually advantageous, there is room for both parties in the negotiation to improve their position by consummating a negotiation instead of breaking off. The likelihood of successful completion of a negotiation is going to be closely related to this fundamental economic character. Consider for example, the case where the joint value of Green and Orange will not be enhanced by the merger. In this case, the only way that either set of shareholders can gain is at the expense of the other. Only naïveté is likely to allow this negotiation to come to fruition.

INSOLVENCY

Two separate definitions of the term insolvency are in use. One refers to a condition where a company's liabilities exceed the value of its assets; the second refers to a condition where a company is unable to meet its obligations as they come due. Often if a company is insolvent in one sense it is insolvent in the other as well, but the two conditions need not coexist. For example, a company may owe $1 million due one year hence, and have no other liabilities. Its assets may have a present market value of $500,000 with no reasonable chance of appreciation before the end of the year. This company has not failed to meet an obligation when it is due, simply because its obligation is not due, but at the same time its liabilities are in excess of its assets. Alternatively, a company might have assets which with sufficient time (say, a year) it could liquidate for $1 million. However, it has an immediate obligation to discharge a debt of $500,000 and no cash available. This company is insolvent in the sense that it is unable to meet its obligations when due, but not in the sense that a reasonable valuation of its assets fails to exceed its liabilities.

Both situations are conditions of serious financial difficulty and both may result in the company's formally being declared bankrupt. However, bankruptcy is not the only possible result of insolvency; we shall explore several in this section.

Negotiations with Creditors

If a company finds itself in financial difficulties, but still has hope of recouping its fortunes, it may undertake negotiations with its creditors. (One may assume, if we regard a company as being insolvent, that it has already made use of normal extensions of its trade credit, by foregoing cash discounts and perhaps slipping behind the credit terms specified on its purchase invoices.) It may, by consultation with its creditors, be able to assure them that all will be well if they will only allow a little more time.

There are both ethical and legal reasons for carrying on these negotiations in a spirit of fairness. For example, Company X obtains a generous credit extension from Trade Creditor A, and then promptly sells major portions of its assets to discharge its unsecured promissory note to Banker B in full. This would not only seem unfair, but could be grounds for legal action from Trade Creditor A as we shall subsequently see.

Sometimes a negotiation with creditors is done on an informal basis; at other times it is in the form of a formal agreement. For example, a company may reach an agreement with a group of its major creditors under which they all agree to delay their claims. The agreement, sometimes called a *composition of creditors,* may permit the company to discharge some of the claims of minor creditors. Such an agreement could be advantageous to all parties involved. Neither trade creditors nor lending institutions desire as a rule to force companies out of business. There are several reasons for this:

1. It is bad for their image.

2. If time is allowed for a debtor company to make a recovery, the debtor may be able to discharge its obligations in full, where if it is currently pressed for payment, the debtor may be only able to make part payments even if all its assets are exhausted.

3. A negotiated settlement, even if it does not ultimately save the financial life of the debtor, may still allow the affected creditors more assets than if they would have forced formal bankruptcy proceedings, with their attendant costs.

Voluntary Reorganization

A company reorganization involves a major change in the company's financing arrangements. Reorganization usually involves some relaxation in the urgency of creditors' claims in exchange for some financial concessions from the shareholders. Consider such an example.

Hurka Limited has committed itself to extensive research and development. These have placed a great drain on its recent cash flows, since large amounts of money have been disbursed in development programs which are expected to generate sales well in the future. As a result of these policies, perhaps coupled with some unforeseen cost overruns or delays in the completion of projects, Hurka Limited is in financial trouble. Its major creditor requires an $800,000 payment of interest and sinking fund on an 8 percent bond issue and Hurka cannot meet this payment. To aggravate matters, the bond indenture contains an acceleration clause so failure to meet the current payment will render the remaining principal of the obligation, $3.2 million, also immediately due.

In addition to its $4 million total liability on the bond issue, Hurka also has $1 million in other short-term obligations of various sorts. It has no other outstanding long-term debt. In spite of these problems, Hurka's management and major shareholders believe that Hurka's long-term prospects are good; their projections indicate a conservative valuation of the present value of future net cash flows is $10 million. They, therefore, value the company's net worth in a long-run sense at $5 million, even though the company cannot pay its bills.

Hurka Limited is at the mercy of its bondholders and perhaps of its other creditors as well. They could force the company into an immediate liquidation. But perhaps this liquidation, if forced, would mean the abandonment of existing Hurka projects. This could mean that the liquidation would yield only small amounts from the sale of Hurka's physical facilities—let us say $2 million.

Now a possible solution may be explored. Representatives of Hurka's directors and management sit down with agents from the bondholders' trustee and discuss the matter, hoping to end up with a mutually beneficial rearrangement of Hurka's affairs.

They agree on the following proposal: the bondholders will fully release Hurka Limited from its $4 million bond obligation. In return Hurka will issue $4 million of 12 percent cumulative preferred shares to the bondholders, in proportion to their bondholdings.

Furthermore, Hurka Limited now has 100,000 shares of common stock outstanding. It will issue an additional 100,000 common shares and these will be also turned over to the bondholders as additional compensation for their discharge of the bond issue.

Finally, after tentatively agreeing to these arrangements, the negotiators call in a representative of the chartered bank with whom Hurka normally does business. The chartered bank agrees that if the above arrangements are concluded, and if Hurka agrees to declare no dividends on either its preferred or common for the next three years, the bank will provide a three-year loan for $1 million to clean up Hurka's remaining obligations.

Once these arrangements have been agreed upon by the bondholders' trustee and by the company's board of directors, they will require ratification by the company's shareholders and, under arrangements specified in the bond indenture, by the company's bondholders. If these agreements are ratified Hurka's short-term financial pressures will be relieved. Where an immediate liquidation would have left the shareholders with nothing, they will now be left with a half-interest in their company. Similarly, where immediate liquidation would have allowed only partial discharge of the company's obligations to its creditors, the bondholders now have a chance of profiting handsomely if Hurka's plans in fact do come to fruition.

Bankruptcy

Negotiations, including those directed toward voluntary reorganization, do not always bear fruit. Creditors may believe that they are better off in forcing a liquidation rather than protracting the company's life. Furthermore, a company may undertake certain actions, called *acts of bankruptcy*, which force the issue and open formal bankruptcy proceedings.

These bankruptcy proceedings are governed by national

legislation—the Bankruptcy Act, administered by a superintendent of bankruptcy. Although the superintendent has general charge this authority will be delegated to a *receiver* who in turn will arrange the appointment of a *licensed trustee* to administer the affairs of the bankrupt company.

Under bankruptcy proceedings, the trustee assumes control of the company and discharges its obligations through liquidation or assignment of company assets. Discharge of liabilities must be done strictly in accordance with legal rules of priority among creditors. Usually, once the assets of the company have been distributed, all the liabilities of the company are deemed discharged. There are exceptions however, where actions of the shareholders may restrict the applicability of the company's limited liability, and the shareholders may find themselves personally responsible for some of the company's obligations. This setting aside of limited liability is most likely to occur when shareholders have attempted to mistreat their creditors in some way, such as by selling company assets at bargain prices to individual shareholders shortly before the company is declared bankrupt.

A considerable number of actions may constitute acts of bankruptcy which place the company in the hands of the trustee. First, the company may formally declare that it cannot meet its obligations and in effect request that bankruptcy proceedings be commenced. Such an action will relieve the shareholders from possible liability they might incur if the company attempted to discharge its obligations without the supervision of a trustee.

Any one creditor may also initiate a bankruptcy process if other acts are perpetrated. Simple failure to discharge an obligation when due is one of these acts. Others are actions that are prejudicial to the interests of the creditor. Favoured treatment of other creditors, removal of company properties or other attempts to transfer assets out of the company, and absconding of company officers are all examples of such acts.

Under the Bankruptcy Act, certain actions of the company made prior to actual bankruptcy may be set aside. For example, if a company has paid some creditors but not others, those creditors who were paid may be required to return the funds to be divided up equitably among all creditors. Similarly, dividends or other disbursements to shareholders could be voided; in fact, dividends declared while insolvent are illegal.

Once the company is in the hands of the trustee, he will liquidate the company assets and disburse the proceeds. The priority of these disbursements is as follows:

1. Settlements are first made with creditors who, by virtue of security arrangements, have property rights in the company's assets. For example, the company's bankruptcy will render a mortgagee the legal owner of property covered by his mortgage.

2. After secured creditors have been satisfied, certain claims of parties other than the company's regular creditors are discharged. For example, the expenses and legal costs of the trustee and charges made by the superintendent of bankruptcy are payable, unpaid employees and landlords have some claim on rent and wages due them, and some municipal taxes and claims for damages must be discharged. Claims of the Crown, including those for unpaid income taxes, are also payable before any distribution is made to the company's unsecured creditors.

3. To the extent that assets are available, unsecured creditors are paid on a pro rata basis. For example, if after the higher priority obligations have been made, the company has $80,000 remaining, and $100,000 of claims from unsecured creditors, each creditor obtains 80 cents for each dollar of his claim.

4. If assets remain after all creditors are paid, any preference in asset distribution specified under the terms of the company's preferred stock has next priority.

5. Finally, anything remaining, after everyone else has had his chance, is the residual possession of the company's shareholders, to be divided up among them in proportion to their shareholdings.

It is possible for the licensed trustee to arrange a reorganization, rather than simply to sell the company's assets and divide the cash. This will preserve the company as a going concern, and may be the most wealth-enhancing procedure for the claimants. If reorganization takes place, it must be done in accordance with the established priorities. For example, reorganization could proceed no further, if a mortgagee of the company dissented, until his claim was fully settled. Without strict observance of priorities the reorganization could be subsequently voided, and the trustee could also be liable for possible damages incurred by neglected claimants.

SUMMARY

The essential ingredient of a new business is an idea for profit. Financing requirements for new businesses are often underestimated, and financing is often inadequate. In addition to the personal resources of the founders, and borrowed money, additional equity or high-risk debt money may be needed. Since public share issues are not feasible for small companies, these companies must often search for venture capital. The venture capital market is not highly organized, so this search may be difficult.

The legal formation of a company is normally a routine procedure. "Going public" is more complex and costly, because of marketing costs and conformity to security regulations.

Companies may wish to join together for a number of reasons, including plant and marketing efficiencies, scale economies in financing, and joint reduction of risk. There is considerable question about the soundness of the last motive.

Companies may be joined in a variety of ways, including one buying out the other, a third company buying the two candidates for juncture, and formal merger. In a joining of companies valuation issues are often vital, and complicated.

A company may find itself in financial difficulties, with obligations exceeding its ability to pay. Sometimes this stress may be relieved through mutually satisfactory readjustments, such as composition of creditors and voluntary reorganizations. In other cases formal bankruptcy proceedings may result.

Under bankruptcy, the company's assets and operations are placed under the control of a trustee. The trustee may liquidate company assets to discharge obligations. Claimants against the company share the proceeds from liquidation in a legally established order of priority, with shareholders last on the list.

QUESTIONS AND PROBLEMS

1. After the graduation from university, a commerce student and an engineering student decide to join forces to produce and sell a novel electronic-measuring device which the engineering student has invented during his fourth year. In the association of the two students, the engineering student agrees to handle production of the device, while the commerce student is to concentrate on finance and marketing.

   Prepare a list of potential assets that may be required in the venture.

   Assume that the total of the assets on the above list is $75,000 and that the two students have $5,000 in personal funds available. How do you think they can finance their venture?

   Return to the list of asset requirements. What possibilities are there for economizing the use of each of the assets you have listed (for example, renting production equipment instead of buying it).

2. A new business is expected to earn $40,000 per year before tax. If incorporated, marginal income tax rate of the business will be 25 percent. The marginal personal tax rate of the developer of the business is expressed in the following schedule:

Range of Personal Income	Marginal Tax Rate (percent)
0–20,000	30%
20,000–30,000	40
30,000–40,000	50

   An individual involved in the business is considering whether to operate as a limited company or as an unincorporated proprietorship. One element that will influence his choice is income tax.

   Suppose the individual desires to maintain personal consumption expenditures of $15,000 per year.

   If the business is left unincorporated, what will be the owners total personal income tax bill, and how much of the company's earnings will be available for after-tax reinvestment in the business?

   Suppose the business is set up as a limited company. How large a salary must the owner pay himself to satisfy his personal consumption desires (he must pay himself enough to pay his personal income tax and have $15,000 available afterwards)? If he pays himself such a salary, what will be the company's income tax bill? How much money will be left for the investment within the company?

3. A company has the following earnings history:

Year	Earnings, After Tax
1975	−$130,000
1976	38,000
1977	625,000

At the end of 1977, the company's management decides that a public issue of shares is essential to sustain the company's growth. The company currently has 10,000 shares of common stock outstanding, all in the hands of company officers. No transactions have ever taken place in the company shares. The company wishes to raise $2 million through issuance of additional common shares.

Company management believes that if no new shares are issued, after-tax earnings of the company will reach $900,000 next year, but that if new shares are issued, company earnings will go to $1.5 million. The officers of the company are reluctant to speculate about what earnings will be in the following years because of the keen competition and rapid rate of technological change in the company's line of business.

Assuming that marketing costs for the new issue will consume 20 percent of the proceeds of the issue, the company will have to sell shares to the public valued at $2.5 million. Discuss how many shares should the company offer, and at what price.

4. What is an arm's-length transaction?

5. Two manufacturing companies decided they could reduce costs substantially if they could market their products through a single sales organization.

How could the companies maintain themselves as separate financial entities, while at the same time obtaining the advantage of a common sales organization? Note at least two alternatives.

What are the pros and cons of merging the companies, as opposed to the alternatives you have listed above?

6. In a composition of creditors, what motivates creditors to relax some of the contractual terms under which they have extended credit?

7. A company is in a position where it cannot discharge its liabilities as they come due. Representatives of the shareholders and creditors discuss a voluntary reorganization. What bargaining power does each group have in this negotiation?

8. A company's assets have the following liquidation values:

Cash	$ 15,000
Accounts receivable	400,000
Inventory	600,000
Plant	800,000
Equipment	250,000

The most recent company balance sheet, prepared on the basis of book value, has the following right-hand side:

Accounts payable	$ 200,000
Income taxes payable	300,000
Bank loans payable, unsecured	450,000
Bank loans payable, secured by mortgage on equipment	150,000
Mortgage on plant	3,000,000
Equity	5,000,000

How would the assets be distributed under a bankruptcy proceeding?

RELATED READINGS

Bankruptcy Act, The. Toronto: The Canadian Credit Institute.

Canadian Imperial Bank of Commerce. *Doing Business in Canada.* A booklet available from the bank.

Furst, R. W. "Does Listing Increase the Market Price of Common Stocks?" *Journal of Business,* April 1970.

Levy, H., and Sarnat, M. "Diversification, Portfolio Analysis and the Uneasy Case for Conglomerate Mergers." *Journal of Finance,* September 1970.

McDonald, J. G., and Fisher, A. K. "New-Issue Stock Price Behavior." *Journal of Finance,* March 1972.

McQuillan, P. *Going Public in Canada.* Toronto: Canadian Institute of Chartered Accountants, 1971.

Morin, D., and Chippindale, W., eds. *Acquisitions and Mergers in Canada.* Toronto: Methuen, 1970.

Murray, R. F. "The Penn Central Debacle: Lessons for Financial Analysis." *Journal of Finance,* May 1971.

Reilly, F. "What Determines the Ratio of Exchange in Corporate Mergers?" *Financial Analysts' Journal,* November–December 1962.

Smyth, J. E., and Soberman, D. A. *The Law and Business Administration in Canada.* Toronto: Prentice-Hall, 1968, chap. 30.

Weston, J. F. "The Industrial Economics Background of the Penn Central Bankruptcy." *Journal of Finance,* May 1971.

20

INTERNATIONAL
ASPECTS OF
BUSINESS FINANCE

There is a great deal of common usage in finance on this continent, and the financial markets of the United States and Canada are intimately intertwined. However, several areas of difference exist. We have noted variation in tax policies which affect financing choices; to some extent these also colour asset selection. There are also other differences in the legal environment scattered throughout the various aspects of finance. In addition, another contrast exists, in degree if not in kind, between the Canadian and U.S. financial systems. Beyond these, stemming from the character of the two economies themselves, Canada's economy is a much more internationally oriented one; in this respect it is more like that of the Western European countries. For example, where under 10 percent of the goods used in the U.S. are imported, the comparable Canadian percentage is about 30 percent.

This international character of the economy reflects itself in the financial problems and opportunities which confront Canadian financial managers. Their financial activities are much

438

more likely to involve them in transactions crossing international boundaries than their U.S. counterparts. (Incidentally, most of the border-crossing, both in terms of flow of exports and imports and the associated financing interrelationships, is between Canada and its immediate southern neighbour.)

WHAT IS DIFFERENT ABOUT INTERNATIONAL FINANCE?

Quantitative Differences

A company undertaking international purchases and sales may find that asset requirements in support of this activity are greater than the corresponding types of domestic activity. Goods in transit, particularly when ocean transportation is involved, constitute the potential for major inventory requirements.

Consider the following example: Vargas Ltd. is a manufacturer located in Halifax. It has previously been relying on a Montreal supplier for component X in its production operation, and obtains this with a two-day delivery time. Vargas buys the component X on a cash basis in Montreal, and normally maintains, in addition to goods in transit, an inventory necessary for ten days' production. Vargas' daily production need for X is about $10,000 worth. Thus it usually has goods on hand of $100,000 plus another $20,000 of goods in transit, or a total X inventory of $120,000.

It now discovers that it is possible to buy component X in Singapore for 40 percent of the Canadian price, or 50 percent after allowing for transport and other noncapital costs, receiving delivery by ocean shipment. Other things being equal, this price reduction would cut Vargas' inventory in half; however, other things are not equal. Suppose that Vargas must make allowance for six weeks' delivery time, using ocean transport and also, because of the uncertainties in the international market, it increases its component X on hand from ten days' supply to 80 days' supply. The result is that instead of having X supplies for 12 days' production, Vargas now requires X inventories for 122 days' production. Thus, while the unit cost of its inventory items decreases by half, the physical quantity of its inventory increases tenfold, with a result that its X inventory value increases by a factor of 5 to about $500,000.

This does not suggest that the policy of purchasing in Singapore rather than Montreal has proved to be an undesirable one; it simply illustrates that it is one which imposes additional financial requirements. Suppose Vargas manufactures 200 days per year; its curtailing of its raw materials cost by $5,000 per day then means a $1 million annual saving. Assuming that it is in a 40 percent marginal tax bracket, this translates to $600,000 after tax, as a return on its $40,000 marginal inventory investment. The result is an after-tax internal rate of return of an estimated 150 percent.

Another inventory need associated with international activity arises from the lack of adequate supply sources in some foreign countries. For example, a construction company building a manufacturing plant in a newly industrializing country may find no local supplies of equipment parts, standard hardware items, lumber, and so forth. All of these items must be stockpiled and the stockpiles must be financed.

Other asset requirements may also change as a result of international activity. Selling abroad may impose extra receivable-carrying requirements on the company. Particularly when a company is endeavouring to sell in "third-world" nations, it may be necessary to assist, either directly or indirectly, in providing long-term financing on long-lived assets sold in those countries. Additionally, an exporting company may find that the counterpart to the inventory requirements in the Vargas example are receivables requirements for the exporter, if the company's selling terms provide financing for customers' goods-in-transit.

Collection delays, and cash transit costs and problems, particularly when transactions are carried on in less developed countries, may also contribute to a company's cash and receivables requirements. A strain may be placed on a company's working capital because of lack of conventional trade credit when foreign purchases are undertaken. Similarly, other types of supplier credit, such as leasing or equipment purchase contracts, may not be as readily available from suppliers outside the country. Thus quantities on both sides of the company's balance sheet may change as a result of the company's international operations. Analysis of these considerations is particularly important for a company that is venturing into an international market as a buyer or seller for the first time.

Qualitative Differences

Beyond the fact that the quantitative dimensions of asset needs may change for the firm entering international trade, there are a number of differences in kind with respect to doing financing business outside of Canada. In one respect, these qualitative differences are not as great in carrying out the finance function as they are in other functions of the business, such as marketing products or producing goods, on foreign soil. One's contacts in finance are likely to be with businessmen, particularly foreign financial managers, who are often cosmopolitan. Thus, while foreign financial operations are not without their "cultural gap" problems, these problems do not appear to be as severe as those in functions requiring interaction with a foreign general public.

Besides possible cultural differences, there are some distinctive types of risk associated with international financial transactions. First, some conventional types of losses, such as default on receivables or misappropriation of inventory, may not be as readily redressed under foreign jurisdiction. These problems are not likely to be significant in such areas as the United States, Great Britain, Australia, or New Zealand, which share a common British legal tradition, but they may pose serious problems in other jurisdictions.

Closely related to this lack of recourse to governmental protection of owners' rights is another issue. The governments in some foreign countries have been known to make legal commissions, instead of omissions, that can make life difficult for the Canadian financial manager. When one does business in a foreign country, assets in that country are subject to the laws of that country (usually anyway—the concept of extraterritoriality, or the extension of one country's laws into another, will be briefly noted in the next chapter) and thus any nation may exercise its sovereignty by expropriating Canadian assets within its boundaries. Sometimes this expropriation takes place with an attempt at an equitable compensation; at other times the action represents a dead loss from the point of view of the Canadian company which once owned the assets. In any event, it is an element to be addressed when committing assets to the jurisdictions of foreign governments, particularly in countries where political instability makes the course of government difficult to predict.

Legal problems associated with doing business on foreign soil, including the possibility of expropriation, may be regarded as risks of extraordinary occurrences. A more everyday variety is found in the fluctuation of the relative value of foreign currencies, and that will be discussed in the following section.

EXCHANGE RATES AND THEIR CONSEQUENCES

Exchange Rates

An exchange rate is a form of price, a value ratio between two things—in this case, currencies of two countries. In 1976, an American dollar was worth approximately $0.99 Canadian and a French franc was worth about $0.23 Canadian. Reciprocally, a Canadian dollar was worth about U.S. $1.01 or about 4.35 francs.

The supply and demand forces that determine these exchange rates are outside the scope of this book. We should note, however, that an orderly market exists between various currencies. The Canadian chartered banks, for example, stand ready to buy and sell a number of foreign currencies on the basis of regular bid and ask quotations. Beyond this they are willing to arrange transactions in currencies in which they do not deal directly. Currency dealing is carried on by many banks outside of Canada and also by dealers specialized in international currency transactions.

Freely Floating Exchange Rates

In the absence of governmental intervention, exchange rates will vary as supply and demand conditions change. As an example, a "tight money" policy on the part of the Canadian government coupled with an increase in Canadian investment opportunities (say, a major ore discovery) would be likely to create a shortage of Canadian dollars and increase the price of that currency.

With freely floating exchange rates, exchange rate consistency is maintained through the actions of professional foreign currency dealers, often called arbitrageurs. Suppose, for example, the following set of exchange rates was temporarily in effect:

One Canadian dollar = one U.S. dollar
One U.S. dollar = 12 Mexican pesos
One Canadian dollar = 13 Mexican pesos

This constitutes a situation which is actionable for an arbitrageur. Suppose he starts with $100,000, and we ignore transaction costs. He uses this to buy 1,300,000 Mexican pesos. Then, using the pesos/U.S. dollar rate, he converts his 1,300,000 pesos into U.S. $108,333. He switches the U.S. dollars back to Canadian on the 1:1 ratio and ends up over $8,000 richer.

But the very existence of arbitrageurs will keep this gross a profit opportunity from occurring. There is enough competition among the arbitrageurs, so that when *any* significant profit opportunity occurs, the same set of actions are set into effect. Canadian dollars are used to buy pesos and then those pesos are sold for American dollars. This creates a supply demand imbalance (Canadian dollars chasing pesos chasing U.S. dollars) which tends to realign the exchange rates into a consistent pattern. For example, the following pattern is consistent. It offers no attraction to arbitrageurs:

One British pound (£1) = 600 Japanese yen
One Japanese yen = 0.0026 Australian dollars (A. $.0026)
One British pound (£1) = 1.763 Australian dollars (A. $1.763)

The reader can verify that these rates are consistent (except for minor rounding) and provide no attraction to arbitrage. Any significant deviation from this pattern of rates, of course, would set the forces of arbitrage into motion and restore consistency.

Note that consistency and fluctuation are not incompatible. For example, inflation in Japan could cause the yen to fall relative to the Australian dollar and the British pound. However, so long as it fell at the same ratio to both of the other currencies, no arbitrage opportunity would exist. We should also note that consistency should be interpreted with a certain looseness; minor inconsistencies can occur without attracting the attention of arbitrageurs; or they may persist if they are sufficiently minor that transaction costs render arbitrage unprofitable. However the discrepancies from perfect consistency that are likely to exist may be regarded as trivial.

Pegged Exchange Rates

Exchange rates subject to the ups and downs of market forces are said to be *floating exchange rates.* As we shall observe later, there may be disadvantages to the fluctuations of floating rates. To eliminate fluctuation countries, either acting on their own or through international agreements, have attempted to impose a form of price control referred to as *pegging* exchange rates. At one time this was done through the use of the international gold standard. Each country participating in the standard defined its currency as a ratio to gold, and stood ready to buy and sell gold at this price. Since all participating currencies were expressed in fixed ratio to a common unit, gold, their values were, by extension, maintained in rigidly fixed ratios to one another. For example, defining a U.S. dollar as equal to $\frac{1}{20}$ ounce of gold and a British pound as equal to $\frac{1}{4}$ ounce of gold would automatically fix the exchange rate between dollars and sterling at £1 = U.S. $5.

A modern variant of the gold standard is the use of international agreements where a group of participating countries agree to "support" their currency at a certain ratio with other countries. They do this by maintaining the equivalent of stockpiles of gold; namely, reserves of foreign currencies. For example, at one time the Canadian government was pegging the Canadian dollar at approximately U.S. $0.92. Under this policy the ratio was maintained by a standing offer of the Canadian government to exchange U.S. dollars (drawn from its reserve holdings) for Canadian dollars at this ratio, or to acquire U.S. dollars at that same ratio.

Compromises between rigidly pegged currencies and freely fluctuating exchange rates exist. A country may ostensibly allow its currency to float freely on the world market and still, usually through its central bank, conduct currency buying and selling operations in an attempt to control the extent of its fluctuation. This modified degree of government intervention is sometimes called a *dirty float*.

In recent years, attempts to peg exchange rates have not proved to be a panacea for the vagaries of exchange rate fluctuation. Instead, they have tended to substitute abrupt revisions in the pegged exchange rates. For example, at one time Britain was pegging the pound at approximately U.S. $2.80. To maintain this exchange rate the Bank of England has to more or less continuously purchase pounds on the world market. Since the Bank's resources were not inexhaustible, eventually the strain became too great, and the value of the pound had to be adjusted downward relative to the dollar. (Downward adjustment of a particular currency relative to another is called a devaluation; the converse is an increase in the relative value of other currencies. When a currency is moved upward in value it is usually said to be revalued.)

It is difficult to predict just where the direction of international monetary policy will lead, whether toward a continuation of a recent trend toward greater freedom of market determination of exchange rates, or a return to greater emphasis on pegs. However, in both cases an element of uncertainty is introduced into a variety of international transactions; namely, that the exchange rates will change, either through market fluctuation or through peg revision.

Foreign Exchange Risks

Exchange rate fluctuations can have a number of serious effects on a company's engaging in international transactions. Consider the following example: Powrie Limited has just successfully completed the sale of 10,000 sewing machines in Colombia. To compete in the Colombian market the sewing machines were priced at 2,500 Colombian pesos each (approximately Can. $100 at a time when the Colombian peso was valued at about Can. $0.04). To make the sale, Powrie agrees to extend credit of 1,500 Colombian pesos (Can. $60) on each machine, thus acquiring receivables valued at $600,000. The terms of the receivables are $n/90$. Before 90 days has expired and the sewing machines have been paid for in full, a drastic deterioration in the world coffee market takes place and along with this, a precipitous decline in the value of the Colombian peso; it falls to Can. $0.025. At the end of the 90 days, the sewing machines are dutifully paid for, under the terms of the contract, in Colombian pesos. However, when these are converted into Canadian dollars the original receivable position of 15 million pesos now converts into Canadian dollars at 15,000,000 × $0.025 = $375,000. Thus even though the Colombian customer perfectly complied with the terms of his credit agreement, the Canadian company found its receivable position shrinking from $600,000 to $375,000.

Similar misfortunes (or just as easily, good luck) arise if a company is holding its cash in the form of a currency of another nation. The same uncertainty applies with respect to debts incurred abroad. A company may "cleverly" borrow abroad to take advantage of a lower interest rate, and then see the Canadian dollar decline on the world currency market. The result is a corresponding increase in the number of Canadian dollars required to discharge the foreign obligation.

Exchange rate changes, whether market fluctuations or peg revisions, are not the only form of risk in transactions involving foreign currencies. Foreign governments may attempt to serve their own economic ends by the imposition of exchange controls, which makes it difficult or impossible to convert their funds into other currencies. For example, it is conceivable that in the Powrie example the Colombian government might have temporarily outlawed conversions of Colombian pesos into other currencies. In this case, the Powrie Company would find itself in a position of holding 1,500,000 Colombian pesos without having a dollar available for paying its bills in Canada. The company would probably derive slight consolation from the fact that it would be allowed to invest the pesos in Colombia and perhaps eventually repatriate them, if in the meantime its inability to translate the funds into dollars caused its insolvency.

Protection against Foreign Exchange Risk

There are two major steps that a company can take to protect itself against exchange rate fluctuations. The first of these relates to its cash, receivables, and debt management and the second to a form of hedging. The first is really a matter of common sense, though its accomplishment may require a very systematic effort for a company with large and complex multi-national operations. It involves attempting to maintain a balance between assets denominated in a particular currency and liabilities denominated in that same currency. To hark back to the Powrie example suppose Powrie was maintaining manufacturing operations in Colombia, and had a payroll to meet there. It might then have less cause for concern about fluctuations in the exchange rate applicable to its receivable position there, since it would probably be using most of the proceeds from the receivables to meet disbursements in Colombian pesos. If this were true, the fall in the Canadian equivalent value of the receivables position would be offset by a fall in the Canadian equivalent value of Powrie's peso obligations.

Similarly Powrie could directly offset the foreign exchange rate risk in its receivable position in Colombia by obtaining a loan there, payable in Colombian pesos. In the absence of these offsetting peso liabilities, Powrie might either wish to take alternative steps, to be discussed in following sections, or else bargain with its Colombian customer on the basis of shorter credit terms, or an obligation payable in Canadian funds. Note, of course, that the latter method would protect against exchange rate fluctuation, but would not protect against possible Colombian foreign exchange controls; though willing, the Colombian customer might be forbidden by his government from buying the necessary Canadian dollars to discharge his obligation.

The technique of managerial matching of assets and liabilities is not always easily practiced. However there are often opportunities for using it advantageously. As another example, suppose that another Canadian company maintains substantial Canadian cash balances as part of its cash reserves policy, and at the same time owes liabilities payable in German marks. One can see a good reason for switching some of the cash reserve holdings out of dollar balances and into mark balances, to protect against possible exchange rate change. If, for example, the mark was revalued upward, increased value of the company's mark balances would help offset the increased dollar value of its mark liabilities.

Hedging Foreign Exchange

Positions in foreign currency (whether positive in the form of cash or receivables, or negative in the form of liabilities) are similar to inventories in the sense that the holder of the position is concerned about price volatility. It is possible to protect many types of inventory positions through hedging in the futures market and this same tactic can be employed with respect to the foreign exchange position. Futures markets exist in the world's major currencies, operating in essentially the same way as commodity futures markets. Major currency futures markets are located in New York, Chicago, and London. Access to these markets is readily available through Canadian banks and investment dealers.

A hedging operation on the currency futures market is again virtually the same as that on the commodities market. For example, a company which owes obligations in British pounds may offset this liability by buying a futures contract in an offsetting amount. Then, should the pound be revalued, the increase in the company's liability will be offset by its profit on the futures contract. Similarly, a company holding receivables denominated in francs, or franc bank balances, could hedge these through a short sale of francs on the futures market. Then, if the franc should be devalued officially, or fall in value through free market fluctuation, the company's loss on its receivables position would be offset by its gain on its short sale in the futures market.

Again, comparably with the commodity futures markets, transaction costs on the foreign exchange futures market are quite low so this is an inexpensive form of protection. Similarly, too, hedging not only protects against possible losses through exchange rate fluctuation but also has the effect of foreclosing possible windfalls.

INTERNATIONAL DIVERSIFICATION

Another risk control device, which is applicable both to the risk of currency fluctuation and to that of other international hazards such as exchange controls and expropriations, is conventional diversification. Particularly when one is dealing with countries with histories of political and exchange rate instability, it is possible to take advantage of the fact that the disturbances that occur in these various countries are probably uncorrelated. Therefore, by carrying on operations in a number of countries, risk reduction is obtained. Multinational mining and oil companies, for example, have long lived with the possibility of expropriation as a fact of life. However, their operations have been distributed over so many countries that the effect of a revolution or other disturbance in one of the countries is not calamitous to the company's operations; indeed these disturbances may become almost a routine part of a company's operating costs.

The holding of foreign assets has by itself been justified as a form of diversification. The ebb of economic tides in Canada may be offset by good fortunes in other countries; in other words, if a company is going to use diversification as a risk reduction tactic, there is a case to be made for this diversification being carried on more efficiently on an international rather than a national level. It should be simultaneously noted, that while this case exists, it is not always a very strong one. When most Canadian firms conduct operations outside of Canada, these are usually conducted principally in the United States and, to a lesser extent, in Western Europe and Japan. The general level of economic activity in all these areas is closely correlated with Canada's. So risk reduction by spreading operations between Canada and these countries or among these countries is not especially compelling. When one leaves this comfortable orbit of conventional trading partners, the potential for meaningful diversification is amplified; but, to be sure, at the cost of a greater degree of complexity and risk in trading with any particular country.

Opportunities for international diversification help explain one curious aspect of international financial relationships. As mentioned earlier, Canada has been a net importer of capital. Canadian investment opportunities have grown more rapidly than Canadian savings with the result that foreign monies have flowed in to fill the gap.

However, the extent of Canada's reliance on investment from foreign countries is greatly increased by the fact that Canadian companies and individuals buy assets abroad. For individuals these are usually in the form of portfolio investments; that is, the purchase of foreign securities. For companies the assets are more likely to be in the form of direct investments; that is, the direct ownership of foreign properties. It is possible that a quest for diversification through international activity helps to explain the simultaneous occurrence of extensive Canadian investment abroad while foreigners are finding attractive investments in Canada. In the absence of some explanation of this type, one would think that, since it is usually more convenient to invest in one's country, these two-way international financial flows would not occur.

INTERNATIONAL FINANCIAL CONNECTIONS

In discussing the operations of chartered banks and investment dealers, we already noted that these financial institutions maintain extensive international connections. The banks (and to some extent the trust companies) maintain branch offices in many foreign countries. Investment dealers also have foreign offices and close ties with their foreign counterparts. To illustrate the degree of interconnection one can observe that as of December 31, 1973, the five major Canadian banks maintained nearly 500 "branches" abroad (including branchlike operations such as subsidiaries). Not only were they well represented in the major industrial countries (62 "branches" in the United States, 27 in Britain and 15 in West Germany and France, for example) but they were also heavily concentrated in the Caribbean area (250 "branches" in Jamaica, the Bahamas, and other parts of the West Indies). In addition to these banking offices owned by the Canadian chartered banks, close working affiliations are in effect between Canadian banks and their international counterparts in all parts of the world. As a further illustration of the international aspect of the Canadian banking system, well over one fourth of the assets held by Canadian banks have recently been denominated in foreign currencies. In 1974, for example, Canadian chartered banks held about $25 billion in foreign currency assets. About 60 percent of this was in the form of deposits in foreign banks, with the remainder mainly in the form of loans made in foreign currencies.

These foreign currency assets are traditionally about equally offset by liabilities denominated in foreign currencies. Again, for example, in 1974 Canadian banks owed $27 million in foreign currency liabilities to depositors.

In addition to the international contacts of financial institutions, many nonfinancial Canadian companies maintain direct contact with foreign banks, particularly those in the United States. Sometimes credit can be obtained on more favourable terms from banks outside the country, or sometimes company reserves can be committed at higher interest rates through deposit with banks outside of Canada. One advantage that extremely large Canadian companies have in maintaining contact with foreign banks lies in their size. While Canadian chartered banks are strong, powerful institutions by international standards, they still cannot match the scale of the giant American banking companies. As a rough generalization for each of the five major Canadian chartered banks, there is a U.S. bank that is two to three times as large.

Besides the advantage of bank size, which admittedly is important only to the very largest of Canadian companies, there are other reasons for going abroad directly for financing. Interest rate differences sometimes reflect themselves in a more favourable market in the United States for commercial paper issued by Canadian companies. In addition, particularly in European banking circles, credit requirements may be somewhat less stringent than in North America, and companies unable to obtain credit in Canada, or perhaps in the United States, too, may find the funds they need in the European market.

This phenomenon may be explained by two reasons. First, as noted earlier, European banks are different creatures than their North American cousins. Their large equity positions permit them to hold more venturesome assets; of course, they expect appropriate compensation for this adventurousness. In addition, a distinct type of banking market has developed in Europe, partly through the actions of North American bankers. This market will be discussed in the following subsection.

Eurodollars, Eurocredits, and Eurobonds

In the course of normal international financial relationships, major banks have normally carried on business outside their own countries, and have normally operated partly with assets and liabilities denominated in foreign currencies. However, during the 1960s, American banks increasingly discovered a way around some restrictive U.S. banking regulations. These rules included ceilings on the interest rates they could charge on loans and pay on deposits, and governmentally imposed requirements for the maintenance of reserves (as in Canada, principally in the form of central bank deposits). To circumvent these regulations an American bank would establish a foreign branch, often in London. This branch would be outside the jurisdiction of American banking laws, and curiously enough would also, at least in the past, have been exempt from a great deal of British banking regulation. The foreign affiliate of the U.S. bank could solicit deposits from U.S. citizens and others at above the allowable interest rate ceiling in the United States, and lend these funds at rates above the lending rates permitted in the United States, even though the loans were made to U.S. borrowers. Furthermore, freedom from reserve requirements allowed them to lend out a higher proportion of their deposits than they would have been allowed to do had they operated domestically.

Banks from other countries also joined in this action, for various reasons, and a special type of international financial market was born. Because most of the transactions carried on, both by U.S. companies and the firms from other countries who also participated, were denominated in U.S. dollars and transacted in Europe, this market, centred in London, became known as the Eurodollar market. Loans in the market also came to be known as Eurocredits or Eurobonds. The absence of regulation made the market a freewheeling one, with deposits which paid high rates of interest and with loans which, correspondingly priced, were often made under conditions of considerable risk. One writer has cleverly compared this market to the European radio stations that operate in Luxembourg, beaming radio programs to other countries where the broadcasters were originally unable to obtain broadcasting licences.

At present, the Eurodollar market is in a state of confusion and change. Some banks participating in the market while freed from government compulsion for the maintenance of prudent banking standards, have found themselves in financial difficulties. (In fact the reserve requirements imposed by governments on banks are usually of such nature that, were they not dictated by government decree, they might often be self-imposed by careful bankers anyway.) In addition to financial difficulties of some market participants, nations are increasingly finding ways to regulate the activities of dealers in Eurodollars, on the grounds that this market contributes to international financial instability.

However, some variant of the Eurodollar market has existed in the past and probably will continue to exist in the future. The term Eurodollar is now being used as a general term for banking activities carried on in another currency. Since the U.S. dollar is still the leading world currency (a position once occupied by the British pound) international transactions are often denominated in dollars, and Canadian banks are likely to continue to maintain a considerable volume of legitimate Euro-dollar activity. The Eurodollar transactions may be denominated in sterling, yen, or other currencies as well; to repeat most are likely to be denominated in U.S. dollars. One of the advantages of this market to the Canadian businessman, aside from its reputation as a source of high-risk debt funds, is the fact that a Canadian company, holding let us say receivables payable in German marks, may incur offsetting mark liabilities without dealing with a German bank. Through a Eurodollar transaction he may obtain a loan in marks from a Canadian or U.S. bank.

Technical Aspects of International Banking

The interrelationships between banks and other financial institutions throughout the world facilitate various financial transactions. For example, suppose that one wishes to discharge an obligation in Capetown, payable in South African rands. Any Canadian chartered bank, and many other financial institutions as well, can arrange this payment quickly and easily. They can arrange for a wire transfer of funds, and also complete the necessary currency exchange transactions. The cost of the currency and the charges for the wire transfer will then simply be charged against the Canadian company's local deposit account. In this way virtually instantaneous money transfer is available between nearly every major trading centre in the world.

A variety of specialized credit instruments are used in international transactions, including variants of time and sight drafts, conventional open account arrangements and such other devices as notes and equipment purchase contracts. One should recall that the bulk of Canadian international transactions are with the United States and with larger Commonwealth countries; here the institutions are so compatible with those in Canada, both in legal environment and method of doing business, that there is very little "foreign" character to the foreign transactions.

One financial arrangement often used in international finance is the *irrevocable letter of credit.* This may be arranged by a Canadian through his local chartered bank, or it may be arranged by a foreign customer with his own bank. The credit reputations of banks often extend much further than that of individual companies; the irrevocable letter of credit, in which a bank gives absolute assurance that it will pay a draft or cheque in the amount specified in the letter, is often used to provide assurance to a foreign seller that goods shipped will be paid for. (Letters of credit may also be issued in revocable form; in this case, the other party in the transaction will normally obtain formal confirmation from the issuing bank.)

GOVERNMENTAL AIDS TO INTERNATIONAL FINANCE

Canadian federal and provincial governments have a long record of aiding Canadian companies in their attempts to sell goods and services outside Canada. Particularly, the governments have encouraged the export of Canadian manufactured goods, since the country's large excesses of imported manufactured goods over exported manufactured goods has persistently caused governmental concern. Aside from economic considerations, there seems to be a certain status or image of modernity associated with countries which export manufactured goods rather than raw materials.

The Federal Department of Trade and Commerce and the Department of External Affairs have a variety of programs to encourage the manufacture and marketing of goods for export.

Other programs exist in most provinces. In addition, again at both governmental levels a network of governmental agents are available throughout the world to provide intelligence and other assistance in consummating international transactions. Consulates and a corps of Trade Commissioners provide federal services in virtually every major world trading centre. In addition, provinces maintain agencies abroad, charged in part with facilitating export trade.

These agencies can aid in finance by providing information about international financing sources, and details on legal and technical aspects associated with international transactions. In addition to these agencies, international organizations, such as the World Bank, may also be helpful, particularly when a Canadian exporter is attempting to arrange credit for a customer in a developing country.

Beyond these contact points mentioned, certain Canadian federal government agencies warrant more detailed discussion.

The Export Development Corporation

The Export Development Corporation is a Crown corporation charged with the promotion of export trade. It provides two major forms of service—insurance to protect against various forms of risk in international transactions, and certain types of export credit.

The insurance takes two forms. The first of these is the insuring of foreign receivables. Insurance is available to exporters of consumer goods sold on credit terms up to 180 days, on capital goods such as industrial equipment sold on credit to a maximum of five-year terms, and on credit extended in connection with the export of various services, such as architectural or advertising firms render. In return for an insurance premium the Export Development Corporation will guarantee payment on these receivables. This coverage includes defaults by foreign buyers, blockage of payments because of exchange controls or other international disturbances, and in general all the risks of holding the receivable with the exception of exchange rate fluctuation (for which other forms of protection are normally available). Additionally the Export Development Corporation will insure business assets owned abroad from the consequences of political action such as expropriation of war.

The Export Development Corporation also offers two forms of credit assistance. It may guarantee loans of Canadian companies who are acquiring assets for international activities; this assures the company of obtaining credit on favourable terms from a chartered bank or other lending source. In addition, on certain types of transactions, the Export Development Corporation will extend direct credit to a foreign customer for the purchase of Canadian goods, thus relieving the Canadian supplier from carrying the international receivable.

Other Federal Financial Aids

The Department of Trade and Commerce, through the General Adjustment Assistance Program, provides financial assistance to Canadian manufacturing companies under certain conditions. These terms of assistance may include the guaranteeing of loans, making of direct governmental loans, and even government grants to foster certain types of international commerce.

The Canadian International Development Administration (CIDA) is charged with providing aid to developing countries. It is particularly concerned with making Canadian expertise available to less affluent nations; this includes fostering the development of financial services abroad, through grants and contracts.

SUMMARY

Canada has an internationally oriented economy, and international transactions have special financial aspects. Relative quantities of assets required for doing business are affected by shipping distances and other aspects of international business. Exposure to differing legal systems and to exchange rate problems, are other important aspects of international transactions.

Exchange rates are value ratios between pairs of currencies. These ratios may be determined by supply and demand, or they may be "managed." When a company holds assets or owes debts valued in foreign currencies, it is exposed to the risk of changing foreign exchange rates. A futures market exists in international currencies, so hedging is available as a protection against exchange rate fluctuation.

One case for participation in international business activity lies in diversification; the ups and downs of foreign economies may differ from those in Canada.

Financial institutions, especially banks, maintain extensive international connections. International market exists in loans and deposits; an important part of this market is characterized as Eurodollar transactions.

Both the federal and provincial governments actively promote international trade.

QUESTIONS AND PROBLEMS

1. Consider the following set of exchange rates.

    > Can. $1.70 = £1.
    > Can. $1.00 = U.S. $1.
    > U.S. $1.80 = £1.

    In this unlikely situation how could an arbitrageur profit? What effect would this arbitrage have on the exchange rate?

2. Explain why a pegged exchange rate does not protect someone engaged in financial transactions from exchange rate risk in the pegged currency.

3. A Canadian company has just borrowed 2 million Swiss francs, payable in six months. How could the borrower be adversely affected by currency fluctuation? What could it do to protect itself?

4. A Canadian individual holds a broadly diversified portfolio of Canadian shares. He decides to increase his degree of diversification by selling part of his Canadian holdings and substituting positions in a broad collection of shares of U.S. companies.

    Would this diversification across the border provide much increase in protection from economic "ups and downs" over the original all-Canadian portfolio? Explain.

    Would your answer be different if the international diversification had been effected with the use of a mixture of French, German, and British securities? Explain.

5. Define Eurodollar.

6. What is an irrevocable letter of credit?

458   Canadian Business Finance

7.   In its guarantees of foreign receivables, the Export Development Corporation excepts one aspect of risk in these receivables. What aspect is omitted, and how can the holder of receivables protect alternatively against this risk?

RELATED READINGS

Department of Trade and Commerce. "Incentive and Development Programs for Canadian Industry." *Information Canada,* 1973.

Eiteman, D. K., and Slonehill, A. I.   *Multinational Business Finance.* Reading, Mass.: Addison-Wesley, 1973.

Landy, L.   "Canada's Foreign Investment Review Act—Origins and Implications." Toronto Dominion Bank research paper, August 1974.

Litvak, I. A., and Maule, C. J.   "Canadian Multinationals in the Western Hemisphere. *The Business Quarterly,* Autumn 1975.

McMillan, C. J.   "After the Gray Report: The Tortuous Evolution of Foreign Investment Policy." *McGill Law Journal,* vol. 20, no. 2 (1974).

Styles, R. "Export Development Corporation." *The Canadian Banker,* September–October 1969.

Weston, J. F., and Sorge, B. W.   *International Financial Management.* Englewood Cliffs, N.J.: Prentice-Hall, 1969.

21

SOCIAL ISSUES
TOUCHING FINANCE

Like other business decisions, financial decisions are not made
in isolation. Decisions may affect other parts of the society, and
be affected by actions of the society at large. Because of this,
financial management touches and is touched by issues of overall social policy. While this textbook is not primarily addressed
to public economic policy, there are several reasons for allowing some room for the topic in the treatment of business
finance. First, an issue arises as to wehther considerations of
public good, instead of sole concern with shareholder wealth
maximization, should be regarded as a relevant aspect to be
considered in financial choices. One supposes that most financial managers already accept some idea of the abridgement of
wealth maximization, at least by amending the expression to
wealth maximization *within the law*. Few (though history is
sprinkled with a substantial number of exceptions) managers
would expect to carry wealth maximization to a point where
they would willfully break the law if the present value of the

cash flows generated by successful breach of the law exceeded the present value of expected fines (and other penalties reduced to monetary equivalents). It is, however, an open and widely debated question about the extent to which business managers, including those charged with the financial aspects of a business, should go beyond legally established minima in their concern with the social consequences of their actions.

The second reason for looking at some of these broader issues is that the consequences of financial decisions can be drastically altered by subsequent changes in policies established by parliaments, courts, and other agents of collective action. As for the third, it is not uncommon for financial managers to find themselves on the other side of the fence, themselves becoming agents rather than objects of social control. Persons involved in financial affairs often become members of provincial securities commissions or royal commissions relating to financial issues, MLAs, MPs, and ministers of the Crown. Even in their role as company officers they, particularly as they attain senior levels, are likely to feel an obligation (or compulsion) to speak out publicly on matters affecting social policy relating to finance.

In this chapter we will look at a number of issues which were topical in 1976. Some of these issues have a way of enduring; others seem to pass quickly from the public stage—whether resolved or not—to be supplanted by others. Incidentally, the writer while anything but neutral on some of these matters, will *attempt* to present alternative viewpoints on most of these issues, leaving resolution of right and wrong for the reader.

One further note. An attempt will be made to confine the discussion to topics directly related to business financial decisions. Broad topics, such as national and international monetary and employment policies, will be excluded; though an understanding of these matters is important for the thoughtful financial manager, they are treated extensively in texts on monetary policy, macroeconomics, and economic principles.

External Effects of Financial Choices

Economists define an *external effect* or *externality* as, in simplified terms, an effect on party C caused by a transaction between parties A and B. Automobile Company A buys steel from Steel Company B. Smoke from B's new steel mill befouls the air of a residential area where Citizen C dwells. As a result of the smoke, Citizen C must paint his house once every two years instead of once every five years—for simplicity, the example uses an effect on C that is easily translated to monetary terms, unlike the respiratory diseases that he may also pick up from the smoke inhalation.

Obviously one of the costs of producing steel has been the damage done to Citizen C. but there is no direct way in which this cost will enter the transaction between companies A and B. This in turn means that Company B may make a profit at C's expense, or—more likely in a competitive environment—sell a product to A at below its full cost of production (where damages to C are counted as part of production cost).

The possibility of a product selling consistently below its full cost of production violates one of the fundamental justifications for the "free enterprise system." This rationale asserts that products will be produced only if they meet a "market test." Unless a buyer wants a product sufficiently to pay all of its marginal cost of production, the resources used to produce the product should be used for other purposes instead. But if some resources are unaccounted for in the bargain between A and B (in our example, the extra paint for C's house) a true market test does not exist. Had B charged a price including all costs of steel, it might have found no buyer for its steel. Company A might have decided to use aluminum instead, or to buy steel elsewhere, or to produce fewer cars and more of other products that did not require as much steel.

There are three major policy approaches to the externality problem, if one reasons within the confines of maintaining an economic system similar to the one currently prevailing in Canada. The first of these is to ignore the externalities, recognizing them as an unfortunate but incorrectible imperfection in an otherwise desirable economic system. The second is to internalize them; this will involve devising a method where the indirect cost to C somehow is worked back directly into B's cost of production. The third alternative is for B to voluntarily avoid doing harm to C, or to compensate him for damages done.

The disadvantages of the first alternative have been looked at; it violates the "market test." The only apparent advantage is that, particularly where externalities are not major, their identification and correction may be so difficult that it is simpler to ignore the problem. Attempting to redress all grievances in any social system is hopelessly utopian.

The second and third alternatives, internalization of the costs or voluntary handling of the matter, directly concern financial management, particularly with respect to capital budgeting decisions. Let us consider the possible impact of either of these approaches in such aspects as the decision to acquire a steel plant, the choice of its location, or the extent to which marginal expenditures should be committed to incorporating pollution control technology within the plant.

Internalization

There are a number of ways in which the costs to C may be internalized to Company B. If Company B, in its capital budgeting process, fails to recognize the possibility of this internalization, it may commit serious capital budgeting errors. Let us look at a number of ways in which these costs inflicted upon C may come home to roost.

a.   Citizen C may be able to bring legal action for damages. This is not a certainty, but the principle of using the courts to obtain compensation for damages is well rooted in the traditions of British common law, which often governs in Canadian courts. To generalize, one component of the cash flow stream associated with the plant which should be included in its associated capital budgeting analysis is the probability of liabilities arising from side effects of its operation.

b.   Internalization may also take the form of direct government regulation. Furthermore, there is nothing to prevent the establishment of air pollution restrictions or taxes on a polluter after a plant has been established. Of course, existing restrictions will be considered when a current plant design is approved; but realistic analysis of the plant's prospects ought to include consideration of the cost of possible modifications, or even plant shutdown, which may result from more restrictive future regulations.

c. Not all of the internationalization need take the form of direct costs, either actual or potential, as in the form of damage liabilities and governmental restrictions. Internalization may also be of an opportunity cost form. Governmental subsidy may be offered for abstinence from an act harmful to a third party. A good example of this is the extraordinary capital consumption allowance currently allowed to those companies who install pollution control equipment. (The effect of this is a substantial increase in the present value of the CCA tax shield.)

d. It is also possible, though practical examples are not easy to find, that affected third parties, such as Citizen C, will negotiate a private subsidization of Company B for abstaining from its externality. Whether from a private or public source, the opportunity of a subsidy constitutes an opportunity cost—the potential loss of the subsidy—associated with generating an external effect. Again the possibility of such subsidies may be relevant in a capital budgeting process.

Internalization of costs, in general, means that effects on outsiders are going to be charged back to the individual firm in the form of money amounts, and these money amounts constitute important variables in the formulation of the company's financial plans.

Voluntary Abstention

To continue with the A, B, and C example, B could voluntarily relocate its plant, or install pollution control equipment, in such a way that Citizen C and others like him are not damaged by the exhalations of steel production. It is important to separate motives here; we are talking about Company B doing this in a strictly voluntary sense, and not in anticipation of subsequent regulation or lawsuits. The question of this voluntary abstention in turn relates to broader problems—the social responsibility of the company. The company is legally a creature apart from its owners, with an identity of its own. Should this artificial person undertake some of the responsibilities that one would expect of a real individual in his role as a good citizen?

Some exercise of social responsibility may be consistent with shareholder wealth maximization. Generous company acts may contribute to its public image, and indirectly help in the sale of its products, procurement of its employees, or other ways. However, such a coincidence begs the central question; there often is a direct conflict. To hark back to the A, B, and C example, should Company B voluntarily compensate C, or incur extra costs to avoid damaging C, when this in effect results in a transfer of wealth from the company's shareholders to C?

There are no easy answers on this issue for company management. Corporate charity donations are a well-established, though not a universally advocated, practice. On the other hand, excessive generosity, even though condoned by majority shareholders, could conceivably constitute grounds for a shareholders' suit. Furthermore, unless competitors also act with voluntary generosity, Company B may not survive its benefactions because of their cost disadvantage.

To recapitulate, in some cases company generosity or concern about damages to others coincides with shareholder wealth maximization. Where these objectives conflict, there is no easy guideline for a choice between "good corporate citizenship," and strict financial stewardship.

Compulsory versus Voluntary Solutions: Pros and Cons

Against voluntarism, there is the question of whether companies should broaden their role beyond simplistic wealth maximization and establish themselves as righters of social wrongs. Perhaps this is expecting too much of company management, or alternatively put, perhaps this is entrusting company officers with a task that is more properly within the jurisdiction of popularly elected public officials?

The second argument against voluntary solutions lies in the fact that they may be inconsistent with the spirit of competition. One company alone may not survive if it undertakes costly activity in favour of the public, when its competitors are not following the same course. Therefore, if a systematic solution is to be obtained voluntarily, it is quite likely that cooperation between companies will be necessary. Unfortunately there is a thin line between co-operation and collusion; when the officers of a number of companies who are otherwise competitors sit down to discuss a joint abrogation of their competitive struggle in some area deemed to be in the public interest, their harmony may extend to other more antisocial forms of co-operation. (The issue becomes analogous to that associated with professional organizations. When chartered accountants establish strict standards for entry into the accounting profession, are they protecting the public from incompetent accountancy or are they protecting themselves from too much potential competition?)

The alternative to voluntarism is usually a governmentally imposed solution either through regulation or tax/subsidy. This approach, too, has its problems. One of these is regulatory overkill. Returning once more to the A, B, and C example, suppose the damages suffered by Citizen C and his counterparts are sufficient to elicit government action in the form of imposing an absolute restriction against B's air pollution. B, lacking technological alternatives, shuts down. A and its customers, deprived of B as a source of supply, suffer damages far in excess of those which would have been suffered by C.

A second problem lies in the cost and controversy associated with precise governmental internalization. Ideally a governmentally imposed solution would give B the option of compensating C for damages sustained and continuing production, or modifying and/or discontinuing production if this alternative was more wealth-enhancing; in other words, a true market test would be reinstated. That the necessary organization and measurement can be mustered to achieve this end is not always clear.

(To return to the analogy of the accounting profession, as self-regulation has its limitations, so do alternatives. One of these is governmentally imposed accreditation of accountants; but this may be done inexpertly, and could conceivably confuse professional and political qualifications. There is a third alternative; no standards or licensure may be imposed by either the profession or the government. Then companies of accountants could establish their own records of achievement and convey them to the public through conventional advertising; or private accrediting agencies could establish themselves. Again, this "pure competition" alternative may be fraught with confusion or hucksterism.)

INCOME DISTRIBUTION EFFECTS OF
FINANCIAL POLICIES

The side effects of financial policies may show up in ways other than physical externalities such as air or river pollution. Apart from direct company charity, the actions of a company can change the distribution of income within the country. Two examples will illustrate this point.

A large company, LaFontaine Ltd., switches from a policy of informal evaluation of its credit customers to a more systematic program based on point scoring backed by statistical studies. On the basis of these studies it discovers that it should, in its point-scoring program, place considerable weight on geographic location. Specifically, it finds that it can predict that default rates are likely to be higher in low-income areas of the major cities in which it operates. If it follows this analysis with corresponding policy changes, the results will be the denial of more credit applications in low-income areas. Previously, the company would have been granting credit in these areas with some economic irrationality, inadvertently accepting disproportionate credit losses in those areas. The effect of its policy "refinement" will be discontinuance of this loss absorption and, along with this, further strain on the finances of persons who are already poor.

The arguments in favour of the refinement of the credit policy are easily mustered. Marginal analysis discloses that transactions with the applicants affected by the new credit-screening process are not wealth maximizing; and perhaps that should end the matter. Additionally, if competitors also adopt the refined analysis, their ability to eliminate bad debt losses in low-income areas may enable them to liberalize their credit terms in other areas. LaFontaine, too, may now be forced to either restrict credit in the problem region or specialize in granting credit there, with interest charges commensurate to the default rates of those regions.

In other words, prior to the refinement of credit application analysis, debtors in affluent areas were unwittingly subsidizing those in low-income areas, by accepting credit terms which were sufficiently rigorous to cover the bad debt losses of others. The result was an income transfer from rich to poor; the "improvement" in credit analysis eliminated this transfer. Again the argument of corporate citizenship comes into play. Should a company leave questions of income distribution entirely to governmental action, or should it actively try to alleviate the lot of the poor. We have used a financial example here; the issue is obviously extensible to employment policies, and perhaps to purchasing and other areas.

For the second example, we turn again to the question of capital budgeting decisions affecting choice of alternative sites for plant construction. The company may be choosing between two manufacturing plant locations, one near a source of raw materials in northern Quebec and another near its major market area, Toronto. Suppose strict wealth maximization dictates in favour of the choice of the Toronto location. Should the company consider the effect of its choice in the matter of where the employment opportunity generated by the manufacturing plant will do the most good.

The question of regional income disparity is a serious one in this country, and has been addressed by a variety of governmental programs at the federal and provincial level. Some of these programs attempt to internalize the income redistribution side effects of plant location by subsidizing, through favourable credit availability or other means, the location of plants in economically disadvantaged parts of the country. Even the strictly wealth-maximizing company may want to reconsider a plant site decision in the light of governmental subsidy for locating in an impoverished region, under such a program as DREE (Department of Regional Economic Expansion).

FOREIGN OWNERSHIP

One of the thorniest national financial issues relates to the extent of ownership of Canadian companies by persons and companies not resident in Canada. Since Canada has regularly relied on foreign monies to finance its economic development, this issue has a long history. However, the contemporary spirit of nationalism, and especially of a desire for an identity separate from the United States, has recently placed the issue in the forefront. The issue has principally focused on U.S. investment in Canada with some concern, especially in the West, about Japanese participation. In 1976, additional concern (this time shared in the United States) was being manifested over the massive investment potentialities of the so-called OPEC countries (Organization of Petroleum Exporting Countries)— petroleum-rich Middle Eastern states such as Saudi Arabia and Iran.

Pros and Cons

The arguments in favour of allowing unlimited international investment are for the most part economic—in fact, they are the classical arguments for economic internationalism. Unrestricted inflow of international money into Canada is likely to have two effects. It will accelerate the pace of economic growth in Canada, by increasing the resources available to support that growth. Second, it will provide increased competition for local capital suppliers. This second effect is likely to result in income redistribution with lower rates of return on their money for Canadian savers; and with the increased availability of capital for industrial expansion creating upward pressure on domestic wage earnings.

The arguments against unrestricted capital inflows are principally political in character. They contend that the activity of companies has a major effect on the character of the country. This is particularly true if companies undertake acts of "social responsibility" rather than confine themselves to a simplistic goal of wealth maximization.

An issue particularly vexing to many Canadians has been that of the extraterritorial extension of laws of other countries, especially the United States, into areas presumably under Canadian sovereignty. For example, under the U.S. Trading with the Enemy Act; subsidiaries of American companies, even though these are themselves companies resident in Canada, were (at the time of writing of this book) forbidden to conduct trading relationships with Cuba. While the United States defines Cuba as an "enemy," Canada maintains normal diplomatic and commercial relations with that nation.

Foreign Ownership and Financial Management

The financial manager may come in direct contact with this issue in at least two ways. A company, in its search for additional capital sources, may find it advantageous to sell new issues of common shares or other equity participations in foreign markets. As we have noted, close international ties of Canadian investment dealers and banks with foreign financial institutions facilitate this international search for capital. The question arises, should a company's financial management sell substantial equity to foreigners, if this represents a least cost financing solution? Or should they depart from strict wealth maximization in the interest of retaining the Canadian character of their ownership.

Similarly, a Canadian company may have the opportunity to sell assets, perhaps even all of its properties or shares, to a non-Canadian investor. Again, one comes back to the question of social responsibility versus wealth maximization. Furthermore, "social responsibility" is not easily definable here, because not all Canadians share an aversion to non-Canadian ownership of Canadian companies.

There has been some recent tendency toward governmental intervention in this type of financial decision. Under existing legislation, the federal government can prohibit proposed foreign acquisitions of Canadian companies. The government would be particularly likely to exercise this right if extra-economic consideration were involved. For example, it would be almost inconceivable now that foreign owners could purchase control of a major Canadian newspaper, because of its potential political and cultural influence.

Like other social issues, this one may abate with the passing of time. On the other hand, governments at both the provincial and federal level could move further toward internalizing the political side effects of the use of foreign capital. Even now, for example, the province of Saskatchewan has restricted nonresident land ownership within the province. (Here the restriction is extended not only to nonresidents of Canada but to Canadian residents who are nonresidents of Saskatchewan.) As another example, even now aspects of Canadian tax legislation discriminate against investment here by nonresidents. One could foresee, if public concern over this issue continues, that there may be increasing internalization of foreign ownership effects through a system of taxes or subsidies.

OTHER GOVERNMENT ACTIVITY IN FINANCIAL MARKETS

Interest Rate Controls

Even in times and in countries where other prices have been determined by free market considerations, interest rates have sometimes been singled out as different. If an individual or company buys the *use* of something on a temporary basis, the benefits conveyed are not as obvious or tangible as if outright ownership of a property is obtained. Accordingly, there is a long tradition of regarding interest (with rent sometimes also included) as a price charged for a "nothing." This concept of interest as exploitative (the term *usury* is often used to denote interest in this context) has led to restrictions on interest charges in many jurisdictions. As we noted earlier, until the 1967 revision of the Bank Act, these restrictions applied in Canada. Canadian companies borrowing or lending in the United States will still encounter an array of these restrictions.

The arguments in favour of interest rate control are that they undoubtedly do prevent some exploitation. Even where full disclosure is required, an interest rate may not be as understandable to the general public as other prices that are couched directly in terms of dollars and cents. This may in turn mean less "shopping around" on the part of the public for the most favourable interest rate, with some resulting freedom for an entrepreneur to take advantage of this lack of competitive exposure.

On the other hand, restrictions on interest rates have the same general consequences as restrictions on other prices. They outlaw many voluntary and mutually beneficial transactions. Under previous Bank Acts, for example, a restriction of bank interest charges made it difficult for banks to compete aggressively in areas of consumer and small business finance. They simply could not charge interest rates which would adequately compensate them for the administrative costs and prospective bad debt losses in these lines of lending. In turn, this meant that many small businessmen and the consumers who could have advantageously used bank credit were denied it.

In addition to prohibition of some transactions, such a price ceiling also tends to encourage circumventions, both legal and illegal. With an interest rate ceiling, legal circumventions would almost certainly include increased reliance on various forms of providing equity capital and leasing or rental arrangements, where the capital supplier was not compensated in the form of an explicit interest rate. The illegal modes are left to the reader's imagination.

An interesting aspect of the interest rate regulation issue has arisen recently in connection with the practice of purchasing the right to income tax refunds. For example, suppose Joe believes that the amount of income tax withheld by his employer exceeds his income tax liability for 1975. Joe may need some ready cash, and may not wish to wait for the government refund cheque to arrive. Entrepreneurs have established themselves to fill this need by offering to buy these income tax claims at a discount. Joe brings his withholding tax statement (T–4 form) to one of these entrepreneurs who, using the T–4 form and other information supplied by Joe, calculates the amount of the tax refund Joe has coming.

Suppose this calculation indicates that Joe can expect $400, and the best guess available is that this $400 will be available about May 1. It is now February 1, and the entrepreneur offers Joe $300 in immediate cash in return for his claim. One can crudely estimate the internal rate on this transaction as 133 percent (33 percent for one fourth of a year). This is a high rate of interest, but Joe may go away very pleased to have the $300 available now rather than waiting for the $400 later.

There are a number of issues involved. There are instances in transactions of this type where the entrepreneur may make a dishonest estimate of the refund; perhaps Joe is really foregoing a future $500 or $600 instead of $400, in exchange for $300 cash in hand. Second, there is the question of disclosure; while the substance of this transaction is a loan to Joe, it is legally a purchase rather than a loan transaction, and as a result interest rate disclosure (truth-in-lending) laws do not apply. The third question relates to whether anyone should have the right, even if the refund estimate is honest and the implicit interest rate is made explicit, to charge 133 percent interest.

In principle, the workings of a competitive marketplace

could solve all three of these problems. Companies could establish reputations for honest estimates; some shopping around by Joe would at least enable him to pick the highest estimate of his potential tax refund. Similarly, if there were public desire to know the interest rate implicit in these transactions, would it not be good business for some aggressive entrepreneur to advertise that he was supplying this information, and would that not force others to emulate him? Finally, if 133 percent was "too high," would not capital flow into this market, intensifying the competition and driving the discount rates on tax refunds down?

But suppose Joe is not a rational shopper, and will accept the first offer he obtains. What rights should he have? The right to an honest estimate? The right to the disclosure of the interest rate? The right to a ceiling on the interest rate charged? The issues are separable; it should be noted that an affirmative answer to the third question probably requires the imposition of a usury law placing a ceiling on interest rates.

(One additional complication should be noted; even though a claim against the government is involved this transaction may not be riskless. Joe, too, may be dishonest. For example, he may have worked for two employers during the year but only show the refund-purchaser one of his T–4 slips.)

TAX EFFECTS ON FINANCIAL CHOICE

Capital Mobility

Under present tax law, we noted that it is somewhat more economical for a company to obtain marginal equity capital from earnings retention rather than from sale of additional common shares, particularly where the earnings retention does not involve total abstinence from dividends. Partly this situation is a creature of the administrative costs of selling new issues of common shares, as compared to the passive retention of earnings already available. Partly, too, the situation is a creature of tax legislation.

Under present Canadian law this tax disadvantage is not severe. Dividends are given favourable personal tax treatment in the form of a dividend credit, because shareholder earnings have already been taxed at the corporate level. The result is that in most cases, the company which would not finance a new asset with the sale of new common shares would not finance it with retained earnings either. (While there are some cost differences between the two, the differences are small.)

However, until recently, and still in many other countries, tax treatment of dividends is much harsher. As a result companies may be encouraged to undertake investments with retained earnings which they would not consider if they had to rely on externally generated funds. The result of this is economic irrationality imposed by the tax system. Company A may, to avoid paying a dividend and exposing its shareholders to the tax consequences of that dividend, purchase assets yielding 10 percent when the prevailing discount rate on comparable common stock is 15 percent.[1] This means that Company A is undertaking marginal investments yielding 10 percent at a time when other companies must have investments yielding over 15 percent available; otherwise a 15 percent return on equity would not persist in the marketplace.

Some students of the subject (and this became the official position of the famous Carter Commission) have argued that the corporate income tax should be abolished and company earnings should be immediately taxable to their shareholders. In this way two aims are achieved. Companies cannot be used as devices for escaping personal taxation. Second, companies have absolutely no tax incentive to abstain from paying dividends since shareholders are taxed as if dividends had been paid whether they actually are disbursed or not. This extreme solution may have disadvantages (for example, it may discourage investment and arrest economic growth) but it does have the advantage of eliminating all "locking in" of capital in one company when it could be more advantageously used in another.

Tax Preference for Debt

Another important tax policy issue relates to tax efficiency obtainable through the use of debt in company financing. As

---

[1] Of course, one company could directly purchase the common shares of another company—if this is allowed. (This action is not readily available as an alternative to dividend payment under U.S. tax legislation.) If unlimited purchase of shares of other companies is allowed, as it is in Canada, no company should be valued at less than a cost of k_i because of opportunity cost considerations.

we noted, under current Canadian tax law there is little reason for a company to prefer debt financing or equity financing for tax efficiency reasons alone.

This is in substantial contrast with the extreme example used in Chapter 18, where returns to equity were subject to full double taxation—corporate income tax plus full personal income tax. The result of introducing tax efficiency in the direction of debt, of the type in this extreme illustration, is to foster the use of debt. Indeed companies must then accumulate high debt ratios for competitive reasons, since these tend to be cost minimizing.

It should be noted that the extreme example presented was not an idle speculation; a strong tax bias in favour of debt exists in the United States and there was probably such a bias under former Canadian tax legislation (though the issue was more ambiguous here). The result of encouraging high debt ratios has two direct effects: an increasing tendency for bankruptcy, with the attendant costs, and an increasing tendency for companies to undertake risk reduction activities, including merger, to avoid the bankruptcy costs.

Experience in the United States has suggested a third more indirect result of such a policy with the encouragement of high debt ratios, and the possibility of waves of bankruptcy. During periods when industries are subject to adverse economic winds, there has been a tendency for government to enter the picture and provide financial assistance for companies whose corporate life is endangered. The effect of this is a curious form of government equity participation—government (or the taxpayers) are absorbing risks previously undertaken by private entrepreneurs. This seems like a particularly ungainly and unrewarding way for government to involve itself in equity participation.[2]

SUMMARY

Financial choices may have external effects; that is, financial transaction may affect others beyond those who are direct

---

[2] The author admits to having been somewhat one-sided in his presentation of this last section. Perhaps the reader can find convincing reasons for favouring tax-induced capital immobility or debt preference; I cannot.

parties in the transaction. The result of these external effects may be injustice, and nonoptimal use of natural resources.

External effects may be internalized; that is, their costs may be assessed to the parties who are direct participants in a transaction. Liability laws, government regulations on external effects, and subsidies for abstaining from external effects all constitute cost internalizations.

Compulsory internalization of external effects often involves the rigidities of governmental intervention. Voluntary solutions, too, have difficulties; the collaboration of businesses in effecting a voluntary solution may lessen competition.

Beyond exposing others to external costs, company actions may affect income distribution.

Foreign ownership is another current policy issue. Is the economic advantage of capital imported from abroad, sufficient to offset surrendering some economic control to foreign shareholders?

Other public policy issues affecting finance relate to controls on interest rates and the effect of tax policies upon capital mobility and financing choice.

RELATED READINGS

Coase, R. H. "The Problem of Social Cost." *Journal of Law and Economics*, October 1960.

Crookel, H., and Wrigley, L. "Canadian Response to Multinational Enterprise." *The Business Quarterly*, Spring 1975.

Dales, J. H. *Pollution, Property and Prices: An Essay in Policy-making and Economics.* Toronto: University of Toronto Press, 1968.

Edelstein, R. H. "Improving the Selection of Credit Risks: An Analysis of Bank Minority Lending Programs." *Journal of Finance*, March, 1975.

Pigou, A. C. *The Economics of Welfare*, 2d ed. London: Macmillan, 1974.

Posner, R. A. *Economic Analysis of Law.* Boston and Toronto: Little, Brown, 1972, Part III.

Tullock, G. "Problems in Theory of Public Choice, Social Cost and Government Action." *American Economic Review*, May 1969.

TABLE A-1
Present Value of $1

Periods until Payment	1%	2%	3%	4%	5%	6%	8%	10%	12%	14%	15%	16%	18%	20%	22%	24%	25%	26%	30%	40%	50%
1	0.990	0.980	0.971	0.962	0.952	0.943	0.926	0.909	0.893	0.877	0.870	0.862	0.847	0.833	0.820	0.806	0.800	0.794	0.769	0.714	0.667
2	0.980	0.961	0.943	0.925	0.907	0.890	0.857	0.826	0.797	0.769	0.756	0.743	0.718	0.694	0.672	0.650	0.640	0.630	0.592	0.510	0.444
3	0.971	0.942	0.915	0.889	0.864	0.840	0.794	0.751	0.712	0.675	0.658	0.641	0.609	0.579	0.551	0.524	0.512	0.500	0.455	0.364	0.296
4	0.961	0.924	0.888	0.855	0.823	0.792	0.735	0.683	0.636	0.592	0.572	0.552	0.516	0.482	0.451	0.423	0.410	0.397	0.350	0.260	0.198
5	0.951	0.906	0.863	0.822	0.784	0.747	0.681	0.621	0.567	0.519	0.497	0.476	0.437	0.402	0.370	0.341	0.328	0.315	0.269	0.186	0.132
6	0.942	0.888	0.837	0.790	0.746	0.705	0.630	0.564	0.507	0.456	0.432	0.410	0.370	0.335	0.303	0.275	0.262	0.250	0.207	0.133	0.088
7	0.933	0.871	0.813	0.760	0.711	0.665	0.583	0.513	0.452	0.400	0.376	0.354	0.314	0.279	0.249	0.222	0.210	0.198	0.159	0.095	0.059
8	0.923	0.853	0.789	0.731	0.677	0.627	0.540	0.467	0.404	0.351	0.327	0.305	0.266	0.233	0.204	0.179	0.168	0.157	0.123	0.068	0.039
9	0.914	0.837	0.766	0.703	0.645	0.592	0.500	0.424	0.361	0.308	0.284	0.263	0.225	0.194	0.167	0.144	0.134	0.125	0.094	0.048	0.026
10	0.905	0.820	0.744	0.676	0.614	0.558	0.463	0.386	0.322	0.270	0.247	0.227	0.191	0.162	0.137	0.116	0.107	0.099	0.073	0.035	0.017
11	0.896	0.804	0.722	0.650	0.585	0.527	0.429	0.350	0.287	0.237	0.215	0.195	0.162	0.135	0.112	0.094	0.086	0.079	0.056	0.025	0.012
12	0.887	0.788	0.701	0.625	0.557	0.497	0.397	0.319	0.257	0.208	0.187	0.168	0.137	0.112	0.092	0.076	0.069	0.062	0.043	0.018	0.008
13	0.879	0.773	0.681	0.601	0.530	0.469	0.368	0.290	0.229	0.182	0.163	0.145	0.116	0.093	0.075	0.061	0.055	0.050	0.033	0.013	0.005
14	0.870	0.758	0.661	0.577	0.505	0.442	0.340	0.263	0.205	0.160	0.141	0.125	0.099	0.078	0.062	0.049	0.044	0.039	0.025	0.009	0.003
15	0.861	0.743	0.642	0.555	0.481	0.417	0.315	0.239	0.183	0.140	0.123	0.108	0.084	0.065	0.051	0.040	0.035	0.031	0.020	0.006	0.002
16	0.853	0.728	0.623	0.534	0.458	0.394	0.292	0.218	0.163	0.123	0.107	0.093	0.071	0.054	0.042	0.032	0.028	0.025	0.015	0.005	0.002
17	0.844	0.714	0.605	0.513	0.436	0.371	0.270	0.198	0.146	0.108	0.093	0.080	0.060	0.045	0.034	0.026	0.023	0.020	0.012	0.003	0.001
18	0.836	0.700	0.587	0.494	0.416	0.350	0.250	0.180	0.130	0.095	0.081	0.069	0.051	0.038	0.028	0.021	0.018	0.016	0.009	0.002	0.001
19	0.828	0.686	0.570	0.475	0.396	0.331	0.232	0.164	0.116	0.083	0.070	0.060	0.043	0.031	0.023	0.017	0.014	0.012	0.007	0.002	
20	0.820	0.673	0.554	0.456	0.377	0.312	0.215	0.149	0.104	0.073	0.061	0.051	0.037	0.026	0.019	0.014	0.012	0.010	0.005	0.001	
21	0.811	0.660	0.538	0.439	0.359	0.294	0.199	0.135	0.093	0.064	0.053	0.044	0.031	0.022	0.015	0.011	0.009	0.008	0.004	0.001	
22	0.803	0.647	0.522	0.422	0.342	0.278	0.184	0.123	0.083	0.056	0.046	0.038	0.026	0.018	0.013	0.009	0.007	0.006	0.003	0.001	
23	0.795	0.634	0.507	0.406	0.326	0.262	0.170	0.112	0.074	0.049	0.040	0.033	0.022	0.015	0.010	0.007	0.006	0.005	0.002		
24	0.788	0.622	0.492	0.390	0.310	0.247	0.158	0.102	0.066	0.043	0.035	0.028	0.019	0.013	0.008	0.006	0.005	0.004	0.002		
25	0.780	0.610	0.478	0.375	0.295	0.233	0.146	0.092	0.059	0.038	0.030	0.024	0.016	0.010	0.007	0.005	0.004	0.003	0.001		
26	0.772	0.598	0.464	0.361	0.281	0.220	0.135	0.084	0.053	0.033	0.026	0.021	0.014	0.009	0.006	0.004	0.003	0.002	0.001		
27	0.764	0.586	0.450	0.347	0.268	0.207	0.125	0.076	0.047	0.029	0.023	0.018	0.011	0.007	0.005	0.003	0.002	0.002	0.001		
28	0.757	0.574	0.437	0.333	0.255	0.196	0.116	0.069	0.042	0.026	0.020	0.016	0.010	0.006	0.004	0.002	0.002	0.002	0.001		
29	0.749	0.563	0.424	0.321	0.243	0.185	0.107	0.063	0.037	0.022	0.017	0.014	0.008	0.005	0.003	0.002	0.002	0.001			
30	0.742	0.552	0.412	0.308	0.231	0.174	0.099	0.057	0.033	0.020	0.015	0.012	0.007	0.004	0.003	0.002	0.001	0.001			
40	0.672	0.453	0.307	0.208	0.142	0.097	0.046	0.022	0.011	0.005	0.004	0.003	0.001	0.001							
50	0.608	0.372	0.228	0.141	0.087	0.054	0.021	0.009	0.003	0.001	0.001	0.001									

Source: Jerome Bracken and Charles J. Christenson, *Tables for Use in Analyzing Business Decisions* (Homewood, Ill.: Richard D. Irwin, Inc., 1965).

TABLE A-2
Present Value of $1 Received Annually

Periods to Be Paid	1%	2%	3%	4%	5%	6%	8%	10%	12%	14%	15%	16%	18%	20%	22%	24%	25%	26%	30%	40%	50%
1	0.990	0.980	0.971	0.962	0.952	0.943	0.926	0.909	0.893	0.877	0.870	0.862	0.847	0.833	0.820	0.806	0.800	0.794	0.769	0.714	0.667
2	1.970	1.942	1.914	1.886	1.859	1.833	1.783	1.736	1.690	1.647	1.626	1.605	1.556	1.528	1.492	1.457	1.440	1.424	1.361	1.224	1.111
3	2.941	2.884	2.829	2.775	2.723	2.673	2.577	2.487	2.402	2.322	2.283	2.246	2.174	2.106	2.042	1.981	1.952	1.923	1.816	1.589	1.407
4	3.902	3.808	3.717	3.630	3.546	3.465	3.312	3.170	3.037	2.914	2.855	2.798	2.690	2.589	2.494	2.404	2.362	2.320	2.166	1.849	1.605
5	4.853	4.713	4.580	4.452	4.330	4.212	3.993	3.791	3.605	3.433	3.352	3.274	3.127	2.991	2.864	2.745	2.689	2.635	2.436	2.035	1.737
6	5.795	5.601	5.417	5.242	5.076	4.917	4.623	4.355	4.111	3.889	3.784	3.685	3.498	3.326	3.167	3.020	2.951	2.885	2.643	2.168	1.824
7	6.728	6.472	6.230	6.002	5.786	5.582	5.206	4.868	4.564	4.288	4.160	4.039	3.812	3.605	3.416	3.242	3.161	3.083	2.802	2.263	1.883
8	7.652	7.325	7.020	6.733	6.463	6.210	5.747	5.335	4.968	4.639	4.487	4.344	4.078	3.837	3.619	3.421	3.329	3.241	2.925	2.331	1.922
9	8.566	8.162	7.786	7.435	7.108	6.802	6.247	5.759	5.328	4.946	4.772	4.607	4.303	4.031	3.786	3.566	3.463	3.366	3.019	2.379	1.948
10	9.471	8.983	8.530	8.111	7.722	7.360	6.710	6.145	5.650	5.216	5.019	4.833	4.494	4.192	3.923	3.682	3.571	3.465	3.092	2.414	1.965
11	10.368	9.787	9.253	8.760	8.306	7.887	7.139	6.495	5.938	5.453	5.234	5.029	4.656	4.327	4.035	3.776	3.656	3.544	3.147	2.438	1.977
12	11.255	10.575	9.954	9.385	8.863	8.384	7.536	6.814	6.194	5.660	5.421	5.197	4.793	4.439	4.127	3.851	3.725	3.606	3.190	2.456	1.985
13	12.134	11.348	10.635	9.986	9.394	8.853	7.904	7.103	6.424	5.842	5.583	5.342	4.910	4.533	4.203	3.912	3.780	3.656	3.223	2.468	1.990
14	13.004	12.106	11.296	10.563	9.899	9.295	8.244	7.367	6.628	6.002	5.724	5.468	5.008	4.611	4.265	3.962	3.824	3.695	3.249	2.478	1.993
15	13.865	12.849	11.938	11.118	10.380	9.712	8.559	7.606	6.811	6.142	5.847	5.576	5.092	4.676	4.315	4.001	3.859	3.726	3.268	2.484	1.995
16	14.718	13.578	12.561	11.652	10.838	10.106	8.851	7.824	6.974	6.265	5.954	5.668	5.162	4.730	4.357	4.033	3.887	3.751	3.283	2.488	1.997
17	15.562	14.292	13.166	12.166	11.274	10.477	9.122	8.022	7.120	6.373	6.047	5.749	5.222	4.775	4.391	4.059	3.910	3.771	3.295	2.492	1.998
18	16.398	14.992	13.754	12.659	11.690	10.828	9.372	8.201	7.250	6.467	6.128	5.818	5.273	4.812	4.419	4.080	3.928	3.786	3.304	2.494	1.999
19	17.226	15.678	14.324	13.134	12.085	11.158	9.604	8.365	7.366	6.550	6.198	5.878	5.316	4.844	4.442	4.097	3.942	3.799	3.311	2.496	1.999
20	18.046	16.351	14.877	13.590	12.462	11.470	9.818	8.514	7.469	6.623	6.259	5.929	5.353	4.870	4.460	4.110	3.954	3.808	3.316	2.497	1.999
21	18.857	17.011	15.415	14.029	12.821	11.764	10.017	8.649	7.562	6.687	6.312	5.973	5.384	4.891	4.476	4.121	3.963	3.816	3.320	2.498	2.000
22	19.660	17.658	15.937	14.451	13.163	12.042	10.201	8.772	7.645	6.743	6.359	6.011	5.410	4.909	4.488	4.130	3.970	3.822	3.323	2.498	2.000
23	20.456	18.292	16.444	14.857	13.489	12.303	10.371	8.883	7.718	6.792	6.399	6.044	5.432	4.924	4.499	4.137	3.976	3.827	3.325	2.499	2.000
24	21.243	18.914	16.936	15.247	13.799	12.550	10.529	8.985	7.784	6.835	6.434	6.073	5.451	4.937	4.507	4.143	3.981	3.831	3.327	2.499	2.000
25	22.023	19.523	17.413	15.622	14.094	12.783	10.675	9.077	7.843	6.873	6.464	6.097	5.467	4.948	4.514	4.147	3.985	3.834	3.329	2.499	2.000
26	22.795	20.121	17.877	15.983	14.375	13.003	10.810	9.161	7.896	6.906	6.491	6.118	5.480	4.956	4.520	4.151	3.988	3.837	3.330	2.500	2.000
27	23.560	20.707	18.327	16.330	14.643	13.211	10.935	9.237	7.943	6.935	6.514	6.136	5.492	4.964	4.524	4.154	3.990	3.839	3.331	2.500	2.000
28	24.316	21.281	18.764	16.663	14.898	13.406	11.051	9.307	7.984	6.961	6.534	6.152	5.502	4.970	4.528	4.157	3.992	3.840	3.331	2.500	2.000
29	25.066	21.844	19.188	16.984	15.141	13.591	11.158	9.370	8.022	6.983	6.551	6.166	5.510	4.975	4.531	4.159	3.994	3.841	3.332	2.500	2.000
30	25.808	22.396	19.600	17.292	15.372	13.765	11.258	9.427	8.055	7.003	6.565	6.177	5.517	4.979	4.534	4.160	3.995	3.842	3.332	2.500	2.000
40	32.835	27.355	23.115	19.793	17.159	15.046	11.925	9.779	8.244	7.105	6.642	6.234	5.548	4.997	4.544	4.166	3.999	3.846	3.333	2.500	2.000
50	39.196	31.424	25.730	21.482	18.256	15.762	12.233	9.915	8.304	7.133	6.660	6.246	5.554	4.999	4.545	4.167	4.000	3.846	3.333	2.500	2.000

Source: Jerome Bracken and Charles J. Christenson, *Tables for Use in Analyzing Business Decisions* (Homewood, Ill.: Richard D. Irwin, Inc., 1965).

INDEX

*This book has been set in 11 point and 10
point Caledonia, leaded 2 points. Chapter
numbers and titles are in 48 and 16 point
Weiss Roman. The size of the type page is
25 by 45 picas.*